Culture and Imperialism

CULTURE

AND

IMPERIALISM

Edward W. Said

ALFRED A. KNOPF / NEW YORK

1 9 9 3

THIS IS A BORZOI BOOK
PUBLISHED BY ALFRED A. KNOPF, INC.

Copyright © 1993 by Edward W. Said

ISBN 0-394-58738-3
LC 92-54380

Manufactured in the United States of America
First Edition

For
Eqbal Ahmad

The conquest of the earth, which mostly means the taking it away from those who have a different complexion or slightly flatter noses than ourselves, is not a pretty thing when you look into it too much. What redeems it is the idea only. An idea at the back of it; not a sentimental pretence but an idea; and an unselfish belief in the idea—something you can set up, and bow down before, and offer a sacrifice to. . . .

JOSEPH CONRAD, *Heart of Darkness*

Contents

CHAPTER THREE
RESISTANCE AND OPPOSITION

CHAPTER FOUR
FREEDOM FROM DOMINATION IN THE FUTURE

Introduction

About five years after *Orientalism* was published in 1978, I began to gather together some ideas about the general relationship between culture and empire that had become clear to me while writing that book. The first result was a series of lectures that I gave at universities in the United States, Canada, and England in 1985 and 1986. These lectures form the core argument of the present work, which has occupied me steadily since that time. A substantial amount of scholarship in anthropology, history, and area studies has developed arguments I put forward in *Orientalism*, which was limited to the Middle East. So I, too, have tried here to expand the arguments of the earlier book to describe a more general pattern of relationships between the modern metropolitan West and its overseas territories.

What are some of the non–Middle Eastern materials drawn on here? European writing on Africa, India, parts of the Far East, Australia, and the Caribbean; these Africanist and Indianist discourses, as some of them have been called, I see as part of the general European effort to rule distant lands and peoples and, therefore, as related to Orientalist descriptions of the Islamic world, as well as to Europe's special ways of representing the Caribbean islands, Ireland, and the Far East. What are striking in these discourses are the rhetorical figures one keeps encountering in their descriptions of "the mysterious East," as well as the stereotypes about "the African [or Indian or Irish or Jamaican or Chinese] mind," the notions about bringing civilization to primitive or barbaric peoples, the disturbingly familiar ideas about flogging or death or extended punishment being required when "they" misbehaved or became rebellious, because "they" mainly understood force or violence best; "they" were not like "us," and for that reason deserved to be ruled.

Yet it was the case nearly everywhere in the non-European world that the coming of the white man brought forth some sort of resistance. What I left out of *Orientalism* was that response to Western dominance which culminated in the great movement of decolonization all across the Third World. Along with armed resistance in places as diverse as nineteenth-century Algeria, Ireland, and Indonesia, there also went considerable efforts in cultural resistance almost everywhere, the assertions of nationalist identities, and, in the political realm, the creation of associations and parties whose common goal was self-determination and national independence. Never was it the case that the imperial encounter pitted an active Western intruder against a supine or inert non-Western native; there was *always* some form of active resistance, and in the overwhelming majority of cases, the resistance finally won out.

These two factors—a general world-wide pattern of imperial culture, and a historical experience of resistance against empire—inform this book in ways that make it not just a sequel to *Orientalism* but an attempt to do something else. In both books I have emphasized what in a rather general way I have called "culture." As I use the word, "culture" means two things in particular. First of all it means all those practices, like the arts of description, communication, and representation, that have relative autonomy from the economic, social, and political realms and that often exist in aesthetic forms, one of whose principal aims is pleasure. Included, of course, are both the popular stock of lore about distant parts of the world and specialized knowledge available in such learned disciplines as ethnography, historiography, philology, sociology, and literary history. Since my exclusive focus here is on the modern Western empires of the nineteenth and twentieth centuries, I have looked especially at cultural forms like the novel, which I believe were immensely important in the formation of imperial attitudes, references, and experiences. I do not mean that only the novel was important, but that I consider it *the* aesthetic object whose connection to the expanding societies of Britain and France is particularly interesting to study. The prototypical modern realistic novel is *Robinson Crusoe*, and certainly not accidentally it is about a European who creates a fiefdom for himself on a distant, non-European island.

A great deal of recent criticism has concentrated on narrative fiction, yet very little attention has been paid to its position in the history and world of empire. Readers of this book will quickly discover that narrative is crucial to my argument here, my basic point being that stories are at the heart of what explorers and novelists say about strange regions of the world; they also become the method colonized people use to assert their own identity and the existence of their own history. The main battle in imperialism is over land, of course; but when it came to who owned the land, who had the right to settle and work on it, who kept it going, who won it back, and who now plans its future—these issues were reflected, contested, and even for a time decided in narrative. As one critic has suggested, nations themselves *are* narrations. The power to narrate, or to block other narratives from forming and emerging, is very important to culture and imperialism, and constitutes one of the main connections between them. Most important, the grand narratives of emancipation and enlightenment mobilized people in the colonial world to rise up and throw off imperial subjection; in the process, many Europeans and Americans were also stirred by these stories and their protagonists, and they too fought for new narratives of equality and human community.

Second, and almost imperceptibly, culture is a concept that includes a refining and elevating element, each society's reservoir of the best that has been known and thought, as Matthew Arnold put it in the 1860s. Arnold believed that culture palliates, if it does not altogether neutralize, the ravages of a modern, aggressive, mercantile, and brutalizing urban existence. You read Dante or Shakespeare in order to keep up with the best that was thought and known, and also to see yourself, your people, society, and tradition in their best lights. In time, culture comes to be associated, often aggressively, with the nation or the state; this differentiates "us" from "them," almost always with some degree of xenophobia. Culture in this sense is a source of identity, and a rather combative one at that, as we see in recent "returns" to culture and tradition. These "returns" accompany rigorous codes of intellectual and moral behavior that are opposed to the permissiveness associated with such relatively liberal philosophies as multiculturalism and hybridity. In the formerly colonized world, these "returns" have produced varieties of religious and nationalist fundamentalism.

In this second sense culture is a sort of theater where various political and ideological causes engage one another. Far from being a placid realm of Apollonian gentility, culture can even be a battleground on which causes expose themselves to the light of day and contend with one another, making it apparent that, for instance, American, French, or Indian students who are taught to read *their* national classics before they read others are expected to appreciate and belong loyally, often uncritically, to their nations and traditions while denigrating or fighting against others.

Now the trouble with this idea of culture is that it entails not only venerating one's own culture but also thinking of it as somehow divorced from, because transcending, the everyday world. Most professional humanists as a result are unable to make the connection between the prolonged and sordid cruelty of practices such as slavery, colonialist and racial oppression, and imperial subjection on the one hand, and the poetry, fiction, philosophy of the society that engages in these practices on the other. One of the difficult truths I discovered in working on this book is how very few of the British or French artists whom I admire took issue with the notion of "subject" or "inferior" races so prevalent among officials who practiced those ideas as a matter of course in ruling India or Algeria. They were widely accepted notions, and they helped fuel the imperial acquisition of territories in Africa throughout the nineteenth century. In thinking of Carlyle or Ruskin, or even of Dickens and Thackeray, critics have often, I believe, relegated these writers' ideas about colonial expansion, inferior races, or "niggers" to a very different department from that of culture, culture being the elevated area of activity in which they "truly" belong and in which they did their "really" important work.

Culture conceived in this way can become a protective enclosure: check your politics at the door before you enter it. As someone who has spent his entire professional life teaching literature, yet who also grew up in the pre–World War Two colonial world, I have found it a challenge *not* to see culture in this way—that is, antiseptically quarantined from its worldly affiliations—but as an extraordinarily varied field of endeavor. The novels and other books I consider here I analyze because first of all I find them estimable and admirable works of art and learning, in which I and many other readers take pleasure and from which we derive profit. Second, the challenge is to connect them not only with that pleasure and profit but also with the imperial process of which they were manifestly and unconcealedly a part; rather than condemning or ignoring their participation in what was an unquestioned reality in their societies, I suggest that what we learn about this hitherto ignored aspect actually and truly *enhances* our reading and understanding of them.

Let me say a little here about what I have in mind, using two well-known and very great novels. Dickens's *Great Expectations* (1861) is primarily a novel about self-delusion, about Pip's vain attempts to become a gentleman with neither the hard work nor the aristocratic source of income required for such a role. Early in life he helps a condemned convict, Abel Magwitch, who, after being transported to Australia, pays back his young benefactor with large sums of money; because the lawyer involved says nothing as he disburses the money, Pip persuades himself that an elderly gentlewoman, Miss Havisham, has been his patron. Magwitch then reappears illegally in London, unwelcomed by Pip because everything about the man reeks of delinquency and unpleasantness. In the end, though, Pip is reconciled to Magwitch and to his reality: he finally acknowledges Magwitch—hunted, apprehended, and fatally ill—as his surrogate father, not as someone to be denied or rejected, though Magwitch is in fact unacceptable, being from Australia, a penal colony designed for the rehabilitation but not the repatriation of transported English criminals.

Most, if not all, readings of this remarkable work situate it squarely within the metropolitan history of British fiction, whereas I believe that it belongs in a history both more inclusive and more dynamic than such interpretations allow. It has been left to two more recent books than Dickens's—Robert Hughes's magisterial *The Fatal Shore* and Paul Carter's brilliantly speculative *The Road to Botany Bay*—to reveal a vast history of speculation about and experience of Australia, a "white" colony like Ireland, in which we can locate Magwitch and Dickens not as mere coincidental references in that history, but as participants in it, through the novel and through a much older and wider experience between England and its overseas territories.

Australia was established as a penal colony in the late eighteenth century mainly so that England could transport an irredeemable, unwanted excess population of felons to a place, originally charted by Captain Cook, that would also function as a colony replacing those lost in America. The pursuit of profit, the building of empire, and what Hughes calls social *apartheid* together produced modern Australia, which by the time Dickens first took an interest in it during the 1840s (in *David Copperfield* Wilkins Micawber happily immigrates there) had progressed somewhat into profitability and a sort of "free system" where laborers could do well on their own if allowed to do so. Yet in Magwitch

> Dickens knotted several strands in the English perception of convicts in Australia at the end of transportation. They could succeed, but they could hardly, in the real sense, return. They could expiate their crimes in a technical, legal sense, but what they suffered there warped them into permanent outsiders. And yet they were capable of redemption— as long as they stayed in Australia.[1]

Carter's exploration of what he calls Australia's spatial history offers us another version of that same experience. Here explorers, convicts, ethnographers, profiteers, soldiers chart the vast and relatively empty continent each in a discourse that jostles, displaces, or incorporates the others. Botany Bay is therefore first of all an Enlightenment discourse of travel and discovery, then a set of travelling narrators (including Cook) whose words, charts, and intentions accumulate the strange territories and gradually turn them into "home." The adjacence between the Benthamite organization of space (which produced the city of Melbourne) and the apparent disorder of the Australian bush is shown by Carter to have become an optimistic transformation of social space, which produced an Elysium for gentlemen, an Eden for laborers in the 1840s.[2] What Dickens envisions for Pip, being Magwitch's "London gentleman," is roughly equivalent to what was envisioned by English benevolence for Australia, one social space authorizing another.

But *Great Expectations* was not written with anything like the concern for native Australian accounts that Hughes or Carter has, nor did it presume or forecast a tradition of Australian writing, which in fact came later to include the literary works of David Malouf, Peter Carey, and Patrick White. The prohibition placed on Magwitch's return is not only penal but imperial: subjects can be taken to places like Australia, but they cannot be allowed a "return" to metropolitan space, which, as all Dickens's fiction testifies, is meticulously charted, spoken for, inhabited by a hierarchy of metropolitan personages. So on the one hand, interpreters like Hughes and Carter expand on the relatively attenuated presence of Australia in nineteenth-century British writing, expressing the fullness and earned integrity of an Australian history that became independent from Britain's in the twentieth century; yet, on the other, an accurate reading of *Great Expectations* must note that after Magwitch's delinquency is expiated, so to speak, after Pip redemptively acknowledges his debt to the old, bitterly energized, and vengeful convict, Pip himself collapses and is revived in two explicitly positive ways. A new Pip appears, less laden than the old Pip with the chains of the past—he is glimpsed in the form of a child, also called Pip; and the old Pip takes on a new career with his boyhood friend Herbert Pocket, this time not as an idle gentleman but as a hardworking trader in the East, where Britain's other colonies offer a sort of normality that Australia never could.

Thus even as Dickens settles the difficulty with Australia, another structure of attitude and reference emerges to suggest Britain's imperial intercourse through trade and travel with the Orient. In his new career as colonial businessman, Pip is hardly an exceptional figure, since nearly all of Dickens's businessmen, wayward relatives, and frightening outsiders have a fairly normal and secure connection with the empire. But it is only in recent years that these connections have taken on interpretative importance. A new generation of scholars and critics—the children of decolonization in some instances, the beneficiaries (like sexual, religious, and racial minorities) of advances in human freedom at home—have seen in such great texts of Western literature a standing interest in what was considered a lesser world, populated with lesser people of color, portrayed as open to the intervention of so many Robinson Crusoes.

By the end of the nineteenth century the empire is no longer merely a shadowy presence, or embodied merely in the unwelcome appearance of a fugitive convict but, in the works of writers like Conrad, Kipling, Gide, and

Loti, a central area of concern. Conrad's *Nostromo* (1904)—my second example—is set in a Central American republic, independent (unlike the African and East Asian colonial settings of his earlier fictions), and dominated at the same time by outside interests because of its immense silver mine. For a contemporary American the most compelling aspect of the work is Conrad's prescience: he forecasts the unstoppable unrest and "misrule" of the Latin American republics (governing them, he says, quoting Bolívar, is like plowing the sea), and he singles out North America's particular way of influencing conditions in a decisive yet barely visible way. Holroyd, the San Francisco financier who backs Charles Gould, the British owner of the San Tomé mine, warns his protégé that "we won't be drawn into any large trouble" as investors. Nevertheless,

> We can sit and watch. Of course, some day we shall step in. We are bound to. But there's no hurry. Time itself has got to wait on the greatest country in the whole of God's universe. We shall be giving the word for everything—industry, trade, law, journalism, art, politics, and religion, from Cape Horn clear over to Surith's Sound, and beyond it, too, if anything worth taking hold of turns up at the North Pole. And then we shall have the leisure to take in hand the outlying islands and continents of the earth. We shall run the world's business whether the world likes it or not. The world can't help it—and neither can we, I guess.[3]

Much of the rhetoric of the "New World Order" promulgated by the American government since the end of the Cold War—with its redolent self-congratulation, its unconcealed triumphalism, its grave proclamations of responsibility—might have been scripted by Conrad's Holroyd: we are number one, we are bound to lead, we stand for freedom and order, and so on. No American has been immune from this structure of feeling, and yet the implicit warning contained in Conrad's portraits of Holroyd and Gould is rarely reflected on since the rhetoric of power all too easily produces an illusion of benevolence when deployed in an imperial setting. Yet it is a rhetoric whose most damning characteristic is that it has been used before, not just once (by Spain and Portugal) but with deafeningly repetitive frequency in the modern period, by the British, the French, the Belgians, the Japanese, the Russians, and now the Americans.

Yet it would be incomplete to read Conrad's great work simply as an early prediction of what we see happening in twentieth-century Latin America, with its string of United Fruit Companies, colonels, liberation forces, and American-financed mercenaries. Conrad is the precursor of the Western views of the Third World which one finds in the work of novelists as different as Graham Greene, V. S. Naipaul, and Robert Stone, of theoreticians of imperialism like Hannah Arendt, and of travel writers, filmmakers, and polemicists whose specialty is to deliver the non-European world either for analysis and judgement or for satisfying the exotic tastes of European and North American audiences. For if it is true that Conrad ironically sees the imperialism of the San Tomé silver mine's British and American owners as doomed by its own pretentious and impossible ambitions, it is also true that he writes as a man whose *Western* view of the non-Western world is so ingrained as to blind him to other histories, other cultures, other aspirations. All Conrad can see is a world totally dominated by the Atlantic West, in which every opposition to the West only confirms the West's wicked power. What Conrad cannot see is an alternative to this cruel tautology. He could neither understand that India, Africa, and South America also had lives and cultures with integrities not totally controlled by the gringo imperialists and reformers of this world, nor allow himself to believe that anti-imperialist independence movements were not all corrupt and in the pay of the puppet masters in London or Washington.

These crucial limitations in vision are as much a part of *Nostromo* as its characters and plot. Conrad's novel embodies the same paternalistic arrogance of imperialism that it mocks in characters like Gould and Holroyd. Conrad seems to be saying, "We Westerners will decide who is a good native or a bad, because all natives have sufficient existence by virtue of our recognition. We created them, we taught them to speak and think, and when they rebel they simply confirm our views of them as silly children, duped by some of their Western masters." This is in effect what Americans have felt about their southern neighbors: that independence is to be wished for them so long as it is the kind of independence *we* approve of. Anything else is unacceptable and, worse, unthinkable.

It is no paradox, therefore, that Conrad was both anti-imperialist and imperialist, progressive when it came to rendering fearlessly and pessimistically the self-confirming, self-deluding corruption of overseas domination, deeply reactionary when it came to conceding that Africa or South America could ever have had an independent history or culture, which the imperialists violently disturbed but by which they were ultimately defeated. Yet lest we think patronizingly of Conrad as the creature of his own time, we had better note that recent attitudes in Washington and among most Western policymakers and intellectuals show little advance over his views. What Conrad discerned as the futility latent in imperialist philanthropy—whose intentions include such ideas as "making the world safe for democracy"—the United States government is still unable to perceive, as it tries to implement its wishes all over the globe, especially in the Middle East. At least Conrad had the courage to see that no such schemes ever succeed—because they trap the planners in more illusions of omnipotence and misleading self-satisfaction (as in Vietnam), and because by their very nature they falsify the evidence.

All this is worth bearing in mind if *Nostromo* is to be read with some attention to its massive strengths and inherent limitations. The newly independent state of Sulaco that emerges at the end of the novel is only a smaller, more tightly controlled and intolerant version of the larger state from which it has seceded and has now come to displace in wealth and importance. Conrad allows the reader to see that imperialism is a system. Life in one subordinate realm of experience is imprinted by the fictions and follies of the dominant realm. But the reverse is true, too, as experience in the dominant society comes to depend uncritically on natives and their territories perceived as in need of *la mission civilisatrice*.

However it is read, *Nostromo* offers a profoundly unforgiving view, and it has quite literally enabled the equally severe view of Western imperialist illusions in Graham Greene's *The Quiet American* or V. S. Naipaul's *A Bend in the River*, novels with very different agendas. Few readers today, after Vietnam, Iran, the Philippines, Algeria, Cuba, Nicaragua, Iraq, would disagree that it is precisely the fervent innocence of Greene's Pyle or Naipaul's Father Huismans, men for whom the native can be educated into "our" civilization, that turns out to produce the murder, subversion, and endless instability of "primitive" societies. A similar anger pervades films like Oliver Stone's *Salvador*, Francis Ford Coppola's *Apocalypse Now*, and Constantin Costa-Gavras's *Missing*, in which unscrupulous CIA operatives and power-mad officers manipulate natives and well-intentioned Americans alike.

Yet all these works, which are so indebted to Conrad's anti-imperialist irony in *Nostromo*, argue that the source of the world's significant action and life is in the West, whose representatives seem at liberty to visit their fantasies and philanthropies upon a mind-deadened Third World. In this view, the outlying regions of the world have no life, history, or culture to speak of, no independence or integrity worth representing without the West. And when there is something to be described it is, following Conrad, unutterably corrupt, degenerate, irredeemable. But whereas Conrad wrote *Nostromo* during a period of Europe's largely uncontested imperialist enthusiasm, contemporary novelists and filmmakers who have learned his ironies so well have done their work *after* decolonization, *after* the massive intellectual, moral, and imaginative overhaul and deconstruction of Western representation of the non-Western world, *after* the work of Frantz Fanon, Amílcar Cabral, C.L.R. James, Walter Rodney, *after* the novels and plays of

Chinua Achebe, Ngugi wa Thiongo, Wole Soyinka, Salman Rushdie, Gabriel García Márquez, and many others.

Thus Conrad has passed along his residual imperialist propensities, although his heirs scarcely have an excuse to justify the often subtle and unreflecting bias of their work. This is not just a matter of Westerners who do not have enough sympathy for or comprehension of foreign cultures—since there are, after all, some artists and intellectuals who have, in effect, crossed to the other side—Jean Genet, Basil Davidson, Albert Memmi, Juan Goytisolo, and others. What is perhaps more relevant is the political willingness to take seriously the alternatives to imperialism, among them the existence of other cultures and societies. Whether one believes that Conrad's extraordinary fiction confirms habitual Western suspicions about Latin America, Africa, and Asia, or whether one sees in novels like *Nostromo* and *Great Expectations* the lineaments of an astonishingly durable imperial worldview, capable of warping the perspectives of reader and author equally: *both* those ways of reading the real alternatives seem outdated. The world today does not exist as a spectacle about which we can be either pessimistic or optimistic, about which our "texts" can be either ingenious or boring. All such attitudes involve the deployment of power and interests. To the extent that we see Conrad both criticizing and reproducing the imperial ideology of his time, to that extent we can characterize our own present attitudes: the projection, or the refusal, of the wish to dominate, the capacity to damn, or the energy to comprehend and engage with other societies, traditions, histories.

The world has changed since Conrad and Dickens in ways that have surprised, and often alarmed, metropolitan Europeans and Americans, who now confront large non-white immigrant populations in their midst, and face an impressive roster of newly empowered voices asking for their narratives to be heard. The point of my book is that such populations and voices have been there for some time, thanks to the globalized process set in motion by modern imperialism; to ignore or otherwise discount the overlapping experience of Westerners and Orientals, the interdependence of cultural terrains in which colonizer and colonized co-existed and battled each other through projections as well as rival geographies, narratives, and histories, is to miss what is essential about the world in the past century.

For the first time, the history of imperialism and its culture can now be studied as neither monolithic nor reductively compartmentalized, separate, distinct. True, there has been a disturbing eruption of separatist and chauvinist discourse, whether in India, Lebanon, or Yugoslavia, or in Afrocentric, Islamocentric, or Eurocentric proclamations; far from invalidating the struggle to be free from empire, these reductions of cultural discourse actually prove the validity of a fundamental liberationist energy that animates the wish to be independent, to speak freely and without the burden of unfair domination. The only way to understand this energy, however, is historically: and hence the rather wide geographical and historical range attempted in this book. In our wish to make ourselves heard, we tend very often to forget that the world is a crowded place, and that if everyone were to insist on the radical purity or priority of one's own voice, all we would have would be the awful din of unending strife, and a bloody political mess, the true horror of which is beginning to be perceptible here and there in the re-emergence of racist politics in Europe, the cacophony of debates over political correctness and identity politics in the United States, and—to speak about my own part of the world—the intolerance of religious prejudice and illusionary promises of Bismarckian despotism, à la Saddam Hussein and his numerous Arab epigones and counterparts.

What a sobering and inspiring thing it is therefore not just to read one's own side, as it were, but also to grasp how a great artist like Kipling (few more imperialist and reactionary than he) rendered India with such skill, and how in doing so his novel *Kim* not only depended on a long history of Anglo-Indian perspective, but also, in spite of itself, forecast the untenability of that perspective in its insistence on the belief that the Indian reality required, indeed beseeched British tutelage more or less indefinitely. The great cultural archive, I argue, is where the intellectual and aesthetic investments in overseas dominion are made. If you were British or French in the 1860s you saw, and you felt, India and North Africa with a combination of familiarity and distance, but never with a sense of their separate sovereignty. In your narratives, histories, travel tales, and explorations your consciousness was represented as the principal authority, an active point of energy that made sense not just of colonizing activities but of exotic geographies and peoples. Above all, your sense of power scarcely imagined that those "natives" who appeared either subservient or sullenly uncooperative were ever going to be capable of finally making you give up India or Algeria. Or of saying anything that might perhaps contradict, challenge, or otherwise disrupt the prevailing discourse.

Imperialism's culture was not invisible, nor did it conceal its worldly affiliations and interests. There is a sufficient clarity in the culture's major lines for us to remark the often scrupulous notations recorded there, and also to remark how they have not been paid much attention. Why they are now of such interest as, for instance, to spur this and other books derives less from a kind of retrospective vindictiveness than from a fortified need for links and connections. One of imperialism's achievements was to bring the world closer together, and although in the process the separation between

Europeans and natives was an insidious and fundamentally unjust one, most of us should now regard the historical experience of empire as a common one. The task then is to describe it as pertaining to Indians *and* Britishers, Algerians *and* French, Westerners *and* Africans, Asians, Latin Americans, and Australians despite the horrors, the bloodshed, and the vengeful bitterness.

My method is to focus as much as possible on individual works, to read them first as great products of the creative or interpretative imagination, and then to show them as part of the relationship between culture and empire. I do not believe that authors are mechanically determined by ideology, class, or economic history, but authors are, I also believe, very much in the history of their societies, shaping and shaped by that history and their social experience in different measure. Culture and the aesthetic forms it contains derive from historical experience, which in effect is one of the main subjects of this book. As I discovered in writing *Orientalism,* you cannot grasp historical experience by lists or catalogues, and no matter how much you provide by way of coverage, some books, articles, authors, and ideas are going to be left out. Instead, I have tried to look at what I consider to be important and essential things, conceding in advance that selectivity and conscious choice have had to rule what I have done. My hope is that readers and critics of this book will use it to further the lines of inquiry and arguments about the historical experience of imperialism put forward in it. In discussing and analyzing what in fact is a global process, I have had to be occasionally both general and summary; yet no one, I am sure, would wish this book any longer than it is!

Moreover, there are several empires that I do not discuss: the Austro-Hungarian, the Russian, the Ottoman, and the Spanish and Portuguese. These omissions, however, are not at all meant to suggest that Russia's domination of Central Asia and Eastern Europe, Istanbul's rule over the Arab world, Portugal's over what are today's Angola and Mozambique, and Spain's domination in both the Pacific and Latin America have been either benign (and hence approved of) or any less imperialist. What I am saying about the British, French, and American imperial experience is that it has a unique coherence and a special cultural centrality. England of course is in an imperial class by itself, bigger, grander, more imposing than any other; for almost two centuries France was in direct competition with it. Since narrative plays such a remarkable part in the imperial quest, it is therefore not surprising that France and (especially) England have an unbroken tradition of novel-writing, unparalleled elsewhere. America began as an empire during the nineteenth century, but it was in the second half of the twentieth, after the decolonization of the British and French empires, that it directly followed its two great predecessors.

There are two additional reasons for focussing as I do on these three. One is that the idea of overseas rule—jumping beyond adjacent territories to very distant lands—has a privileged status in these three cultures. This idea has a lot to do with projections, whether in fiction or geography or art, and it acquires a continuous presence through actual expansion, administration, investment, and commitment. There is something systematic about imperial culture therefore that is not as evident in any other empire as it is in Britain's or France's and, in a different way, the United States'. When I use the phrase "a structure of attitude and reference," this is what I have in mind. Second is that these countries are the three in whose orbits I was born, grew up, and now live. Although I feel at home in them, I have remained, as a native from the Arab and Muslim world, someone who also belongs to the other side. This has enabled me in a sense to live on both sides, and to try to mediate between them.

In fine, this is a book about the past and the present, about "us" and "them," as each of these things is seen by the various, and usually opposed and separated, parties. Its moment, so to speak, is that of the period after the Cold War, when the United States has emerged as the last superpower. To live there during such a time means, for an educator and intellectual with a background in the Arab world, a number of quite particular concerns, all of which have inflected this book, as indeed they have influenced everything I have written since *Orientalism*.

First is a depressing sense that one has seen and read about current American policy formulations before. Each great metropolitan center that aspired to global dominance has said, and alas done, many of the same things. There is always the appeal to power and national interest in running the affairs of lesser peoples; there is the same destructive zeal when the going gets a little rough, or when natives rise up and reject a compliant and unpopular ruler who was ensnared and kept in place by the imperial power; there is the horrifically predictable disclaimer that "we" are exceptional, not imperial, not about to repeat the mistake of earlier powers, a disclaimer that has been routinely followed by making the mistake, as witness the Vietnam and Gulf wars. Worse yet has been the amazing, if often passive, collaboration with these practices on the part of intellectuals, artists, journalists whose positions at home are progressive and full of admirable sentiments, but the opposite when it comes to what is done abroad in their name.

It is my (perhaps illusory) hope that a history of the imperial adventure rendered in cultural terms might therefore serve some illustrative and even deterrent purpose. Yet though imperialism implacably advanced during the nineteenth and twentieth centuries, resistance to it also advanced. Methodologically then I try to show the two forces together. This by no means exempts the aggrieved colonized peoples from criticism; as any survey of post-colonial states will reveal, the fortunes and misfortunes of nationalism, of what can be called separatism and nativism, do not always make up a flattering story. It too must be told, if only to show that there have always been alternatives to Idi Amin and Saddam Hussein. Western imperialism and Third World nationalism feed off each other, but even at their worst they are neither monolithic nor deterministic. Besides, culture is not monolithic either, and is not the exclusive property of East or West, nor of small groups of men or women.

Nonetheless the story is a gloomy and often discouraging one. What tempers it today is, here and there, the emergence of a new intellectual and political conscience. This is the second concern that went into the making of this book. However much there are laments that the old course of humanistic study has been subject to politicized pressures, to what has been called the culture of complaint, to all sorts of egregiously overstated claims on behalf of "Western" or "feminist" or "Afrocentric" and "Islamocentric" values, that is not all there is today. Take as an example the extraordinary change in studies of the Middle East, which when I wrote *Orientalism* were still dominated by an aggressively masculine and condescending ethos. To mention only works that have appeared in the last three or four years—Lila Abu-Lughod's *Veiled Sentiments,* Leila Ahmed's *Women and Gender in Islam,* Fedwa Malti-Douglas's *Woman's Body, Woman's World*[4]—a very different sort of idea about Islam, the Arabs, and the Middle East has challenged, and to a considerable degree undermined, the old despotism. Such works are feminist, but not exclusivist; they demonstrate the diversity and complexity of experience that works beneath the totalizing discourses of Orientalism and of Middle East (overwhelmingly male) nationalism; they are both intellectually and politically sophisticated, attuned to the best theoretical and historical scholarship, engaged but not demagogic, sensitive to but not maudlin about women's experience; finally, while written by scholars of different backgrounds and education, they are works that are in dialogue with, and contribute to, the political situation of women in the Middle East.

Along with Sara Suleri's *The Rhetoric of English India* and Lisa Lowe's *Critical Terrains,*[5] revisionist scholarship of this sort has varied, if it has not altogether broken up the geography of the Middle East and India as homogenous, reductively understood domains. Gone are the binary oppositions dear to the nationalist and imperialist enterprise. Instead we begin to sense that old authority cannot simply be replaced by new authority, but that new alignments made across borders, types, nations, and essences are rapidly coming into view, and it is those new alignments that now provoke and challenge the fundamentally static notion of *identity* that has been the core of cultural thought during the era of imperialism. Throughout the exchange between Europeans and their "others" that began systematically half a millennium ago, the one idea that has scarcely varied is that there is an "us" and a "them," each quite settled, clear, unassailably self-evident. As I discuss it in *Orientalism,* the division goes back to Greek thought about barbarians, but, whoever originated this kind of "identity" thought, by the nineteenth century it had become the hallmark of imperialist cultures as well as those cultures trying to resist the encroachments of Europe.

We are still the inheritors of that style by which one is defined by the nation, which in turn derives its authority from a supposedly unbroken tradition. In the United States this concern over cultural identity has of course yielded up the contest over what books and authorities constitute "our" tradition. In the main, trying to say that this or that book is (or is not) part of "our" tradition is one of the most debilitating exercises imaginable. Besides, its excesses are much more frequent than its contributions to historical accuracy. For the record then, I have no patience with the position that "we" should only or mainly be concerned with what is "ours," any more than I can condone reactions to such a view that require Arabs to read Arab books, use Arab methods, and the like. As C.L.R. James used to say, Beethoven belongs as much to West Indians as he does to Germans, since his music is now part of the human heritage.

Yet the ideological concern over identity is understandably entangled with the interests and agendas of various groups—not all of them oppressed minorities—that wish to set priorities reflecting these interests. Since a great deal of this book is all about what to read of recent history and how to read it, I shall only quickly summarize my ideas here. Before we can agree on what the American identity is made of, we have to concede that as an immigrant settler society superimposed on the ruins of considerable native presence, American identity is too varied to be a unitary and homogenous thing; indeed the battle within it is between advocates of a unitary identity and those who see the whole as a complex but not reductively unified one. This opposition implies two different perspectives, two historiographies, one linear and subsuming, the other contrapuntal and often nomadic.

My argument is that only the second perspective is fully sensitive to the reality of historical experience. Partly because of empire, all cultures are involved in one another; none is single and pure, all are hybrid, heterogenous, extraordinarily differentiated, and unmonolithic. This, I believe, is as true of the contemporary United States as it is of the modern Arab world, where in each instance respectively so much has been made of the dangers of "un-Americanism" and the threats to "Arabism." Defensive, reactive, and even paranoid nationalism is, alas, frequently woven into the very fabric of education, where children as well as older students are taught to venerate and celebrate the uniqueness of *their* tradition (usually and invidiously at the expense of others). It is to such uncritical and unthinking forms of education and thought that this book is addressed—as a corrective, as a patient alternative, as a frankly exploratory possibility. In its writing I have availed myself of the utopian space still provided by the university, which I believe must remain a place where such vital issues are investigated, discussed, reflected on. For it to become a site where social and political issues are actually either imposed or resolved would be to remove the university's function and turn it into an adjunct to whatever political party is in power.

I do not wish to be misunderstood. Despite its extraordinary cultural diversity, the United States is, and will surely remain, a coherent nation. The same is true of other English-speaking countries (Britain, New Zealand, Australia, Canada) and even of France, which now contains large groups of immigrants. Much of the polemical divisiveness and polarized debate that Arthur Schlesinger speaks of as hurting the study of history in *The Disuniting of America* is there of course, but it does not, in my opinion, portend a dissolution of the republic.[6] On the whole it is better to explore history rather than to repress or deny it; the fact that the United States contains so many histories, many of them now clamoring for attention, is by no means to be suddenly feared since many of them were always there, and out of them *an* American society and politics (and even a style of historical writing) were in fact created. In other words, the result of present debates over multiculturalism is hardly likely to be "Lebanonization," and if these debates point a way for political changes and changes in the way women, minorities, and recent immigrants see themselves, then that is not to be feared or defended against. What does need to be remembered is that narratives of emancipation and enlightenment in their strongest form were also narratives of *integration* not separation, the stories of people who had been excluded from the main group but who were now fighting for a place in it. And if the old and habitual ideas of the main group were not flexible or generous enough to admit new groups, then these ideas need changing, a far better thing to do than reject the emerging groups.

The last point I want to make is that this book is an exile's book. For objective reasons that I had no control over, I grew up as an Arab with a Western education. Ever since I can remember, I have felt that I belonged to both worlds, without being completely *of* either one or the other. During my lifetime, however, the parts of the Arab world that I was most attached to either have been changed utterly by civil upheavals and war, or have simply ceased to exist. And for long periods of time I have been an outsider in the United States, particularly when it went to war against, and was deeply opposed to, the (far from perfect) cultures and societies of the Arab world. Yet when I say "exile" I do not mean something sad or deprived. On the contrary belonging, as it were, to both sides of the imperial divide enables you to understand them more easily. Moreover New York, where the whole of this book was written, is in so many ways the exilic city *par excellence;* it also contains within itself the Manichean structure of the colonial city described by Fanon. Perhaps all this has stimulated the kinds of interests and interpretations ventured here, but these circumstances certainly made it possible for me to feel as if I belonged to more than one history and more than one group. As to whether such a state can be regarded as really a salutary alternative to the normal sense of belonging to only one culture and feeling a sense of loyalty to only one nation, the reader must now decide.

The argument of this book was first presented in various lecture series given at universities in the United Kingdom, the United States, and Canada from 1985 to 1988. For these extended opportunities, I am greatly indebted to faculty and students at the University of Kent, Cornell University, the University of Western Ontario, the University of Toronto, the University of Essex, and, in a considerably earlier version of the argument, the University of Chicago. Later versions of individual sections of this book were also delivered as lectures at the Yeats International School at Sligo, Oxford University (as the George Antonius Lecture at St. Antony's College), the University of Minnesota, King's College of Cambridge University, the Princeton University Davis Center, Birkbeck College of London University, and the University of Puerto Rico. My gratitude to Declan Kiberd, Seamus Deane, Derek Hopwood, Peter Nesselroth, Tony Tanner, Natalie Davis and Gayan Prakash, A. Walton Litz, Peter Hulme, Deirdre David, Ken Bates, Tessa Blackstone, Bernard Sharrett, Lyn Innis, Peter Mulford, Gervasio Luis Garcia, and Maria de los Angeles Castro for the favor of inviting, and then hosting, me is warm and sincere. In 1989 I was honored when I was asked to give the first Raymond Williams Memorial Lecture in London; I spoke about Camus on that occasion, and thanks to Graham Martin and the late Joy Williams, it was a memorable experience for me. I need hardly say that many parts of this book are suffused with the ideas and the human and moral example of Raymond Williams, a good friend and a great critic.

I shamelessly availed myself of various intellectual, political, and cultural associations as I worked on this book. Those include close personal friends who are also editors of journals in which some of these pages first appeared: Tom Mitchell (of *Critical Inquiry*), Richard Poirier (of *Raritan Review*), Ben Sonnenberg (of *Grand Street*), A. Sivanandan (of *Race and Class*), Joanne Wypejewski (of *The Nation*), and Karl Miller (of *The London Review of Books*). I am also grateful to editors of *The Guardian* (London) and to Paul Keegan of Penguin under whose auspices some of the ideas in this book were first expressed. Other friends on whose indulgence, hospitality, and criticisms I depended were Donald Mitchell, Ibrahim Abu-Lughod, Masao Miyoshi, Jean Franco, Marianne McDonald, Anwar Abdel-Malek, Eqbal Ahmad, Jonathan Culler, Gayatri Spivak, Homi Bhabha, Benita Parry, and Barbara Harlow. It gives me particular pleasure to acknowledge the brilliance and perspicacity of several students of mine at Columbia University, for whom any teacher would have been grateful. These young scholars and critics gave me the full benefit of their exciting work, which is now both well published and well known: Anne McClintock, Rob Nixon, Suvendi Perera, Gauri Viswanathan, and Tim Brennan.

In the preparation of the manuscript, I have been very ably helped in different ways by Yumna Siddiqi, Aamir Mufti, Susan Lhota, David Beams, Paola di Robilant, Deborah Poole, Ana Dopico, Pierre Gagnier, and Kieran Kennedy. Zaineb Istrabadi performed the difficult task of deciphering my appalling handwriting and then putting it into successive drafts with admirable patience and skill. I am very indebted to her for unstinting support, good humor, and intelligence. At various stages of editorial preparation Frances Coady and Carmen Callil were helpful readers and good friends of what I was trying to present here. I must also record my deep gratitude and almost thunderstruck admiration for Elisabeth Sifton: friend of many years, superb editor, exacting and always sympathetic critic. George Andreou was unfailingly helpful in getting things right as the book moved through the publishing process. To Mariam, Wadie, and Najla Said, who lived with the author of this book in often trying circumstances, heartfelt thanks for their constant love and support.

New York, New York
July 1992

Culture and Imperialism

CHAPTER ONE

OVERLAPPING TERRITORIES, INTERTWINED HISTORIES

Silence from and about the subject was the order of the day. Some of the silences were broken, and some were maintained by authors who lived with and within the policing strategies. What I am interested in are the strategies for breaking it.

TONI MORRISON, *Playing in the Dark*

History, in other words, is not a calculating machine. It unfolds in the mind and the imagination, and it takes body in the multifarious responses of a people's culture, itself the infinitely subtle mediation of material realities, of underpinning economic fact, of gritty objectivities.

BASIL DAVIDSON, *Africa in Modern History*

(I)

Empire, Geography, and Culture

Appeals to the past are among the commonest of strategies in interpretations of the present. What animates such appeals is not only disagreement about what happened in the past and what the past was, but uncertainty about whether the past really is past, over and concluded, or whether it continues, albeit in different forms, perhaps. This problem animates all sorts of discussions—about influence, about blame and judgement, about present actualities and future priorities.

In one of his most famous early critical essays, T. S. Eliot takes up a similar constellation of issues, and although the occasion as well as the intention of his essay is almost purely aesthetic, one can use his formulations to inform other realms of experience. The poet, Eliot says, is obviously an individual talent, but he works within a tradition that cannot be merely inherited but can only be obtained "by great labour." Tradition, he continues,

> involves, in the first place, the historical sense, which we may call nearly indispensable to anyone who would continue to be a poet beyond his twenty-fifth year; and the historical sense involves a perception, not only of the pastness of the past, but of its presence; the historical sense compels a man to write not merely with his own generation in his bones, but with a feeling that the whole of the literature of Europe from Homer and within it the whole of the literature of his own country has a simultaneous existence and composes a simultaneous order. This historical sense, which is a sense of the timeless as well as of the temporal and of the timeless and of the temporal together, is what makes a writer traditional. And it is at the same time what makes a writer most acutely conscious of his place in time, of his own contemporaneity.
>
> No poet, no artist of any art, has his complete meaning alone.[1]

The force of these comments is directed equally, I think, at poets who think critically and at critics whose work aims at a close appreciation of the poetic process. The main idea is that even as we must fully comprehend the pastness of the past, there is no just way in which the past can be quarantined from the present. Past and present inform each other, each implies the other and, in the totally ideal sense intended by Eliot, each co-exists with the other. What Eliot proposes, in short, is a vision of literary tradition that, while it respects temporal succession, is not wholly commanded by it. Neither past nor present, any more than any poet or artist, has a complete meaning alone.

Eliot's synthesis of past, present, and future, however, is idealistic and in important ways a function of his own peculiar history;[2] also, its conception of time leaves out the combativeness with which individuals and institutions decide on what is tradition and what is not, what relevant and what not. But his central idea is valid: how we formulate or represent the past shapes our understanding and views of the present. Let me give an example. During the Gulf War of 1990–91, the collision between Iraq and the United States was a function of two fundamentally opposed histories, each used to advantage by the official establishment of each country. As construed by the Iraqi Baath Party, modern Arab history shows the unrealized, unfulfilled promise of Arab independence, a promise traduced both by "the West" and by a whole array of more recent enemies, like Arab reaction and Zionism. Iraq's bloody occupation of Kuwait was, therefore, justified not only on Bismarckian grounds, but also because it was believed that the Arabs had to right the wrongs done against them and wrest from imperialism one of its greatest prizes. Conversely, in the American view of the past, the United States was not a classical imperial power, but a righter of wrongs around the world, in pursuit of tyranny, in defense of freedom no matter the place or cost. The war inevitably pitted these versions of the past against each other.

Eliot's ideas about the complexity of the relationship between past and present are particularly suggestive in the debate over the meaning of "imperialism," a word and an idea today so controversial, so fraught with all sorts of questions, doubts, polemics, and ideological premises as nearly to resist use altogether. To some extent of course the debate involves definitions and attempts at delimitations of the very notion itself: was imperialism principally economic, how far did it extend, what were its causes, was it systematic, when (or whether) did it end? The roll call of names who have contributed to the discussion in Europe and America is impressive: Kautsky, Hilferding, Luxemburg, Hobson, Lenin, Schumpeter, Arendt, Magdoff, Paul Kennedy. And in recent years such works published in the United States as Paul Kennedy's *The Rise and Fall of the Great Powers,* the revisionist history of William Appleman Williams, Gabriel Kolko, Noam Chomsky, Howard Zinn, and Walter Lefeber, and studious defenses or explanations of American policy as non-imperialist written by various strategists, theoreticians, and sages—all this has kept the question of imperialism, and its applicability (or not) to the United States, the main power of the day, very much alive.

These authorities debated largely political and economic questions. Yet scarcely any attention has been paid to what I believe is the privileged role of culture in the modern imperial experience, and little notice taken of the fact that the extraordinary global reach of classical nineteenth- and early-twentieth-century European imperialism still casts a considerable shadow over our own times. Hardly any North American, African, European, Latin American, Indian, Caribbean, Australian individual—the list is very long—who is alive today has not been touched by the empires of the past. Britain and France between them controlled immense territories: Canada, Australia, New Zealand, the colonies in North and South America and the Caribbean, large swatches of Africa, the Middle East, the Far East (Britain will hold

Hong Kong as a colony until 1997), and the Indian subcontinent in its entirety—all these fell under the sway of and in time were liberated from British or French rule; in addition, the United States, Russia, and several lesser European countries, to say nothing of Japan and Turkey, were also imperial powers for some or all of the nineteenth century. This pattern of dominions or possessions laid the groundwork for what is in effect now a fully global world. Electronic communications, the global extent of trade, of availability of resources, of travel, of information about weather patterns and ecological change have joined together even the most distant corners of the world. This set of patterns, I believe, was first established and made possible by the modern empires.

Now I am temperamentally and philosophically opposed to vast system-building or to totalistic theories of human history. But I must say that having studied and indeed lived within the modern empires, I am struck by how constantly expanding, how inexorably integrative they were. Whether in Marx, or in conservative works like those by J. R. Seeley, or in modern analyses like those by D. K. Fieldhouse and C. C. Eldridge (whose *England's Mission* is a central work),[3] one is made to see that the British empire integrated and fused things within it, and taken together it and other empires made the world one. Yet no individual, and certainly not I, can see or fully grasp this whole imperial world.

When we read the debate between contemporary historians Patrick O'Brien[4] and Davis and Huttenback (whose important book *Mammon and the Pursuit of Empire* tries to quantify the actual profitability of imperial activities),[5] or when we look at earlier debates such as the Robinson-Gallagher controversy,[6] or at the work of the dependency and world-accumulation economists André Gunder Frank and Samir Amin,[7] as literary and cultural historians, we are compelled to ask what all this means for interpretations of the Victorian novel, say, or of French historiography, of Italian grand opera, of German metaphysics of the same period. We are at a point in our work when we can no longer ignore empires and the imperial context in our studies. To speak, as O'Brien does, of "the propaganda for an expanding empire [which] created illusions of security and false expectations that high returns would accrue to those who invested beyond its boundaries"[8] is in effect to speak of an atmosphere created by both empire and novels, by racial theory and geographical speculation, by the concept of national identity and urban (or rural) routine. The phrase "false expectations" suggests *Great Expectations,* "invested beyond its boundaries" suggests Joseph Sedley and Becky Sharp, "created illusions," suggests *Illusions perdues*—the crossings over between culture and imperialism are compelling.

It is difficult to connect these different realms, to show the involvements of culture with expanding empires, to make observations about art that preserve its unique endowments and at the same time map its affiliations, but, I submit, we must attempt this, and set the art in the global, earthly context. Territory and possessions are at stake, geography and power. Everything about human history is rooted in the earth, which has meant that we must think about habitation, but it has also meant that people have planned to *have* more territory and therefore must do something about its indigenous residents. At some very basic level, imperialism means thinking about, settling on, controlling land that you do not possess, that is distant, that is lived on and owned by others. For all kinds of reasons it attracts some people and often involves untold misery for others. Yet it is generally true that literary historians who study the great sixteenth-century poet Edmund Spenser, for example, do not connect his bloodthirsty plans for Ireland, where he imagined a British army virtually exterminating the native inhabitants, with his poetic achievement or with the history of British rule over Ireland, which continues today.

For the purposes of this book, I have maintained a focus on actual contests over land and the land's people. What I have tried to do is a kind of geographical inquiry into historical experience, and I have kept in mind the idea that the earth is in effect one world, in which empty, uninhabited spaces virtually do not exist. Just as none of us is outside or beyond geography, none of us is completely free from the struggle over geography. That struggle is complex and interesting because it is not only about soldiers and cannons but also about ideas, about forms, about images and imaginings.

A whole range of people in the so-called Western or metropolitan world, as well as their counterparts in the Third or formerly colonized world, share a sense that the era of high or classical imperialism, which came to a climax in what the historian Eric Hobsbawm has so interestingly described as "the age of empire" and more or less formally ended with the dismantling of the great colonial structures after World War Two, has in one way or another continued to exert considerable cultural influence in the present. For all sorts of reasons, they feel a new urgency about understanding the pastness *or not* of the past, and this urgency is carried over into perceptions of the present and the future.

At the center of these perceptions is a fact that few dispute, namely, that during the nineteenth century unprecedented power—compared with which the powers of Rome, Spain, Baghdad, or Constantinople in their day were far less formidable—was concentrated in Britain and France, and later in other Western countries (the United States, especially). This century climaxed "the rise of the West," and Western power allowed the imperial metropolitan centers to acquire and accumulate territory and subjects on a truly astonishing scale. Consider that in 1800 Western powers claimed 55 percent but actually held approximately 35 percent of the earth's surface, and that by 1878 the proportion was 67 percent, a rate of increase of 83,000 square miles per year. By 1914, the annual rate had risen to an astonishing 240,000 square miles, and Europe held a grand total of roughly 85 percent of the earth as colonies, protectorates, dependencies, dominions, and common-wealths.[9] No other associated set of colonies in history was as large, none so totally dominated, none so unequal in power to the Western metropolis. As a result, says William McNeill in *The Pursuit of Power*, "the world was united into a single interacting whole as never before."[10] And in Europe itself at the end of the nineteenth century, scarcely a corner of life was untouched by the facts of empire; the economies were hungry for overseas markets, raw materials, cheap labor, and hugely profitable land, and defense and foreign-policy establishments were more and more committed to the maintenance of vast tracts of distant territory and large numbers of subjugated peoples. When the Western powers were not in close, sometimes ruthless competi-tion with one another for more colonies—all modern empires, says V. G. Kiernan,[11] imitated one another—they were hard at work settling, survey-ing, studying, and of course ruling the territories under their jurisdictions.

The American experience, as Richard Van Alstyne makes clear in *The Rising American Empire*, was from the beginning founded upon the idea of "an *imperium*—a dominion, state or sovereignty that would expand in population and territory, and increase in strength and power."[12] There were claims for North American territory to be made and fought over (with astonishing success); there were native peoples to be dominated, variously exterminated, variously dislodged; and then, as the republic increased in age and hemi-spheric power, there were distant lands to be designated vital to American interests, to be intervened in and fought over—e.g., the Philippines, the Caribbean, Central America, the "Barbary Coast," parts of Europe and the Middle East, Vietnam, Korea. Curiously, though, so influential has been the discourse insisting on American specialness, altruism, and opportunity that "imperialism" as a word or ideology has turned up only rarely and recently in accounts of United States culture, politics, history. But the connection between imperial politics and culture is astonishingly direct. American attitudes to American "greatness," to hierarchies of race, to the perils of *other* revolutions (the American revolution being considered unique and some-how unrepeatable anywhere else in the world)[13] have remained constant, have dictated, have obscured, the realities of empire, while apologists for overseas American interests have insisted on American innocence, doing good, fighting for freedom. Graham Greene's character Pyle, in *The Quiet American*, embodies this cultural formation with merciless accuracy.

Yet for citizens of nineteenth-century Britain and France, empire was a major topic of unembarrassed cultural attention. British India and French North Africa alone played inestimable roles in the imagination, economy, political life, and social fabric of British and French society, and if we mention names like Delacroix, Edmund Burke, Ruskin, Carlyle, James and John Stuart Mill, Kipling, Balzac, Nerval, Flaubert, or Conrad, we shall be mapping a tiny corner of a far vaster reality than even their immense collective talents cover. There were scholars, administrators, travellers, traders, parliamentarians, merchants, novelists, theorists, speculators, adventurers, visionaries, poets, and every variety of outcast and misfit in the outlying possessions of these two imperial powers, each of whom contributed to the formation of a colonial actuality existing at the heart of metropolitan life.

As I shall be using the term, "imperialism" means the practice, the theory, and the attitudes of a dominating metropolitan center ruling a distant territory; "colonialism," which is almost always a consequence of imperialism, is the implanting of settlements on distant territory. As Michael Doyle puts it: "Empire is a relationship, formal or informal, in which one state controls the effective political sovereignty of another political society. It can be achieved by force, by political collaboration, by economic, social, or cultural dependence. Imperialism is simply the process or policy of establishing or maintaining an empire."[14] In our time, direct colonialism has largely ended; imperialism, as we shall see, lingers where it has always been, in a kind of general cultural sphere as well as in specific political, ideological, economic, and social practices.

Neither imperialism nor colonialism is a simple act of accumulation and acquisition. Both are supported and perhaps even impelled by impressive ideological formations that include notions that certain territories and people *require* and beseech domination, as well as forms of knowledge affiliated with domination: the vocabulary of classic nineteenth-century imperial culture is plentiful with words and concepts like "inferior" or "subject races," "subordinate peoples," "dependency," "expansion," and "authority." Out of the imperial experiences, notions about culture were clarified, reinforced, criticized, or rejected. As for the curious but perhaps allowable idea propagated a century ago by J. R. Seeley that some of Europe's overseas empires were originally acquired absentmindedly, it does not by any stretch of the imagination account for their inconsistency, persistence, and systematized acquisition and administration, let alone their augmented rule and sheer presence. As David Landes has said in *The Unbound Prometheus*, "the decision of certain European powers . . . to establish 'plantations,' that is to treat their colonies as continuous enterprises was, whatever one may think of the morality, a momentous innovation."[15] That is the question that concerns me here: given the initial, perhaps obscurely derived and motivated move toward empire from Europe to the rest of the world, how did the idea and the practice of it gain the consistency and density of continuous enterprise, which it did by the latter part of the nineteenth century?

The primacy of the British and French empires by no means obscures the quite remarkable modern expansion of Spain, Portugal, Holland, Belgium, Germany, Italy, and, in a different way, Russia and the United States. Russia, however, acquired its imperial territories almost exclusively by adjacence. Unlike Britain or France, which jumped thousands of miles beyond their own borders to other continents, Russia moved to swallow whatever land or peoples stood next to its borders, which in the process kept moving farther and farther east and south. But in the English and French cases, the sheer distance of attractive territories summoned the projection of far-flung interests, and that is my focus here, partly because I am interested in examining the set of cultural forms and structures of feeling which it produces, and partly because overseas domination is the world I grew up in and still live in. Russia's and America's joint superpower status, enjoyed for a little less than half a century, derives from quite different histories and from different imperial trajectories. There are several varieties of domination and responses to it, but the "Western" one, along with the resistance it provoked, is the subject of this book.

In the expansion of the great Western empires, profit and hope of further profit were obviously tremendously important, as the attractions of spices, sugar, slaves, rubber, cotton, opium, tin, gold, and silver over centuries amply testify. So also was inertia, the investment in already going enterprises, tradition, and the market or institutional forces that kept the enterprises going. But there is more than that to imperialism and colonialism. There was a commitment to them over and above profit, a commitment in constant circulation and recirculation, which, on the one hand, allowed decent men and women to accept the notion that distant territories and their native peoples *should* be subjugated, and, on the other, replenished metropolitan energies so that these decent people could think of the *imperium* as a protracted, almost metaphysical obligation to rule subordinate, inferior, or less advanced peoples. We must not forget that there was very little domestic resistance to these empires, although they were very frequently established and maintained under adverse and even disadvantageous conditions. Not only were immense hardships endured by the colonizers, but there was always the tremendously risky physical disparity between a small number of

Europeans at a very great distance from home and the much larger number of natives on their home territory. In India, for instance, by the 1930s "a mere 4,000 British civil servants assisted by 60,000 soldiers and 90,000 civilians (businessmen and clergy for the most part) had billeted themselves upon a country of 300 million persons."[16] The will, self-confidence, even arrogance necessary to maintain such a state of affairs can only be guessed at, but, as we shall see in the texts of *A Passage to India* and *Kim*, these attitudes are at least as significant as the number of people in the army or civil service, or the millions of pounds England derived from India.

For the enterprise of empire depends upon the *idea* of *having an empire*, as Conrad so powerfully seems to have realized, and all kinds of preparations are made for it within a culture; then in turn imperialism acquires a kind of coherence, a set of experiences, and a presence of ruler and ruled alike within the culture. As an acute modern student of imperialism has put it:

> Modern imperialism has been an accretion of elements, not all of equal weight, that can be traced back through every epoch of history. Perhaps its ultimate causes, with those of war, are to be found less in tangible material wants than in the uneasy tensions of societies distorted by class division, with their reflection in distorted ideas in men's minds.[17]

One acute indication of how crucially the tensions, inequalities, and injustices of the home or metropolitan society were refracted and elaborated in the imperial culture is given by the distinguished conservative historian of empire D. K. Fieldhouse: "The basis of imperial authority," he says, "was the mental attitude of the colonist. His acceptance of subordination—whether through a positive sense of common interest with the parent state, or through inability to conceive of any alternative—made empire durable."[18] Fieldhouse was discussing white colonists in the Americas, but his general point goes beyond that: the durability of empire was sustained on both sides, that of the rulers and that of the distant ruled, and in turn each had a set of interpretations of their common history with its own perspective, historical sense, emotions, and traditions. What an Algerian intellectual today remembers of his country's colonial past focusses severely on such events as France's military attacks on villages and the torture of prisoners during the war of liberation, on the exultation over independence in 1962; for his French counterpart, who may have taken part in Algerian affairs or whose family lived in Algeria, there is chagrin at having "lost" Algeria, a more positive attitude toward the French colonizing mission—with its schools, nicely planned cities, pleasant life—and perhaps even a sense that "troublemakers" and communists disturbed the idyllic relationship between "us" and "them."

To a very great degree the era of high nineteenth-century imperialism is over: France and Britain gave up their most splendid possessions after World War Two, and lesser powers also divested themselves of their far-flung dominions. Yet, once again recalling the words of T. S. Eliot, although that era clearly had an identity all its own, the meaning of the imperial past is not totally contained within it, but has entered the reality of hundreds of millions of people, where its existence as shared memory and as a highly conflictual texture of culture, ideology, and policy still exercises tremendous force. Frantz Fanon says, "We should flatly refuse the situation to which the Western countries wish to condemn us. Colonialism and imperialism have not paid their score when they withdraw their flags and their police forces from our territories. For centuries the [foreign] capitalists have behaved in the underdeveloped world like nothing more than criminals."[19] We must take stock of the nostalgia for empire, as well as the anger and resentment it provokes in those who were ruled, and we must try to look carefully and integrally at the culture that nurtured the sentiment, rationale, and above all the imagination of empire. And we must also try to grasp the hegemony of the imperial ideology, which by the end of the nineteenth century had become completely embedded in the affairs of cultures whose less regrettable features we still celebrate.

There is, I believe, a quite serious split in our critical consciousness today, which allows us to spend a great deal of time elaborating Carlyle's and Ruskin's aesthetic theories, for example, without giving attention to the authority that their ideas simultaneously bestowed on the subjugation of inferior peoples and colonial territories. To take another example, unless we can comprehend how the great European realistic novel accomplished one of its principal purposes—almost unnoticeably sustaining the society's consent in overseas expansion, a consent that, in J. A. Hobson's words, "the selfish forces which direct Imperialism should utilize the protective colours of . . . disinterested movements"[20] such as philanthropy, religion, science and art—we will misread both the culture's importance and its resonances in the empire, then and now.

Doing this by no means involves hurling critical epithets at European or, generally, Western art and culture by way of wholesale condemnation. Not at all. What I want to examine is how the processes of imperialism occurred beyond the level of economic laws and political decisions, and—by predisposition, by the authority of recognizable cultural formations, by continuing consolidation within education, literature, and the visual and musical arts— were manifested at another very significant level, that of the national culture, which we have tended to sanitize as a realm of unchanging intellectual monuments, free from worldly affiliations. William Blake is unrestrained on this point: "The Foundation of Empire," he says in his annotations to Reynolds's *Discourses,* "is Art and Science. Remove them or Degrade them and the Empire is No more. Empire follows Art and not vice versa as Englishmen suppose."[21]

What, then, is the connection between the pursuit of national imperial aims and the general national culture? Recent intellectual and academic discourse has tended to separate and divide these: most scholars are specialists; most of the attention that is endowed with the status of expertise is given to fairly autonomous subjects, e.g., the Victorian industrial novel, French colonial policy in North Africa, and so forth. The tendency for fields and specializations to subdivide and proliferate, I have for a long while argued, is contrary to an understanding of the whole, when the character, interpretation, and direction or tendency of cultural experience are at issue. To lose sight of or ignore the national and international context of, say, Dickens's representations of Victorian businessmen, and to focus only on the internal coherence of their roles in his novels is to miss an essential connection between his fiction and its historical world. And understanding that connection does not reduce or diminish the novels' value as works of art: on the contrary, because of their *worldliness,* because of their complex affiliations with their real setting, they are *more* interesting and *more* valuable as works of art.

At the opening of *Dombey and Son,* Dickens wishes to underline the importance to Dombey of his son's birth:

> The earth was made for Dombey and Son to trade in, and the sun and moon were made to give them light. Rivers and seas were formed to float their ships; rainbows gave them promise of fair weather; winds blew for or against their enterprises; stars and planets circled in their orbits, to preserve inviolate a system of which they were the centre. Common abbreviations took new meanings in his eyes, and had sole reference to them: A. D. had no concern with anno Domini, but stood for anno Dombei—and Son.[22]

As a description of Dombey's overweening self-importance, his narcissistic obliviousness, his coercive attitude to his barely born child, the service performed by this passage is clear. But one must also ask, how *could* Dombey think that the universe, and the whole of time, was his to trade in? We should also see in this passage—which is by no means a central one in the novel—

an assumption specific to a British novelist in the 1840s: that, as Raymond Williams has it, this was "the decisive period in which the consciousness of a new phase of civilization was being formed and expressed." But then, why does Williams describe "this transforming, liberating, and threatening time"[23] *without* reference to India, Africa, the Middle East, and Asia, since that is where transformed British life expanded to and filled, as Dickens slyly indicates?

Williams is a great critic, whose work I admire and have learned much from, but I sense a limitation in his feeling that English literature is mainly about England, an idea that is central to his work as it is to that of most scholars and critics. Moreover, scholars who write about novels deal more or less exclusively with them (though Williams is not one of those). These habits seem to be guided by a powerful if imprecise notion that works of literature are autonomous, whereas, as I shall be trying to show throughout this book, the literature itself makes constant references to itself as somehow participating in Europe's overseas expansion, and therefore creates what Williams calls "structures of feeling" that support, elaborate, and consolidate the practice of empire. True, Dombey is neither Dickens himself nor the whole of English literature, but the way in which Dickens expresses Dombey's egoism recalls, mocks, yet ultimately depends on the tried and true discourses of imperial free trade, the British mercantile ethos, its sense of all but unlimited opportunities for commercial advancement abroad.

These matters should not be severed from our understanding of the nineteenth-century novel, any more than literature can be chopped off from history and society. The supposed autonomy of works of art enjoins a kind of separation which, I think, imposes an uninteresting limitation that the works themselves resolutely will not make. Still, I have deliberately abstained from advancing a completely worked out theory of the connection between literature and culture on the one hand, and imperialism on the other. Instead, I hope the connections will emerge from their explicit places in the various texts, with the enveloping setting—empire—there to make connections with, to develop, elaborate, expand, or criticize. Neither culture nor imperialism is inert, and so the connections between them as historical experiences are dynamic and complex. My principal aim is not to separate but to connect, and I am interested in this for the main philosophical and methodological reason that cultural forms are hybrid, mixed, impure, and the time has come in cultural analysis to reconnect their analysis with their actuality.

(II)

Images of the Past, Pure and Impure

A s the twentieth century moves to a close, there has been a gathering
awareness nearly everywhere of the lines *between* cultures, the divisions and differences that not only allow us to discriminate one culture from
another, but also enable us to see the extent to which cultures are humanly
made structures of both authority and participation, benevolent in what they
include, incorporate, and validate, less benevolent in what they exclude and
demote.

There is in all nationally defined cultures, I believe, an aspiration to
sovereignty, to sway, and to dominance. In this, French and British, Indian
and Japanese cultures concur. At the same time, paradoxically, we have
never been as aware as we now are of how oddly hybrid historical and
cultural experiences are, of how they partake of many often contradictory
experiences and domains, cross national boundaries, defy the *police* action of
simple dogma and loud patriotism. Far from being unitary or monolithic or
autonomous things, cultures actually assume more "foreign" elements, al-
terities, differences, than they consciously exclude. Who in India or Algeria
today can confidently separate out the British or French component of the
past from present actualities, and who in Britain or France can draw a clear
circle around British London or French Paris that would exclude the impact
of India and Algeria upon those two imperial cities?

These are not nostalgically academic or theoretical questions, for as a
brief excursion or two will ascertain, they have important social and political
consequences. Both London and Paris have large immigrant populations
from the former colonies, which themselves have a large residue of British
and French culture in their daily life. But that is obvious. Consider, for a
more complex example, the well-known issues of the image of classical
Greek antiquity or of tradition as a determinant of national identity. Studies
such as Martin Bernal's *Black Athena* and Eric Hobsbawm and Terence
Ranger's *The Invention of Tradition* have accentuated the extraordinary influence of today's anxieties and agendas on the pure (even purged) images
we construct of a privileged, genealogically useful past, a past in which we
exclude unwanted elements, vestiges, narratives. Thus, according to Bernal,
whereas Greek civilization was known originally to have roots in Egyptian,
Semitic, and various other southern and eastern cultures, it was redesigned

as "Aryan" during the course of the nineteenth century, its Semitic and African roots either actively purged or hidden from view. Since Greek writers themselves openly acknowledged their culture's hybrid past, European philologists acquired the ideological habit of passing over these embarrassing passages without comment, in the interests of Attic purity.[24] (One also recalls that only in the nineteenth century did European historians of the Crusades begin *not* to allude to the practice of cannibalism among the Frankish knights, even though eating human flesh is mentioned unashamedly in contemporary Crusader chronicles.)

No less than the image of Greece, images of European authority were buttressed and shaped during the nineteenth century, and where but in the manufacture of rituals, ceremonies, and traditions could this be done? This is the argument put forward by Hobsbawm, Ranger, and the other contributors to *The Invention of Tradition.* At a time when the older filaments and organizations that bound pre-modern societies internally were beginning to fray, and when the social pressures of administering numerous overseas territories and large new domestic constituencies mounted, the ruling elites of Europe felt the clear need to project their power backward in time, giving it a history and legitimacy that only tradition and longevity could impart. Thus in 1876 Victoria was declared Empress of India, her Viceroy Lord Lytton was sent there on a visit, greeted and celebrated in "traditional" jamborees and durbars all over the country, as well as in a great Imperial Assemblage in Delhi, as if her rule was not mainly a matter of power and unilateral edict, rather than age-old custom.[25]

Similar constructions have been made on the opposite side, that is, by insurgent "natives" about their pre-colonial past, as in the case of Algeria during the War of Independence (1954–1962), when decolonization encouraged Algerians and Muslims to create images of what they supposed themselves to have been prior to French colonization. This strategy is at work in what many national poets or men of letters say and write during independence or liberation struggles elsewhere in the colonial world. I want to underline the mobilizing power of the images and traditions brought forth, and their fictional, or at least romantically colored, fantastic quality. Think of what Yeats does for the Irish past, with its Cuchulains and its great houses, which give the nationalist struggle something to revive and admire. In post-colonial national states, the liabilities of such essences as the Celtic spirit, *négritude,* or Islam are clear: they have much to do not only with the native manipulators, who also use them to cover up contemporary faults, corruptions, tyrannies, but also with the embattled imperial contexts out of which they came and in which they were felt to be necessary.

Though for the most part the colonies have won their independence, many of the imperial attitudes underlying colonial conquest continue. In 1910 the French advocate of colonialism Jules Harmand said:

> It is necessary, then, to accept as a principle and point of departure the fact that there is a hierarchy of races and civilizations, and that we belong to the superior race and civilization, still recognizing that, while superiority confers rights, it imposes strict obligations in return. The basic legitimation of conquest over native peoples is the conviction of our superiority, not merely our mechanical, economic, and military superiority, but our moral superiority. Our dignity rests on that quality, and it underlies our right to direct the rest of humanity. Material power is nothing but a means to that end.[26]

As a precursor of today's polemics about the superiority of Western civilization over others, the supreme value of purely Western humanities as extolled by conservative philosophers like Allan Bloom, the essential inferiority (and threat) of the non-Westerner as claimed by Japan-bashers, ideological Orientalists, and critics of "native" regression in Africa and Asia, Harmand's declaration has a stunning prescience.

More important than the past itself, therefore, is its bearing upon cultural attitudes in the present. For reasons that are partly embedded in the imperial experience, the old divisions between colonizer and colonized have re-emerged in what is often referred to as the North-South relationship, which has entailed defensiveness, various kinds of rhetorical and ideological combat, and a simmering hostility that is quite likely to trigger devastating wars—in some cases it already has. Are there ways we can reconceive the imperial experience in other than compartmentalized terms, so as to transform our understanding of both the past and the present and our attitude toward the future?

We must start by characterizing the commonest ways that people handle the tangled, many-sided legacy of imperialism, not just those who left the colonies, but also those who were there in the first place and who remained, the natives. Many people in England probably feel a certain remorse or regret about their nation's Indian experience, but there are also many people who miss the good old days, even though the value of those days, the reason they ended, and their own attitudes toward native nationalism are all unresolved, still volatile issues. This is especially the case when race relations are involved, for instance during the crisis over the publication of Salman Rushdie's *The Satanic Verses* and the subsequent *fatwa* calling for Rushdie's death issued by Ayatollah Khomeini.

But, equally, debate in Third World countries about colonialist practice and the imperialist ideology that sustained it is extremely lively and diverse. Large groups of people believe that the bitterness and humiliations of the experience which virtually enslaved them nevertheless delivered benefits— liberal ideas, national self-consciousness, and technological goods—that over time seem to have made imperialism much less unpleasant. Other people in the post-colonial age retrospectively reflected on colonialism the better to understand the difficulties of the present in newly independent states. Real problems of democracy, development, and destiny, are attested to by the state persecution of intellectuals who carry on their thought and practice publicly and courageously—Eqbal Ahmad and Faiz Ahmad Faiz in Pakistan, Ngugi wa Thiongo in Kenya, or Abdelrahman el Munif in the Arab world—major thinkers and artists whose sufferings have not blunted the intransigence of their thought, or inhibited the severity of their punishment.

Neither Munif, Ngugi, nor Faiz, nor any other like them, was anything but unstinting in his hatred of implanted colonialism or the imperialism that kept it going. Ironically, they were listened to only partially, whether in the West or by the ruling authorities in their own societies. They were likely, on the one hand, to be considered by many Western intellectuals retrospective Jeremiahs denouncing the evils of a past colonialism, and, on the other, to be treated by their governments in Saudi Arabia, Kenya, Pakistan as agents of outside powers who deserved imprisonment or exile. The tragedy of this experience, and indeed of so many post-colonial experiences, derives from the limitations of the attempts to deal with relationships that are polarized, radically uneven, remembered differently. The spheres, the sites of intensity, the agendas, and the constituencies in the metropolitan and ex-colonized worlds appear to overlap only partially. The small area that is perceived as common does not, at this point, provide for more than what might be called a *rhetoric of blame.*

I want first to consider the actualities of the intellectual terrains both common and discrepant in post-imperial public discourse, especially concentrating on what in this discourse gives rise to and encourages the rhetoric and politics of blame. Then, using the perspectives and methods of what might be called a comparative literature of imperialism, I shall consider the ways in which a reconsidered or revised notion of how a post-imperial intellectual attitude might expand the overlapping community between metropolitan and formerly colonized societies. By looking at the different experiences contrapuntally, as making up a set of what I call intertwined and overlapping histories, I shall try to formulate an alternative both to a politics of blame and to the even more destructive politics of confrontation and hostility. A more interesting type of secular interpretation can emerge, altogether more rewarding than the denunciations of the past, the expressions of regret for its having ended, or—even more wasteful because violent and far too easy and attractive—the hostility between Western and non-Western cultures that leads to crises. The world is too small and interdependent to let these passively happen.

(III)

Two Visions in Heart of Darkness

Domination and inequities of power and wealth are perennial facts of human society. But in today's global setting they are also interpretable as having something to do with imperialism, its history, its new forms. The nations of contemporary Asia, Latin America, and Africa are politically independent but in many ways are as dominated and dependent as they were when ruled directly by European powers. On the one hand, this is the consequence of self-inflicted wounds, critics like V. S. Naipaul are wont to say: *they* (everyone knows that "they" means coloreds, wogs, niggers) are to blame for what "they" are, and it's no use droning on about the legacy of imperialism. On the other hand, blaming the Europeans sweepingly for the misfortunes of the present is not much of an alternative. What we need to do is to look at these matters as a network of interdependent histories that it would be inaccurate and senseless to repress, useful and interesting to understand.

The point here is not complicated. If while sitting in Oxford, Paris, or New York you tell Arabs or Africans that they belong to a basically sick or unregenerate culture, you are unlikely to convince them. Even if you prevail over them, they are not going to concede to you your essential superiority or your right to rule them despite your evident wealth and power. The history of this stand-off is manifest throughout colonies where white masters were once unchallenged but finally driven out. Conversely, the triumphant natives soon enough found that they needed the West and that the idea of *total* independence was a nationalist fiction designed mainly for what Fanon calls the "nationalist bourgeoisie," who in turn often ran the new countries with a callous, exploitative tyranny reminiscent of the departed masters.

And so in the late twentieth century the imperial cycle of the last century in some way replicates itself, although today there are really no big empty spaces, no expanding frontiers, no exciting new settlements to establish. We live in one global environment with a huge number of ecological, economic, social, and political pressures tearing at its only dimly perceived, basically uninterpreted and uncomprehended fabric. Anyone with even a vague consciousness of this whole is alarmed at how such remorselessly selfish and narrow interests—patriotism, chauvinism, ethnic, religious, and racial hatreds—can in fact lead to mass destructiveness. The world simply cannot afford this many more times.

One should not pretend that models for a harmonious world order are ready at hand, and it would be equally disingenuous to suppose that ideas of peace and community have much of a chance when power is moved to action by aggressive perceptions of "vital national interests" or unlimited sovereignty. The United States' clash with Iraq and Iraq's aggression against Kuwait concerning oil are obvious examples. The wonder of it is that the schooling for such relatively provincial thought and action is still prevalent, unchecked, uncritically accepted, recurringly replicated in the education of generation after generation. We are all taught to venerate our nations and admire our traditions: we are taught to pursue their interests with toughness and in disregard for other societies. A new and in my opinion appalling tribalism is fracturing societies, separating peoples, promoting greed, bloody conflict, and uninteresting assertions of minor ethnic or group particularity. Little time is spent not so much in "learning about other cultures"—the phrase has an inane vagueness to it—but in studying the map of interactions, the actual and often productive traffic occurring on a day-by-day, and even minute-by-minute basis among states, societies, groups, identities.

No one can hold this entire map in his or her head, which is why the geography of empire and the many-sided imperial experience that created its fundamental texture should be considered first in terms of a few salient configurations. Primarily, as we look back at the nineteenth century, we see that the drive toward empire in effect brought most of the earth under the domination of a handful of powers. To get hold of part of what this means, I propose to look at a specific set of rich cultural documents in which the interaction between Europe or America on the one hand and the imperialized world on the other is animated, informed, made explicit as an experience for both sides of the encounter. Yet before I do this, historically and systematically, it is a useful preparation to look at what still remains of imperialism in recent cultural discussion. This is the residuum of a dense, interesting history that is parodoxically global and local at the same time, and it is also a sign of how the imperial past lives on, arousing argument and counter-argument with surprising intensity. Because they are contemporary and easy at hand, these traces of the past in the present point the way to a study of the histories—the plural is used advisedly—created by empire, not just the stories of the white man and woman, but also those of the non-whites whose lands and very being were at issue, even as their claims were denied or ignored.

One significant contemporary debate about the residue of imperialism—the matter of how "natives" are represented in the Western media—illustrates the persistence of such interdependence and overlapping, not only in the debate's content but in its form, not only in what is said but also in how it is said, by whom, where, and for whom. This bears looking into, although it requires a self-discipline not easily come by, so well-developed, tempting, and ready at hand are the confrontational strategies. In 1984, well before *The Satanic Verses* appeared, Salman Rushdie diagnosed the spate of films and articles about the British Raj, including the television series *The Jewel in the Crown* and David Lean's film of *A Passage to India.* Rushdie noted that the nostalgia pressed into service by these affectionate recollections of British rule in India coincided with the Falklands War, and that "the rise of Raj revisionism, exemplified by the huge success of these fictions, is the artistic counterpart to the rise of conservative ideologies in modern Britain." Commentators responded to what they considered Rushdie's wailing and whining in public and seemed to disregard his principal point. Rushdie was trying to make a larger argument, which presumably should have appealed to intellectuals for whom George Orwell's well-known description of the intellectual's place in society as being inside and outside the whale no longer applied; modern reality in Rushdie's terms was actually "whaleless, this world without quiet corners [in which] there can be no easy escapes from history, from hullabaloo, from terrible, unquiet fuss."[27] But Rushdie's main point was *not* the point considered worth taking up and debating. Instead the main issue for contention was whether things in the Third World hadn't in fact declined after the colonies had been emancipated, and whether it might not be better on the whole to listen to the rare—luckily, I might add, extremely rare—Third World intellectuals who manfully ascribed most of their present barbarities, tyrannies, and degradations to their own native histories, histories that were pretty bad before colonialism and that reverted to that state after colonialism. Hence, ran *this* argument, better a ruthlessly honest V. S. Naipaul than an absurdly posturing Rushdie.

One could conclude from the emotions stirred up by Rushdie's own case, then and later, that many people in the West came to feel that enough was enough. After Vietnam and Iran—and note here that these labels are usually employed equally to evoke American domestic traumas (the student insurrections of the 1960s, the public anguish about the hostages in the 1970s) as much as international conflict and the "loss" of Vietnam and Iran to radical nationalisms—after Vietnam and Iran, lines had to be defended. Western democracy had taken a beating, and even if the physical damage had been done abroad, there was a sense, as Jimmy Carter once rather oddly put it, of "mutual destruction." This feeling in turn led to Westerners rethinking the whole process of decolonization. Was it not true, ran their new evaluation, that "we" had given "them" progress and modernization? Hadn't we provided them with order and a kind of stability that they haven't been able since to provide for themselves? Wasn't it an atrocious misplaced trust to believe in their capacity for independence, for it had led to Bokassas and Amins, whose intellectual correlates were people like Rushdie? Shouldn't we have held on to the colonies, kept the subject or inferior races in check, remained true to our civilizational responsibilities?

I realize that what I have just reproduced is not entirely the thing itself, but perhaps a caricature. Nevertheless it bears an uncomfortable resemblance to what many people who imagined themselves speaking for the West said. There seemed little skepticism that a monolithic "West" in fact existed, any more than an entire ex-colonial world described in one sweeping generalization after another. The leap to essences and generalizations was accompanied by appeals to an imagined history of Western endowments and free hand-outs, followed by a reprehensible sequence of ungrateful bitings of that grandly giving "Western" hand. "Why don't they appreciate us, after what we did for them?"[28]

How easily so much could be compressed into that simple formula of unappreciated magnanimity! Dismissed or forgotten were the ravaged colonial peoples who for centuries endured summary justice, unending economic oppression, distortion of their social and intimate lives, and a recourseless submission that was the function of unchanging European superiority. Only to keep in mind the millions of Africans who were supplied to the slave trade is to acknowledge the unimaginable cost of maintaining that superiority. Yet dismissed most often are precisely the infinite number of traces in the immensely detailed, violent history of colonial intervention—minute by minute, hour by hour—in the lives of individuals and collectivities, on both sides of the colonial divide.

The thing to be noticed about this kind of contemporary discourse, which assumes the primacy and even the complete centrality of the West, is how totalizing is its form, how all-enveloping its attitudes and gestures, how much it shuts out even as it includes, compresses, and consolidates. We suddenly find ourselves transported backward in time to the late nineteenth century.

This imperial attitude is, I believe, beautifully captured in the complicated and rich narrative form of Conrad's great novella *Heart of Darkness*, written between 1898 and 1899. On the one hand, the narrator Marlow acknowledges the tragic predicament of all speech—that "it is impossible to convey the life-sensation of any given epoch of one's existence—that which makes its truth, its meaning—its subtle and penetrating essence.... We live, as we dream—alone"[29]—yet still manages to convey the enormous power of Kurtz's African experience through his own overmastering narrative of his voyage into the African interior toward Kurtz. This narrative in turn is connected directly with the redemptive force, as well as the waste and horror, of Europe's mission in the dark world. Whatever is lost or elided or even simply made up in Marlow's immensely compelling recitation is compensated for in the narrative's sheer historical momentum, the temporal forward movement—with digressions, descriptions, exciting encounters, and all. Within the narrative of how he journeyed to Kurtz's Inner Station, whose source and authority he now becomes, Marlow moves backward and forward materially in small and large spirals, very much the way episodes in the course of his journey up-river are then incorporated by the principal forward trajectory into what he renders as "the heart of Africa."

Thus Marlow's encounter with the improbably white-suited clerk in the middle of the jungle furnishes him with several digressive paragraphs, as does his meeting later with the semi-crazed, harlequin-like Russian who has been so affected by Kurtz's gifts. Yet underlying Marlow's inconclusiveness, his evasions, his arabesque meditations on his feelings and ideas, is the unrelenting course of the journey itself, which, despite all the many obstacles, is sustained through the jungle, through time, through hardship, to the heart of it all, Kurtz's ivory-trading empire. Conrad wants us to see how Kurtz's great looting adventure, Marlow's journey up the river, and the narrative itself all share a common theme: Europeans performing acts of imperial mastery and will in (or about) Africa.

What makes Conrad different from the other colonial writers who were his contemporaries is that, for reasons having partly to do with the colonialism that turned him, a Polish expatriate, into an employee of the imperial system, he was so self-conscious about what he did. Like most of his other tales, therefore, *Heart of Darkness* cannot just be a straightforward recital of Marlow's adventures: it is also a dramatization of Marlow himself, the former wanderer in colonial regions, telling his story to a group of British listeners at a particular time and in a specific place. That this group of people is drawn largely from the business world is Conrad's way of emphasizing the fact that during the 1890s the business of empire, once an adventurous and often individualistic enterprise, had become the empire of business. (Coincidentally we should note that at about the same time Halford Mackinder, an explorer, geographer, and Liberal Imperialist, gave a series of lectures on imperialism at the London Institute of Bankers:[30] perhaps Conrad knew about this.) Although the almost oppressive force of Marlow's narrative leaves us with a quite accurate sense that there is no way out of the sovereign historical force of imperialism, and that it has the power of a system representing as well as speaking for everything within its dominion, Conrad shows us that what Marlow does is contingent, acted out for a set of like-minded British hearers, and limited to that situation.

Yet neither Conrad nor Marlow gives us a full view of what is *outside* the world-conquering attitudes embodied by Kurtz, Marlow, the circle of listeners on the deck of the *Nellie,* and Conrad. By that I mean that *Heart of Darkness* works so effectively because its politics and aesthetics are, so to speak, imperialist, which in the closing years of the nineteenth century seemed to be at the same time an aesthetic, politics, and even epistemology inevitable and unavoidable. For if we cannot truly understand someone else's experience and if we must therefore depend upon the assertive authority of the sort of power that Kurtz wields as a white man in the jungle or that Marlow, another white man, wields as narrator, there is no use looking for other, non-imperialist alternatives; the system has simply eliminated them and made them unthinkable. The circularity, the perfect closure of the whole thing is not only aesthetically but also mentally unassailable.

Conrad is so self-conscious about situating Marlow's tale in a narrative moment that he allows us simultaneously to realize after all that imperialism, far from swallowing up its own history, was taking place in and was circumscribed by a larger history, one just outside the tightly inclusive circle of Europeans on the deck of the *Nellie.* As yet, however, no one seemed to inhabit that region, and so Conrad left it empty.

Conrad could probably never have used Marlow to present anything other than an imperialist world-view, given what was available for either Conrad or Marlow to see of the non-European at the time. Independence was for whites and Europeans; the lesser or subject peoples were to be ruled; science, learning, history emanated from the West. True, Conrad scrupulously recorded the differences between the disgraces of Belgian and British colonial attitudes, but he could only imagine the world carved up into one or another Western sphere of dominion. But because Conrad also had an extraordinarily persistent residual sense of his own exilic marginality, he quite carefully (some would say maddeningly) qualified Marlow's narrative with the provisionality that came from standing at the very juncture of this world with another, unspecified but different. Conrad was certainly not a great imperialist entrepreneur like Cecil Rhodes or Frederick Lugard, even though he understood perfectly how for each of them, in Hannah Arendt's words, to enter "the maelstrom of an unending process of expansion, he will, as it were, cease to be what he was and obey the laws of the process, identify himself with anonymous forces that he is supposed to serve in order to keep the whole process in motion, he will think of himself as mere function, and eventually consider such functionality, such an incarnation of the dynamic trend, his highest possible achievement."[31] Conrad's realization is that if, like narrative, imperialism has monopolized the entire system of representation—which in the case of *Heart of Darkness* allowed it to speak for Africans as well as for Kurtz and the other adventurers, including Marlow and his audience—your self-consciousness as an outsider can allow you actively to comprehend how the machine works, given that you and it are fundamentally not in perfect synchrony or correspondence. Never the wholly incorporated and fully acculturated Englishman, Conrad therefore preserved an ironic distance in each of his works.

The form of Conrad's narrative has thus made it possible to derive two possible arguments, two visions, in the post-colonial world that succeeded his. One argument allows the old imperial enterprise full scope to play itself out conventionally, to render the world as official European or Western imperialism saw it, and to consolidate itself after World War Two. Westerners may have physically left their old colonies in Africa and Asia, but they retained them not only as markets but as locales on the ideological map over which they continued to rule morally and intellectually. "Show me the Zulu Tolstoy," as one American intellectual has recently put it. The assertive sovereign inclusiveness of this argument courses through the words of those who speak today for the West and for what the West did, as well as for what the rest of the world is, was, and may be. The assertions of this discourse exclude what has been represented as "lost" by arguing that the colonial world was in some ways ontologically speaking lost to begin with, irredeemable, irrecusably inferior. Moreover, it focusses not on what was shared in the colonial experience, but on what must never be shared, namely the authority and rectitude that come with greater power and development. Rhetorically, its terms are the organization of political passions, to borrow from Julien Benda's critique of modern intellectuals, terms which, he was sensible enough to know, lead inevitably to mass slaughter, and if not to literal mass slaughter then certainly to rhetorical slaughter.

The second argument is considerably less objectionable. It sees itself as Conrad saw his own narratives, local to a time and place, neither unconditionally true nor unqualifiedly certain. As I have said, Conrad does not give us the sense that he could imagine a fully realized alternative to imperialism: the natives he wrote about in Africa, Asia, or America were incapable of independence, and because he seemed to imagine that European tutelage was a given, he could not foresee what would take place when it came to an end. But come to an end it would, if only because—like all human effort, like speech itself—it would have its moment, then it would have to pass. Since Conrad *dates* imperialism, shows its contingency, records its illusions and tremendous violence and waste (as in *Nostromo*), he permits his later readers to imagine something other than an Africa carved up into dozens of European colonies, even if, for his own part, he had little notion of what that Africa might be.

To return to the first line out of Conrad, the discourse of resurgent empire proves that the nineteenth-century imperial encounter continues today to draw lines and defend barriers. Strangely, it persists also in the enormously complex and quietly interesting interchange between former colonial partners, say between Britain and India, or between France and the Francophone countries of Africa. But these exchanges tend to be overshadowed by the loud antagonisms of the polarized debate of pro- and anti-imperialists, who speak stridently of national destiny, overseas interests, neo-imperialism, and the like, drawing like-minded people—aggressive Westerners and, ironically, those non-Westerners for whom the new nationalist and resurgent Ayatollahs speak—away from the other ongoing interchange. Inside each regrettably constricted camp stand the blameless, the just, the faithful, led by the omnicompetent, those who know the truth about themselves and others; outside stands a miscellaneous bunch of querulous intellectuals and wishy-washy skeptics who go on complaining about the past to little effect.

An important ideological shift occurred during the 1970s and 1980s, accompanying this contraction of horizons in what I have been calling the first of the two lines leading out of *Heart of Darkness*. One can locate it, for instance, in the dramatic change in emphasis and, quite literally, direction among thinkers noted for their radicalism. The later Jean-François Lyotard and Michel Foucault, eminent French philosophers who emerged during the 1960s as apostles of radicalism and intellectual insurgency, describe a striking new lack of faith in what Lyotard calls the great legitimizing narratives of emancipation and enlightenment. Our age, he said in the 1980s, is postmodernist, concerned only with local issues, not with history but with problems to be solved, not with a grand reality but with games.[32] Foucault also turned his attention away from the oppositional forces in modern society which he had studied for their undeterred resistance to exclusion and confinement—delinquents, poets, outcasts, and the like—and decided that since power was everywhere it was probably better to concentrate on the local micro-physics of power that surround the individual. The self was therefore to be studied, cultivated, and, if necessary, refashioned and constituted.[33] In both Lyotard and Foucault we find precisely the same trope employed to explain the disappointment in the politics of liberation: narrative, which posits an enabling beginning point and a vindicating goal, is no longer adequate for plotting the human trajectory in society. There is nothing to look forward to: we are stuck within our circle. And now the line is enclosed by a circle. After years of support for anti-colonial struggles in Algeria, Cuba, Vietnam, Palestine, Iran, which came to represent for many Western intellectuals their deepest engagement in the politics and philosophy of anti-imperialist decolonization, a moment of exhaustion and disappointment was reached.[34] One began to hear and read how futile it was to support revolutions, how barbaric were the new regimes that came to power, how—this is an extreme case—decolonization had benefitted "world communism."

Enter now terrorism and barbarism. Enter also the ex-colonial experts whose well-publicized message was these colonial peoples deserve only colonialism or, since "we" were foolish to pull out of Aden, Algeria, India, Indochina, and everywhere else, it might be a good idea to reinvade their territories. Enter also various experts and theoreticians of the relationship between liberation movements, terrorism, and the KGB. There was a resurgence of sympathy for what Jeane Kirkpatrick called authoritarian (as opposed to totalitarian) regimes who were Western allies. With the onset of Reaganism, Thatcherism, and their correlates, a new phase of history began.

However else it might have been historically understandable, peremptorily withdrawing "the West" from its own experiences in the "peripheral world" certainly was and is not an attractive or edifying activity for an intellectual today. It shuts out the possibility of knowledge and of discovery of what it means to be outside the whale. Let us return to Rushdie for another insight:

> We see that it can be as false to create a politics-free fictional universe as to create one in which nobody needs to work or eat or hate or love or sleep. Outside the whale it becomes necessary, and even exhilarating, to grapple with the special problems created by the incorporation of political material, because politics is by turns farce and tragedy, and sometimes (e.g., Zia's Pakistan) both at once. Outside the whale the writer is obliged to accept that he (or she) is part of the crowd, part of the ocean, part of the storm, so that objectivity becomes a great dream, like perfection, an unattainable goal for which one must struggle in spite of the impossibility of success. Outside the whale is the world of Samuel Beckett's famous formula: *I can't go on, I'll go on.*[35]

The terms of Rushdie's description, while they borrow from Orwell, seem to me to resonate even more interestingly with Conrad. For here is the second consequence, the second line leading out of Conrad's narrative form;

in its explicit references to the outside, it points to a perspective outside the basically imperialist representations provided by Marlow and his listeners. It is a profoundly secular perspective, and it is beholden neither to notions about historical destiny and the essentialism that destiny always seems to entail, nor to historical indifference and resignation. Being on the inside shuts out the full experience of imperialism, edits it and subordinates it to the dominance of one Eurocentric and totalizing view; this other perspective suggests the presence of a field without special historical privileges for one party.

I don't want to overinterpret Rushdie, or put ideas in his prose that he may not have intended. In this controversy with the local British media (before *The Satanic Verses* sent him into hiding), he claimed that he could not recognize the truth of his own experience in the popular media representations of India. Now I myself would go further and say that it is one of the virtues of such conjunctures of politics with culture and aesthetics that they permit the disclosure of a common ground obscured by the controversy itself. Perhaps it is especially hard for the combatants directly involved to see this common ground when they are fighting back more than reflecting. I can perfectly understand the anger that fuelled Rushdie's argument because like him I feel outnumbered and outorganized by a prevailing Western consensus that has come to regard the Third World as an atrocious nuisance, a culturally and politically inferior place. Whereas we write and speak as members of a small minority of marginal voices, our journalistic and academic critics belong to a wealthy system of interlocking informational and academic resources with newspapers, television networks, journals of opinion, and institutes at its disposal. Most of them have now taken up a strident chorus of rightward-tending damnation, in which they separate what is non-white, non-Western, and non-Judeo-Christian from the acceptable and designated Western ethos, then herd it all together under various demeaning rubrics such as terrorist, marginal, second-rate, or unimportant. To attack what is contained in these categories is to defend the Western spirit.

Let us return to Conrad and to what I have been referring to as the second, less imperialistically assertive possibility offered by *Heart of Darkness*. Recall once again that Conrad sets the story on the deck of a boat anchored in the Thames; as Marlow tells his story the sun sets, and by the end of the narrative the heart of darkness has reappeared in England; outside the group of Marlow's listeners lies an undefined and unclear world. Conrad sometimes seems to want to fold that world into the imperial metropolitan discourse represented by Marlow, but by virtue of his own dislocated subjectivity he resists the effort and succeeds in so doing, I have always believed, largely through formal devices. Conrad's self-consciously circular narrative forms draw attention to themselves as artificial constructions, encouraging us to sense the potential of a reality that seemed inaccessible to imperialism, just beyond its control, and that only well after Conrad's death in 1924 acquired a substantial presence.

This needs more explanation. Despite their European names and mannerisms, Conrad's narrators are not average unreflecting witnesses of European imperialism. They do not simply accept what goes on in the name of the imperial idea: they think about it a lot, they worry about it, they are actually quite anxious about whether they can make it seem like a routine thing. But it never is. Conrad's way of demonstrating this discrepancy between the orthodox and his own views of empire is to keep drawing attention to how ideas and values are constructed (and deconstructed) through dislocations in the narrator's language. In addition, the recitations are meticulously staged: the narrator is a speaker whose audience and the reason for their being together, the quality of whose voice, the effect of what he says—are all important and even insistent aspects of the story he tells. Marlow, for example, is never straightforward. He alternates between garrulity and stunning eloquence, and rarely resists making peculiar things seem more peculiar by surprisingly misstating them, or rendering them vague and contradictory. Thus, he says, a French warship fires "into a continent"; Kurtz's eloquence is enlightening as well as fraudulent; and so on—his speech so full of these odd discrepancies (well discussed by Ian Watt as "delayed decoding"[36]) that the net effect is to leave his immediate audience as well as the reader with the acute sense that what he is presenting is not quite as it should be or appears to be.

Yet the whole point of what Kurtz and Marlow talk about is in fact imperial mastery, white European *over* black Africans, and their ivory, civilization *over* the primitive dark continent. By accentuating the discrepancy between the official "idea" of empire and the remarkably disorienting actuality of Africa, Marlow unsettles the reader's sense not only of the very idea of empire, but of something more basic, reality itself. For if Conrad can show that all human activity depends on controlling a radically unstable reality to which words approximate only by will or convention, the same is true of empire, of venerating the idea, and so forth. With Conrad, then, we are in a world being made and unmade more or less all the time. What appears stable and secure—the policeman at the corner, for instance—is only slightly more secure than the white men in the jungle, and requires the same continuous (but precarious) triumph over an all-pervading darkness, which by the end of the tale is shown to be the same in London and in Africa.

Conrad's genius allowed him to realize that the ever-present darkness could be colonized or illuminated—*Heart of Darkness* is full of references to the *mission civilisatrice*, to benevolent as well as cruel schemes to bring light to the dark places and peoples of this world by acts of will and deployments of power—but that it also had to be acknowledged as independent. Kurtz and Marlow acknowledge the darkness, the former as he is dying, the latter as he reflects retrospectively on the meaning of Kurtz's final words. They (and of course Conrad) are ahead of their time in understanding that what they call "the darkness" has an autonomy of its own, and can reinvade and reclaim what imperialism had taken for *its* own. But Marlow and Kurtz are also creatures of their time and cannot take the next step, which would be to recognize that what they saw, disablingly and disparagingly, as a non-European "darkness" was in fact a non-European world *resisting* imperialism so as one day to regain sovereignty and independence, and not, as Conrad reductively says, to reestablish the darkness. Conrad's tragic limitation is that even though he could see clearly that on one level imperialism was essentially pure dominance and land-grabbing, he could not then conclude that imperialism had to end so that "natives" could lead lives free from European domination. As a creature of his time, Conrad could not grant the natives their freedom, despite his severe critique of the imperialism that enslaved them.

The cultural and ideological evidence that Conrad was wrong in his Eurocentric way is both impressive and rich. A whole movement, literature, and theory of resistance and response to empire exists—it is the subject of Chapter Three of this book—and in greatly disparate post-colonial regions one sees tremendously energetic efforts to engage with the metropolitan world in equal debate so as to testify to the diversity and differences of the non-European world and to its own agendas, priorities, and history. The purpose of this testimony is to inscribe, reinterpret, and expand the areas of engagement as well as the terrain contested with Europe. Some of this activity—for example, the work of two important and active Iranian intellectuals, Ali Shariati and Jalal Ali i-Ahmed, who by means of speeches, books, tapes, and pamphlets prepared the way for the Islamic Revolution—interprets colonialism by asserting the absolute opposition of the native culture: the West is an enemy, a disease, an evil. In other instances, novelists like the Kenyan Ngugi and the Sudanese Tayeb Salih appropriate for their fiction such great *topoi* of colonial culture as the quest and the voyage into the unknown, claiming them for their own, post-colonial purposes. Salih's hero in *Season of Migration to the North* does (and is) the reverse of what Kurtz does (and is): the Black man journeys north into white territory.

Between classical nineteenth-century imperialism and what it gave rise to in resistant native cultures, there is thus both a stubborn confrontation and a crossing over in discussion, borrowing back and forth, debate. Many of the most interesting post-colonial writers bear their past within them—as scars of humiliating wounds, as instigation for different practices, as potentially revised visions of the past tending toward a new future, as urgently reinterpretable and redeployable experiences, in which the formerly silent native speaks and acts on territory taken back from the empire. One sees these aspects in Rushdie, Derek Walcott, Aimé Césaire, Chinua Achebe, Pablo Neruda, and Brian Friel. And now these writers can truly read the great colonial masterpieces, which not only misrepresented them but assumed they were unable to read and respond directly to what had been written about them, just as European ethnography presumed the natives' incapacity to intervene in scientific discourse about them. Let us try now to review this new situation more fully.

(IV)

Discrepant Experiences

Let us begin by accepting the notion that although there is an irreducible subjective core to human experience, this experience is also historical and secular, it is accessible to analysis and interpretation, and—centrally important—it is not exhausted by totalizing theories, not marked and limited by doctrinal or national lines, not confined once and for all to analytical constructs. If one believes with Gramsci that an intellectual vocation is socially possible as well as desirable, then it is an inadmissible contradiction at the same time to build analyses of historical experience around exclusions, exclusions that stipulate, for instance, that only women can understand feminine experience, only Jews can understand Jewish suffering, only formerly colonial subjects can understand colonial experience.

I do not mean what people mean when they say glibly that there are two sides to every question. The difficulty with theories of essentialism and exclusiveness, or with barriers and sides, is that they give rise to polarizations that absolve and forgive ignorance and demagogy more than they enable knowledge. Even the most cursory look at the recent fortunes of theories about race, the modern state, modern nationalism itself verifies this sad truth. If you know in advance that the African or Iranian or Chinese or Jewish or German experience is fundamentally integral, coherent, separate, and therefore comprehensible only to Africans, Iranians, Chinese, Jews, or Germans, you first of all posit as essential something which, I believe, is both historically created and the result of interpretation—namely the existence of Africanness, Jewishness, or Germanness, or for that matter Orientalism and Occidentalism. And second, you are likely as a consequence to defend the essence or experience itself rather than promote full knowledge of it and its entanglements and dependencies on other knowledges. As a result, you will demote the different experience of others to a lesser status.

If at the outset we acknowledge the massively knotted and complex histories of special but nevertheless overlapping and interconnected experiences—of women, of Westerners, of Blacks, of national states and cultures—there is no particular intellectual reason for granting each and all of them an ideal and essentially separate status. Yet we would wish to preserve what is unique about each so long as we also preserve some sense of the human community and the actual contests that contribute to its formation, and of which they are all a part. An excellent example of this approach is one I have already referred to, the essays in *The Invention of Tradition,* essays which consider invented traditions that are highly specialized and local (e.g., Indian durbars and European football games) yet, even though they are very different, share similar characteristics. The point of the book is that these quite various practices can be read and understood together since they belong to comparable fields of human experience, those Hobsbawm describes as attempting "to establish continuity with a suitable historic past."[37]

A comparative or, better, a contrapuntal perspective is required in order to see a connection between coronation rituals in England and the Indian durbars of the late nineteenth century. That is, we must be able to think through and interpret together experiences that are discrepant, each with its particular agenda and pace of development, its own internal formations, its internal coherence and system of external relationships, all of them coexisting and interacting with others. Kipling's novel *Kim,* for example, occupies a very special place in the development of the English novel and in late Victorian society, but its picture of India exists in a deeply antithetical relationship with the development of the movement for Indian independence. Either the novel or the political movement represented or interpreted without the other misses the crucial discrepancy between the two given to them by the actual experience of empire.

One point needs further clarification. The notion of "discrepant experiences" is not intended to circumvent the problem of ideology. On the contrary, no experience that is interpreted or reflected on can be characterized as immediate, just as no critic or interpreter can be entirely believed if he or she claims to have achieved an Archimedean perspective that is subject neither to history nor to a social setting. In juxtaposing experiences with each other, in letting them play off each other, it is my interpretative political aim (in the broadest sense) to make concurrent those views and experiences that are ideologically and culturally closed to each other and that attempt to distance or suppress other views and experiences. Far from seeking to reduce the significance of ideology, the exposure and dramatization of discrepancy highlights its cultural importance; this enables us to appreciate its power and understand its continuing influence.

So let us contrast two roughly contemporary early-nineteenth-century texts (both date from the 1820s): the *Description de l'Egypte* in all its massive, impressive coherence, and a comparatively slender volume, 'Abd al-Rahman al-Jabarti's *'Aja'ib al-Athar*. The *Description* was the twenty-four-volume account of Napoleon's expedition to Egypt, produced by the team of French scientists which he took with him. 'Abd al-Rahman al-Jabarti was an Egyptian notable and *'alim*, or religious leader, who witnessed and lived through the French expedition. Take first the following passage from the general introduction to the *Description* written by Jean-Baptiste-Joseph Fourier:

> Placed between Africa and Asia, and communicating easily with Europe, Egypt occupies the center of the ancient continent. This country presents only great memories; it is the homeland of the arts and conserves innumerable monuments; its principal temples and the palaces inhabited by its kings still exist, even though its least ancient edifices had already been built by the time of the Trojan War. Homer, Lycurgus, Solon, Pythagoras, and Plato all went to Egypt to study the sciences, religion, and the laws. Alexander founded an opulent city there, which for a long time enjoyed commercial supremacy and which witnessed Pompey, Caesar, Mark Antony, and Augustus deciding between them the fate of Rome and that of the entire world. It is therefore proper for this country to attract the attention of illustrious princes who rule the destiny of nations.
>
> No considerable power was ever amassed by any nation, whether in the West or in Asia, that did not also turn that nation toward Egypt, which was regarded in some measure as its natural lot.[38]

Fourier speaks as the rationalizing mouthpiece of Napoleon's invasion of Egypt in 1798. The resonances of the great names he summons, the placing, the grounding, the normalizing of foreign conquest within the cultural orbit of European existence—all this transforms conquest from a clash between a conquering and a defeated army into a much longer, slower process, obviously more acceptable to the European sensibility enfolded within its own cultural assumptions than the shattering experience could have been for an Egyptian who endured the conquest.

At almost the same time Jabarti records in his book a series of anguished and perceptive reflections on the conquest; he writes as an embattled religious notable recording the invasion of his country and the destruction of his society.

> This year is the beginning of a period marked by great battles; serious results were suddenly produced in a frightening manner; miseries multiplied without end, the course of things was troubled, the common meaning of life was corrupted and destruction overtook it and the devastation was general. [Then, as a good Muslim, he turns back to reflect on himself and his people.] "God," says the Koran (xi, 9) "does not unjustly ruin cities whose inhabitants are just."³⁹

The French expedition was accompanied by a whole team of scientists whose job it was to survey Egypt as it had never been surveyed before—the result was the gigantic *Description* itself—but Jabarti has eyes for, and only appreciates, the facts of power, whose meaning he senses as constituting a punishment for Egypt. French power bears upon his existence as a conquered Egyptian, an existence for him compressed into that of a subjugated particle, barely able to do more than record the French army's comings and goings, its imperious decrees, its overwhelmingly harsh measures, its awesome and seemingly unchecked ability to do what it wants according to imperatives that Jabarti's compatriots could not affect. The discrepancy between the politics producing the *Description* and that of Jabarti's immediate response is stark, and highlights the terrain they contest so unequally.

Now it is not difficult to follow out the results of Jabarti's attitude, and generations of historians have in fact done this, as I shall do to some extent later in this book. His experience produced a deep-seated anti-Westernism that is a persistent theme of Egyptian, Arab, Islamic, and Third World history; one can also find in Jabarti the seeds of Islamic reformism which, as promulgated later by the great Azhar cleric and reformer Muhammad 'Abdu and his remarkable contemporary Jamal al-Din al-Afghani, argued either that Islam had better modernize in order to compete with the West, or that it should return to its Meccan roots the better to combat the West; in addition, Jabarti speaks at an early moment in the history of the immense wave of national self-consciousness that culminated in Egyptian independence, in Nasserite theory and practice, and in contemporary movements of so-called Islamic fundamentalism.

Nevertheless historians have not so readily read the development of French culture and history in terms of Napoleon's Egyptian expedition. (The same is true of the British reign in India, a reign of such immense range and wealth as to have become a fact of nature for members of the imperial culture.) Yet what later scholars and critics say about the European texts literally made possible by the *Description*'s consolidation of the conquest of the Orient is also, interestingly, a somewhat attenuated and highly implicit function of that earlier contest. To write today about Nerval and Flaubert, whose work depended so massively upon the Orient, is to work in territory originally charted by the French imperial victory, to follow in its steps, and to extend them into 150 years of European experience, although in saying this one once again highlights the symbolic discrepancy between Jabarti and Fourier. The imperial conquest was not a one-time tearing of the veil, but a continually repeated, institutionalized presence in French life, where the response to the silent and incorporated disparity between French and subjugated cultures took on a variety of forms.

The asymmetry is striking. In one instance, we assume that the better part of history in colonial territories was a function of the imperial intervention; in the other, there is an equally obstinate assumption that colonial undertakings were marginal and perhaps even eccentric to the central activities of the great metropolitan cultures. Thus, the tendency in anthropology, history, and cultural studies in Europe and the United States is to treat the whole of world history as viewable by a kind of Western super-subject, whose historicizing and disciplinary rigor either takes away or, in the post-colonial period, restores history to people and cultures "without" history. Few full-scale critical studies have focussed on the relationship between modern Western imperialism and its culture, the occlusion of that deeply symbiotic relationship being a result of the relationship itself. More particularly, the extraordinary formal and ideological dependence of the great French and English realistic novels on the facts of empire has also never been studied from a general theoretical standpoint. These elisions and denials are all reproduced, I believe, in the strident journalistic debates about decolonization, in which imperialism is repeatedly on record as saying, in effect, You are what you are because of us; when we left, you reverted to your deplorable state; know that or you will know nothing, for certainly there is little to be known about imperialism that might help either you or us in the present.

Were the disputed value of knowledge about imperialism merely a controversy about methodology or academic perspectives in cultural history, we would be justified in regarding it as not really serious, though perhaps worth notice. In fact, however, we are talking about a compellingly important and interesting configuration in the world of power and nations. There is no question, for example, that in the past decade the extraordinarily intense reversion to tribal and religious sentiments all over the world has accompanied and deepened many of the discrepancies among polities that have continued since—if they were not actually created by—the period of high European imperialism. Moreover, the various struggles for dominance among states, nationalisms, ethnic groups, regions, and cultural entities have conducted and amplified a manipulation of opinion and discourse, a production and consumption of ideological media representations, a simplification and reduction of vast complexities into easy currency, the easier to deploy and exploit them in the interest of state policies. In all of this intellectuals have played an important role, nowhere in my opinion more crucial *and* more compromised than in the overlapping region of experience and culture that is colonialism's legacy where the politics of secular interpretation is carried on for very high stakes. Naturally the preponderance of power has been on the side of the self-constituted "Western" societies and the public intellectuals who serve as their apologists and ideologists.

But there have been interesting responses to this imbalance in many formerly colonized states. Recent work on India and Pakistan in particular (e.g., *Subaltern Studies*) has highlighted the complicities between the post-colonial security state and the intellectual nationalist elite; Arab, African, and Latin American oppositional intellectuals have produced similar critical studies. But I shall focus here more closely on the unfortunate convergence that uncritically propels the Western powers into action against ex-colonial peoples. During the time I have been writing this book, the crisis caused by Iraq's invasion and annexation of Kuwait has been in full flower: hundreds of thousands of the United States' troops, planes, ships, tanks, missiles arrived in Saudi Arabia; Iraq appealed to the Arab world (badly split among the United States' supporters like Mubarak of Egypt, the Saudi royal family, the remaining Gulf sheikhs, Moroccans, and outright opponents like Libya and Sudan, or caught-in-the-middle powers like Jordan and Palestine) for help; the United Nations was divided between sanctions and the United States' blockade; and in the end the United States prevailed and a devastating war was fought. Two central ideas clearly were held over from the past and still hold sway: one was the great power's right to safeguard its distant interests even to the point of military invasion; the second was that lesser powers were also lesser peoples, with lesser rights, morals, claims.

Perceptions and political attitudes molded and manipulated by the media were significant here. In the West, representations of the Arab world ever since the 1967 War have been crude, reductionist, coarsely racialist, as much critical literature in Europe and the United States has ascertained and verified. Yet films and television shows portraying Arabs as sleazy "camel-jockeys," terrorists, and offensively wealthy "sheikhs" pour forth anyway. When the media mobilized behind President Bush's instructions to preserve the American way of life and to roll Iraq back, little was said or shown about the political, social, cultural actualities of the Arab world (many of them deeply influenced by the United States), actualities that made possible both the appalling figure of Saddam Hussein and at the same time a complex set of other, radically different configurations—the Arabic novel (whose pre-eminent practitioner, Naguib Mahfouz, won the 1988 Nobel Prize) and the many institutions surviving in what was left of civil society. While it is certainly true that the media is far better equipped to deal with caricature and sensation than with the slower processes of culture and society, the deeper reason for these misconceptions is the imperial dynamic and above all its separating, essentializing, dominating, and reactive tendencies.

Self-definition is one of the activities practiced by all cultures: it has a rhetoric, a set of occasions and authorities (national feasts, for example, times of crisis, founding fathers, basic texts, and so on), and a familiarity all its own. Yet in a world tied together as never before by the exigencies of electronic communication, trade, travel, environmental and regional conflicts that can expand with tremendous speed, the assertion of identity is by no means a mere ceremonial matter. What strikes me as especially dangerous is that it can mobilize passions atavistically, throwing people back to an earlier imperial time when the West and its opponents championed and even embodied virtues designed not as virtues so to speak but for war.

One perhaps trivial example of this atavism occurred in a column written for *The Wall Street Journal* on May 2, 1989, by Bernard Lewis, one of the senior Orientalists working in the United States. Lewis was entering the debate about changing the "Western canon." To the students and professors at Stanford University who had voted to modify the curriculum to include texts by more non-Europeans, women, and so on, Lewis—speaking as an authority on Islam—took the extreme position that "if Western culture does indeed go a number of things would go with it and others would come in their place." No one had said anything so ludicrous as "Western culture must go," but Lewis's argument, focussed on much grander matters than strict accuracy, lumbered forward with the remarkable proposition that since modifications in the reading list would be equivalent to the demise of Western culture, such subjects (he named them specifically) as the restoration of slavery, polygamy, and child marriage would ensue. To this amazing thesis Lewis added that "curiosity about other cultures," which he believes is unique to the West, would also come to an end.

This argument, symptomatic and even a trifle comic, is an indication not only of a highly inflated sense of Western exclusivity in cultural accomplishment, but also of a tremendously limited, almost hysterically antagonistic view of the rest of the world. To say that without the West, slavery and bigamy would return is to foreclose the possibility that any advance over tyranny and barbarism could or did occur outside the West. Lewis's argument has the effect of driving the non-Westerner into a violent rage or, with equally unedifying consequences, into boasting about the achievements of non-Western cultures. Rather than affirming the interdependence of various histories *on* one another, and the necessary interaction of contemporary societies *with* one another, the rhetorical separation of cultures assured a murderous imperial contest between them—the sorry tale is repeated again and again.

Another example occurred in late 1986, during the broadcast and subsequent discussion of a television documentary called *The Africans*. Originally commissioned and mostly funded by the BBC, this series was written and narrated by a distinguished scholar and professor of political science at the University of Michigan, Ali Mazrui, a Kenyan and a Muslim, whose competence and credibility as a first-rank academic authority were unquestioned. Mazrui's series had two premises: one, that for the first time in a history dominated by Western representations of Africa (to use the phrase from Christopher Miller's book *Blank Darkness*, by a discourse that is thoroughly Africanist in every instance and inflection)[40] an African was representing himself and Africa before a Western audience, precisely that audience whose societies for several hundred years had pillaged, colonized, enslaved Africa; second, that African history was made up of three elements or, in Mazrui's language, concentric circles: the native African experience, the experience of Islam, and the experience of imperialism.

For a start, the National Endowment for the Humanities removed its financial support for the broadcast of the documentaries, although the series ran on PBS anyway. Then *The New York Times*, the leading American newspaper, ran consecutive attacks on the series in articles (September 14, October 9 and 26, 1986) by the (then) television correspondent John Corry. To describe Corry's pieces as insensate or semi-hysterical would not be an exaggeration. Mostly Corry accused Mazrui personally of "ideological" exclusions and emphases, for example, that he nowhere mentioned Israel (in a program about African history Israel may have appeared to Mazrui as not relevant) and that he vastly exaggerated the evils of Western colonialism. Corry's attack especially singled out Mazrui's "moralistic and political ordinates," a peculiar euphemism implying that Mazrui was little more than an unscrupulous propagandist, the better to be able to challenge Mazrui's figures about such things as the number of people who died in building the Suez Canal, the number killed during the Algerian war of liberation, and so on. Lurking near the turbulent and disorderly surface of Corry's prose was the (to him) disturbing and unacceptable reality of Mazrui's performance itself. Here at last was an African on prime-time television, in the West, daring to accuse the West of what it had done, thus reopening a file considered closed. That Mazrui also spoke well of Islam, that he showed a command of "Western" historical method and political rhetoric, that, in fine, he appeared as a convincing model of a real human being—all these ran contrary to the reconstituted imperial ideology for which Corry was, perhaps inadvertently, speaking. At its heart lay the axiom that non-Europeans should not represent their views of European and American history as those histories impinged on the colonies; if they did, they had to be very firmly resisted.

The entire legacy of what can metaphorically be called the tension between Kipling, who finally saw only the politics of empire, and Fanon, who tried to look past the nationalist assertions succeeding classical imperialism, has been disastrous. Let us allow that, given the discrepancy between European colonial power and that of the colonized societies, there was a kind of historical necessity by which colonial pressure created anti-colonial resistance. What concerns me is the way in which, generations later, the conflict continues in an impoverished and for that reason all the more dangerous form, thanks to an uncritical alignment between intellectuals and institutions of power which reproduces the pattern of an earlier imperialist history. This results, as I noted earlier, in an intellectual politics of blame and a drastic reduction in the range of material proposed for attention and controversy by public intellectuals and cultural historians.

What is the inventory of the various strategies that might be employed to widen, expand, and deepen our awareness of the way the past and present of the imperial encounter interact with each other? This seems to me a question of immediate importance, and indeed explains the idea behind this book. Let me very briefly illustrate my idea with two examples that are usefully presented, I think, in anecdotal form; in subsequent pages I shall present a more formal and methodological account of the issues and of the cultural interpretations and politics that follow.

A few years ago I had a chance encounter with an Arab Christian clergyman who had come to the United States, he told me, on an exceedingly urgent and unpleasant mission. As I myself happened to be a member by birth of the small but significant minority he served—Arab Christian Protestants—I was most interested in what he had to say. Since the 1860s there has been a Protestant community comprising a few sects scattered throughout the Levant, largely the result of the imperial competition for converts and constituents in the Ottoman Empire, principally in Syria, Lebanon, and Palestine. In time of course these congregations—Presbyterian, Evangelical, Episcopalian, Baptist, among others—acquired their own identities and traditions, their own institutions, all of which without exception played an honorable role during the period of the Arab Renaissance.

Roughly 110 years later, however, the very same European and American synods and churches who had authorized and indeed sustained the early missionary efforts appeared, quite without warning, to be reconsidering the matter. It had become clear to them that Eastern Christianity was really constituted by the Greek Orthodox Church (from which, it should be noted, the overwhelming majority of Levantine converts to Protestantism came: the nineteenth-century Christian missionaries were totally unsuccessful in converting either Muslims or Jews). Now, in the 1980s, the Western principals of the Arab Protestant communities were encouraging their acolytes to return to the Orthodox fold. There was talk of withdrawing financial support, of disbanding the churches and schools, of cancelling the whole thing in a sense. The missionary authorities had made a mistake one hundred years ago in severing Eastern Christians from the main church. Now they should go back.

To my clergyman friend this was a truly drastic eventuality; were it not for the genuinely aggrieved sensibility involved, one might have considered the whole matter merely a cruel joke. What struck me most strongly, however, was the way in which my friend put his argument. This was what he was in America to say to his ecclesiastical principals: he could understand the new doctrinal point being put forward, that modern ecumenism ought generally to go in the direction of dissolving small sects and preserving the dominant community, rather than encouraging these sects to remain independent from the main church. That you could discuss. But what seemed horrendously imperialist and entirely of the realm of power politics was, he said, the total disregard with which over a century of Arab Protestant experience was simply scratched off as if it had never happened. They do not seem to realize, my gravely affected friend told me, that while once we were their converts and students, we have in fact been their partners for well over a century. We have trusted them and our own experience. We have developed our own integrity and lived our own Arab Protestant identity within our sphere, but also spiritually within theirs. How do they expect us to efface our modern history, which is an autonomous one? How can they say that the mistake they made a century ago can be rectified today by a stroke of the pen in New York or London?

One should note that this touching story concerns an experience of imperialism that is essentially one of sympathy and congruence, not of antagonism, resentment, or resistance. The appeal by one of the parties was to the value of a mutual experience. True, there had once been a principal and a subordinate, but there had also been dialogue and communication.

One can see in the story, I think, the power to give or withhold attention, a power utterly essential to interpretation and to politics. The implicit argument made by the Western missionary authorities was that the Arabs had gotten something valuable out of what had been given them, but in this relationship of historical dependence and subordination, all the giving went one way, the value was mainly on one side. Mutuality was considered to be basically impossible.

This is a parable about the area of attention, greater or lesser in size, more or less equal in value and quality, that is furnished for interpretation by the post-imperial situation.

The second general point I want to make can also be made by example. One of the canonical topics of modern intellectual history has been the development of dominant discourses and disciplinary traditions in the main fields of scientific, social, and cultural inquiry. Without exceptions I know of, the paradigms for this topic have been drawn from what are considered exclusively Western sources. Foucault's work is one instance and so, in another domain, is Raymond Williams's. In the main I am in considerable sympathy with the genealogical discoveries of these two formidable scholars, and greatly indebted to them. Yet for both the imperial experience is quite irrelevant, a theoretical oversight that is the norm in Western cultural and scientific disciplines except in occasional studies of the history of anthropology—like Johannes Fabian's *Time and the Other* and Talal Asad's *Anthropology and the Colonial Encounter*—or the development of sociology, such as Brian Turner's *Marx and the End of Orientalism*.[41] Part of the impulse behind what I tried to do in my book *Orientalism* was to show the dependence of what appeared to be detached and apolitical cultural disciplines upon a quite sordid history of imperialist ideology and colonialist practice.

But I will confess that I was also consciously trying to express dissatisfaction at the consolidated walls of denial that had been built around policy studies passing themselves off as uncontroversial, essentially pragmatic scholarly enterprises. Whatever effect my book achieved would not have occurred had there not also been some readiness on the part of a younger generation of scholars, in the West and in the formerly colonized world, to take a fresh look at their collective histories. Despite the acrimony and recriminations that followed their efforts, many important revisionary works have appeared. (Actually, they started to appear as early as one hundred years ago, during the resistance to empire all through the non-Western world.) Many of these more recent works, which I discuss elsewhere in this book, are valuable because they get beyond the reified polarities of East versus West, and in an intelligent and concrete way attempt to understand the heterogenous and often odd developments that used to elude the so-called world historians as well as the colonial Orientalists, who have tended to herd immense amounts of material under simple and all-encompassing rubrics. Examples worth mentioning include Peter Gran's study on the Islamic roots of modern capitalism in Egypt, Judith Tucker's research on Egyptian family and village structure under the influence of imperialism, Hanna Batatu's monumental work on the formation of modern state institutions in the Arab world, and S. H. Alatas's great study *The Myth of the Lazy Native*.[42]

Yet few works have dealt with the more complex genealogy of contemporary culture and ideology. One notable effort has been the recently published work of a Columbia doctoral student from India, a trained scholar and teacher of English literature whose historical and cultural research has, I think, uncovered the political origins of modern English studies and located them to a significant extent in the system of colonial education imposed on natives in nineteenth-century India. A great deal about Gauri Viswanathan's work, *The Masks of Conquest*, has unusual interest, but her central point alone is important: that what has conventionally been thought of as a discipline created entirely by and for British youth was first created by early-nineteenth-century colonial administrators for the ideological pacification and re-formation of a potentially rebellious Indian population, and then imported into England for a very different but related use there.[43] The evidence, I think, is incontrovertible and free from "nativism," an especially besetting hobble of most post-colonial work. Most important, though, this kind of study maps out a varied and intertwined archeology for knowledge whose actualities lie considerably below the surface hitherto assumed to be the true locus, and textuality, of what we study as literature, history, culture, and philosophy. The implications are vast, and they pull us away from routinized polemics on the superiority of Western over non-Western models.

There is no way of dodging the truth that the present ideological and political moment is a difficult one for the alternative norms for intellectual work that I propose in this book. There is also no escape from the pressing and urgent calls many of us are likely to respond to from embattled causes and turbulent fields of battle. The ones that involve me as an Arab are, alas, perfect cases in point, and they are exacerbated by pressures exerted on me as an American. Nevertheless, a resistant, perhaps ultimately subjective component of oppositional energy resides in the intellectual or critical vocation itself, and one has to rely on mobilizing this, particularly when collective passions seem mostly harnessed to movements for patriotic domination and nationalist coercion, even in studies and disciplines that claim to be humanistic. In standing up to and challenging their power, we should try to enlist what we can truly comprehend of other cultures and periods.

For the trained scholar of comparative literature, a field whose origin and purpose is to move beyond insularity and provincialism and to see several cultures and literatures together, contrapuntally, there is an already considerable investment in precisely this kind of antidote to reductive nationalism and uncritical dogma: after all, the constitution and early aims of comparative literature were to get a perspective beyond one's own nation, to see some sort of whole instead of the defensive little patch offered by one's own culture, literature, and history. I suggest that we look first at what comparative literature originally was, as vision and as practice; ironically, as we shall see, the study of "comparative literature" originated in the period of high European imperialism and is irrecusably linked to it. Then we can draw out of comparative literature's subsequent trajectory a better sense of what it can do in modern culture and politics, which imperialism continues to influence.

(v)

Connecting Empire to Secular Interpretation

From long before World War Two until the early 1970s, the main tradition of comparative-literature studies in Europe and the United States was heavily dominated by a style of scholarship that has now almost disappeared. The main feature of this older style was that it was scholarship principally, and not what we have come to call criticism. No one today is trained as were Erich Auerbach and Leo Spitzer, two of the great German comparatists who found refuge in the United States as a result of fascism: this is as much a quantitative as a qualitative fact. Whereas today's comparatist will present his or her qualifications in Romanticism between 1795 and 1830 in France, England, and Germany, yesterday's comparatist was more likely, first, to have studied an earlier period; second, to have done a long apprenticeship with various philological and scholarly experts in various universities in various fields over many years; third, to have a secure grounding in all or most of the classical languages, the early European vernaculars, and their literatures. The early-twentieth-century comparatist was a *philolog* who, as Francis Fergusson put it in a review of Auerbach's *Mimesis,* was so learned and had so much stamina as to make "our most intransigent 'scholars'—those who pretend with the straightest faces to scientific rigor and exhaustiveness—[appear to be] timid and relaxed."[44]

Behind such scholars was an even longer tradition of humanistic learning that derived from that efflorescence of secular anthropology—which included a revolution in the philological disciplines—we associate with the late eighteenth century and with such figures as Vico, Herder, Rousseau, and the brothers Schlegel. And underlying *their* work was the belief that mankind formed a marvelous, almost symphonic whole whose progress and formations, again as a whole, could be studied exclusively as a concerted and secular historical experience, not as an exemplification of the divine. Because "man" has made history, there was a special hermeneutical way of studying history that differed in intent as well as method from the natural sciences. These great Enlightenment insights became widespread, and were accepted in Germany, France, Italy, Russia, Switzerland, and subsequently, England.

It is not a vulgarization of history to remark that a major reason why such a view of human culture became current in Europe and America in several different forms during the two centuries between 1745 and 1945 was the striking rise of nationalism during the same period. The interrelationships between scholarship (or literature, for that matter) and the institutions of nationalism have not been as seriously studied as they should, but it is nevertheless evident that when most European thinkers celebrated humanity or culture they were principally celebrating ideas and values they ascribed to their own national culture, or to Europe as distinct from the Orient, Africa, and even the Americas. What partly animated my study of Orientalism was my critique of the way in which the alleged universalism of fields such as the classics (not to mention historiography, anthropology, and sociology) was Eurocentric in the extreme, as if other literatures and societies had either an inferior or a transcended value. (Even the comparatists trained in the dignified tradition that produced Curtius and Auerbach showed little interest in Asian, African, or Latin American texts.) And as the national and international competition between European countries increased during the nineteenth century, so too did the level of intensity in competition between one national scholarly interpretative tradition and another. Ernest Renan's polemics on Germany and the Jewish tradition are a well-known example of this.

Yet this narrow, often strident nationalism was in fact counteracted by a more generous cultural vision represented by the intellectual ancestors of Curtius and Auerbach, scholars whose ideas emerged in pre-imperial Germany (perhaps as compensation for the political unification eluding the country), and, a little later, in France. These thinkers took nationalism to be a transitory, finally secondary matter: what mattered far more was the concert of peoples and spirits that transcended the shabby political realm of bureaucracy, armies, customs barriers, and xenophobia. Out of this catholic tradition, to which European (as opposed to national) thinkers appealed in times of severe conflict, came the idea that the comparative study of literature could furnish a trans-national, even trans-human perspective on literary performance. Thus the idea of comparative literature not only expressed universality and the kind of understanding gained by philologists about language families, but also symbolized the crisis-free serenity of an almost ideal realm. Standing above small-minded political affairs were both a kind of anthropological Eden in which men and women happily produced something called literature, and a world that Matthew Arnold and his disciples designated as that of "culture," where only "the best that is thought and known" could be admitted.

Goethe's idea of *Weltliteratur*—a concept that waffled between the notion of "great books" and a vague synthesis of *all* the world's literatures—was very important to professional scholars of comparative literature in the early twentieth century. But still, as I have suggested, its practical meaning and operating ideology were that, so far as literature and culture were concerned, Europe led the way and was the main subject of interest. In the world of great scholars such as Karl Vossler and De Sanctis, it is most specifically Romania that makes intelligible and provides a center for the enormous grouping of literatures produced world-wide; Romania underpins Europe, just as (in a curiously regressive way) the Church and the Holy Roman Empire guarantee the integrity of the core European literatures. At a still deeper level, it is from the Christian Incarnation that Western realistic literature as we know it emerges. This tenaciously advanced thesis explained Dante's supreme importance to Auerbach, Curtius, Vossler, and Spitzer.

To speak of comparative literature therefore was to speak of the interaction of world literatures with one another, but the field was epistemologically organized as a sort of hierarchy, with Europe and its Latin Christian literatures at its center and top. When Auerbach, in a justly famous essay entitled "Philologie der *Weltliteratur*," written after World War Two, takes note of how many "other" literary languages and literatures seemed to have emerged (as if from nowhere: he makes no mention of either colonialism or decolonization), he expresses more anguish and fear than pleasure at the prospect of what he seems so reluctant to acknowledge. Romania is under threat.[45]

Certainly American practitioners and academic departments found this European pattern a congenial one to emulate. The first American department of comparative literature was established in 1891 at Columbia University, as was the first journal of comparative literature. Consider what George Edward Woodberry—the department's first chaired professor—had to say about his field:

The parts of the world draw together, and with them the parts of knowledge, slowly knitting into that one intellectual state which, above the sphere of politics and with no more institutional machinery than tribunals of jurists and congresses of gentlemen, will be at last the true bond of all the world. The modern scholar shares more than other citizens in the benefits of this enlargement and intercommunication, this age equally of expansion and concentration on the vast scale, this infinitely extended and intimate commingling of nations with one another and with the past; his ordinary mental experience includes more of race-memory and of race-imagination than belonged to his predecessors, and his outlook before and after is on greater horizons; he lives in a larger world—is, in fact, born no longer to the freedom of a city merely, however noble, but to that new citizenship in the rising state which—the obscurer or brighter dream of all great scholars from Plato to Goethe—is without frontiers or race or force, but there is reason supreme. The emergence and growth of the new study known as Comparative Literature are incidental to the coming of this larger world and the entrance of scholars upon its work: the study will run its course, and together with other converging elements goes to its goal in the unity of mankind found in the spiritual unities of science, art and love.[46]

Such rhetoric uncomplicatedly and naively resonates with the influence of Croce and De Sanctis, and also with the earlier ideas of Wilhelm von Humboldt. But there is a certain quaintness in Woodberry's "tribunals of jurists and congresses of gentlemen," more than a little belied by the actualities of life in the "larger world" he speaks of. In a time of the greatest Western imperial hegemony in history, Woodberry manages to overlook that dominating form of political unity in order to celebrate a still higher, strictly ideal unity. He is unclear about how "the spiritual unities of science, art and love" are to deal with less pleasant realities, much less how "spiritual unities" can be expected to overcome the facts of materiality, power, and political division.

Academic work in comparative literature carried with it the notion that Europe and the United States together were the center of the world, not simply by virtue of their political positions, but also because their literatures were the ones most worth studying. When Europe succumbed to fascism and when the United States benefitted so richly from the many emigré scholars who came to it, understandably little of their sense of crisis took root with them. *Mimesis,* for example, written while Auerbach was in exile from Nazi Europe in Istanbul, was not simply an exercise in textual explication, but— he says in his 1952 essay to which I have just referred—an act of civilizational survival. It had seemed to him that his mission as a comparatist was to present, perhaps for the last time, the complex evolution of European literature in all its variety from Homer to Virginia Woolf. Curtius's book on the Latin Middle Ages was composed out of the same driven fear. Yet how little of that spirit survived in the thousands of academic literary scholars who were influenced by these two books! *Mimesis* was praised for being a remarkable work of rich analysis, but the sense of its mission died in the often trivial uses made of it.[47] Finally in the late 1950s *Sputnik* came along, and transformed the study of foreign languages—and of comparative litera- ture—into fields directly affecting national security. The National Defense Education Act[48] promoted the field and, with it, alas, an even more compla- cent ethnocentrism and covert Cold Warriorism than Woodberry could have imagined.

As *Mimesis* immediately reveals, however, the notion of Western litera- ture that lies at the very core of comparative study centrally highlights, dramatizes, and celebrates a certain idea of history, and at the same time obscures the fundamental geographical and political reality empowering that idea. The idea of European or Western literary history contained in it and the other scholarly works of comparative literature is essentially idealis- tic and, in an unsystematic way, Hegelian. Thus the principle of develop- ment by which Romania is said to have acquired dominance is incorporative and synthetic. More and more reality is included in a literature that expands and elaborates from the medieval chronicles to the great edifices of nine- teenth-century narrative fiction—in the works of Stendhal, Balzac, Zola, Dickens, Proust. Each work in the progression represents a synthesis of problematic elements that disturb the basic Christian order so memorably laid out in the *Divine Comedy.* Class, political upheavals, shifts in economic patterns and organization, war: all these subjects, for great authors like Cervantes, Shakespeare, Montaigne, as well as for a host of lesser writers, are enfolded within recurringly renewed structures, visions, stabilities, all of them attesting to the abiding dialectical order represented by Europe itself.

The salutary vision of a "world literature" that acquired a redemptive status in the twentieth century coincides with what theorists of colonial geography also articulated. In the writings of Halford Mackinder, George Chisolm, Georges Hardy, Leroy-Beaulieu, and Lucien Fevre, a much franker appraisal of the world system appears, equally metrocentric and imperial; but instead of history alone, now both empire and actual geographical space collaborate to produce a "world-empire" commanded by Europe. But in this geographically articulated vision (much of it based, as Paul Carter shows in *The Road to Botany Bay*, on the cartographic results of actual geographical exploration and conquest) there is no less strong a commitment to the belief that European pre-eminence is natural, the culmination of what Chisolm calls various "historical advantages" that allowed Europe to override the "natural advantages" of the more fertile, wealthy, and accessible regions it controlled.[49] Fevre's *La Terre et l'evolution humaine* (1922), a vigorous and integral encyclopedia, matches Woodberry for its scope and utopianism.

To their audience in the late nineteenth and early twentieth centuries, the great geographical synthesizers offered technical explanations for ready political actualities. Europe *did* command the world; the imperial map *did* license the cultural vision. To us, a century later, the coincidence or similarity between one vision of a world system and the other, between geography and literary history, seems interesting but problematic. What should we do with this similarity?

First of all, I believe, it needs *articulation* and *activation*, which can only come about if we take serious account of the present, and notably of the dismantling of the classical empires and the new independence of dozens of formerly colonized peoples and territories. We need to see that the contemporary global setting—overlapping territories, intertwined histories—was already prefigured and inscribed in the coincidences and convergences among geography, culture, and history that were so important to the pioneers of comparative literature. Then we can grasp in a new and more dynamic way both the idealist historicism which fuelled the comparatist "world literature" scheme and the concretely imperial world map of the same moment.

But that cannot be done without accepting that what is common to both is an elaboration of power. The genuinely profound scholarship of the people who believed in and practiced *Weltliteratur* implied the extraordinary privilege of an observer located in the West who could actually survey the world's literary output with a kind of sovereign detachment. Orientalists and other specialists about the non-European world—anthropologists, historians, philologists—had that power, and, as I have tried to show elsewhere, it often went hand in glove with a consciously undertaken imperial enterprise. We must articulate these various sovereign dispositions and see their common methodology.

An explicitly geographical model is provided in Gramsci's essay *Some Aspects of the Southern Question*. Under-read and under-analyzed, this study is the only sustained piece of political and cultural analysis Gramsci wrote (although he never finished it); it addresses the geographical conundrum posed for action and analysis by his comrades as to how to think about, plan for, and study southern Italy, given that its social disintegration made it seem incomprehensible yet paradoxically crucial to an understanding of the north. Gramsci's brilliant analysis goes, I think, beyond its tactical relevance to Italian politics in 1926, for it provides a culmination to his journalism before 1926 and also a prelude to *The Prison Notebooks*, in which he gave, as his towering counterpart Lukacs did not, paramount focus to the territorial, spatial, geographical foundations of social life.

Lukacs belongs to the Hegelian tradition of Marxism, Gramsci to a Vichian, Crocean departure from it. For Lukacs the central problematic in his major work through *History and Class Consciousness* (1923) is temporality; for Gramsci, as even a cursory examination of his conceptual vocabulary immediately reveals, social history and actuality are grasped in geographical terms—such words as "terrain," "territory," "blocks," and "region" predominate. In *The Southern Question*, Gramsci not only is at pains to show that the division between the northern and southern regions of Italy is basic to the challenge of what to do politically about the national working-class movement at a moment of impasse, but also is fastidious in describing the peculiar topography of the south, remarkable, as he says, for the striking contrast between the large undifferentiated mass of peasants on the one hand, and the presence of "big" landowners, important publishing houses, and distinguished cultural formations on the other. Croce himself, a most impressive and notable figure in Italy, is seen by Gramsci with characteristic shrewdness as a southern philosopher who finds it easier to relate to Europe and to Plato than to his own crumbling meridional environment.

The problem therefore is how to connect the south, whose poverty and vast labor pool are inertly vulnerable to northern economic policies and powers, with a north that is dependent on it. Gramsci formulates the answer in ways that forecast his celebrated animadversions on the intellectual in the *Quaderni:* he considers Piero Gobetti, who as an intellectual understood the need for connecting the northern proletariat with the southern peasantry, a strategy that stood in stark contrast with the careers of Croce and Guistino Fortunato, and who linked north and south by virtue of his capacity for organizing culture. His work "posed the Southern question on a terrain different from the traditional one [which regarded the south simply as a backward region of Italy] by introducing into it the proletariat of the North."[50] But this introduction could not occur, Gramsci continues, unless one remembered that intellectual work is slower, works according to more extended calendars than that of any other social group. Culture cannot be looked at as an immediate fact but has to be seen (as he was to say in the *Quaderni*) *sub specie aeternitatis.* Much time elapses before new cultural formations emerge, and intellectuals, who depend on long years of preparation, action, and tradition, are necessary to the process.

Gramsci also understands that in the extended time span during which the coral-like formation of a culture occurs, one needs "breaks of an organic kind." Gobetti represents one such break, a fissure that opened up within the cultural structures that supported and occluded the north-south discrepancy for so long in Italian history. Gramsci regards Gobetti with evident warmth, appreciation, and cordiality as an individual, but his political and social significance for Gramsci's analysis of the southern question—and it is appropriate that the unfinished essay ends abruptly with this consideration of Gobetti—is that he accentuates the need for a social formation to develop, elaborate, build upon the break instituted by his work, and by his insistence that intellectual effort itself furnishes the link between disparate, apparently autonomous regions of human history.

What we might call the Gobetti factor functions like an animating connective that expresses and represents the relationship between the development of comparative literature and the emergence of imperial geography, and does so dynamically and organically. To say of both discourses merely that they are imperialist is to say little about where and how they take place. Above all it leaves out what makes it possible for us to articulate them *together,* as an ensemble, as having a relationship that is more than coincidental, conjunctural, mechanical. For this we must look at the domination of the non-European world from the perspective of a resisting, gradually more and more challenging alternative.

Without significant exception the universalizing discourses of modern Europe and the United States assume the silence, willing or otherwise, of the non-European world. There is incorporation; there is inclusion; there is direct rule; there is coercion. But there is only infrequently an acknowledgement that the colonized people should be heard from, their ideas known.

It is possible to argue that the continued production and interpretation of Western culture itself made exactly the same assumption well on into the twentieth century, even as political resistance grew to the West's power in the "peripheral" world. Because of that, and because of where it led, it becomes possible now to reinterpret the Western cultural archive as if fractured geographically by the activated imperial divide, to do a rather different kind of reading and interpretation. In the first place, the history of fields like comparative literature, English studies, cultural analysis, anthropology can be seen as affiliated with the empire and, in a manner of speaking, even contributing to its methods for maintaining Western ascendancy over non-Western natives, especially if we are aware of the spatial consciousness exemplified in Gramsci's "southern question." And in the second place our interpretative change of perspective allows us to challenge the sovereign and unchallenged authority of the allegedly detached Western observer.

Western cultural forms can be taken out of the autonomous enclosures in which they have been protected, and placed instead in the dynamic global environment created by imperialism, itself revised as an ongoing contest between north and south, metropolis and periphery, white and native. We may thus consider imperialism as a process occurring as part of the metropolitan culture, which at times acknowledges, at other times obscures the sustained business of the empire itself. The important point—a very Gramscian one—is how the national British, French, and American cultures maintained hegemony over the peripheries. How within them was consent gained and continuously consolidated for the distant rule of native peoples and territories?

As we look back at the cultural archive, we begin to reread it not univocally but *contrapuntally*, with a simultaneous awareness both of the metropolitan history that is narrated and of those other histories against which (and together with which) the dominating discourse acts. In the counterpoint of Western classical music, various themes play off one another, with only a provisional privilege being given to any particular one; yet in the resulting polyphony there is concert and order, an organized interplay that derives from the themes, not from a rigorous melodic or formal principle outside the work. In the same way, I believe, we can read and interpret English novels, for example, whose engagement (usually suppressed for the most part) with the West Indies or India, say, is shaped and perhaps even determined by the specific history of colonization, resistance, and finally native nationalism. At this point alternative or new narratives emerge, and they become institutionalized or discursively stable entities.

It should be evident that no one overarching theoretical principle governs the whole imperialist ensemble, and it should be just as evident that the principle of domination and resistance based on the division between the West and the rest of the world—to adapt freely from the African critic Chinweizu—runs like a fissure throughout. That fissure affected all the many local engagements, overlappings, interdependencies in Africa, India, and elsewhere in the peripheries, each different, each with its own density of associations and forms, its own motifs, works, institutions, and—most important from our point of view as rereaders—its own possibilities and conditions of knowledge. For each locale in which the engagement occurs, and the imperialist model is disassembled, its incorporative, universalizing, and totalizing codes rendered ineffective and inapplicable, a particular type of research and knowledge begins to build up.

An example of the new knowledge would be the study of Orientalism or Africanism and, to take a related set, the study of Englishness and Frenchness. These identities are today analyzed not as god-given essences, but as results of collaboration between African history and the study of Africa in England, for instance, or between the study of French history and the reorganization of knowledge during the First Empire. In an important sense, we are dealing with the formation of cultural identities understood not as essentializations (although part of their enduring appeal is that they seem and are considered to be like essentializations) but as contrapuntal ensembles, for it is the case that no identity can ever exist by itself and without an array of opposites, negatives, oppositions: Greeks always require barbarians, and Europeans Africans, Orientals, etc. The opposite is certainly true as well. Even the mammoth engagements in our own time over such essentializations as "Islam," the "West," the "Orient," "Japan," or "Europe" admit to a particular knowledge and structures of attitude and reference, and those require careful analysis and research.

If one studies some of the major metropolitan cultures—England's, France's and the United States', for instance—in the geographical context of their struggles for (and over) empires, a distinctive cultural topography becomes apparent. In using the phrase "structures of attitude and reference" I have this topography in mind, as I also have in mind Raymond Williams's seminal phrase "structures of feeling." I am talking about the way in which structures of location and geographical reference appear in the cultural languages of literature, history, or ethnography, sometimes allusively and sometimes carefully plotted, across several individual works that are not otherwise connected to one another or to an official ideology of "empire."

In British culture, for instance, one may discover a consistency of concern in Spenser, Shakespeare, Defoe, and Austen that fixes socially desirable, empowered space in metropolitan England or Europe and connects it by design, motive, and development to distant or peripheral worlds (Ireland, Venice, Africa, Jamaica), conceived of as desirable but subordinate. And with these meticulously maintained references come attitudes—about rule, control, profit and enhancement and suitability—that grow with astonishing power from the seventeenth to the end of the nineteenth century. These structures do not arise from some pre-existing (semi-conspiratorial) design that the writers then manipulate, but are bound up with the development of Britain's cultural identity, as that identity imagines itself in a geographically conceived world. Similar structures may be remarked in French and American cultures, growing for different reasons and obviously in different ways. We are not yet at the stage where we can say whether these globally integral structures are preparations for imperial control and conquest, or whether they accompany such enterprises, or whether in some reflective or careless way they are a result of empire. We are only at a stage where we must look at the astonishing frequency of geographical articulations in the three Western cultures that most dominated far-flung territories. In the second chapter of this book I explore this question and advance further arguments about it.

To the best of my ability to have read and understood these "structures of attitude and reference," there was scarcely any dissent, any departure, any demurral from them: there was virtual unanimity that subject races should be ruled, that they *are* subject races, that one race deserves and has consistently earned the right to be considered the race whose main mission is to expand beyond its own domain. (Indeed, as Seeley was to put it in 1883, about Britain—France and the United States had their own theorists—the British could only be understood as such.) It is perhaps embarrassing that sectors of the metropolitan cultures that have since become vanguards in the social contests of our time were uncomplaining members of this imperial consensus. With few exceptions, the women's as well as the working-class movement was pro-empire. And, while one must always be at great pains to show that different imaginations, sensibilities, ideas, and philosophies were at work, and that each work of literature or art is special, there was virtual unity of purpose on this score: the empire must be maintained, and it *was* maintained.

Reading and interpreting the major metropolitan cultural texts in this newly activated, reinformed way could not have been possible without the movements of resistance that occurred everywhere in the peripheries against the empire. In the third chapter of this book I make the claim that a new global consciousness connects all the various local arenas of anti-imperial contest. And today writers and scholars from the formerly colonized world have imposed their diverse histories on, have mapped their local geographies in, the great canonical texts of the European center. And from these overlapping yet discrepant interactions the new readings and knowledges are beginning to appear. One need only think of the tremendously powerful upheavals that occurred at the end of the 1980s—the breaking down of barriers, the popular insurgencies, the drift across borders, the looming problems of immigrant, refugee, and minority rights in the West—to see how obsolete are the old categories, the tight separations, and the comfortable autonomies.

It is very important, though, to assess how these entities were built, and to understand how patiently the idea of an unencumbered English culture, for example, acquired its authority and its power to impose itself across the seas. This is a tremendous task for any individual, but a whole new generation of scholars and intellectuals from the Third World is engaged on just such an undertaking.

Here a word of caution and prudence is required. One theme I take up is the uneasy relationship between nationalism and liberation, two ideals or goals for people engaged against imperialism. In the main it is true that the creation of very many newly independent nation-states in the post-colonial world has succeeded in re-establishing the primacy of what have been called imagined communities, parodied and mocked by writers like V. S. Naipaul and Conor Cruise O'Brien, hijacked by a host of dictators and petty tyrants, enshrined in various state nationalisms. Nevertheless in general there is an oppositional quality to the consciousness of many Third World scholars and intellectuals, particularly (but not exclusively) those who are exiles, expatriates, or refugees and immigrants in the West, many of them inheritors of the work done by earlier twentieth-century expatriates like George Antonius and C.L.R. James. Their work in trying to connect experiences across the imperial divide, in re-examining the great canons, in producing what in effect is a critical literature cannot be, and generally has not been, co-opted by the resurgent nationalisms, despotisms, and ungenerous ideologies that betrayed the liberationist ideal in favor of the nationalist independence actuality.

Moreover their work should be seen as sharing important concerns with minority and "suppressed" voices within the metropolis itself: feminists, African-American writers, intellectuals, artists, among others. But here too vigilance and self-criticism are crucial, since there is an inherent danger to oppositional effort of becoming institutionalized, marginality turning into separatism, and resistance hardening into dogma. Surely the activism that reposits and reformulates the political challenges in intellectual life is safeguarded against orthodoxy. But there is always a need to keep community before coercion, criticism before mere solidarity, and vigilance ahead of assent.

Since my themes here are a sort of sequel to *Orientalism*, which like this book was written in the United States, some consideration of America's cultural and political environment is warranted. The United States is no ordinary large country. The United States is the last superpower, an enormously influential, frequently interventionary power nearly everywhere in the world. Citizens and intellectuals of the United States have a particular responsibility for what goes on between the United States and the rest of the world, a responsibility that is in no way discharged or fulfilled by saying that the Soviet Union, Britain, France, or China were, or are, worse. The fact is that we are indeed responsible for, and therefore more capable of, influencing *this* country in ways that we were not for the pre-Gorbachev Soviet Union, or other countries. So we should first take scrupulous note of how in Central and Latin America—to mention the most obvious—as well as in the Middle East, Africa, and Asia, the United States has replaced the great earlier empires and is *the* dominant outside force.

Looked at honestly, the record is not a good one. United States military interventions since World War Two have occurred (and are still occurring) on nearly every continent, many of great complexity and extent, with tremendous national investment, as we are now only beginning to understand. All of this is, in William Appleman Williams's phrase, empire as a way of life. The continuing disclosures about the war in Vietnam, about the United States' support of "contras" in Nicaragua, about the crisis in the Persian Gulf, are only part of the story of this complex of interventions. Insufficient attention is paid to the fact that United States Middle Eastern and Central American policies—whether exploiting a geo-political opening among Iranian so-called moderates, or aiding the so-called Contra Freedom Fighters in overthrowing the elected, legal government of Nicaragua, or coming to the aid of the Saudi and Kuwaiti royal families—can only be described as imperialist.

Even if we were to allow, as many have, that United States foreign policy is principally altruistic and dedicated to such unimpeachable goals as freedom and democracy, there is considerable room for skepticism. The relevance of T. S. Eliot's remarks in "Tradition and the Individual Talent" about the historical sense are demonstrably important. Are we not as a nation repeating what France and Britain, Spain and Portugal, Holland and Germany, did before us? And yet do we not tend to regard ourselves as somehow exempt from the more sordid imperial adventures that preceded ours? Besides, is there not an unquestioned assumption on our part that our destiny is to rule and lead the world, a destiny that we have assigned ourselves as part of our errand into the wilderness?

In short, we face as a nation the deep, profoundly perturbed and perturbing question of our relationship to others—other cultures, states, histories, experiences, traditions, peoples, and destinies. There is no Archimedean point beyond the question from which to answer it; there is no vantage outside the actuality of relationships among cultures, among unequal imperial and non-imperial powers, among us and others; no one has the epistemological privilege of somehow judging, evaluating, and interpreting the world free from the encumbering interests and engagements of the ongoing relationships themselves. We are, so to speak, *of* the connections, not outside and beyond them. And it behooves us as intellectuals and humanists and secular critics to understand the United States in the world of nations and power from *within* the actuality, as participants in it, not detached outside observers who, like Oliver Goldsmith, in Yeats's perfect phrase, deliberately sip at the honeypots of our minds.

Contemporary travails in recent European and American anthropology reflect these conundrums and embroilments in a symptomatic and interesting way. That cultural practice and intellectual activity carry, as a major constitutive element, an unequal relationship of force between the outside Western ethnographer-observer and the primitive, or at least different, but certainly weaker and less developed non-European, non-Western person. In the extraordinarily rich text of *Kim*, Kipling extrapolates the political meaning of that relationship and embodies it in the figure of Colonel Creighton, an ethnographer in charge of the Survey of India, also the head of British intelligence services in India, the "Great Game" to which young Kim belongs. Modern Western anthropology frequently repeated that problematic relationship, and in recent works of a number of theoreticians deals with the almost insuperable contradiction between a political actuality based on force, and a scientific and humane desire to understand the Other hermeneutically and sympathetically in modes not influenced by force.

Whether these efforts succeed or fail is a less interesting matter than what distinguishes them, what makes them possible: an acute and embarrassed awareness of the all-pervasive, unavoidable imperial setting. In fact, there is no way that I know of apprehending the world from within American culture (with a whole history of exterminism and incorporation behind it) without also apprehending the imperial contest itself. This, I would say, is a cultural fact of extraordinary political as well as interpretative importance, yet it has not been recognized as such in cultural and literary theory, and is routinely circumvented or occluded in cultural discourses. To read most cultural deconstructionists, or Marxists, or new historicists is to read writers whose political horizon, whose historical location is within a society and culture deeply enmeshed in imperial domination. Yet little notice is taken of this horizon, few acknowledgements of the setting are advanced, little realization of the imperial closure itself is allowed for. Instead, one has the impression that interpretation of other cultures, texts, and peoples—which at bottom is what all interpretation is about—occurs in a timeless vacuum, so forgiving and permissive as to deliver the interpretation directly into a universalism free from attachment, inhibition, and interest.

We live of course in a world not only of commodities but also of representation, and representations—their production, circulation, history, and interpretation—are the very element of culture. In much recent theory the problem of representation is deemed to be central, yet rarely is it put in its full political context, a context that is primarily imperial. Instead we have on the one hand an isolated cultural sphere, believed to be freely and unconditionally available to weightless theoretical speculation and investigation, and, on the other, a debased political sphere, where the real struggle between interests is supposed to occur. To the professional student of culture—the humanist, the critic, the scholar—only one sphere is relevant, and, more to the point, it is accepted that the two spheres are separated, whereas the two are not only connected but ultimately the same.

A radical falsification has become established in this separation. Culture is exonerated of any entanglements with power, representations are considered only as apolitical images to be parsed and construed as so many grammars of exchange, and the divorce of the present from the past is assumed to be complete. And yet, far from this separation of spheres being a neutral or accidental choice, its real meaning is as an act of complicity, the humanist's choice of a disguised, denuded, systematically purged textual model over a more embattled model, whose principal features would inevitably coalesce around the continuing struggle over the question of empire itself.

Let me put this differently, using examples that will be familiar to everyone. For at least a decade, there has been a decently earnest debate in the United States over the meaning, contents, and goals of liberal education. Much but not all of this debate was stimulated in the university after the upheavals of the 1960s, when it appeared for the first time in this century that the structure, authority, and tradition of American education were challenged by marauding energies, released by socially and intellectually inspired provocations. The newer currents in the academy, and the force of what is called theory (a rubric under which were herded many new disciplines like psychoanalysis, linguistics, and Nietzschean philosophy, unhoused from the traditional fields such as philology, moral philosophy, and the natural sciences), acquired prestige and interest; they appeared to undermine the authority and the stability of established canons, well-capitalized fields, long-standing procedures of accreditation, research, and the division of intellectual labor. That all this occurred in the modest and circumscribed terrain of cultural-academic praxis simultaneously with the great wave of anti-war, anti-imperialist protest was not fortuitous but, rather, a genuine political and intellectual conjuncture.

There is considerable irony that our search in the metropolis for a newly invigorated, reclaimed tradition follows the exhaustion of modernism and is expressed variously as post-modernism or, as I said earlier, citing Lyotard, as the loss of the legitimizing power of the narratives of Western emancipation and enlightenment; simultaneously, modernism is rediscovered in the formerly colonized, peripheral world, where resistance, the logic of daring, and various investigations of age-old tradition (*al-Turath*, in the Islamic world) together set the tone.

One response in the West to the new conjunctures, then, has been profoundly reactionary: the effort to reassert old authorities and canons, the effort to reinstate ten or twenty or thirty essential Western books without which a Westerner would not be educated—these efforts are couched in the rhetoric of embattled patriotism.

But there can be another response, worth returning to here, for it offers an important theoretical opportunity. Cultural experience or indeed every cultural form is radically, quintessentially hybrid, and if it has been the practice in the West since Immanuel Kant to isolate cultural and aesthetic realms from the worldly domain, it is now time to rejoin them. This is by no means a simple matter, since—I believe—it has been the essence of experience in the West at least since the late eighteenth century not only to acquire distant domination and reinforce hegemony, but also to divide the realms of culture and experience into apparently separate spheres. Entities such as races and nations, essences such as Englishness or Orientalism, modes of production such as the Asiatic or Occidental, all of these in my opinion testify to an ideology whose cultural correlatives well precede the actual accumulation of imperial territories world-wide.

Most historians of empire speak of the "age of empire" as formally beginning around 1878, with "the scramble for Africa." A closer look at the cultural actuality reveals a much earlier, more deeply and stubbornly held view about overseas European hegemony; we can locate a coherent, fully mobilized system of ideas near the end of the eighteenth century, and there follows the set of integral developments such as the first great systematic conquests under Napoleon, the rise of nationalism and the European nation-state, the advent of large-scale industrialization, and the consolidation of power in the bourgeoisie. This is also the period in which the novel form and the new historical narrative become pre-eminent, and in which the importance of subjectivity to historical time takes firm hold.

Yet most cultural historians, and certainly all literary scholars, have failed to remark the *geographical* notation, the theoretical mapping and charting of territory that underlies Western fiction, historical writing, and philosophical discourse of the time. There is first the authority of the European observer—traveller, merchant, scholar, historian, novelist. Then there is the hierarchy of spaces by which the metropolitan center and, gradually, the metropolitan economy are seen as dependent upon an overseas system of territorial control, economic exploitation, and a socio-cultural vision; without these stability and prosperity at home—"home" being a word with extremely potent resonances—would not be possible. The perfect example of what I mean is to be found in Jane Austen's *Mansfield Park,* in which Thomas Bertram's slave plantation in Antigua is mysteriously necessary to the poise and the beauty of Mansfield Park, a place described in moral and aesthetic terms well before the scramble for Africa, or before the age of empire officially began. As John Stuart Mill puts it in the *Principles of Political Economy:*

> These [outlying possessions of ours] are hardly to be looked upon as countries, ... but more properly as outlying agricultural or manufacturing estates belonging to a larger community. Our West Indian colonies, for example, cannot be regarded as countries with a productive capital of their own ... [but are rather] the place where England finds it convenient to carry on the production of sugar, coffee and a few other tropical commodities.[51]

Read this extraordinary passage together with Jane Austen, and a much less benign picture stands forth than the usual one of cultural formations in the pre-imperialist age. In Mill we have the ruthless proprietary tones of the white master used to effacing the reality, work, and suffering of millions of slaves, transported across the middle passage, reduced only to an incorporated status "for the benefit of the proprietors." These colonies are, Mill says, to be considered as hardly anything more than a convenience, an attitude confirmed by Austen, who in *Mansfield Park* sublimates the agonies of Caribbean existence to a mere half dozen passing references to Antigua. And much the same processes occur in other canonical writers of Britain and France; in short, the metropolis gets its authority to a considerable extent from the devaluation as well as the exploitation of the outlying colonial possession. (Not for nothing, then, did Walter Rodney entitle his great decolonizing treatise of 1972 *How Europe Underdeveloped Africa.*)

Lastly, the authority of the observer, and of European geographical centrality, is buttressed by a cultural discourse relegating and confining the non-European to a secondary racial, cultural, ontological status. Yet this secondariness is, paradoxically, essential to the primariness of the European; this of course is the paradox explored by Césaire, Fanon, and Memmi, and it is but one among many of the ironies of modern critical theory that it has rarely been explored by investigators of the aporias and impossibilities of reading. Perhaps that is because it places emphasis not so much on *how* to read, but rather on *what* is read and *where* it is written about and represented. It is to Conrad's enormous credit to have sounded in such a complex and riven prose the authentic imperialist note—how you supply the forces of

world-wide accumulation and rule with a self-confirming ideological motor
(what Marlow in *Heart of Darkness* calls efficiency with devotion to an idea
at the back of it, "it" being the taking away of the earth from those with
darker complexions and flatter noses) and simultaneously draw a screen
across the process, saying that art and culture have nothing to do with "it."

What to read and what to do with that reading, that is the full form of the
question. All the energies poured into critical theory, into novel and demystifying theoretical praxes like the new historicism and deconstruction and
Marxism have avoided the major, I would say determining, political horizon
of modern Western culture, namely imperialism. This massive avoidance
has sustained a canonical inclusion and exclusion: you include the Rous-
seaus, the Nietzsches, the Wordsworths, the Dickenses, Flauberts, and so on,
and at the same you exclude their relationships with the protracted, complex, and striated work of empire. But why is this a matter of what to read
and about where? Very simply, because critical discourse has taken no
cognizance of the enormously exciting, varied post-colonial literature produced in resistance to the imperialist expansion of Europe and the United
States in the past two centuries. To read Austen without also reading Fanon
and Cabral—and so on and on—is to disaffiliate modern culture from its
engagements and attachments. That is a process that should be reversed.

But there is more to be done. Critical theory and literary historical
scholarship have reinterpreted and revalidated major swatches of Western
literature, art, and philosophy. Much of this has been exciting and powerful work, even though one often senses more an energy of elaboration and
refinement than a committed engagement to what I would call secular and
affiliated criticism; such criticism cannot be undertaken without a fairly
strong sense of how consciously chosen historical models are relevant to
social and intellectual change. Yet if you read and interpret modern European and American culture as having had something to do with imperialism, it becomes incumbent upon you also to reinterpret the canon in the
light of texts whose place there has been insufficiently linked to, insufficiently weighted toward the expansion of Europe. Put differently, this procedure entails reading the canon as a polyphonic accompaniment to the
expansion of Europe, giving a revised direction and valence to writers
such as Conrad and Kipling, who have always been read as sports, not as
writers whose manifestly imperialist subject matter has a long subterranean or implicit and proleptic life in the earlier work of writers like, say,
Austen or Chateaubriand.

Second, theoretical work must begin to formulate the relationship between empire and culture. There have been a few milestones—Kiernan's
work, for instance, and Martin Green's—but concern with the issue has not

been intense. Things, however, are beginning to change, as I noted earlier. A whole range of work in other disciplines, a new group of often younger scholars and critics—here, in the Third World, in Europe—are beginning to embark on the theoretical and historical enterprises; many of them seem in one way or another to be converging on questions of imperialist discourse, colonialist practice, and so forth. Theoretically we are only at the stage of trying to inventory the *interpellation* of culture by empire, but the efforts so far made are only slightly more than rudimentary. And as the study of culture extends into the mass media, popular culture, micro-politics, and so forth, the focus on modes of power and hegemony grows sharper.

Third, we should keep before us the prerogatives of the present as signposts and paradigms for the study of the past. If I have insisted on integration and connections between the past and the present, between imperializer and imperialized, between culture and imperialism, I have done so not to level or reduce differences, but rather to convey a more urgent sense of the interdependence between things. So vast and yet so detailed is imperialism as an experience with crucial cultural dimensions, that we must speak of overlapping territories, intertwined histories common to men and women, whites and non-whites, dwellers in the metropolis and on the peripheries, past as well as present and future; these territories and histories can only be seen from the perspective of the whole of secular human history.

CHAPTER TWO

CONSOLIDATED VISION

We called ourselves "Intrusive" as a band; for we meant to break into the accepted halls of English foreign policy, and build a new people in the East, despite the rails laid down for us by our ancestors.

T. E. LAWRENCE, *The Seven Pillars of Wisdom*

(I)

Narrative and Social Space

N early everywhere in nineteenth- and early-twentieth-century British and French culture we find allusions to the facts of empire, but perhaps nowhere with more regularity and frequency than in the British novel. Taken together, these allusions constitute what I have called a structure of attitude and reference. In *Mansfield Park,* which within Jane Austen's work carefully defines the moral and social values informing her other novels, references to Sir Thomas Bertram's overseas possessions are threaded through; they give him his wealth, occasion his absences, fix his social status at home and abroad, and make possible his values, to which Fanny Price (and Austen herself) finally subscribes. If this is a novel about "ordination," as Austen says, the right to colonial possessions helps directly to establish social order and moral priorities at home. Or again, Bertha Mason, Rochester's deranged wife in *Jane Eyre,* is a West Indian, and also a threatening presence, confined to an attic room. Thackeray's Joseph Sedley in *Vanity Fair* is an Indian nabob whose rambunctious behavior and excessive (perhaps undeserved) wealth is counterpointed with Becky's finally unacceptable deviousness, which in turn is contrasted with Amelia's propriety, suitably rewarded in the end; Joseph Dobbin is seen at the end of the novel engaged serenely in writing a history of the Punjab. The good ship *Rose* in Charles Kingsley's *Westward Ho!* wanders through the Caribbean and South America. In Dickens's *Great Expectations,* Abel Magwitch is the convict transported to Australia whose wealth—conveniently removed from Pip's triumphs as a provincial lad flourishing in London in the guise of a gentleman—ironically makes possible the great expectations Pip entertains. In many other Dickens novels businessmen have connections with the empire, Dombey and Quilp being two noteworthy examples. For Disraeli's *Tancred* and Eliot's *Daniel Deronda,* the East is partly a habitat for native peoples (or immigrant European populations), but also partly incorporated under the sway of empire. Henry James's Ralph Touchett in *Portrait of a Lady* travels in Algeria and Egypt. And when we come to Kipling, Conrad, Arthur Conan Doyle, Rider Haggard, R. L. Stevenson, George Orwell, Joyce Cary, E. M. Forster, and T. E. Lawrence, the empire is everywhere a crucial setting.

The situation in France was different, insofar as the French imperial vocation during the early nineteenth century was different from England's, buttressed as it was by the continuity and stability of the English polity itself. The reverses of policy, losses of colonies, insecurity of possession, and shifts in philosophy that France suffered during the Revolution and the Napoleonic era meant that its empire had a less secure identity and presence in French culture. In Chateaubriand and Lamartine one hears the rhetoric of imperial grandeur; and in painting, in historical and philological writing, in music and theater one has an often vivid apprehension of France's outlying possessions. But in the culture at large—until after the middle of the century—there is rarely that weighty, almost philosophical sense of imperial mission that one finds in Britain.

There is also a dense body of American writing, contemporary with this British and French work, which shows a peculiarly acute imperial cast, even though paradoxically its ferocious anti-colonialism, directed at the Old World, is central to it. One thinks, for example, of the Puritan "errand into the wilderness" and, later, of that extraordinarily obsessive concern in Cooper, Twain, Melville, and others with United States expansion westward, along with the wholesale colonization and destruction of native American life (as memorably studied by Richard Slotkin, Patricia Limerick, and Michael Paul Rogin);[1] an imperial motif emerges to rival the European one. (In Chapter Four of this book I shall deal with other and more recent aspects of the United States in its late-twentieth-century imperial form.)

As a reference, as a point of definition, as an easily assumed place of travel, wealth, and service, the empire functions for much of the European nineteenth century as a codified, if only marginally visible, presence in fiction, very much like the servants in grand households and in novels, whose work is taken for granted but scarcely ever more than named, rarely studied (though Bruce Robbins has recently written on them),[2] or given density. To cite another intriguing analogue, imperial possessions are as usefully *there,* anonymous and collective, as the outcast populations (analyzed by Gareth Stedman Jones)[3] of transient workers, part-time employees, seasonal artisans; their existence always counts, though their names and identities do not, they are profitable without being fully there. This is a literary equivalent, in Eric Wolf's somewhat self-congratulatory words, of "people without History,"[4] people on whom the economy and polity sustained by empire depend, but whose reality has not historically or culturally required attention.

In all of these instances the facts of empire are associated with sustained possession, with far-flung and sometimes unknown spaces, with eccentric or unacceptable human beings, with fortune-enhancing or fantasized activities like emigration, money-making, and sexual adventure. Disgraced younger sons are sent off to the colonies, shabby older relatives go there to try to recoup lost fortunes (as in Balzac's *La Cousine Bette*), enterprising young travellers go there to sow wild oats and to collect exotica. The colonial territories are realms of possibility, and they have always been associated with the realistic novel. Robinson Crusoe is virtually unthinkable without the colonizing mission that permits him to create a new world of his own in the distant reaches of the African, Pacific, and Atlantic wilderness. But most of the great nineteenth-century realistic novelists are less assertive about colonial rule and possessions than either Defoe or late writers like Conrad and Kipling, during whose time great electoral reform and mass participation in politics meant that imperial competition became a more intrusive domestic topic. In the closing year of the nineteenth century, with the scramble for Africa, the consolidation of the French imperial Union, the American annexation of the Philippines, and British rule in the Indian subcontinent at its height, empire was a universal concern.

What I should like to note is that these colonial and imperial realities are overlooked in criticism that has otherwise been extraordinarily thorough and resourceful in finding themes to discuss. The relatively few writers and critics who discuss the relationship between culture and empire—among them Martin Green, Molly Mahood, John McClure, and, in particular, Patrick Brantlinger—have made excellent contributions, but their mode is essentially narrative and descriptive—pointing out the presence of themes, the importance of certain historical conjunctures, the influence or persistence of ideas about imperialism—and they cover huge amounts of material.[5] In almost all cases they write critically of imperialism, of that way of life that William Appleman Williams describes as being compatible with all sorts of other ideological persuasions, even antinomian ones, so that during the nineteenth century "imperial outreach made it necessary to develop an appropriate ideology" in alliance with military, economic, and political methods. These made it possible to "preserve and extend the empire without wasting its psychic or cultural or economic substance." There are hints in these scholars' work that, again to quote Williams, imperialism produces troubling self-images, for example, that of "a benevolent progressive policeman."[6]

But these critics are mainly descriptive and positivist writers strikingly different from the small handful of generally theoretical and ideological contributions—among them Jonah Raskin's *The Mythology of Imperialism,* Gordon K. Lewis's *Slavery, Imperialism, and Freedom,* and V. G. Kiernan's *Marxism and Imperialism* and his crucial work, *The Lords of Human Kind.*[7] All these books, which owe a great deal to Marxist analysis and premises, point out the centrality of imperialist thought in modern Western culture.

Yet none of them has been anywhere as influential as they should have been in changing our ways of looking at the canonical works of nineteenth- and twentieth-century European culture. The major critical practitioners simply ignore imperialism. In recently rereading Lionel Trilling's fine little book on E. M. Forster, for instance, I was struck that in his otherwise perceptive consideration of *Howards End* he does not once mention imperialism, which, in my reading of the book, is hard to miss, much less ignore. After all, Henry Wilcox and his family are colonial rubber growers: "They had the colonial spirit, and were always making for some spots where the white man might carry his burden unobserved."[8] And Forster frequently contrasts and associates that fact with the changes taking place in England, changes that affect Leonard and Jacky Bast, the Schlegels, and Howards End itself. Or there is the more surprising case of Raymond Williams, whose *Culture and Society* does not deal with the imperial experience at all. (When in an interview Williams was challenged about this massive absence, since imperialism "was not something which was secondary and external—it was absolutely constitutive of the whole nature of the English political and social order . . . *the* salient fact"[9]—he replied that his Welsh experience, which ought to have enabled him to think about the imperial experience, was "very much in abeyance" at the time he wrote *Culture and Society.*)[10] The few tantalizing pages in *The Country and the City* that touch on culture and imperialism are peripheral to the book's main idea.

Why did these lapses occur? And how was the centrality of the imperial vision registered and supported by the culture that produced it, then to some extent disguised it, and also was transformed by it? Naturally, if you yourself happen to have a colonial background, the imperial theme is a determining one in your formation, and it will draw you to it if you also happen to be a dedicated critic of European literature. An Indian or African scholar of English literature reads *Kim,* say, or *Heart of Darkness* with a critical urgency not felt in quite the same way by an American or British one. But in what way can we formulate the relationship between culture and imperialism beyond the asseverations of personal testimony? The emergence of formerly colonial subjects as interpreters of imperialism and its great cultural works has given imperialism a perceptible, not to say obtrusive identity as a subject for study and vigorous revision. But how can that particular kind of post-imperial testimony and study, usually left at the margins of critical discourse, be brought into active contact with current theoretical concerns?

To regard imperial concerns as constitutively significant to the culture of the modern West is, I have suggested, to consider that culture from the perspective provided by anti-imperialist resistance as well as pro-imperialist apology. What does this mean? It means remembering that Western writers until the middle of the twentieth century, whether Dickens and Austen, Flaubert or Camus, wrote with an exclusively Western audience in mind, even when they wrote of characters, places, or situations that referred to, made use of, overseas territories held by Europeans. But just because Austen referred to Antigua in *Mansfield Park* or to realms visited by the British navy in *Persuasion* without any thought of possible responses by the Caribbean or Indian natives resident there is no reason for us to do the same. We now know that these non-European peoples did not accept with indifference the authority projected over them, or the general silence on which their presence in variously attenuated forms is predicated. We must therefore read the great canonical texts, and perhaps also the entire archive of modern and pre-modern European and American culture, with an effort to draw out, extend, give emphasis and voice to what is silent or marginally present or ideologically represented (I have in mind Kipling's Indian characters) in such works.

In practical terms, "contrapuntal reading" as I have called it means reading a text with an understanding of what is involved when an author shows, for instance, that a colonial sugar plantation is seen as important to the process of maintaining a particular style of life in England. Moreover, like all literary texts, these are not bounded by their formal historic beginnings and endings. References to Australia in *David Copperfield* or India in *Jane Eyre* are made because they *can be*, because British power (and not just the novelist's fancy) made passing references to these massive appropriations possible; but the further lessons are no less true: that these colonies were subsequently liberated from direct and indirect rule, a process that began and unfolded while the British (or French, Portuguese, Germans, etc.) were still there, although as part of the effort at suppressing native nationalism only occasional note was taken of it. The point is that contrapuntal reading must take account of both processes, that of imperialism and that of resistance to it, which can be done by extending our reading of the texts to include what was once forcibly excluded—in *L'Etranger,* for example, the whole previous history of France's colonialism and its destruction of the Algerian state, and the later emergence of an independent Algeria (which Camus opposed).

Each text has its own particular genius, as does each geographical region of the world, with its own overlapping experiences and interdependent histories of conflict. As far as the cultural work is concerned, a distinction between particularity and sovereignty (or hermetic exclusiveness) can usefully be made. Obviously no reading should try to generalize so much as to efface the identity of a particular text, author, or movement. By the same token it should allow that what was, or appeared to be, certain for a given work or author may have become subject to disputation. Kipling's India, in *Kim,* has a quality of permanence and inevitability that belongs not just to that wonderful novel, but to British India, its history, administrators, and apologists and, no less important, to the India fought for by Indian nationalists as their country to be won back. By giving an account of this series of pressures and counter-pressures in Kipling's India, we understand the process of imperialism itself as the great work of art engages them, and of later anti-imperialist resistance. In reading a text, one must open it out both to what went into it and to what its author excluded. Each cultural work is a vision of a moment, and we must juxtapose that vision with the various revisions it later provoked—in this case, the nationalist experiences of post-independence India.

In addition, one must connect the structures of a narrative to the ideas, concepts, experiences from which it draws support. Conrad's Africans, for example, come from a huge library of *Africanism,* so to speak, as well as from Conrad's personal experiences. There is no such thing as a *direct* experience, or reflection, of the world in the language of a text. Conrad's impressions of Africa were inevitably influenced by lore and writing about Africa, which he alludes to in *A Personal Record;* what he supplies in *Heart of Darkness* is the result of his impressions of those texts interacting creatively, together with the requirements and conventions of narrative and his own special genius and history. To say of this extraordinarily rich mix that it "reflects" Africa, or even that it reflects an experience of Africa, is somewhat pusillanimous and surely misleading. What we have in *Heart of Darkness*—a work of immense influence, having provoked many readings and images—is a politicized, ideologically saturated Africa which to some intents and purposes was the imperialized place, with those many interests and ideas furiously at work in it, not just a photographic literary "reflection" of it.

This is, perhaps, to overstate the matter, but I want to make the point that far from *Heart of Darkness* and its image of Africa being "only" literature, the work is extraordinarily caught up in, is indeed an organic part of, the "scramble for Africa" that was contemporary with Conrad's composition. True, Conrad's audience was small, and, true also, he was very critical of Belgian colonialism. But to most Europeans, reading a rather rarefied text like *Heart of Darkness* was often as close as they came to Africa, and in that limited sense it was part of the European effort to hold on to, think about, plan for Africa. To represent Africa is to enter the battle over Africa, inevitably connected to later resistance, decolonization, and so forth.

Works of literature, particularly those whose manifest subject is empire, have an inherently untidy, even unwieldy aspect in so fraught, so densely charged a political setting. Yet despite their formidable complexity, literary works like *Heart of Darkness* are distillations, or simplifications, or a set of choices made by an author that are far less messy and mixed up than the reality. It would not be fair to think of them as abstractions, although fictions such as *Heart of Darkness* are so elaborately fashioned by authors and so worried over by readers as to suit the necessities of narrative which as a result, we must add, makes a highly specialized entry into the struggle over Africa.

So hybrid, impure, and complex a text requires especially vigilant attention as it is interpreted. Modern imperialism was so global and all-encompassing that virtually nothing escaped it; besides, as I have said, the nineteenth-century contest over empire is still continuing today. Whether or not to look at the connections between cultural texts and imperialism is therefore to take a position *in fact taken*—either to study the connection in order to criticize it and think of alternatives for it, or not to study it in order to let it stand, unexamined and, presumably, unchanged. One of my reasons for writing this book is to show how far the quest for, concern about, and consciousness of overseas dominion extended—not just in Conrad but in figures we practically never think of in that connection, like Thackeray and Austen—and how enriching and important for the critic is attention to this material, not only for the obvious political reasons, but also because, as I have been arguing, this particular kind of attention allows the reader to interpret canonical nineteenth- and twentieth-century works with a newly engaged interest.

Let us return to *Heart of Darkness*. In it Conrad offers an uncannily suggestive starting point for grappling at close quarters with these difficult matters. Recall that Marlow contrasts Roman colonizers with their modern counterparts in an oddly perceptive way, illuminating the special mix of power, ideological energy, and practical attitude characterizing European imperialism. The ancient Romans, he says, were "no colonists; their administration was merely a squeeze and nothing more." Such people conquered and did little else. By contrast, "what saves us is efficiency—the devotion to efficiency," unlike the Romans, who relied on brute force, which is scarcely more than "an accident arising from the weakness of others." Today, however,

> the conquest of the earth, which mostly means the taking it away from those who have a different complexion or slightly flatter noses than ourselves, is not a pretty thing when you look into it too much. What redeems it is the idea only. An idea at the back of it; not a sentimental pretence but an idea; and an unselfish belief in the idea—something you can set up, and bow down before, and offer a sacrifice to. . . .[11]

In his account of his great river journey, Marlow extends the point to mark a distinction between Belgian rapacity and (by implication) British rationality in the conduct of imperialism.[12]

Salvation in this context is an interesting notion. It sets "us" off from the damned, despised Romans and Belgians, whose greed radiates no benefits onto either their consciences or the lands and bodies of their subjects. "We" are saved because first of all we needn't look directly at the results of what we do; we are ringed by and ring ourselves with the practice of efficiency, by which land and people are put to use completely; the territory and its inhabitants are totally incorporated by our rule, which in turn totally incorporates us as we respond efficiently to its exigencies. Further, through Marlow, Conrad speaks of redemption, a step in a sense beyond salvation. If salvation saves us, saves time and money, and also saves us from the ruin of mere short-term conquest, then redemption extends salvation further still. Redemption is found in the self-justifying practice of an idea or mission over time, in a structure that completely encircles and is revered by you, even though you set up the structure in the first place, ironically enough, and no longer study it closely because you take it for granted.

Thus Conrad encapsulates two quite different but intimately related aspects of imperialism: the idea that is based on the power to take over territory, an idea utterly clear in its force and unmistakable consequences; and the practice that essentially disguises or obscures this by developing a justificatory regime of self-aggrandizing, self-originating authority interposed between the victim of imperialism and its perpetrator.

We would completely miss the tremendous power of this argument if we were merely to lift it out of *Heart of Darkness,* like a message out of a bottle. Conrad's argument is inscribed right in the very form of narrative as he inherited it and as he practiced it. Without empire, I would go so far as saying, there is no European novel as we know it, and indeed if we study the impulses giving rise to it, we shall see the far from accidental convergence between the patterns of narrative authority constitutive of the novel on the one hand, and, on the other, a complex ideological configuration underlying the tendency to imperialism.

Every novelist and every critic or theorist of the European novel notes its institutional character. The novel is fundamentally tied to bourgeois society; in Charles Morazé's phrase, it accompanies and indeed is a part of the conquest of Western society by what he calls *les bourgeois conquérants*. No less significantly, the novel is inaugurated in England by *Robinson Crusoe*, a work whose protagonist is the founder of a new world, which he rules and reclaims for Christianity and England. True, whereas Crusoe is explicitly enabled by an ideology of overseas expansion—directly connected in style and form to the narratives of sixteenth- and seventeenth-century exploration voyages that laid the foundations of the great colonial empires—the major novels that come after Defoe, and even Defoe's later works, seem not to be single-mindedly compelled by the exciting overseas prospects. *Captain Singleton* is the story of a widely travelled pirate in India and Africa, and *Moll Flanders* is shaped by the possibility in the New World of the heroine's climactic redemption from a life of crime, but Fielding, Richardson, Smollett, and Sterne do not connect their narratives so directly to the act of accumulating riches and territories abroad.

These novelists do, however, situate their work in and derive it from a carefully surveyed territorial greater Britain, and that *is* related to what Defoe so presciently began. Yet while distinguished studies of eighteenth-century English fiction—by Ian Watt, Lennard Davis, John Richetti, and Michael McKeon—have devoted considerable attention to the relationship between the novel and social space, the imperial perspective has been neglected.[13] This is not simply a matter of being uncertain whether, for example, Richardson's minute constructions of bourgeois seduction and rapacity actually relate to British military moves against the French in India occurring at the same time. Quite clearly they do not in a literal sense; but in both realms we find common values about contest, surmounting odds and obstacles, and patience in establishing authority through the art of connecting principle with profit over time. In other words, we need to have a critical sense of how the great spaces of *Clarissa* or *Tom Jones* are two things together: a domestic accompaniment to the imperial project for presence and control abroad, and a practical narrative about expanding and moving about in space that must be actively inhabited and enjoyed before its discipline or limits can be accepted.

I am not trying to say that the novel—or the culture in the broad sense—"caused" imperialism, but that the novel, as a cultural artefact of bourgeois society, and imperialism are unthinkable without each other. Of all the major literary forms, the novel is the most recent, its emergence the most datable, its occurrence the most Western, its normative pattern of social authority the most structured; imperialism and the novel fortified each other to such a degree that it is impossible, I would argue, to read one without in some way dealing with the other.

Nor is this all. The novel is an incorporative, quasi-encyclopedic cultural form. Packed into it are both a highly regulated plot mechanism and an entire system of social reference that depends on the existing institutions of bourgeois society, their authority and power. The novelistic hero and heroine exhibit the restlessness and energy characteristic of the enterprising bourgeoisie, and they are permitted adventures in which their experiences reveal to them the limits of what they can aspire to, where they can go, what they can become. Novels therefore end either with the death of a hero or heroine (Julien Sorel, Emma Bovary, Bazarov, Jude the Obscure) who by virtue of overflowing energy does not fit into the orderly scheme of things, or with the protagonists' accession to stability (usually in the form of marriage or confirmed identity, as is the case with novels of Austen, Dickens, Thackeray, and George Eliot).

But, one might ask, why give so much emphasis to novels, and to England? And how can we bridge the distance separating this solitary aesthetic form from large topics and undertakings like "culture" or "imperialism"? For one thing, by the time of World War One the British empire had become unquestionably dominant, the result of a process that had started in the late sixteenth century; so powerful was the process and so definitive its result that, as Seeley and Hobson argued toward the end of the nineteenth century, it was the central fact in British history, and one that included many disparate activities.[14] It is not entirely coincidental that Britain also produced and sustained a novelistic institution with no real European competitor or equivalent. France had more highly developed intellectual institutions—academies, universities, institutes, journals, and so on—for at least the first half of the nineteenth century, as a host of British intellectuals, including Arnold, Carlyle, Mill, and George Eliot, noted and lamented. But the extraordinary compensation for this discrepancy came in the steady rise and gradually undisputed dominance of the British novel. (Only as North Africa assumes a sort of metropolitan presence in French culture after 1870 do we see a comparable aesthetic and cultural formation begin to flow: this is the period when Loti, the early Gide, Daudet, Maupassant, Mille, Psichari, Malraux, the exoticists like Segalen, and of course Camus project a global concordance between the domestic and imperial situations.)

By the 1840s the English novel had achieved eminence as *the* aesthetic form and as a major intellectual voice, so to speak, in English society. Because the novel gained so important a place in "the condition of England" question, for example, we can see it also as participating in England's overseas empire. In projecting what Raymond Williams calls a "knowable community" of Englishmen and women, Jane Austen, George Eliot, and Mrs. Gaskell shaped the idea of England in such a way as to give it identity, presence, ways of reusable articulation.[15] And part of such an idea was the relationship between "home" and "abroad." Thus England was surveyed, evaluated, made known, whereas "abroad" was only referred to or shown briefly without the kind of presence or immediacy lavished on London, the countryside, or northern industrial centers such as Manchester or Birmingham.

This steady, almost reassuring work done by the novel is unique to England and has to be taken as an important cultural affiliation domestically speaking, as yet undocumented and unstudied, for what took place in India, Africa, Ireland, or the Caribbean. An analogy is the relationship between Britain's foreign policy and its finance and trade, a relationship which *has* been studied. We get a lively sense of how dense and complex it was from D.C.M. Platt's classic (but still debated) study of it, *Finance, Trade and Politics in British Foreign Policy, 1815–1914,* and how much the extraordinary twinning of British trade and imperial expansion depended on cultural and social factors such as education, journalism, intermarriage, and class. Platt speaks of "social and intellectual contact [friendship, hospitality, mutual aid, common social and educational background] which energized the actual pressure on British foreign policy," and he goes on to say that "concrete evidence [for the actual accomplishments of this set of contacts] has probably never existed." Nevertheless, if one looks at how the government's attitude to such issues as "foreign loans . . . the protection of bondholders, and the promotion of contracts and concessions overseas" developed, one can see what he calls a "departmental view," a sort of consensus about the empire held by a whole range of people responsible for it. This would "suggest how officials and politicians were likely to react."[16]

How best to characterize this view? There seems to be agreement among scholars that until about 1870 British policy was (according to the early Disraeli, for example) not to expand the empire but "to uphold and maintain it and to protect it from disintegration."[17] Central to this task was India, which acquired a status of astonishing durability in "departmental" thought. After 1870 (Schumpeter cites Disraeli's Crystal Palace speech in 1872 as the hallmark of aggressive imperialism, "the catch phrase of domestic policy")[18] protecting India (the parameters kept getting larger) and defending against other competing powers, e.g., Russia, necessitated British imperial expansion in Africa, and the Middle and Far East. Thereafter, in one area of the globe after another, "Britain was indeed preoccupied with holding what she already had," as Platt puts it, "and whatever she gained was demanded because it helped her to preserve the rest. She belonged to the party of *les satisfaits,* but she had to fight ever harder to stay with them, and she had by far the most to lose."[19] A "departmental view" of British policy was fundamentally careful; as Ronald Robinson and John Gallagher put it in their redefinition of Platt's thesis, "the British would expand by trade and influence if they could, but by imperial rule if they must."[20] We should not minimize or forget, they remind us, that the Indian army was used in China three times between 1829 and 1856, at least once in Persia (1856), Ethiopia and Singapore (1867), Hong Kong (1868), Afghanistan (1878), Egypt (1882), Burma (1885), Ngasse (1893), Sudan and Uganda (1896).

In addition to India, British policy obviously made the bulwark for imperial commerce mainland Britain itself (with Ireland a continuous colonial problem), as well as the so-called white colonies (Australia, New Zealand, Canada, South Africa, and even the former American possessions). Continuous investment and routine conservation of Britain's overseas and home territories were without significant parallel in other European or American powers, where lurches, sudden acquisitions or losses, and improvisations occurred far more frequently.

In short, British power was durable and continually reinforced. In the related and often adjacent cultural sphere, that power was elaborated and articulated in the novel, whose central continuous presence is not comparably to be found elsewhere. But we must be as fastidious as possible. A novel is neither a frigate nor a bank draft. A novel exists first as a novelist's effort and second as an object read by an audience. In time novels accumulate and become what Harry Levin has usefully called an institution of literature, but they do not ever lose either their status as events or their specific density as part of a continuous enterprise recognized and accepted as such by readers and other writers. But for all their social presence, novels are not reducible to a sociological current and cannot be done justice to aesthetically, culturally, and politically as subsidiary forms of class, ideology, or interest.

Equally, however, novels are not *simply* the product of lonely genius (as a school of modern interpreters like Helen Vendler try to suggest), to be regarded only as manifestations of unconditioned creativity. Some of the most exciting recent criticism—Fredric Jameson's *The Political Unconscious* and David Miller's *The Novel and the Police* are two celebrated examples[21]— shows the novel generally, and narrative in particular, to have a sort of regulatory social presence in West European societies. Yet missing from these otherwise valuable descriptions are adumbrations of the actual world in which the novels and narratives take place. Being an English writer meant something quite specific and different from, say, being a French or Portuguese writer. For the British writer, "abroad" was felt vaguely and ineptly to be out there, or exotic and strange, or in some way or other "ours" to control, trade in "freely," or suppress when the natives were energized into overt military or political resistance. The novel contributed significantly to these feelings, attitudes, and references and became a main element in the consolidated vision, or departmental cultural view, of the globe.

I should specify how the novelistic contribution was made and also, conversely, how the novel neither deterred nor inhibited the more aggressive and popular imperialist feelings manifest after 1880.[22] Novels are pictures of reality at the very early or the very late stage in the reader's experience of them: in fact they elaborate and maintain a reality they inherit from other novels, which they rearticulate and repopulate according to their creator's situation, gifts, predilections. Platt rightly stresses *conservation* in the "departmental view"; this is significant for the novelist, too: the nineteenth-century English novels stress the continuing existence (as opposed to revolutionary overturning) of England. Moreover, they *never* advocate giving up colonies, but take the long-range view that since they fall within the orbit of British dominance, *that* dominance is a sort of norm, and thus conserved along with the colonies.

What we have is a slowly built up picture with England—socially, politically, morally charted and differentiated in immensely fine detail—at the center and a series of overseas territories connected to it at the peripheries. The *continuity* of British imperial policy throughout the nineteenth century—in fact a narrative—is actively accompanied by this novelistic process, whose main purpose is not to raise more questions, not to disturb or otherwise preoccupy attention, but to keep the empire more or less in place. Hardly ever is the novelist interested in doing a great deal more than mentioning or referring to India, for example, in *Vanity Fair* and *Jane Eyre,* or Australia in *Great Expectations.* The idea is that (following the general principles of free trade) outlying territories are available for use, at will, at the novelist's discretion, usually for relatively simple purposes such as immigration, fortune, or exile. At the end of *Hard Times,* for example, Tom is shipped off to the colonies. Not until well after mid-century did the empire become a principal subject of attention in writers like Haggard, Kipling, Doyle, Conrad as well as in emerging discourses in ethnography, colonial administration, theory and economy, the historiography of non-European regions, and specialized subjects like Orientalism, exoticism, and mass psychology.

The actual interpretative consequences of this slow and steady structure of attitude and reference articulated by the novel are diverse. I shall specify four. The first is that, in literary history, an unusual organic continuity can be seen between the earlier narratives that are normally not considered to have much to do with empire and the later ones explicitly *about* it. Kipling and Conrad are prepared for by Austen and Thackeray, Defoe, Scott, and Dickens; they are also interestingly connected with their contemporaries like Hardy and James, regularly supposed to be only coincidentally associated with the overseas exhibits presented by their rather more peculiar novelistic counterparts. But both the formal characteristics and the contents of all these novelists' works belong to the same cultural formation, the differences being those of inflection, emphasis, stress.

Second, the structure of attitude and reference raises the whole question of power. Today's critic cannot and should not suddenly give a novel legislative or direct political authority: we must continue to remember that novels participate in, are part of, contribute to an extremely slow, infinitesimal politics that clarifies, reinforces, perhaps even occasionally advances perceptions and attitudes about England and the world. It is striking that never, in the novel, is that world beyond seen except as subordinate and dominated, the English presence viewed as regulative and normative. Part of the extraordinary novelty of Aziz's trial in *A Passage to India* is that Forster admits that "the flimsy framework of the court"[23] cannot be sustained because it is a "fantasy" that compromises British power (real) with impartial justice for Indians (unreal). Therefore he readily (even with a sort of frustrated impatience) dissolves the scene into India's "complexity," which twenty-four years before in Kipling's *Kim* was just as present. The main difference between the two is that the impinging disturbance of resisting natives had been thrust on Forster's awareness. Forster could not ignore something that Kipling easily incorporated (as when he rendered even the famous "Mutiny" of 1857 as mere waywardness, not as a serious Indian objection to British rule).

There can be no awareness that the novel underscores and accepts the disparity in power unless readers actually register the signs in individual works, and unless the history of the novel is seen to have the coherence of a continuous enterprise. Just as the sustained solidity and largely unwavering "departmental view" of Britain's outlying territories were maintained throughout the nineteenth century, so too, in an altogether literary way, was the aesthetic (hence cultural) grasp of overseas lands maintained as a part of the novel, sometimes incidental, sometimes very important. Its "consolidated vision" came in a whole series of overlapping affirmations, by which a near unanimity of view was sustained. That this was done within the terms of each medium or discourse (the novel, travel writing, ethnography) and not in terms imposed from outside, suggests conformity, collaboration, willingness but not necessarily an overtly or explicitly held political agenda, at least not until later in the century, when the imperial program was itself more explicit and more a matter of direct popular propaganda.

A third point can best be made by rapid illustration. All through *Vanity Fair* there are allusions to India, but none is anything more than incidental to the changes in Becky's fortunes, or in Dobbin's, Joseph's, and Amelia's positions. All along, though, we are made aware of the mounting contest between England and Napoleon, with its climax at Waterloo. This overseas dimension scarcely makes *Vanity Fair* a novel exploiting what Henry James was later to call "the international theme," any more than Thackeray belongs to the club of Gothic novelists like Walpole, Radcliffe, or Lewis who set their works rather fancifully abroad. Yet Thackeray and, I would argue, all the major English novelists of the mid–nineteenth century, accepted a globalized world-view and indeed could not (in most cases did not) ignore the vast overseas reach of British power. As we saw in the little example cited earlier from *Dombey and Son,* the domestic order was tied to, located in, even illuminated by a specifically *English* order abroad. Whether it is Sir Thomas Bertram's plantation in Antigua or, a hundred years later, the Wilcox Nigerian rubber estate, novelists aligned the holding of power and privilege abroad with comparable activities at home.

When we read the novels attentively, we get a far more discriminating and subtle view than the baldly "global" and imperial vision I have described thus far. This brings me to the fourth consequence of what I have been calling the structure of attitude and reference. In insisting on the integrity of an artistic work, as we must, and refusing to collapse the various contributions of individual authors into a general scheme, we must accept that the structure connecting novels to one another has no existence outside the novels themselves, which means that one gets the particular, concrete experience of "abroad" only in individual novels; conversely that only individual novels can animate, articulate, embody the relationship, for instance, between England and Africa. This obliges critics to read and analyze, rather than only to summarize and judge, works whose paraphrasable content they might regard as politically and morally objectionable. On the one hand, when in a celebrated essay Chinua Achebe criticizes Conrad's racism, he either says nothing about or overrides the limitations placed on Conrad by the novel as an aesthetic form. On the other hand, Achebe shows that he understands how the form works when, in some of his own novels, he rewrites—painstakingly and with originality—Conrad.[24]

All of this is especially true of English fiction because only England had an overseas empire that sustained and protected itself over such an area, for such a long time, with such envied eminence. It is true that France rivalled it, but, as I have said elsewhere, the French imperial consciousness is intermittent until the late nineteenth century, the actuality too impinged on by England, too lagging in system, profit, extent. In the main, though, the nineteenth-century European novel is a cultural form consolidating but also refining and articulating the authority of the *status quo*. However much Dickens, for example, stirs up his readers against the legal system, provincial schools, or the bureaucracy, his novels finally enact what one critic has called a "fiction of resolution."[25] The most frequent figure for this is the reunification of the family, which in Dickens's case always serves as a microcosm of society. In Austen, Balzac, George Eliot, and Flaubert—to take several prominent names together—the consolidation of authority includes, indeed is built into the very fabric of, both private property and marriage, institutions that are only rarely challenged.

The crucial aspect of what I have been calling the novel's consolidation of authority is not simply connected to the functioning of social power and governance, but made to appear both normative and sovereign, that is, self-validating in the course of the narrative. This is paradoxical only if one forgets that the constitution of a narrative subject, however abnormal or unusual, is still a social act *par excellence,* and as such has behind or inside it the authority of history and society. There is first the authority of the author—someone writing out the processes of society in an acceptable institutionalized manner, observing conventions, following patterns, and so forth. Then there is the authority of the narrator, whose discourse anchors the narrative in recognizable, and hence existentially referential, circumstances. Last, there is what might be called the authority of the community, whose representative most often is the family but also is the nation, the specific locality, and the concrete historical moment. Together these functioned most energetically, most noticeably, during the early nineteenth century as the novel opened up to history in an unprecedented way. Conrad's Marlow inherits all this directly.

Lukacs studied with remarkable skill the emergence of history in the European novel[26]—how Stendhal and particularly Scott place their narratives in and as part of a public history, making that history accessible to everyone and not, as before, only to kings and aristocrats. The novel is thus a concretely historical narrative shaped by the real history of real nations. Defoe locates Crusoe on an unnamed island somewhere in an outlying region, and Moll is sent to the vaguely apprehended Carolinas, but Thomas Bertram and Joseph Sedley derive specific wealth and specific benefits from historically annexed territories—the Caribbean and India, respectively—at specific historical moments. And, as Lukacs shows so persuasively, Scott constructs the British polity in the form of a historical society working its way out of foreign adventures[27] (the Crusades, for example) and internecine domestic conflict (the 1745 rebellion, the warring Highland tribes) to become the settled metropolis resisting local revolution and continental provocation with equal success. In France, history confirms the post-revolutionary reaction embodied by the Bourbon restoration, and Stendhal chronicles its—to him—lamentable achievements. Later Flaubert does much the same for 1848. But the novel is assisted also by the historical work of Michelet and Macaulay, whose narratives add density to the texture of national identity.

The appropriation of history, the historicization of the past, the narrativization of society, all of which give the novel its force, include the accumulation and differentiation of social space, space to be used for social purposes. This is much more apparent in late-nineteenth-century, openly colonial fiction: in Kipling's India, for example, where the natives and the Raj inhabit differently ordained spaces, and where with his extraordinary genius Kipling devised Kim, a marvelous character whose youth and energy allow him to explore both spaces, crossing from one to the other with daring grace as if to confound the authority of colonial barriers. The barriers within social space exist in Conrad too, and in Haggard, in Loti, in Doyle, in Gide, Psichari, Malraux, Camus, and Orwell.

Underlying social space are territories, lands, geographical domains, the actual geographical underpinnings of the imperial, and also the cultural contest. To think about distant places, to colonize them, to populate or depopulate them: all of this occurs on, about, or because of land. The actual geographical possession of land is what empire in the final analysis is all about. At the moment when a coincidence occurs between real control and power, the idea of what a given place was (could be, might become), and an actual place—at that moment the struggle for empire is launched. This coincidence is the logic both for Westerners taking possession of land and, during decolonization, for resisting natives reclaiming it. Imperialism and the culture associated with it affirm both the primacy of geography and an ideology about control of territory. The geographical sense makes projections—imaginative, cartographic, military, economic, historical, or in a general sense cultural. It also makes possible the construction of various kinds of knowledge, all of them in one way or another dependent upon the perceived character and destiny of a particular geography.

Three fairly restricted points should be made here. First, the spatial differentiations so apparent in late-nineteenth-century novels do not simply and suddenly appear there as a passive reflection of an aggressive "age of empire," but are derived in a continuum from earlier social discriminations already authorized in earlier historical and realistic novels.

Jane Austen sees the legitimacy of Sir Thomas Bertram's overseas proper-
ties as a natural extension of the calm, the order, the beauties of Mansfield
Park, one central estate validating the economically supportive role of the
peripheral other. And even where colonies are not insistently or even per-
ceptibly in evidence, the narrative sanctions a spatial moral order, whether
in the communal restoration of the town of Middlemarch centrally important during a period of national turbulence, or in the outlying spaces of
deviation and uncertainty seen by Dickens in London's underworld, or in
the Brontë stormy heights.

A second point. As the conclusions of the novel confirm and highlight an
underlying hierarchy of family, property, nation, there is also a very strong
spatial *hereness* imparted to the hierarchy. The astounding power of the
scene in *Bleak House* where Lady Dedlock is seen sobbing at the grave of her
long dead husband *grounds* what we have felt about her secret past—her cold
and inhuman presence, her disturbingly unfertile authority—in the grave-
yard to which as a fugitive she has fled. This contrasts not only with the
disorderly jumble of the Jellyby establishment (with its eccentric ties to
Africa), but also with the favored house in which Esther and her guardian-
husband live. The narrative explores, moves through, and finally endows
these places with confirmatory positive and/or negative values.

This moral commensuration in the interplay between narrative and domestic space is extendable, indeed reproducible, in the world beyond metropolitan centers like Paris or London. In turn such French or English places
have a kind of export value: whatever is good or bad about places at home
is shipped out and assigned comparable virtue or vice abroad. When in his
inaugural lecture in 1870 as Slade Professor at Oxford, Ruskin speaks of
England's pure race, he can then go on to tell his audience to turn England
into a "country again [that is] a royal throne of kings; a sceptred isle, for all
the world a source of light, a centre of peace." The allusion to Shakespeare
is meant to re-establish and relocate a preferential feeling for England. This
time, however, Ruskin conceives of England as functioning *formally* on a
world scale; the feelings of approbation for the island kingdom that Shakespeare had imagined principally but not exclusively confined at home are
rather startlingly mobilized for imperial, indeed aggressively colonial service. Become colonists, found "colonies as fast and as far as [you are] able,"
he seems to be saying.[28]

My third point is that such domestic cultural enterprises as narrative
fiction and history (once again I emphasize the narrative component) are
premised on the recording, ordering, observing powers of the central authorizing subject, or ego. To say of this subject, in a quasi-tautological manner,
that it writes because it *can* write is to refer not only to domestic society but

to the outlying world. The capacity to represent, portray, characterize, and depict is not easily available to just any member of just any society; moreover, the "what" and "how" in the representation of "things," while allowing for considerable individual freedom, are circumscribed and socially regulated. We have become very aware in recent years of the constraints upon the cultural representation of women, and the pressures that go into the created representations of inferior classes and races. In all these areas—gender, class, and race—criticism has correctly focussed upon the institutional forces in modern Western societies that shape and set limits on the representation of what are considered essentially subordinate beings; thus representation itself has been characterized as keeping the subordinate subordinate, the inferior inferior.

(II)

Jane Austen and Empire

We are on solid ground with V. G. Kiernan when he says that "empires must have a mould of ideas or conditioned reflexes to flow into, and youthful nations dream of a great place in the world as young men dream of fame and fortunes."[29] It is, as I have been saying throughout, too simple and reductive to argue that everything in European or American culture therefore prepares for or consolidates the grand idea of empire. It is also, however, historically inaccurate to ignore those tendencies—whether in narrative, political theory, or pictorial technique—that enabled, encouraged, and otherwise assured the West's readiness to assume and enjoy the experience of empire. If there was cultural resistance to the notion of an imperial mission, there was not much support for that resistance in the main departments of cultural thought. Liberal though he was, John Stuart Mill—as a telling case in point—could still say, "The sacred duties which civilized nations owe to the independence and nationality of each other, are not binding towards those to whom nationality and independence are certain evil, or at best a questionable good." Ideas like this were not original with Mill; they were already current in the English subjugation of Ireland during the sixteenth century and, as Nicholas Canny has persuasively demonstrated, were equally useful in the ideology of English colonization in the Americas.[30] Almost all colonial schemes begin with an assumption of native backwardness and general inadequacy to be independent, "equal," and fit.

Why that should be so, why sacred obligation on one front should not be binding on another, why rights accepted in one may be denied in another, are questions best understood in the terms of a culture well-grounded in moral, economic, and even metaphysical norms designed to approve a satisfying local, that is European, order and to permit the abrogation of the right to a similar order abroad. Such a statement may appear preposterous or extreme. In fact, it formulates the connection between Europe's well-being and cultural identity on the one hand and, on the other, the subjugation of imperial realms overseas rather too fastidiously and circumspectly. Part of our difficulty today in accepting any connection at all is that we tend to reduce this complicated matter to an apparently simple causal one, which in turn produces a rhetoric of blame and defensiveness. I am *not* saying that the major factor in early European culture was that it *caused* late-nineteenth-century imperialism, and I am not implying that all the problems of the formerly colonial world should be blamed on Europe. I am saying, however, that European culture often, if not always, characterized itself in such a way as simultaneously to validate its own preferences while also advocating those preferences in conjunction with distant imperial rule. Mill certainly did: he always recommended that India *not* be given independence. When for various reasons imperial rule concerned Europe more intensely after 1880, this schizophrenic habit became useful.

The first thing to be done now is more or less to jettison simple causality in thinking through the relationship between Europe and the non-European world, and lessening the hold on our thought of the equally simple temporal sequence. We must not admit any notion, for instance, that proposes to show that Wordsworth, Austen, or Coleridge, because they wrote *before* 1857, actually caused the establishment of formal British governmental rule over India *after* 1857. We should try to discern instead a counterpoint between overt patterns in British writing about Britain and representations of the world beyond the British Isles. The inherent mode for this counterpoint is not temporal but spatial. How do writers in the period before the great age of explicit, programmatic colonial expansion—the "scramble for Africa," say—situate and see themselves and their work in the larger world? We shall find them using striking but careful strategies, many of them derived from expected sources—positive ideas of home, of a nation and its language, of proper order, good behavior, moral values.

But positive ideas of this sort do more than validate "our" world. They also tend to devalue other worlds and, perhaps more significantly from a retrospective point of view, they do not prevent or inhibit or give resistance to horrendously unattractive imperialist practices. No, cultural forms like the novel or the opera do not cause people to go out and imperialize—

Carlyle did not drive Rhodes directly, and he certainly cannot be "blamed" for the problems in today's southern Africa—but it is genuinely troubling to see how little Britain's great humanistic ideas, institutions, and monuments, which we still celebrate as having the power ahistorically to command our approval, how little they stand in the way of the accelerating imperial process. We are entitled to ask how this body of humanistic ideas co-existed so comfortably with imperialism, and why—until the resistance to imperialism *in the imperial domain,* among Africans, Asians, Latin Americans, developed—there was little significant opposition or deterrence to empire at home. Perhaps the custom of distinguishing "our" home and order from "theirs" grew into a harsh political rule for accumulating more of "them" to rule, study, and subordinate. In the great, humane ideas and values promulgated by mainstream European culture, we have precisely that "mould of ideas or conditioned reflexes" of which Kiernan speaks, into which the whole business of empire later flowed.

The extent to which these ideas are actually invested in geographical distinctions between real places is the subject of Raymond Williams's richest book, *The Country and the City.* His argument concerning the interplay between rural and urban places in England admits of the most extraordinary transformations—from the pastoral populism of Langland, through Ben Jonson's country-house poems and the novels of Dickens's London, right up to visions of the metropolis in twentieth-century literature. Mainly, of course, the book is about how English culture has dealt with land, its possession, imagination, and organization. And while he does address the export of England to the colonies, Williams does so, as I suggested earlier, in a less focussed way and less expansively than the practice actually warrants. Near the end of *The Country and the City* he volunteers that "from at least the mid–nineteenth century, and with important instances earlier, there was this larger context [the relationship between England and the colonies, whose effects on the English imagination "have gone deeper than can easily be traced"] within which every idea and every image was consciously and unconsciously affected." He goes on quickly to cite "the idea of emigration to the colonies" as one such image prevailing in various novels by Dickens, the Brontës, Gaskell, and rightly shows that "new rural societies," all of them colonial, enter the imaginative metropolitan economy of English literature via Kipling, early Orwell, Maugham. After 1880 there comes a "dramatic extension of landscape and social relations": this corresponds more or less exactly with the great age of empire.[31]

It is dangerous to disagree with Williams, yet I would venture to say that if one began to look for something like an imperial map of the world in English literature, it would turn up with amazing insistence and frequency well before the mid–nineteenth century. And turn up not only with the inert regularity suggesting something taken for granted, but—more interestingly—threaded through, forming a vital part of the texture of linguistic and cultural practice. There were established English offshore interests in Ireland, America, the Caribbean, and Asia from the sixteenth century on, and even a quick inventory reveals poets, philosophers, historians, dramatists, statesmen, novelists, travel writers, chroniclers, soldiers, and fabulists who prized, cared for, and traced these interests with continuing concern. (Much of this is well discussed by Peter Hulme in *Colonial Encounters*.)[32] Similar points may be made for France, Spain, and Portugal, not only as overseas powers in their own right, but as competitors with the British. How can we examine these interests at work in modern England before the age of empire, i.e., during the period between 1800 and 1870?

We would do well to follow Williams's lead, and look first at that period of crisis following upon England's wide-scale land enclosure at the end of the eighteenth century. The old organic rural communities were dissolved and new ones forged under the impulse of parliamentary activity, industrialization, and demographic dislocation, but there also occurred a new process of relocating England (and in France, France) within a much larger circle of the world map. During the first half of the eighteenth century, Anglo-French competition in North America and India was intense; in the second half there were numerous violent encounters between England and France in the Americas, the Caribbean, and the Levant, and of course in Europe itself. The major pre-Romantic literature in France and England contains a constant stream of references to the overseas dominions: one thinks not only of various Encyclopedists, the Abbé Raynal, de Brosses, and Volney, but also of Edmund Burke, Beckford, Gibbon, Johnson, and William Jones.

In 1902 J. A. Hobson described imperialism as the expansion of nationality, implying that the process was understandable mainly by considering *expansion* as the more important of the two terms, since "nationality" was a fully formed, fixed quantity,[33] whereas a century before it was still in the process of *being formed*, at home and abroad as well. In *Physics and Politics* (1887) Walter Bagehot speaks with extraordinary relevance of "nation-making." Between France and Britain in the late eighteenth century there were two contests: the battle for strategic gains abroad—in India, the Nile delta, the Western Hemisphere—and the battle for a triumphant nationality. Both battles contrast "Englishness" with "the French," and no matter how intimate and closeted the supposed English or French "essence" appears to be, it was almost always thought of as being (as opposed to already) made, and being fought out with the other great competitor. Thackeray's Becky Sharp, for example, is as much an upstart as she is because of her half-French heritage.

Earlier in the century, the upright abolitionist posture of Wilberforce and his allies developed partly out of a desire to make life harder for French hegemony in the Antilles.[34]

These considerations suddenly provide a fascinatingly expanded dimension to *Mansfield Park* (1814), the most explicit in its ideological and moral affirmations of Austen's novels. Williams once again is in general dead right: Austen's novels express an "attainable quality of life," in money and property acquired, moral discriminations made, the right choices put in place, the correct "improvements" implemented, the finely nuanced language affirmed and classified. Yet, Williams continues,

> What [Cobbett] names, riding past on the road, are classes. Jane Austen, from inside the houses, can never see that, for all the intricacy of her social description. All her discrimination is, understandably, internal and exclusive. She is concerned with the conduct of people who, in the complications of improvement, are repeatedly trying to make themselves into a class. But where only one class is seen, no classes are seen.[35]

As a general description of how Austen manages to elevate certain "moral discriminations" into "an independent value," this is excellent. Where *Mansfield Park* is concerned, however, a good deal more needs to be said, giving greater explicitness and width to Williams's survey. Perhaps then Austen, and indeed, pre-imperialist novels generally, will appear to be more implicated in the rationale for imperialist expansion than at first sight they have been.

After Lukacs and Proust, we have become so accustomed to thinking of the novel's plot and structure as constituted mainly by temporality that we have overlooked the function of space, geography, and location. For it is not only the very young Stephen Dedalus, but every other young protagonist before him as well, who sees himself in a widening spiral at home, in Ireland, in the world. Like many other novels, *Mansfield Park* is very precisely about a series of both small and large dislocations and relocations in space that occur before, at the end of the novel, Fanny Price, the niece, becomes the spiritual mistress of Mansfield Park. And that place itself is located by Austen at the center of an arc of interests and concerns spanning the hemisphere, two major seas, and four continents.

As in Austen's other novels, the central group that finally emerges with marriage and property "ordained" is not based exclusively upon blood. Her novel enacts the disaffiliation (in the literal sense) of some members of a family, and the affiliation between others and one or two chosen and tested outsiders: in other words, blood relationships are not enough to assure continuity, hierarchy, authority, both domestic and international. Thus Fanny Price—the poor niece, the orphaned child from the outlying city of Portsmouth, the neglected, demure, and upright wallflower—gradually acquires a status commensurate with, even superior to, that of most of her more fortunate relatives. In this pattern of affiliation and in her assumption of authority, Fanny Price is relatively passive. She resists the misdemeanors and the importunings of others, and very occasionally she ventures actions on her own: all in all, though, one has the impression that Austen has designs for her that Fanny herself can scarcely comprehend, just as throughout the novel Fanny is thought of by everyone as "comfort" and "acquisition" despite herself. Like Kipling's Kim O'Hara, Fanny is both device and instrument in a larger pattern, as well as a fully fledged novelistic character.

Fanny, like Kim, requires direction, requires the patronage and outside authority that her own impoverished experience cannot provide. Her conscious connections are to some people and to some places, but the novel reveals other connections of which she has faint glimmerings that nevertheless demand her presence and service. She comes into a situation that opens with an intricate set of moves which, taken together, demand sorting out, adjustment, and rearrangement. Sir Thomas Bertram has been captivated by one Ward sister, the others have not done well, and "an absolute breach" opens up; their "circles were so distinct," the distances between them so great that they have been out of touch for eleven years;[36] fallen on hard times, the Prices seek out the Bertrams. Gradually, and even though she is not the eldest, Fanny becomes the focus of attention as she is sent to Mansfield Park, there to begin her new life. Similarly, the Bertrams have given up London (the result of Lady Bertram's "little ill health and a great deal of indolence") and come to reside entirely in the country.

What sustains this life materially is the Bertram estate in Antigua, which is not doing well. Austen takes pains to show us two apparently disparate but actually convergent processes: the growth of Fanny's importance to the Bertrams' economy, including Antigua, and Fanny's own steadfastness in the face of numerous challenges, threats, and surprises. In both, Austen's imagination works with a steel-like rigor through a mode that we might call geographical and spatial clarification. Fanny's ignorance when she arrives at Mansfield as a frightened ten-year-old is signified by her inability to "put the map of Europe together,"[37] and for much of the first half of the novel the action is concerned with a whole range of issues whose common denominator, misused or misunderstood, is space: not only is Sir Thomas in Antigua to make things better there and at home, but at Mansfield Park, Fanny, Edmund, and her aunt Norris negotiate where she is to live, read, and work, where fires are to be lit; the friends and cousins concern themselves with the improvement of estates, and the importance of chapels (i.e., religious authority) to domesticity is envisioned and debated. When, as a device for stirring things up, the Crawfords suggest a play (the tinge of France that hangs a little suspiciously over their background is significant), Fanny's discomfiture is polarizingly acute. She cannot participate, cannot easily accept that rooms for living are turned into theatrical space, although, with all its confusion of roles and purposes, the play, Kotzebue's *Lovers' Vows,* is prepared for anyway.

We are to surmise, I think, that while Sir Thomas is away tending his colonial garden, a number of inevitable mismeasurements (explicitly associated with feminine "lawlessness") will occur. These are apparent not only in innocent strolls by the three pairs of young friends through a park, in which people lose and catch sight of one another unexpectedly, but most clearly in the various flirtations and engagements between the young men and women left without true parental authority, Lady Bertram being indifferent, Mrs. Norris unsuitable. There is sparring, innuendo, perilous taking on of roles: all of this of course crystallizes in preparations for the play, in which something dangerously close to libertinage is about to be (but never is) enacted. Fanny, whose earlier sense of alienation, distance, and fear derives from her first uprooting, now becomes a sort of surrogate conscience about what is right and how far is too much. Yet she has no power to implement her uneasy awareness, and until Sir Thomas suddenly returns from "abroad," the rudderless drift continues.

When he does appear, preparations for the play are immediately stopped, and in a passage remarkable for its executive dispatch, Austen narrates the re-establishment of Sir Thomas's local rule:

> It was a busy morning with him. Conversation with any of them occupied but a small part of it. He had to reinstate himself in all the wonted concerns of his Mansfield life, to see his steward and his bailiff—to examine and compute—and, in the intervals of business, to walk into his stables and his gardens, and nearest plantations; but active and methodical, he had not only done all this before he resumed his seat as master of the house at dinner, he had also set the carpenter to work in pulling down what had been so lately put up in the billiard room, and given the scene painter his dismissal, long enough to justify the pleasing belief of his being then at least as far off as Northampton. The scene painter was gone, having spoilt only the floor of one room, ruined all the coachman's sponges, and made five of the under-servants idle and dissatisfied; and Sir Thomas was in hopes that another day or two would suffice to wipe away every outward memento of what had

been, even to the destruction of every unbound copy of 'Lovers' Vows'
in the house, for he was burning all that met his eye.[38]

The force of this paragraph is unmistakable. Not only is this a Crusoe
setting things in order: it is also an early Protestant eliminating all traces of
frivolous behavior. There is nothing in *Mansfield Park* that would contradict
us, however, were we to assume that Sir Thomas does exactly the same
things—on a larger scale—in his Antigua "plantations." Whatever was
wrong there—and the internal evidence garnered by Warren Roberts suggests that economic depression, slavery, and competition with France were
at issue[39]—Sir Thomas was able to fix, thereby maintaining his control over
his colonial domain. More clearly than anywhere else in her fiction, Austen
here synchronizes domestic with international authority, making it plain
that the values associated with such higher things as ordination, law, and
propriety must be grounded firmly in actual rule over and possession of
territory. She sees clearly that to hold and rule Mansfield Park is to hold and
rule an imperial estate in close, not to say inevitable association with it.
What assures the domestic tranquility and attractive harmony of one is the
productivity and regulated discipline of the other.

Before both can be fully secured, however, Fanny must become more
actively involved in the unfolding action. From frightened and often victim-
ized poor relation she is gradually transformed into a directly participating
member of the Bertram household at Mansfield Park. For this, I believe,
Austen designed the second part of the book, which contains not only the
failure of the Edmund–Mary Crawford romance as well as the disgraceful
profligacy of Lydia and Henry Crawford, but Fanny Price's rediscovery and
rejection of her Portsmouth home, the injury and incapacitation of Tom
Bertram (the eldest son), and the launching of William Price's naval career.
This entire ensemble of relationships and events is finally capped with
Edmund's marriage to Fanny, whose place in Lady Bertram's household is
taken by Susan Price, her sister. It is no exaggeration to interpret the
concluding sections of *Mansfield Park* as the coronation of an arguably
unnatural (or at very least, illogical) principle at the heart of a desired
English order. The audacity of Austen's vision is disguised a little by her
voice, which despite its occasional archness is understated and notably
modest. But we should not misconstrue the limited references to the outside
world, her lightly stressed allusions to work, process, and class, her apparent
ability to abstract (in Raymond Williams's phrase) "an everyday uncompromising morality which is in the end separable from its social basis." In fact
Austen is far less diffident, far more severe.

The clues are to be found in Fanny, or rather in how rigorously we are able to consider her. True, her visit to her original Portsmouth home, where her immediate family still resides, upsets the aesthetic and emotional balance she has become accustomed to at Mansfield Park, and true she has begun to take its wonderful luxuries for granted, even as being essential. These are fairly routine and natural consequences of getting used to a new place. But Austen is talking about two other matters we must not mistake. One is Fanny's newly enlarged sense of what it means to be *at home*; when she takes stock of things after she gets to Portsmouth, this is not merely a matter of expanded space.

> Fanny was almost stunned. The smallness of the house, and thinness of the walls, brought every thing so close to her, that, added to the fatigue of her journey, and all her recent agitation, she hardly knew how to bear it. *Within* the room all was tranquil enough, for Susan having disappeared with the others, there were soon only her father and herself remaining; and he taking out a newspaper—the accustomary loan of a neighbour, applied himself to studying it, without seeming to recollect her existence. The solitary candle was held between himself and the paper, without any reference to her possible convenience; but she had nothing to do, and was glad to have the light screened from her aching head, as she sat in bewildered, broken, sorrowful contemplation.
>
> She was at home. But alas! it was not such a home, she had not such a welcome, as—she checked herself; she was unreasonable. . . . A day or two might shew the difference. *She* only was to blame. Yet she thought it would not have been so at Mansfield. No, in her uncle's house there would have been a consideration of times and seasons, a regulation of subject, a propriety, an attention towards every body which there was not here.[40]

In too small a space, you cannot see clearly, you cannot think clearly, you cannot have regulation or attention of the proper sort. The fineness of Austen's detail ("the solitary candle was held between himself and the paper, without any reference to her possible convenience") renders very precisely the dangers of unsociability, of lonely insularity, of diminished awareness that are rectified in larger and better administered spaces.

That such spaces are not available to Fanny by direct inheritance, legal title, by propinquity, contiguity, or adjacence (Mansfield Park and Portsmouth are separated by many hours' journey) is precisely Austen's point. To earn the right to Mansfield Park you must first leave home as a kind of indentured servant or, to put the case in extreme terms, as a kind of transported commodity—this, clearly, is the fate of Fanny and her brother

William—but then you have the promise of future wealth. I think Austen sees what Fanny does as a domestic or small-scale movement in space that corresponds to the larger, more openly colonial movements of Sir Thomas, her mentor, the man whose estate she inherits. The two movements depend on each other.

The second more complex matter about which Austen speaks, albeit indirectly, raises an interesting theoretical issue. Austen's awareness of empire is obviously very different, alluded to very much more casually, than Conrad's or Kipling's. In her time the British were extremely active in the Caribbean and in South America, notably Brazil and Argentina. Austen seems only vaguely aware of the details of these activities, although the sense that extensive West Indian plantations were important was fairly widespread in metropolitan England. Antigua and Sir Thomas's trip there have a definitive function in *Mansfield Park*, which, I have been saying, is both incidental, referred to only in passing, and absolutely crucial to the action. How are we to assess Austen's few references to Antigua, and what are we to make of them interpretatively?

My contention is that by that very odd combination of casualness and stress, Austen reveals herself to be *assuming* (just as Fanny assumes, in both senses of the word) the importance of an empire to the situation at home. Let me go further. Since Austen refers to and uses Antigua as she does in *Mansfield Park*, there needs to be a commensurate effort on the part of her readers to understand concretely the historical valences in the reference; to put it differently, we should try to understand *what* she referred to, why she gave it the importance she did, and why indeed she made the choice, for she might have done something different to establish Sir Thomas's wealth. Let us now calibrate the signifying power of the references to Antigua in *Mansfield Park*; how do they occupy the place they do, what are they doing there?

According to Austen we are to conclude that no matter how isolated and insulated the English place (e.g., Mansfield Park), it requires overseas sustenance. Sir Thomas's property in the Caribbean would have had to be a sugar plantation maintained by slave labor (not abolished until the 1830s): these are not dead historical facts but, as Austen certainly knew, evident historical realities. Before the Anglo-French competition the major distinguishing characteristic of Western empires (Roman, Spanish, and Portuguese) was that the earlier empires were bent on loot, as Conrad puts it, on the transport of treasure from the colonies to Europe, with very little attention to development, organization, or system within the colonies themselves; Britain and, to a lesser degree, France both wanted to make their empires long-term, profitable, ongoing concerns, and they competed in this enterprise, nowhere more so than in the colonies of the Caribbean, where the transport of slaves, the functioning of large sugar plantations, and the development of sugar markets, which raised the issues of protectionism, monopolies, and price—all these were more or less constantly, competitively at issue.

Far from being nothing much "out there," British colonial possessions in the Antilles and Leeward Islands were during Jane Austen's time a crucial setting for Anglo-French colonial competition. Revolutionary ideas from France were being exported there, and there was a steady decline in British profits: the French sugar plantations were producing more sugar at less cost. However, slave rebellions in and out of Haiti were incapacitating France and spurring British interests to intervene more directly and to gain greater local power. Still, compared with its earlier prominence for the home market, British Caribbean sugar production in the nineteenth century had to compete with alternative sugar-cane supplies in Brazil and Mauritius, the emergence of a European beet-sugar industry, and the gradual dominance of free-trade ideology and practice.

In *Mansfield Park*—both in its formal characteristics and in its contents—a number of these currents converge. The most important is the avowedly complete subordination of colony to metropolis. Sir Thomas, absent from Mansfield Park, is never seen as *present* in Antigua, which elicits at most a half dozen references in the novel. There is a passage, a part of which I quoted earlier, from John Stuart Mill's *Principles of Political Economy* that catches the spirit of Austen's use of Antigua. I quote it here in full:

These [outlying possessions of ours] are hardly to be looked upon as countries, carrying on an exchange of commodities with other countries, but more properly as outlying agricultural or manufacturing estates belonging to a larger community. Our West Indian colonies, for example, cannot be regarded as countries with a productive capital of their own . . . [but are rather] the place where England finds it convenient to carry on the production of sugar, coffee and a few other tropical commodities. All the capital employed is English capital; almost all the industry is carried on for English uses; there is little production of anything except for staple commodities, and these are sent to England, not to be exchanged for things exported to the colony and consumed by its inhabitants, but to be sold in England for the benefit of the proprietors there. The trade with the West Indies is hardly to be considered an external trade, but more resembles the traffic between town and country.[41]

To some extent Antigua is like London or Portsmouth, a less desirable setting than a country estate like Mansfield Park, but producing goods to be consumed by everyone (by the early nineteenth century every Britisher used sugar), although owned and maintained by a small group of aristocrats and gentry. The Bertrams and the other characters in *Mansfield Park* are a subgroup within the minority, and for them the island is wealth, which Austen regards as being converted to propriety, order, and, at the end of the novel, comfort, an added good. But why "added"? Because, Austen tells us pointedly in the final chapters, she wants to "restore every body, not greatly in fault themselves, to tolerable comfort, and to have done with all the rest."[42]

This can be interpreted to mean first that the novel has done enough in the way of destabilizing the lives of "every body" and must now set them at rest: actually Austen says this explicitly, in a bit of meta-fictional impatience, the novelist commenting on her own work as having gone on long enough and now needing to be brought to a close. Second, it can mean that "every body" may now be finally permitted to realize what it means to be properly at home, and at rest, without the need to wander about or to come and go. (This does not include young William, who, we assume, will continue to roam the seas in the British navy on whatever commercial and political missions may still be required. Such matters draw from Austen only a last brief gesture, a passing remark about William's "continuing good conduct and rising fame.") As for those finally resident in Mansfield Park itself, more in the way of domesticated advantages is given to these now fully acclimatized souls, and to none more than to Sir Thomas. He understands for the first time what has been missing in his education of his children, and he understands it in the terms paradoxically provided for him by unnamed outside forces, so to speak, the wealth of Antigua and the imported example of Fanny Price. Note here how the curious alternation of outside and inside follows the pattern identified by Mill of the outside *becoming* the inside by use and, to use Austen's word, "disposition":

Here [in his deficiency of training, of allowing Mrs. Norris too great a role, of letting his children dissemble and repress feeling] had been grievous mismanagement; but, bad as it was, he gradually grew to feel that it had not been the most direful mistake in his plan of education. Some thing must have been wanting *within*, or time would have worn away much of its ill effect. He feared that principle, active principle, had been wanting, that they had never been properly taught to govern their inclinations and tempers, by that sense of duty which can alone suffice. They had been instructed theoretically in their religion, but never required to bring it into daily practice. To be distinguished for elegance and accomplishments—the authorized object of their youth—

could have had no useful influence that way, no moral effect on the mind. He had meant them to be good, but his cares had been directed to the understanding and manners, not the disposition; and of the necessity of self-denial and humility, he feared they had never heard from any lips that could profit them.[43]

What was wanting *within* was in fact supplied by the wealth derived from a West Indian plantation and a poor provincial relative, both brought in to Mansfield Park and set to work. Yet on their own, neither the one nor the other could have sufficed; they require each other and then, more important, they need executive disposition, which in turn helps to reform the rest of the Bertram circle. All this Austen leaves to her reader to supply in the way of literal explication.

And that is what reading her entails. But all these things having to do with the outside brought in seem unmistakably *there* in the suggestiveness of her allusive and abstract language. A principle "wanting *within*" is, I believe, intended to evoke for us memories of Sir Thomas's absences in Antigua, or the sentimental and near-whimsical vagary on the part of the three variously deficient Ward sisters by which a niece is displaced from one household to another. But that the Bertrams did become better if not altogether good, that some sense of duty was imparted to them, that they learned to govern their inclinations and tempers and brought religion into daily practice, that they "directed disposition": all of this did occur because outside (or rather outlying) factors were lodged properly inward, became native to Mansfield Park, with Fanny the niece its final spiritual mistress, and Edmund the second son its spiritual master.

An additional benefit is that Mrs. Norris is dislodged; this is described as "the great supplementary comfort of Sir Thomas's life."[44] Once the principles have been interiorized, the comforts follow: Fanny is settled for the time being at Thornton Lacey "with every attention to her comfort"; her home later becomes "the home of affection and comfort"; Susan is brought in "first as a comfort to Fanny, then as an auxiliary, and at last as her substitute"[45] when the new import takes Fanny's place by Lady Bertram's side. The pattern established at the outset of the novel clearly continues, only now it has what Austen intended to give it all along, an internalized and retrospectively guaranteed rationale. This is the rationale that Raymond Williams describes as "an everyday, uncompromising morality which is in the end separable from its social basis and which, in other hands, can be turned against it."

I have tried to show that the morality in fact is not separable from its social basis: right up to the last sentence, Austen affirms and repeats the geographical process of expansion involving trade, production, and consumption that predates, underlies, and guarantees the morality. And expansion, as Gallagher reminds us, whether "through colonial rule was liked or disliked, [its] desirability through one mode or another was generally accepted. So in the event there were few domestic constraints upon expansion."[46] Most critics have tended to forget or overlook that process, which has seemed less important to critics than Austen herself seemed to think. But interpreting Jane Austen depends on *who* does the interpreting, *when* it is done, and no less important, from *where* it is done. If with feminists, with great cultural critics sensitive to history and class like Williams, with cultural and stylistic interpreters, we have been sensitized to the issues their interests raise, we should now proceed to regard the geographical division of the world—after all significant to *Mansfield Park*—as not neutral (any more than class and gender are neutral) but as politically charged, beseeching the attention and elucidation its considerable proportions require. The question is thus not only how to understand and with what to connect Austen's morality and its social basis, but also *what* to read of it.

Take once again the casual references to Antigua, the ease with which Sir Thomas's needs in England are met by a Caribbean sojourn, the uninflected, unreflective citations of Antigua (or the Mediterranean, or India, which is where Lady Bertram, in a fit of distracted impatience, requires that William should go " 'that I may have a shawl. I think I will have two shawls.' ")[47] They stand for a significance "out there" that frames the genuinely important action *here*, but not for a great significance. Yet these signs of "abroad" include, even as they repress, a rich and complex history, which has since achieved a status that the Bertrams, the Prices, and Austen herself would not, could not recognize. To call this "the Third World" begins to deal with the realities but by no means exhausts the political or cultural history.

We must first take stock of *Mansfield Park*'s prefigurations of a later English history as registered in fiction. The Bertrams' usable colony in *Mansfield Park* can be read as pointing forward to Charles Gould's San Tomé mine in *Nostromo*, or to the Wilcoxes' Imperial and West African Rubber Company in Forster's *Howards End*, or to any of these distant but convenient treasure spots in *Great Expectations*, Jean Rhys's *Wide Sargasso Sea*, *Heart of Darkness*—resources to be visited, talked about, described, or appreciated for domestic reasons, for local metropolitan benefit. If we think ahead to these other novels, Sir Thomas's Antigua readily acquires a slightly greater density than the discrete, reticent appearances it makes in the pages of *Mansfield Park*. And already our reading of the novel begins to open up at those points where ironically Austen was most economical and her critics most (dare one say it?) negligent. Her "Antigua" is therefore not just a slight but a definite

way of marking the outer limits of what Williams calls domestic improvements, or a quick allusion to the mercantile venturesomeness of acquiring
overseas dominions as a source for local fortunes, or one reference among
many attesting to a historical sensibility suffused not just with manners and
courtesies but with contests of ideas, struggles with Napoleonic France,
awareness of seismic economic and social change during a revolutionary
period in world history.

Second, we must see "Antigua" held in a precise place in Austen's moral
geography, and in her prose, by historical changes that her novel rides like
a vessel on a mighty sea. The Bertrams could not have been possible without
the slave trade, sugar, and the colonial planter class; as a social type Sir
Thomas would have been familiar to eighteenth- and early-nineteenth-
century readers who knew the powerful influence of the class through
politics, plays (like Cumberland's *The West Indian*), and many other public
activities (large houses, famous parties and social rituals, well-known commercial enterprises, celebrated marriages). As the old system of protected
monopoly gradually disappeared and as a new class of settler-planters displaced the old absentee system, the West Indian interest lost dominance:
cotton manufacture, an even more open system of trade, and abolition of the
slave trade reduced the power and prestige of people like the Bertrams,
whose frequency of sojourn in the Caribbean then decreased.

Thus Sir Thomas's infrequent trips to Antigua as an absentee plantation
owner reflect the diminishment in his class's power, a reduction directly
expressed in the title of Lowell Ragatz's classic *The Fall of the Planter Class
in the British Caribbean, 1763–1833* (1928). But is what is hidden or allusive in
Austen made sufficiently explicit more than one hundred years later in
Ragatz? Does the aesthetic silence or discretion of a great novel in 1814
receive adequate explication in a major work of historical research a full
century later? Can we assume that the process of interpretation is fulfilled,
or will it continue as new material comes to light?

For all his learning Ragatz still finds it in himself to speak of "the Negro
race" as having the following characteristics: "he stole, he lied, he was
simple, suspicious, inefficient, irresponsible, lazy, superstitious, and loose in
his sexual relations."[48] Such "history" as this therefore happily gave way to
the revisionary work of Caribbean historians like Eric Williams and C.L.R.
James, and more recently Robin Blackburn, in *The Overthrow of Colonial
Slavery, 1776–1848*; in these works slavery and empire are shown to have
fostered the rise and consolidation of capitalism well beyond the old plantation monopolies, as well as to have been a powerful ideological system
whose original connection to specific economic interests may have gone, but
whose effects continued for decades.

The political and moral ideas of the age are to be examined in the very closest relation to the economic development. . . .

An outworn interest, whose bankruptcy smells to heaven in historical perspective, can exercise an obstructionist and disruptive effect which can only be explained by the powerful services it had previously rendered and the entrenchment previously gained. . . .

The ideas built on these interests continue long after the interests have been destroyed and work their old mischief, which is all the more mischievous because the interests to which they corresponded no longer exist.[49]

Thus Eric Williams in *Capitalism and Slavery* (1961). The question of interpretation, indeed of writing itself, is tied to the question of interests, which we have seen are at work in aesthetic as well as historical writing, then and now. We must not say that since *Mansfield Park* is a novel, its affiliations with a sordid history are irrelevant or transcended, not only because it is irresponsible to do so, but because we know too much to say so in good faith. Having read *Mansfield Park* as part of the structure of an expanding imperialist venture, one cannot simply restore it to the canon of "great literary masterpieces"—to which it most certainly belongs—and leave it at that. Rather, I think, the novel steadily, if unobtrusively, opens up a broad expanse of domestic imperialist culture without which Britain's subsequent acquisition of territory would not have been possible.

I have spent time on *Mansfield Park* to illustrate a type of analysis infrequently encountered in mainstream interpretations, or for that matter in readings rigorously based in one or another of the advanced theoretical schools. Yet only in the global perspective implied by Jane Austen and her characters can the novel's quite astonishing general position be made clear. I think of such a reading as completing or complementing others, not discounting or displacing them. And it bears stressing that because *Mansfield Park* connects the actualities of British power overseas to the domestic imbroglio within the Bertram estate, there is no way of doing such readings as mine, no way of understanding the "structure of attitude and reference" except by working through the novel. Without reading it in full, we would fail to understand the strength of that structure and the way it was activated and maintained in literature. But in reading it carefully, we can sense how ideas about dependent races and territories were held both by foreign-office executives, colonial bureaucrats, and military strategists and by intelligent novel-readers educating themselves in the fine points of moral evaluation, literary balance, and stylistic finish.

There is a paradox here in reading Jane Austen which I have been impressed by but can in no way resolve. All the evidence says that even the most routine aspects of holding slaves on a West Indian sugar plantation were cruel stuff. And everything we know about Austen and her values is at odds with the cruelty of slavery. Fanny Price reminds her cousin that after asking Sir Thomas about the slave trade, "There was such a dead silence"[50] as to suggest that one world could not be connected with the other since there simply is no common language for both. That is true. But what stimulates the extraordinary discrepancy into life is the rise, decline, and fall of the British empire itself and, in its aftermath, the emergence of a post-colonial consciousness. In order more accurately to read works like *Mansfield Park*, we have to see them in the main as resisting or avoiding that other setting, which their formal inclusiveness, historical honesty, and prophetic suggestiveness cannot completely hide. In time there would no longer be a dead silence when slavery was spoken of, and the subject became central to a new understanding of what Europe was.

It would be silly to expect Jane Austen to treat slavery with anything like the passion of an abolitionist or a newly liberated slave. Yet what I have called the rhetoric of blame, so often now employed by subaltern, minority, or disadvantaged voices, attacks her, and others like her, retrospectively, for being white, privileged, insensitive, complicit. Yes, Austen belonged to a slave-owning society, but do we therefore jettison her novels as so many trivial exercises in aesthetic frumpery? Not at all, I would argue, if we take seriously our intellectual and interpretative vocation to make connections, to deal with as much of the evidence as possible, fully and actually, to read what is there or not there, above all, to see complementarity and interdependence instead of isolated, venerated, or formalized experience that excludes and forbids the hybridizing intrusions of human history.

Mansfield Park is a rich work in that its aesthetic intellectual complexity requires that longer and slower analysis that is also required by its geographical problematic, a novel based in an England relying for the maintenance of its style on a Caribbean island. When Sir Thomas goes to and comes from Antigua, where he has property, that is not at all the same thing as coming to and going from Mansfield Park, where his presence, arrivals, and departures have very considerable consequences. But precisely because Austen is so summary in one context, so provocatively rich in the other, precisely because of that imbalance we are able to move in on the novel, reveal and accentuate the interdependence scarcely mentioned on its brilliant pages. A lesser work wears its historical affiliation more plainly; its worldliness is simple and direct, the way a jingoistic ditty during the Mahdist uprising or the 1857 Indian Rebellion connects directly to the situation and constituency that coined it. *Mansfield Park* encodes experiences and does not simply repeat them. From our later perspective we can interpret Sir Thomas's power to come and go in Antigua as stemming from the muted national experience of individual identity, behavior, and "ordination," enacted with such irony and taste at Mansfield Park. The task is to lose neither a true historical sense of the first, nor a full enjoyment or appreciation of the second, all the while seeing both together.

(iii)

The Cultural Integrity of Empire

Until after the mid–nineteenth century the kind of easy yet sustained commerce between Mansfield Park (novel and place) and an overseas territory has little equivalent in French culture. Before Napoleon, there existed of course an ample French literature of ideas, travels, polemics, and speculation about the non-European world. One thinks of Volney, for instance, or Montesquieu (some of this is discussed in Tzvetan Todorov's recent *Nous et les autres*).[51] Without significant exception this literature either was specialized—as, for example, in the Abbé Raynal's celebrated report on the colonies—or belonged to a genre (e.g., moral debate) that used such issues as mortality, slavery, or corruption as instances in a general argument about mankind. The Encyclopedists and Rousseau are excellent illustrations of this latter case. As traveller, memoirist, eloquent self-psychologist and romantic, Chateaubriand embodies an individualism of accent and style without peer; certainly, it would be very hard to show that in *René* or *Atala* he belonged to a literary institution like the novel, or to learned discourses such as historiography or linguistics. Besides, his narratives of American and Near Eastern life are too eccentric to be easily domesticated or emulated.

France thus shows a somewhat fitful, perhaps even sporadic but certainly limited and specialized literary or cultural concern with those realms where traders, scholars, missionaries, or soldiers went and where in the East or the Americas they encountered their British counterparts. Before taking Algeria in 1830, France had no India and, I've argued elsewhere, it had momentarily brilliant experiences abroad that were returned to more in memory or literary trope than in actuality. One celebrated example is the Abbé Poiret's *Lettres de Barbarie* (1785), which describes an often uncomprehending but stimulating encounter between a Frenchman and Muslim Africans. The best intellectual historian of French imperialism, Raoul Girardet, suggests that between 1815 and 1870 colonial currents in France existed aplenty, but none of them dominated the others, or was situated prominently or crucially in French society. He specifies arms dealers, economists, the military, and missionary circles as responsible for keeping French imperial institutions alive domestically, although unlike Platt and other students of British imperialism, Giradet cannot identify anything so evident as a French "departmental view."[52]

About French literary culture it would be easy to draw the wrong conclusions, and so a series of contrasts with England are worth listing. England's widespread, unspecialized, and easily accessible awareness of overseas interests has no direct French equivalent. The French equivalents of Austen's country gentry or Dickens's business people who make casual references to the Caribbean or India are not easily to be found. Still, in two or three rather specialized ways France's overseas interests appear in cultural discourse. One, interestingly enough, is the huge, almost iconic figure of Napoleon (as in Hugo's poem "Lui"), who embodies the romantic French spirit abroad, less a conqueror (which in fact he was, in Egypt) than a brooding, melodramatic presence whose persona acts as a mask through which reflections are expressed. Lukacs has astutely remarked on the tremendous influence exerted by Napoleon's career on those of novelistic heroes in French and Russian literature; in the early nineteenth century the Corsican Napoleon also has an exotic aura.

Stendhal's young men are incomprehensible without him. In *Le Rouge et le noir* Julien Sorel is completely dominated by his reading of Napoleon (in particular the St. Helena memoirs), with their fitful grandeur, sense of Mediterranean dash, and impetuous *arrivisme*. The replication of such an ambiance in Julien's career takes an extraordinary series of turns, all of them, in a France now marked by mediocrity and scheming reaction, deflating the Napoleonic legend without detracting from its power over Sorel. So powerful is the Napoleonic ambiance in *Le Rouge et le noir* that it comes as an instructive surprise to note that Napoleon's career is not directly alluded to anywhere in the novel. In fact the only reference to a world outside France comes after Mathilde has sent her declaration of love to Julien, and Stendhal characterizes her Parisian existence as involving more risk than a voyage to Algeria. Typically, then, at exactly the moment in 1830 when France secures its major imperial province, it turns up in a lone Stendhalian reference connoting danger, surprise, and a sort of calculated indifference. This is remarkably unlike the easy allusions to Ireland, India, and the Americas that slip in and out of British literature at the same time.

A second vehicle for culturally appropriating French imperial concerns is the set of new and rather glamorous sciences originally enabled by Napoleonic overseas adventures. This perfectly reflects the social structure of French knowledge, dramatically unlike England's amateurish, often embarrassingly *démodé* intellectual life. The great institutes of learning in Paris (enhanced by Napoleon) have a dominating influence in the rise of archeology, linguistics, historiography, Orientalism, and experimental biology (many of them actively participating in the *Description de l'Egypte*). Typically, novelists cite academically regulated discourse about the East, India, and Africa—Balzac in *La Peau de chagrin* or *La Cousine Bette,* for instance—with a knowingness and sheen of expertise quite un-English. In the writings of British residents abroad, from Lady Wortley Montagu to the Webbs, one finds a language of casual observation; and in colonial "experts" (like Sir Thomas Bertram and the Mills) a studied but basically unincorporated and unofficial attitude; in administrative or official prose, of which Macaulay's 1835 Minute on Indian Education is a famous example, a haughty but still somehow personal obduracy. Rarely is any of this the case in early-nineteenth-century French culture, where the official prestige of the academy and of Paris shape every utterance.

As I have argued, the power even in casual conversation to represent what is beyond metropolitan borders derives from the power of an imperial society, and that power takes the discursive form of a reshaping or reordering of "raw" or primitive data into the local conventions of European narrative and formal utterance, or, in the case of France, the systematics of disciplinary order. And these were under no obligation to please or persuade a "native" African, Indian, or Islamic audience: indeed they were in most influential instances premised on the silence of the native. When it came to what lay beyond metropolitan Europe, the arts and the disciplines of representation—on the one hand, fiction, history and travel writing, painting; on the other, sociology, administrative or bureaucratic writing, philology, racial theory—depended on the powers of Europe to bring the non-European world into representations, the better to be able to see it, to master it, and, above all, to hold it. Philip Curtin's two-volume *Image of Africa* and Bernard Smith's *European Vision and the South Pacific* are perhaps the most extended analyses of the practice available. A good popular characterization is provided by Basil Davidson in his survey of writing about Africa until the mid–twentieth century:

> The literature of [African] exploration and conquest is as vast and varied as those processes themselves. Yet with a few outstanding exceptions the records are built uniquely to a single domination attitude: they are the journals of men who look at Africa resolutely from the outside. I am not saying that many of them could have been expected

to do otherwise: the important point is that the quality of their observation was circumscribed within a cramping limit, and they must be read today with this in mind. If they tried to understand the minds and actions of Africans they knew, it was by the way, and it was rare. Nearly all of them were convinced they were faced by "primeval man," by humanity as it had been before history began, by societies which lingered in the dawn of time. [Brian Street's important book *The Savage in Literature* details the steps by which in academic and popular literature this was shown to be true.] This point of view marched in step with Europe's overwhelming expansion of power and wealth, with its political strength and resilience and sophistication, with its belief in somehow being the elected continent of God. What otherwise honorable explorers thought and did may be seen in the writings of men like Henry Stanley or in the actions of men like Cecil Rhodes and his mineral-hunting agents, ready as they were to represent themselves as honest allies of their African friends so long as the treaties were secured—the treaties through which "effective occupation" could be proved to each other by the governments or private interests which they served and formed.[53]

All cultures tend to make representations of foreign cultures the better to master or in some way control them. Yet not all cultures make representations of foreign cultures *and* in fact master or control them. This is the distinction, I believe, of modern Western cultures. It requires the study of Western knowledge or representations of the non-European world to be a study of both those representations and the political power they express. Late-nineteenth-century artists like Kipling and Conrad, or for that matter mid-century figures like Gérôme and Flaubert, do not merely reproduce the outlying territories: they work them out, or animate them, using narrative technique and historical and exploratory attitudes and positive ideas of the sort provided by thinkers like Max Müller, Renan, Charles Temple, Darwin, Benjamin Kidd, Emerich de Vattel. All of these developed and accentuated the essentialist positions in European culture proclaiming that Europeans should rule, non-Europeans be ruled. And Europeans *did* rule.

We are now reasonably well aware of how dense this material is, and how widespread its influence. Take, for example, studies by Stephen Jay Gould and Nancy Stepan on the power of racial ideas in the world of nineteenth-century scientific discovery, practice, and institutions.[54] As they show, there was no significant dissent from theories of Black inferiority, from hierarchies of advanced or undeveloped (later "subject") races. These conditions were either derived from or in many instances applied sometimes wordlessly to overseas territories where Europeans had what they regarded as direct evidence of lesser species. And even as European power grew disproportionately with that of the enormous non-European *imperium*, so too grew the power of schemata that assured the white race its unchallenged authority.

No area of experience was spared the unrelenting application of these hierarchies. In the system of education designed for India, students were taught not only English literature but the inherent superiority of the English race. Contributors to the emerging science of ethnographic observation in Africa, Asia, and Australia, as described by George Stocking, carried with them scrupulous tools of analysis and also an array of images, notions, quasi-scientific concepts about barbarism, primitivism, and civilization; in the nascent discipline of anthropology, Darwinism, Christianity, utilitarianism, idealism, racial theory, legal history, linguistics, and the lore of intrepid travellers mingled in bewildering combination, none of which wavered, however, when it came to affirming the superlative values of white (i.e., English) civilization.[55]

The more one reads in this matter, and the more one reads the modern scholars on it, the more impressive is its fundamental insistence and repetitiveness when it came to "others." To compare Carlyle's grandiose revaluations of English spiritual life in *Past and Present*, for instance, with what he says about Blacks there or in his "Occasional Discourse on the Nigger Question" is to note two strikingly apparent factors. One is that Carlyle's energetic animadversions on revitalizing Britain, awakening it to work, organic connections, love of unrestricted industrial and capitalist development, and the like do nothing to animate "Quashee," the emblematic Black whose "ugliness, idleness, rebellion" are doomed forever to subhuman status. Carlyle is frank about this in *The Nigger Question:*

No: the gods wish besides pumpkins [the particular plant favored by Carlyle's "niggers"], that spices and valuable products be grown in their West Indies; this much they have declared in so making the West Indies:—infinitely more they wish, that industrious men occupy their West Indies, not indolent two-legged cattle however "happy" over their abundant pumpkins! Both these things, we may be assured, the immortal gods have decided upon, passed their eternal Act of Parliament for: and both of them, though all terrestrial Parliaments and entities oppose it to the death, shall be done. Quashee, if he will not help in bringing-out the spices will get himself made a slave again (which state will be a little less ugly than his present one), and with beneficent whip, since other methods avail not, will be compelled to work.[56]

The lesser species are offered nothing to speak of, while England is expanding tremendously, its culture changing to one based upon industrialization at home and protected free trade abroad. The status of the Black is decreed by "eternal Act of Parliament," so there is no real opportunity for self-help, upward mobility, or even something better than outright slavery (although Carlyle says he opposes slavery). The question is whether Carlyle's logic and attitudes are entirely his own (and therefore eccentric) or whether they articulate, in an extreme and distinctive way, essential attitudes that are not so very different from Austen's a few decades before or John Stuart Mill's a decade after.

The similarities are remarkable, and the differences between the individuals equally great, for the whole weight of the culture made it hard to be otherwise. Neither Austen nor Mill offers a non-white Caribbean any status imaginatively, discursively, aesthetically, geographically, economically other than that of sugar producer in a permanently subordinate position to the English. This, of course, is the concrete meaning of domination whose other side is *productivity.* Carlyle's Quashee is like Sir Thomas's Antiguan possessions: designed to produce wealth intended for English use. So the opportunity for Quashee to be silently *there* for Carlyle is equivalent to working obediently and unobtrusively to keep the British economy and trade going.

The second thing to note about Carlyle's writing on the subject is that it is not obscure, or occult, or esoteric. What he means about Blacks he says, and he is also very frank about the threats and punishments he intends to mete out. Carlyle speaks a language of total generality, anchored in unshakable certainties about the essence of races, peoples, cultures, all of which need little elucidation because they are familiar to his audience. He speaks a *lingua franca* for metropolitan Britain: global, comprehensive, and with so vast a social authority as to be accessible to anyone speaking to and about the nation. This *lingua franca* locates England at the focal point of a world also presided over by its power, illuminated by its ideas and culture, kept productive by the attitudes of its moral teachers, artists, legislators.

One hears similar accents in Macaulay in the 1830s and then again four decades later, largely unchanged, in Ruskin, whose 1870 Slade Lectures at Oxford begin with a solemn invocation to England's destiny. This is worth quoting from at length, not because it shows Ruskin in a bad light, but because it frames nearly everything in Ruskin's copious writings on art. The authoritative Cook and Weddenburn edition of Ruskin's work includes a footnote to this passage underscoring its importance for him; he regarded it "as 'the most pregnant and essential' of all his teaching."[57]

There is a destiny now possible to us—the highest ever set before a nation to be accepted or refused. We are still undegenerate in race; a race mingled of the best northern blood. We are not yet dissolute in temper, but still have the firmness to govern, and the grace to obey. We have taught a religion of pure mercy, which we must either now betray, or learn to defend by fulfilling. And we are rich in an inheritance of honour, bequeathed to us through a thousand years of noble history, which it should be our daily thirst to increase with splendid avarice, so that Englishmen, if it be a sin to covet honour, should be the most offending souls alive. Within the last few years we have had the laws of natural science opened to us with a rapidity which has been blinding by its brightness; and means of transit and communication given to us, which have made but one kingdom of the habitable globe. One kingdom;—but who is to be its king? Is there to be no king in it, think you, and every man to do that which is right in his own eyes? Or only kings of terror, and the obscene empires of Mammon and Belial? Or will you, youths of England, make your country again a royal throne of kings; a sceptred isle, for all the world a source of light, a centre of peace; mistress of Learning and of the Arts;—faithful guardian of great memories in the midst of irreverent and ephemeral visions;—faithful servant to time-tried principles, under temptation from fond experiments and licentious desires; and amidst the cruel and clamorous jealousies of the nations, worshipped in her strange valour of goodwill towards men? 29. "Vexilla regis prodeunt." Yes, but of which king? There are the two oriflammes; which shall we plant on the farthest island,—the one that floats in heavenly fire, or that hangs heavy with foul tissue of terrestrial gold? There is indeed a course of beneficent glory open to us, such as never was yet offered to any poor groups of mortal souls. But it must be—it *is* with us, now, "Reign or Die." And it shall be said of this country, "Fece per viltate, il gran rifiuto," that refusal of the crown will be, of all yet recorded in history, the shamefullest and most untimely. And this is what she must either do, or perish: she must found colonies as fast and as far as she is able, formed of her most energetic and worthiest men;—seizing every piece of fruitful waste ground she can set her foot on, and there teaching these her colonists that their chief virtue is to be fidelity to their country, and that their first aim is to be to advance the power of England by land and sea: and that, though they live off a distant plot of ground, they are no more to consider themselves therefore disfranchised from their native land, than the sailors of her fleets do, because they float of distant waves. So that literally, these colonies must be fastened fleets; and every man of them must be under authority of captains and officers, whose better command is to be over fields and streets instead of ships of the line; and England, in these her motionless navies (or, in the true and mightiest sense, motionless *churches,* ruled by pilots on the Galilean lake of all the world), is to "expect every man to do his duty"; recognizing that duty is indeed possible no less in peace than war; and that if we can get men, for little pay, to cast themselves against cannon-mouths for love of England, we may find men also who will plough and sow for her, who will behave kindly and righteously for her, who will bring up their children to love her, and who will gladden themselves in the brightness of her glory, more than in all the light of tropic skies. But that they may be able to do this, she must make her own majesty stainless; she must give them thoughts of their home of which they can be proud. The England who is to be mistress of half the earth, cannot remain herself a heap of cinders, trampled by contending and miserable crowds; she must yet again become the England she was once, and in all beautiful ways,— more: so happy, so secluded, and so pure, that in her sky—polluted by no unholy clouds—she may be able to spell rightly of every star that heaven doth show; and in her fields, ordered and wide and fair, of every herb that ships the dew; and under the green avenues of her enchanted garden, a sacred Circe, true Daughter of the Sun, she must guide the human arts, and gather the divine knowledge, of distant nations, trans-formed from savageness to manhood, and redeemed from despairing into peace.[58]

Most, if not all, discussions of Ruskin avoid this passage. Yet, like Carlyle, Ruskin speaks plainly; his meaning, while draped in allusions and tropes, is unmistakable. England is to rule the world because it is the best; power is to be used; its imperial competitors are unworthy; its colonies are to in-crease, prosper, remain tied to it. What is compelling in Ruskin's hortatory tones is that he not only believes fervently in what he is advocating, but also connects his political ideas about British world domination to his aesthetic and moral philosophy. Insofar as he believes passionately in the one, he also believes passionately in the other, the political and imperial aspect enfolding and in a sense guaranteeing the aesthetic and moral one. Because England is to be "king" of the globe, "a sceptred isle, for all the world a source of light," its youth are to be colonists whose first aim is to advance the power of England by land and sea; *because* England must do that "or perish," its art and culture depend, in Ruskin's view, on an enforced imperialism.

Simply ignoring these views—which are readily at hand in almost any text one looks at in the nineteenth century—is, I believe, like describing a road without its setting in the landscape. Whenever a cultural form or discourse aspired to wholeness or totality, most European writers, thinkers, politicians, and mercantilists tended to think in global terms. And these were not rhetorical flights but fairly accurate correspondences with their nations' actual and expanding global reach. In an especially trenchant essay on Tennyson, Ruskin's contemporary, and the imperialism of *The Idylls of the King,* V. G. Kiernan examines the quite staggering range of British overseas campaigns, all of them resulting in the consolidation or acquisition of territorial gain, to which Tennyson was sometimes witness, sometimes (through relatives) directly connected. Since the list was contemporaneous with Ruskin's life, let us look at the items cited by Kiernan:

1839–42	opium wars in China
1840s	wars against South African Kaffirs, New Zealand Maoris; conquest of Punjab
1854–6	the Crimean war
1854	conquest of lower Burma
1856–60	second China war
1857	attack on Persia
1857–8	suppression of Indian Mutiny
1865	Governor Eyre case in Jamaica
1866	Abyssinian expedition
1870	repulse of Fenian expansion in Canada
1871	Maori resistance destroyed
1874	decisive campaign against Ashantis in West Africa
1882	conquest of Egypt

In addition, Kiernan refers to Tennyson as being "all for putting up with no nonsense from the Afghans."[59] What Ruskin, Tennyson, Meredith, Dickens, Arnold, Thackeray, George Eliot, Carlyle, Mill—in short, the full roster of significant Victorian writers—saw was a tremendous international display of British power virtually unchecked over the entire world. It was both logical and easy to identify themselves in one way or another with this power, having through various means already identified themselves with Britain domestically. To speak of culture, ideas, taste, morality, the family, history, art, and education as they did, to represent these subjects, try to influence them or intellectually and rhetorically mold them was perforce to recognize them on a world scale. The British international identity, the scope of British mercantile and trade policy, the efficacy and mobility of British arms provided irresistible models to emulate, maps to follow, actions to live up to.

Thus representations of what lay beyond insular or metropolitan boundaries came, almost from the start, to *confirm* European power. There is an impressive circularity here: we are dominant because we have the power (industrial, technological, military, moral), and they don't, because of which they are *not* dominant; they are inferior, we are superior . . . and so on and on. One sees this tautology holding with a particular tenacity in British views of Ireland and the Irish as early as the sixteenth century; it will operate during the eighteenth century with opinions about white colonists in Australia and the Americas (Australians remained an inferior race well into the twentieth century); it gradually extends its sway to include practically the whole world beyond British shores. A comparably repetitive and inclusive tautology about what is overseas beyond France's frontiers emerges in French culture. At the margins of Western society, all the non-European regions, whose inhabitants, societies, histories, and beings represented a non-European essence, were made subservient to Europe, which in turn demonstrably continued to control what was not Europe, and represented the non-European in such a way as to sustain control.

This sameness and circularity were far from being either inhibiting or repressive so far as thought, art, literature, and cultural discourse were concerned. This centrally important truth needs constantly to be insisted upon. The one relationship that does not change is the hierarchical one between the metropole and overseas generally, between European-Western-white-Christian-male and those peoples who geographically and morally inhabit the realm beyond Europe (Africa, Asia, plus Ireland and Australia in the British case).[60] Otherwise, a fantastic elaboration is permitted on both sides of the relationship, with the general result being that the identity of each is reinforced even as its variations on the Western side increase. When the basic theme of imperialism is stated—for example, by writers like Carlyle, who puts things very frankly—it gathers to it by affiliation a vast number of assenting, yet at the same time more interesting, cultural versions, each with its own inflections, pleasures, formal characteristics.

The problem for the contemporary cultural critic is how to bring them together meaningfully. It is certainly true, as various scholars have shown, that an active consciousness of imperialism, of an aggressive, self-aware imperial mission, does not become inescapable—often accepted, referred to, actively concurred in—for European writers until the second part of the nineteenth century. (In England in the 1860s it was often the case that the word "imperialism" was used to refer, with some distaste, to France as a country ruled by an emperor.)

But by the end of the nineteenth century, high or official culture still managed to escape scrutiny for its role in shaping the imperial dynamic and was mysteriously exempted from analysis whenever the causes, benefits, or evils of imperialism were discussed, as they were almost obsessively. This is one fascinating aspect of my subject—how culture participates in imperialism yet is somehow excused for its role. Hobson, for instance, speaks disparagingly of Giddings's incredible idea of "retrospective consent"[61] (that subject people be subjugated first and then assumed retroactively to have consented to their enslavement), but he does not venture to ask where, or how, the idea arose with people such as Giddings, with their fluent jargon of self-congratulatory force. The great rhetoricians of theoretical justification for empire after 1880—in France, Leroy-Beaulieu, in England, Seeley— deploy a language whose imagery of growth, fertility, and expansion, whose teleological structure of property and identity, whose ideological discrimination between "us" and "them" had already matured elsewhere—in fiction, political science, racial theory, travel writing. In colonies like the Congo and Egypt people such as Conrad, Roger Casement, and Wilfrid Scawen Blunt record the abuses and the almost mindlessly unchecked tyrannies of the white man, whereas at home Leroy-Beaulieu rhapsodizes that the essence of colonization:

> c'est dans l'ordre social ce qu'est dans l'ordre de la famille, je ne dis pas la génération seulement, mais l'education. . . . Elle mène à la virilité une nouvelle sortie de ses entrailles. . . . La formation des sociétés humaines, pas plus que la formation des hommes, ne doit être abandonnée au hasard. . . . La colonisation est donc un art qui se forme à l'école de l'experience. . . . Le but de la colonisation, c'est de mettre une société nouvelle dans les meilleures conditions de prosperité et de progrès.[62] (the social order is like the familial order in which not only generation but education is important. . . . It gives to virility a new product from its entrails. . . . The formation of human societies, any more than the formation of men, must not be left to chance. . . . Therefore colonization is an art formed in the school of experience. . . . The goal of colonization is to place a new society in the best conditions for prosperity and progress.)

In England by the late nineteenth century, imperialism was considered essential to the well-being of British fertility generally and of motherhood in particular;[63] and, as a close reading of Baden-Powell's career reveals, his

Boy Scout movement may be directly traced to the connection established between empire and the nation's health (fear of masturbation, degeneration, eugenics).[64]

There are hardly any exceptions then to the overwhelming prevalence of ideas suggesting, often ideologically implementing, imperial rule. Let us bring together what we can in a brief synthesis from a whole battery of modern studies in different fields of scholarly endeavor, in my opinion belonging together in the study of "culture and imperialism." This may be laid out systematically as follows:

1. On the fundamental ontological distinction between the West and the rest of the world there is no disagreement. So strongly felt and perceived are the geographical and cultural boundaries between the West and its non-Western peripheries that we may consider these boundaries absolute. With the supremacy of the distinction there goes what Johannes Fabian calls a denial of "coevalness" in time, and a radical discontinuity in terms of human space.[65] Thus "the Orient," Africa, India, Australia are places dominated by Europe, although populated by different species.

2. With the rise of ethnography—as described by Stocking, and also as demonstrated in linguistics, racial theory, historical classification—there is a codification of difference, and various evolutionary schemes going from primitive to subject races, and finally to superior or civilized peoples. Gobineau, Maine, Renan, Humboldt are centrally important. Such commonly used categories as the primitive, savage, degenerate, natural, unnatural also belong here.[66]

3. Active domination of the non-Western world by the West, now a canonically accepted branch of historical research, is appropriately global in its scope (e.g., K. M. Panikar, *Asia and Western Dominance,* or Michael Adas, *Machines as the Measure of Men: Science, Technology, and Ideologies of Western Dominance*).[67] There is a convergence between the great geographical scope of the empires, especially the British one, and universalizing cultural discourses. Power makes this convergence possible, of course; with it goes the ability to be in far-flung places, to learn about other people, to codify and disseminate knowledge, to characterize, transport, install, and display instances of other cultures (through exhibits, expeditions, photographs, paintings, surveys, schools), and above all to rule them. All this in turn produces what has been called "a duty" to natives, the requirement in Africa and elsewhere to establish colonies for the "benefit" of the natives[68] or for the "prestige" of the mother country. The rhetoric of *la mission civilisatrice.*

4. The domination is not inert, but informs metropolitan cultures in many ways; in the imperial domain itself, its influence is only now beginning to be studied on even the minutiae of daily life. A series of recent works[69] has

described the imperial motif woven into the structures of popular culture, fiction, and the rhetoric of history, philosophy, and geography. Thanks to the work of Gauri Viswanathan, the system of British education in India, whose ideology derives from Macaulay and Bentinck, is seen to be permeated with ideas about unequal races and cultures that were transmitted in the classroom; they were part of the curriculum and a pedagogy whose purpose, according to Charles Trevelyan, an apologist, was

> in a Platonic sense, to awaken the colonial subjects to a memory of their innate character, corrupted as it had become . . . through the feudalistic character of Oriental society. In this universalizing narrative, rescripted from a scenario furnished earlier by missionaries, the British government was refashioned as the ideal republic to which Indians must naturally aspire as a spontaneous expression of self, a state in which the British rulers won a figurative place as Platonic Guardians.[70]

Since I am discussing an ideological vision implemented and sustained not only by direct domination and physical force but much more effectively over a long time by *persuasive means,* the quotidian processes of hegemony—very often creative, inventive, interesting, and above all executive—yield surprisingly well to analysis and elucidation. At the most visible level there was the physical transformation of the imperial realm, whether through what Alfred Crosby calls "ecological imperialism,"[71] the reshaping of the physical environment, or administrative, architectural, and institutional feats such as the building of colonial cities (Algiers, Delhi, Saigon); at home, the emergence of new imperial elites, cultures, and subcultures (schools of imperial "hands," institutes, departments, sciences—such as geography, anthropology, etc.—dependent on a continuing colonial policy), new styles of art, including travel photography, exotic and Orientalist painting, poetry, fiction, and music, monumental sculpture, and journalism (as memorably characterized by Maupassant's *Bel-Ami.*)[72]

The underpinnings of such hegemony have been studied with considerable insight in works such as Fabian's *Language and Colonial Power,* Ranajit Guha's *A Rule of Property for Bengal,* and, as part of the Hobsbawm and Ranger collection, Bernard Cohn's "Representing Authority in Victorian India" (also his remarkable studies on the British representation and surveying of Indian society in *An Anthropologist Among the Historians*).[73] These works show the daily imposition of power in the dynamics of everyday life, the back-and-forth of interaction among natives, the white man, and the institutions of authority. But the important factor in these micro-physics of imperialism is that in passing from "communication to command" and back again, a

unified discourse—or rather, as Fabian puts it, "a field of passages, of crossing and criss-crossing ideas"[74]—develops that is based on a distinction
between the Westerner and the native so integral and adaptable as to make
change almost impossible. We sense the anger and frustration this produced
over time from Fanon's comments on the Manicheanism of the colonial
system and the consequent need for violence.

5. The imperial attitudes had scope and *authority,* but also, in a period of
expansion abroad and social dislocation at home, great creative power. I
refer here not only to "the invention of tradition" generally, but also to the
capacity to produce strangely autonomous intellectual and aesthetic images.
Orientalist, Africanist, and Americanist discourses developed, weaving in
and out of historical writing, painting, fiction, popular culture. Foucault's
ideas about *discourses* are apt here; and, as Bernal has described it, a coherent
classical philology developed during the nineteenth century that purged
Attic Greece of its Semitic-African roots. In time—as Ronald Inden's *Imagining India*[75] tries to show—entire semi-independent metropolitan formations appeared, having to do with imperial possessions and their interests.
Conrad, Kipling, T. E. Lawrence, Malraux are among its narrators; its
ancestors and curators include Clive, Hastings, Dupleix, Bugeaud, Brooke,
Eyre, Palmerston, Jules Ferry, Lyautey, Rhodes; in these and the great
imperial narratives *(The Seven Pillars of Wisdom, Heart of Darkness, Lord Jim,
Nostromo, La Voie royale),* an imperial personality becomes distinct. The discourse of late-nineteenth-century imperialism is further fashioned by the
arguments of Seeley, Dilke, Froude, Leroy-Beaulieu, Harmand, and others,
many of them forgotten and unread today, but powerfully influential, even
prophetic then.

The images of Western imperial authority remain—haunting, strangely
attractive, compelling: Gordon at Khartoum, fiercely staring down the Sudanese dervishes in G. W. Joy's famous painting, armed only with revolver and
sheathed sword; Conrad's Kurtz in the center of Africa, brilliant, crazed,
doomed, brave, rapacious, eloquent; Lawrence of Arabia, at the head of his
Arab warriors, living the romance of the desert, inventing guerilla warfare,
hobnobbing with princes and statesmen, translating Homer, and trying to
hold on to Britain's "Brown Dominion"; Cecil Rhodes, establishing countries, estates, funds as easily as other men might have children or start
businesses; Bugeaud, bringing Abdel Qader's forces to heel, making Algeria
French; the concubines, dancing girls, odalisques of Gérôme, Delacroix's
Sardanapalus, Matisse's North Africa, Saint-Saëns's *Samson and Delilah.* The
list is long and its treasures massive.

(IV)

The Empire at Work: Verdi's Aida

I should like now to demonstrate how far and how inventively this material affects certain areas of cultural activity, even those realms not today
associated with sordid imperial exploitation. We are fortunate that several
young scholars have developed the study of imperial power sufficiently so
as to let us observe the aesthetic component involved in the survey and
administration of Egypt and India. I have in mind, for example, Timothy
Mitchell's *Colonising Egypt*,[76] where it is shown that the practice of building
model villages, discovering the intimacy of harem life, and instituting new
modes of military behavior in an ostensibly Ottoman, but really European,
colony not only reconfirmed European power, but also produced the added
pleasure of surveying and ruling the place. That bond between power and
pleasure in imperial rule is marvelously demonstrated by Leila Kinney and
Zeynep Çelik in their study of belly-dancing, where the quasi-ethnographic
displays afforded by European expositions in fact came to be associated with
consumerist leisure based in Europe.[77] Two related offshoots of this are
excavated in T. J. Clark's study of Manet and other Parisian painters, *The
Painting of Modern Life*, in particular the emergence of unusual leisure and
eroticism in metropolitan France, some of it affected by exotic models; and
Malek Alloula's deconstructive reading of early-twentieth-century French
postcards of Algerian women, *The Colonial Harem*.[78] Obviously the Orient as
a place of promise and power is very important here.

I want to suggest, however, why it is that my attempts at a contrapuntal
reading are perhaps eccentric or odd. First, although I proceed along generally chronological lines, from the beginning to the end of the nineteenth
century, I am not in fact trying to provide a consecutive sequence of events,
trends, or works. Each individual work is seen in terms both of its own past
and of later interpretations. Second, the overall argument is that these
cultural works which interest me irradiate and interfere with apparently
stable and impermeable categories founded on genre, periodization, nationality, or style, those categories presuming that the West and its culture are
largely independent of other cultures, and of the worldly pursuits of power,
authority, privilege, and dominance. Instead, I want to show that the "structure of attitude and reference" is prevalent and influential in all sorts of
ways, forms, and places, even well before the officially designated age of

empire; far from being autonomous or transcendent, it is close to the historical world; and far from being fixed and pure, it is hybrid, partaking of racial
superiority as much as of artistic brilliance, of political as of technical
authority, of simplifyingly reductive as of complex techniques.

Consider *Aida*, Verdi's famous "Egyptian" opera. As a visual, musical, and
theatrical spectacle, *Aida* does a great many things for and in European
culture, one of which is to confirm the Orient as an essentially exotic, distant,
and antique place in which Europeans can mount certain shows of force.
Concurrently with the composition of *Aida*, European "universal" expositions routinely contained models of colonial villages, towns, courts, and the
like; the malleability and transportability of secondary or lesser cultures was
underlined. These subaltern cultures were exhibited before Westerners as
microcosms of the larger imperial domain. Little, if any, allowance was made
for the non-European except within this framework.[79]

Aida is synonymous with "grand opera" of the uniquely high nineteenth-
century type. Along with a very small group of others, it has survived for
more than a century both as an immensely popular work and as one for
which musicians, critics, and musicologists have a healthy respect. Yet *Aida*'s
grandeur and eminence, although evident to anyone who has seen or heard
it, are complex matters about which all sorts of speculative theories exist,
mostly about what connects *Aida* to its historical and cultural moment in the
West. In *Opera: The Extravagant Art*, Herbert Lindenberger puts forward the
imaginative theory that *Aida*, *Boris Godunov*, and *Götterdämmerung* are operas
of 1870, tied respectively to archeology, nationalist historiography, and
philology.[80] Wieland Wagner, who produced *Aida* at Berlin in 1962, treats the
opera, in his words, as "an African mystery." He sees in it a prefiguration of
his grandfather's *Tristan*, with an irreducible conflict at its core between
Ethos and Bios ("Verdis *Aida* ist ein Drama des anauflösbaren Konflikts
zwischen Ethos und Bios, zwischen dem moralischer Gesetz und den For-
derungen des Lebens").[81] In his scheme, Amneris is the central figure,
dominated by a "Riesenphallus," which hangs over her like a mighty club;
according to *Opera*, "Aida was mostly seen prostrate or cowering in the
background."[82]

Even if we overlook the vulgarity to which the famous Triumphal scene
in Act II has often lent itself, we should note that *Aida* climaxes a development in style and vision that brought Verdi from *Nabucco* and *I Lombardi* in
the 1840s, through *Rigoletto*, *Trovatore*, *Traviata*, *Simon Boccanegra*, and *Un Ballo
in Maschera* in the 1850s, to the problematic *Forza del Destino* and *Don Carlos*
in the 1860s. During three decades Verdi had become the pre-eminent Italian
composer of his day, his career accompanying and seeming to comment on
the Risorgimento. *Aida* was the last public and political opera he wrote

before he turned to the essentially domestic, albeit intense pair of operas with which he ended his composing life, *Otello* and *Falstaff.* All the major Verdi scholars—Julian Budden, Frank Walker, William Weaver, Andrew Porter, Joseph Wechsberg—note that *Aida* not only reuses traditional music forms like the *cabaletta* and *concertato* but adds to them a new chromaticism, subtlety of orchestration, and dramatic streamlining not found in the work of any other composer of the time except Wagner. Joseph Kerman's demurral, in *Opera as Drama*, is interesting for how much it acknowledges about *Aida's* singularity:

> The result in *Aida* is, in my opinion, an almost constant disparity between the particular glib simplicity of the libretto and the alarming complexity of the musical expression—for of course Verdi's technique had never been so rich. Only Amneris comes to life; Aida is thoroughly confused; Rhadames seems like a throwback, if not to Metastasio, at least to Rossini. It goes without saying that some pages, numbers, and scenes are beyond praise, reason enough for this opera's great popularity. Nevertheless, there is a curious falsity about *Aida* which is quite unlike Verdi, and which recalls Meyerbeer more disturbingly than the grand-opera apparatus of triumphs, consecrations, and brass bands.[83]

This is undeniably persuasive as far as it goes; Kerman is correct about *Aida's* falsity, but he cannot quite explain what causes it. We should remember first of all that Verdi's previous work attracted attention because it involved and drew in its mostly Italian audience directly. His music-dramas portrayed incorrigibly red-blooded heroes and heroines in the full splendor of contests (often incestuous) over power, fame, and honor, but—as Paul Robinson has convincingly argued in *Opera and Ideas*—they were almost all intended as political operas, replete with rhetorical stridency, martial music, and unbuttoned emotions. "Perhaps the most obvious component of Verdi's rhetorical style—to put the matter bluntly—is sheer loudness. He is with Beethoven, among the noisiest of all major composers. . . . Like a political orator, Verdi can't remain still for long. Drop the needle at random on a recording of a Verdi opera, and you will usually be rewarded with a substantial racket."[84] Robinson goes on to say that Verdi's splendid noisiness is effectively harnessed to such occasions as "parades, rallies and speeches",[85] which during the Risorgimento were heard as Verdi's amplifications of real-life occurrences. (*Aida* is no exception, with, for example, early in Act II the tremendous ensemble piece "Su del nilo," for several soloists and a massed chorus.) It is now commonplace knowledge that tunes in Verdi's earlier operas (*Nabucco, I Lombardi,* and *Attila* in particular) stimulated his audiences to frenzies of participation, so immediate was their impact, the clarity of their contemporary reference, and the sheer skill of his efficiency at whipping everyone into urgent, big theatrical climaxes.

Whereas it had been Italy and Italians (with special force, paradoxically enough, in *Nabucco*) who were addressed in Verdi's earlier operas, despite the often exotic or *outré* subject matter, in *Aida* it was Egypt and Egyptians of early antiquity, a far remoter and less engaging phenomenon than Verdi had ever set to music. Not that *Aida* wants for his customary political noisiness, for surely Act II, scene 2 (the so-called Triumphal scene) is the biggest thing Verdi wrote for the stage, a virtual jamboree of everything an opera house can collect and parade. But *Aida* is self-limiting, atypically held in, and there is no record of any participatory enthusiasm connected with it, even though at New York's Metropolitan Opera, for instance, it has been performed more times than any other work. Verdi's other works that dealt with remote or alien cultures did not inhibit his audiences from identifying with them anyway, and, like the earlier operas, *Aida* is about a tenor and a soprano who want to make love but are prevented by a baritone and a mezzo. What are the differences in *Aida*, and why did Verdi's habitual mix produce so unusual a blend of masterly competence and affective neutrality?

The circumstances of *Aida*'s first production and under which it was written are unique in Verdi's career. The political and certainly the cultural setting in which Verdi worked between early 1870 and late 1871 included not only Italy, but imperial Europe and viceregal Egypt, an Egypt technically within the Ottoman Empire but now gradually being established as a dependent and subsidiary part of Europe. *Aida*'s peculiarities—its subject matter and setting, its monumental grandeur, its strangely unaffecting visual and musical effects, its overdeveloped music and constricted domestic situation, its eccentric place in Verdi's career—require what I have been calling a contrapuntal interpretation, assimilable neither to the standard view of Italian opera nor more generally to prevailing views of the great masterpieces of nineteenth-century European civilization. *Aida*, like the opera form itself, is a hybrid, radically impure work that belongs equally to the history of culture and the historical experience of overseas domination. It is a composite work, built around disparities and discrepancies that have been either ignored or unexplored, that can be recalled and mapped descriptively; they are interesting in and of themselves, and they make more sense of *Aida*'s unevenness, its anomalies, its restrictions and silences, than analyses of the kind that focus on Italy and European culture exclusively.

I shall put before the reader material that paradoxically cannot be overlooked but systematically has been. This is mostly because the embarrassment of *Aida* is finally that it is not so much *about* but *of* imperial domination.

Similarities with Jane Austen's work—equally improbable as art involved with empire—will emerge. If one interprets *Aida* from that perspective, aware that the opera was written for and first produced in an African country with which Verdi had no connection, a number of new features will stand out.

Verdi himself says something to this effect in a letter that inaugurates his as yet almost completely latent connection with an Egyptian opera. Writing to Camille du Locle, a close friend who had just returned from a *voyage en Orient,* Verdi remarks on February 19, 1868: "When we see each other, you must describe all the events of your voyage, the wonders you have seen, and the beauty and ugliness of a country which once had a greatness and a civilization I had never been able to admire."[86]

On November 1, 1869, the inauguration of the Cairo Opera House was a brilliant event during celebrations for the opening of the Suez Canal; *Rigoletto* was the opera performed. A few weeks before, Verdi had turned down Khedive Ismail's offer to write a hymn for the occasion, and in December he wrote du Locle a long letter on the dangers of "patchwork" operas: "I want *art* in any of its manifestations, not the *arrangement,* the *artifice,* and the *system* that you prefer," he said, arguing that for his part he wanted "unified" works, in which "the idea is ONE, and everything must converge to form this ONE."[87] Although these assertions were made in response to du Locle's suggestions that Verdi write an opera for Paris, they turn up enough times in the course of his work on *Aida* to become an important theme. On January 5, 1871, he wrote Nicola de Giosa, "Today operas are written with so many different dramatic and musical intentions that it is almost impossible to interpret them; and it seems to me that no one can take offense if the author, when one of his productions is given for the first time, sends a person who has carefully studied the work under the direction of the author himself."[88] To Ricordi he wrote on April 11, 1871, that he permitted "only one creator" for his work, himself; "I don't concede the right to 'create' to singers and conductors because, as I said before, it is a principle that leads into the abyss."[89]

Why, then, did Verdi finally accept Khedive Ismail's offer to write a special opera for Cairo? Money certainly was a reason: he was given 150,000 francs in gold. He was also flattered, since after all he was choice number one, ahead of Wagner and Gounod. Just as important, I think, was the story offered him by du Locle, who had received a sketch for a possible operatic treatment from Auguste Mariette, a renowned French Egyptologist. On May 26, 1870, Verdi had indicated in a letter to du Locle that he had read "the Egyptian outline," that it was well done, and that "it offers a splendid *mise-en-scène.*"[90] He had noted also that the work shows "a very expert hand

in it, one accustomed to writing and one who knows the theatre very well."
By early June he began work on *Aida,* immediately expressing his impatience
to Ricordi at how slowly things were progressing, even as he requested the
services of one Antonio Ghislanzoni as librettist. "These things should be
done very fast," he says at this point.

In the simple, intense, and above all authentically "Egyptian" scenarios by
Mariette, Verdi perceived a unitary intention, the imprint or trace of a
masterly and expert will that he hoped to match in music. At a time when
his career had been marked with disappointments, unfulfilled intentions,
unsatisfying collaborations with impresarios, ticket sellers, singers—the
Paris premiere of *Don Carlos* was a recent, still smarting instance—Verdi saw
a chance to create a work whose every detail he could supervise from
beginning sketch to opening night. In addition, he was to be supported in this
enterprise by royalty: indeed, du Locle suggested that the Viceroy not only
desperately wanted the piece for himself, but also had helped Mariette in
writing it. Verdi could assume that a wealthy Oriental potentate had joined
with a genuinely brilliant and single-minded Western archeologist to give
him an occasion in which he could be a commanding and undistracted
artistic presence. The story's alienating Egyptian provenance and setting
paradoxically seem to have stimulated his sense of technical mastery.

So far as I have been able to ascertain, Verdi had no feelings at all about
modern Egypt, in contrast with his fairly developed notions about Italy,
France, and Germany, even though during the two years he worked on the
opera he kept getting assurances that he was doing something for Egypt on
a national level, as it were. Draneht Bey (né Pavlos Pavlidis), the Cairo
Opera manager, told him this, and Mariette, who came to Paris to get
costumes and scenery ready in the summer of 1870 (and was subsequently
caught there during the Franco-Prussian War), frequently reminded him
that no expense was being spared to mount a truly spectacular show. Verdi
was intent on getting words and music right, making certain that Ghislanzoni found the perfect "theatrical word," *parola scenica,*[91] overseeing performance details with unflagging attention. In the immensely complicated
negotiations for casting the first Amneris, Verdi's contribution to the imbroglio earned him the title of "the world's foremost Jesuit."[92] Egypt's
submissive or at least indifferent presence in his life allowed him to pursue his artistic intentions with what appeared to be an uncompromising
intensity.

But I believe Verdi fatally confused this complex and in the end col-
laborative capacity to bring a distant operatic fable to life with the Romantic
ideal of an organically integrated, seamless work of art, informed only by the
aesthetic intention of a single creator. Thus an imperial notion of the artist

dovetailed conveniently with an imperial notion of a non-European world whose claims on the European composer were either minimal or non-existent. To Verdi the conjunction must have seemed to be eminently worth nursing along. For years subject to the obtrusive vagaries of opera house personnel, he could now rule his domain unchallenged; as he prepared the opera for performance in Cairo and a couple of months later (February 1872) for its Italian premiere at La Scala, he was told by Ricordi that "you will be the Moltke of La Scala" (September 2, 1871).[93] So strong were the attractions of this martially dominating role that at one point, in a letter to Ricordi, Verdi explicitly connects his aesthetic aims with Wagner's and, more significantly, with Bayreuth (as yet only a theoretical proposal), over whose performances Wagner intended himself to have virtually total dominion.

> The seating arrangement of the orchestra is of much greater importance than is commonly believed—for the *blending* of the instruments, for the sonority, and for the effect. These small improvements will afterward open the way for other innovations, which will surely come one day; among them taking the spectators' boxes off the stage, bringing the curtain to the footlights; another, making the *orchestra invisible*. This is not my idea but Wagner's. It's excellent. It seems impossible that today we tolerate the sight of shabby *tails* and white ties, for example, mixed with Egyptian, Assyrian and Druidic costumes, etc., etc., and, even more, almost in the middle of the floor, of seeing the tops of the harps, the necks of the double basses and the baton of the conductor all up in the air.[94]

Verdi speaks here of a theatrical presentation *removed* from the customary interferences of opera houses, removed and isolated in such a way as to impress the audience with a novel blend of authority and verisimilitude. The parallels are evident with what Stephen Bann, in *The Clothing of Clio,* has called "the historical composition of place" in historical writers like Walter Scott and Byron.[95] The difference is that Verdi could and indeed, for the first time in European opera, did avail himself of Egyptology's historical vision and academic authority. This science was embodied at close hand for Verdi in the person of Auguste Mariette, whose French nationality and training were part of a crucial imperial genealogy. Verdi perhaps had no way of knowing much in detail about Mariette, but he was strongly impressed by Mariette's initial scenario and recognized a qualified expert whose competence could represent ancient Egypt with a legitimate credibility.

The simple point to be made here is that Egyptology is Egyptology and not Egypt. Mariette was made possible by two important predecessors, both

French, both imperial, both reconstructive, and, if I can use a word that I shall borrow from Northrop Frye, both presentational: the first is the archeological volumes of Napoleon's *Description de l'Egypte;* and the second is Champollion's deciphering of hieroglyphics presented in 1822 in his *Lettre à M. Dacier* and in 1824 in his *Précis du système hiéroglyphique.* By "presentational" and "reconstructive" I mean a number of characteristics that seemed tailormade for Verdi: Napoleon's military expedition to Egypt was motivated by a desire to capture Egypt, to threaten the British, to demonstrate French power; but Napoleon and his scholarly experts were there also to put Egypt before Europe, in a sense to stage its antiquity, its wealth of associations, cultural importance, and unique aura *for* a European audience. Yet this could not be done without an aesthetic as well as a political intention. What Napoleon and his teams found was an Egypt whose antique dimensions were screened by the Muslim, Arab, and even Ottoman presence standing everywhere between the invading French army and ancient Egypt. How was one to get to that other, older, and more prestigious part?

Here began the particularly French aspect of Egyptology, which continued in the work of Champollion and Mariette. Egypt had to be reconstructed in models or drawings, whose scale, projective grandeur (I say "projective" because as you leaf through the *Description* you know that what you are looking at are drawings, diagrams, paintings of dusty, decrepit, and neglected pharaonic sites looking ideal and splendid as if there were no modern Egyptians but only European spectators), and exotic distance were truly unprecedented. The reproductions of the *Description* therefore are not descriptions but *ascriptions.* First the temples and palaces were reproduced in an orientation and perspective that staged the actuality of ancient Egypt as reflected through the imperial eye; then—since all of them were empty or lifeless—in the words of Ampère, they had to be made to speak, and hence the efficacy of Champollion's decipherment; then, finally, they could be dislodged from their context and transported to Europe for use there. This, as we shall see, was Mariette's contribution.

This continuous process went on roughly from 1798 until the 1860s, and it is French. Unlike England, which had India, and Germany, which, at a remove, had the organized learning that went with Persia and India, France had this rather imaginative and enterprising field in which, as Raymond Schwab says in *The Oriental Renaissance,* scholars "from Rougé to Mariette at the end of the line [started by Champollion's work] . . . were . . . explorers with isolated careers who learned everything on their own."[96] The Napoleonic *savants* were explorers who learned everything on their own, since there was no body of organized, truly modern and scientific knowledge about Egypt on which they could draw. As Martin Bernal has characterized it, although the prestige of Egypt throughout the eighteenth century was considerable, it was associated with esoteric and mystifying currents like Masonry.[97] Champollion and Mariette were eccentrics and autodidacts, but they were moved by scientific and rationalistic energies. The meaning of this in the ideological terms of Egypt's presentation in French archeology is that Egypt could be described "as the first and essential oriental influence on the West," a claim that Schwab quite rightly regards as false, since it ignores Orientalist work done by European scholars on other parts of the ancient world. In any event, Schwab says:

> Writing in the *Revue des Deux-Mondes* in June 1868 [just at the point that Draneht, Khedive Ismail, and Mariette began to conceive of what was to become *Aida*] Ludovic Vitet hailed "the unparalleled discoveries" of the orientalists over the preceding fifty years. He even spoke of "the archeological revolution for which the Orient is the theatre," but calmly asserted that "the movement started with Champollion and everything began because of him. He is the point of departure for all these discoveries." Vitet's own progression following the one already established in the public mind, he then passed on to the Assyrian monuments and finally to a few words on the Vedas. Vitet did not linger. Clearly, after Napoleon's expedition to Egypt, the monuments there and the scholarly missions to Egyptian sites had already spoken to everyone. India never revived except on paper.[98]

Auguste Mariette's career is significant for *Aida* in many interesting ways. Although there has been some dispute about his exact contribution to the *Aida* libretto, his intervention has been vindicated definitively by Jean Humbert as *the* important inaugurating one for the opera.[99] (Immediately behind the libretto was his role as principal designer of antiquities at the Egyptian pavilion in the Paris International Exhibition of 1867, one of the greatest and earliest displays of imperial potency.)

Although archeology, grand opera, and the European universal expositions are obviously different worlds, someone like Mariette connects them in suggestive ways. There is a perspicacious account of what might have made possible Mariette's passages between the three worlds:

> The universal expositions of the nineteenth century were intended as microcosms that would summarize the entire human experience—past and present, with projections into the future. In their carefully articulated order, they also signified the dominant relation of power. Ordering and characterization ranked, rationalized, and objectified dif-

ferent societies. The resulting hierarchies portrayed a world where races, sexes, and nations occupied fixed places assigned to them by the exposition committees of host countries. The forms through which non-Western cultures were represented at the fairs were predicated upon the social arrangements already established in the "host" culture, France; thus it is important to describe the parameters for they set the patterns of national representation and provided the channels of cultural expression through which the knowledge produced by the expositions would be fashioned.[100]

In the catalogue he wrote for the 1867 exhibition, Mariette rather strenuously stressed the *reconstructive* aspects, leaving little doubt in anyone's mind that he, Mariette, had brought Egypt to Europe for the first time, as it were. He could do so because of his spectacular archeological successes at some thirty-five sites, including those at Giza, Sakkarah, Edfu, and Thebes where, in Brian Fagan's apt words, he "excavated with complete abandon."[101] In addition, Mariette was engaged regularly in both excavating and emptying sites, so that as the European museums (especially the Louvre) grew in Egyptian treasure, Mariette rather cynically displayed the actual tombs in Egypt empty, keeping a bland composure in his explanations to "disappointed Egyptian officials."[102]

In service to the Khedive, Mariette encountered Ferdinand de Lesseps, the canal's architect. We know that the two collaborated in various restorative and curatorial schemes, and I am convinced that both men had a similar vision—perhaps going back to earlier Saint-Simonian, Masonic, and theosophic European ideas about Egypt—out of which they spun their quite extraordinary schemes, whose effectiveness, it is important to note, was increased by the alliance in each of them of personal will, a penchant for theatricality, and scientific dispatch.

Mariette's libretto for *Aida* led to his design for costumes and sets, and this, in turn, back to the remarkably prophetic scenic designs of the *Description*. The most striking pages of the *Description* seem to beseech some very grand actions or personages to fill them, and their emptiness and scale look like opera sets waiting to be populated. Their implied European context is a theater of power and knowledge, while their actual Egyptian setting in the nineteenth century has simply dropped away.

The temple at Phylae as rendered in the *Description* (and not a supposed original at Memphis) was almost certainly in Mariette's mind as he designed the first scene in *Aida,* and although it is unlikely that Verdi saw these very prints, he did see reproduced versions of them that circulated widely in Europe; having seen them made it easier for him to house the loud military music that occurs so frequently in *Aida*'s first two acts. It is also likely that Mariette's notions about costumes came from illustrations in the *Description* which he adapted for the opera, though there are substantial differences. I think that Mariette had in his own mind's eye transmuted the pharaonic originals into a rough modern equivalent, into what pre-historic Egyptians would look like accoutered in styles prevalent in 1870: Europeanized faces, moustaches, and beards are the giveaway.

The result was an Orientalized Egypt, which Verdi had arrived at in the music quite on his own. Well-known examples occur mostly in the second act: the chant of the priestess and, a little later, the ritual dance. We know that Verdi was most concerned with the accuracy of this scene, since it required the most authentication and caused him to ask the most detailed historical questions. A document sent by Ricordi to Verdi in the summer of 1870 contains material on ancient Egypt, of which the most detailed was about consecrations, priestly rites, and other facts concerning ancient Egyptian religion. Verdi used little of it, but the sources are indicative of a generalized European awareness of the Orient as derived from Volney and Creuzer, to which was added Champollion's more recent archeological work. All of this, however, concerns priests: no women are mentioned.

Verdi does two things to this material. He converts some of the priests into priestesses, following the conventional European practice of making Oriental women central to any exotic practice: the functional equivalents of his priestesses are the dancing girls, slaves, concubines, and bathing harem beauties prevalent in mid-nineteenth-century European art and, by the 1870s, entertainment. These displays of feminine eroticism *à l'orientale* "articulated power relations and revealed a desire to enhance supremacy through representation."[103] Some of this is easy to spot in the scene in Act II set inside Amneris's chamber, in which sensuality and cruelty are inevitably associated (for example, in the dance of Moorish slaves). The other thing Verdi does is to convert the general Orientalist cliché of life at court into a more directly allusive barb against the male priesthood. Ramfis the High Priest is, I think, informed both by Verdi's Risorgimento anti-clericalism and by his ideas about the despotic Oriental potentate, a man who will exact vengeance out of sheer bloodthirst masked in legalism and scriptural precedent.

As for the modally exotic music, we know from his letters that Verdi consulted the work of Francois-Joseph Fétis, a Belgian musicologist who seems to have irritated and fascinated him in equal measure. Fétis was the first European to attempt a study of non-European music as a separate part of the general history of music, in his *Resumé philosophique de l'histoire de la musique* (1835). His unfinished *Histoire générale de la musique depuis les temps anciens à nos jours* (1869–76) carried the project further, emphasizing the unique particularity of exotic music and its integral identity. Fétis seems to have known E. W. Lane's work on nineteenth-century Egypt, as well as the two volumes on Egyptian music in the *Description.*

Fétis's value for Verdi was that he could read examples in his work of "Oriental" music—the harmonic clichés, much used in carnival hoochy-kooch, are based on a flattening of the hypertonic—and instances of Oriental instruments, which in some cases corresponded to representation in the *Description:* harps, flutes, and the by now well-known ceremonial trumpet, which Verdi went to somewhat comic effort to have built in Italy.

Lastly, Verdi and Mariette collaborated imaginatively—and in my opinion, most successfully—in creating the quite wonderful atmospherics of Act III, the so-called Nile scene. Here too an idealized representation in the Napoleonic *Description* was the probable model for Mariette's image of the scene, whereas Verdi heightened his conception of an antique Orient by using less literal and more suggestive musical means. The result is a superb tonal picture with a permeable outline that sustains the quiet scene-painting of the act's opening, and then opens out to the turbulent and conflicted climax among Aida, her father, and Radames. Mariette's sketch for the setting of this magnificent scene is like a synthesis of *his* Egypt: "The set represents a garden of the palace. At the left, the oblique facade of a pavilion—*or tent.* At the back of the stage flows the Nile. On the horizon the mountains of the Libyan chain, vividly illuminated by the setting sun. Statues, palms, tropical shrubs."[104] No wonder that, like Verdi, he saw himself as a creator: *"Aida,"* he said in a letter to the patient and ever-resourceful Draneht (July 19, 1871), "is in effect a product of my work. I am the one who convinced the Viceroy to order its presentation; *Aida* in a word, is a creation of my brain."[105]

Aida thus incorporates and fuses material about Egypt in a form that both Verdi and Mariette could claim with justification to be of their making. Yet I suggest that the work suffers—or is at least peculiar—because of the selectivity of and emphases in what is included and, by implication, excluded. Verdi must have had opportunities to wonder what modern Egyptians thought of his work, how individual listeners responded to his music, what would become of the opera after the premiere. But little of this has found its way into the record, except a few ill-tempered letters rebuking European critics at the *premiere;* they gave him unwelcome publicity, he said rather churlishly. In a letter to Filippi we already begin to get a sense of Verdi's distance from the opera, a *Verfremdungseffekt,* I believe, already written into *Aida*'s scene and libretto:

. . . You in Cairo? This is the most powerful *publicity* for *Aida* one could imagine! It seems to me that in this way art is no longer art but a business, a game of pleasure, a hunt, something to be chased after, something which must be given if not success, at least notoriety at any cost! My reaction to this is one of disgust and humiliation! I always remember with joy my early days when, with almost no friends, without anyone to talk about me, without preparations, without influence of any kind, I went before the public with my operas, ready to be *blasted* and quite happy if I could succeed in stirring up some favorable impression. Now, what pomposity for an opera!!!! Journalists, artists, choristers, conductors, instrumentalists, etc., etc. All of them must carry their stone to the edifice of *publicity* and thus fashion a framework of little trifles that add nothing to the worth of an opera; in fact they obscure the real value (if there is any). This is deplorable, profoundly deplorable!!!!

I thank you for your courteous offers for Cairo, but I wrote to Bottesini the day before yesterday everything concerning *Aida*. For this opera I want only a good and above all, an *intelligent* vocal and instrumental performance and mise-en-scène. As for the rest, à la grace de Dieu; for so I began and so I wish to finish my career . . .[106]

The protestations here extend his attitudes about the opera's single intention: *Aida* is a self-sufficient work of art, he seems to be saying, and let's leave it at that. But isn't there something else going on here too, some sense on Verdi's part of an opera written for a place he cannot relate to, with a plot that ends in hopeless deadlock and literal entombment?

Verdi's awareness of *Aida*'s incongruities appears elsewhere. At one point he speaks ironically of adding Palestrina to the harmony of Egyptian music, and he seems also to have been conscious of the extent to which ancient Egypt was not only a dead civilization but also a culture of death, whose apparent ideology of conquest (as he adapted it from Herodotus and Mariette) was related to an ideology of the afterlife. The rather somber, disenchanted, and vestigial attachment that Verdi had to the politics of the Risorgimento as he worked on *Aida* appears in the work as military success entailing personal failure or, as it can also be described, as political triumph rendered in the ambivalent tones of human impasse, in short, of *Realpolitik*. Verdi seems to have imagined the positive attributes of Radames's *patria* as ending up in the funereal tones of *terra addio*, and certainly the divided stage in Act IV—a possible source is one of the plates in the *Description*—powerfully impressed on his mind the *discordia concors* of Amneris's unrequited passion and Aida's and Radames's blissful deaths.

Aida's airlessness and immobility are relieved only by ballets and triumphal parades, but even these displays are undermined in some way: Verdi was too intelligent and single-minded to have left them untouched. The dance of Ramfis's triumphant consecration in Act I of course leads to Radames's demise in Acts III and IV, so there is little to be pleased about; the dance of the Moorish slaves in Act II, scene 1, is a dance of slaves, who entertain Amneris as she malevolently plays with Aida, her slave rival. As for the really famous part of Act II, scene 2, here we have perhaps the core of *Aida*'s egregious appeal to audiences and directors alike, who take it as an opportunity to do more or less anything so long as it is excessive and full of display. This in fact may not be far from Verdi's intention.

Take as three modern examples the following: One—

Aida in Cincinnati (March 1986). A press release from the Cincinnati Opera announces that for its performance of *Aida* this season the following animals would take part in the Triumph scene: 1 aardvark, 1 donkey, 1 elephant, 1 boa constrictor, 1 peacock, 1 toucan, 1 red-tail hawk, 1 white tiger, 1 Siberian lynx, 1 cockatoo, and 1 cheetah—total 11; and that the body count for the production will total 261, being made up of 8 principals, 117 chorus (40 regular chorus, 77 extras), 24 ballet, 101 supernumeraries (including 12 zoo keepers), and 11 animals.[107]

This is *Aida* as a more or less untreated, partly comic outpouring of opulence, a feat played and replayed with matchless vulgarity at the Baths of Caracalla.

In contrast there is Wieland Wagner's Act II, scene 2, a parade of Ethiopian prisoners carrying totems, masks, ritual objects as elements of an ethnographic exhibition presented to the audience. This "was the transference of the whole setting of the work from the Egypt of the Pharaohs to the darker Africa of a prehistoric age":

What I was trying to do, in regard to the scenery, was to give *Aida* the colourful fragrance that is in it—deriving it not from an Egyptian museum, but from the atmosphere inherent in the work itself. I wanted to get away from false Egyptian artiness and false operatic monumentality, from Hollywoodish historical painting, and return to archaic— which is to say, in terms of Egyptology—to pre-dynastic times.[108]

Wagner's emphasis is on the difference between "our" world and "theirs," surely something that Verdi emphasized too, with his recognition that the opera was first composed and designed for a place that was decidedly *not*

Paris, Milan, or Vienna. And this recognition, interestingly enough, brings us to *Aida* in Mexico 1952, where the leading singer, Maria Callas, outperforms the whole ensemble by ending up on a high E-flat, one octave above the note written by Verdi.

In all three examples the effort is made to exploit this one opening that Verdi allowed in the work, an aperture through which he seems to be letting in an outside world otherwise banned from entry. His terms, though, are astringent. He seems to be saying, Come in as exotica or as captives, stay awhile, and then leave me to my business. And to shore up his territory, he resorts musically to devices he hardly ever used before, all of them designed to signal to the audience that a musical master, steeped in the learned traditional techniques scorned by his bel canto contemporaries, was at work. On February 20, 1871, he wrote a correspondent, Giuseppe Piroli, that "for the young composer, then, I would want very long and rigorous exercises in all branches of counterpoint. . . . *No study of the moderns!*"[109] This was in keeping with the mortuary aspects of the opera he was writing (making the mummies sing, he once said), which opens with a piece of strict canon writing; Verdi's contrapuntal and *stretto* techniques in *Aida* reach a heightened intensity and rigor of an order he rarely achieved. Along with the martial music dotting *Aida*'s score (some of which was later to become the Khedival Egyptian national anthem), these learned passages strengthen the opera's monumentality and—more to the point—its wall-like structure.

In short, *Aida* quite precisely recalls the enabling circumstances of its commission and composition, and, like an echo to an original sound, conforms to aspects of the contemporary context it works so hard to exclude. As a highly specialized form of aesthetic memory, *Aida* embodies, as it was intended to do, the authority of Europe's version of Egypt at a moment in its nineteenth-century history, a history for which Cairo in the years 1869–1871 was an extraordinarily suitable site. A full contrapuntal appreciation of *Aida* reveals a structure of reference and attitude, a web of affiliations, connections, decisions, and collaborations, which can be read as leaving a set of ghostly notations in the opera's visual and musical text.

Consider the story: an Egyptian army defeats an Ethiopian force, but the young Egyptian hero of the campaign is impugned as a traitor, sentenced to death, and dies by asphyxiation. This episode of antiquarian inter-African rivalry acquires considerable resonance when one reads it against the background of Anglo-Egyptian rivalry in East Africa from the 1840s till the 1860s. The British regarded Egyptian objectives there under Khedive Ismail, who was eager to expand southward, as a threat to their Red Sea hegemony, and the safety of their route to India; nevertheless, prudently shifting policy, the British encouraged Ismail's moves in East Africa as a way of blocking French

and Italian ambitions in Somalia and Ethiopia. By the early 1870s the change
was completed, and by 1882 Britain occupied Egypt entirely. From the
French point of view, incorporated by Mariette, *Aida* dramatized the dangers
of a successful Egyptian policy of force in Ethiopia, especially since Ismail
himself—as Ottoman Viceroy—was interested in such ventures as a way of
achieving more independence from Istanbul.[110]

There is more than that in *Aida*'s simplicity and severity, especially since
so much about the opera, and the Opera House, which was built to house
Verdi's work, concerns Ismail himself and his reign (1863–1879). A fair amount
of work has been done recently on the economic and political history of
European involvement in Egypt during the eighty years after Napoleon's
expedition; much of this concurs with the position taken by Egyptian nationalist historians (Sabry, Rafi', Ghorbal) that the viceregal heirs who composed
Mohammad Ali's dynasty, in a descending order of merit (with the exception of the intransigent Abbas), involved Egypt ever more deeply in what has
been called the "world economy"[111] but more accurately was the loose
agglomeration of *European* financiers, merchant bankers, loan corporations,
and commercial adventures. This led ineluctably to the British occupation
of 1882, and, just as ineluctably, to the eventual reclamation of the Suez Canal
by Gamal Abdel Nasser in July 1956.

By the 1860s and 1870s the most striking feature of the Egyptian economy
was the boom in cotton sales that occurred when the American Civil War
closed off American supply to European mills; this only accelerated the
various distortions in the local economy (by the 1870s, according to Owen,
"the entire Delta had been converted into an export sector devoted to the
production, processing and export of two or three crops,"[112]) which were
part of a much larger, more depressing situation. Egypt was opened to
schemes of every sort, some crazy, some beneficial (like the constructions of
railroads and roads), all costly, especially the canal. Development was fi-
nanced by issuing treasury bonds, printing money, increasing the budgetary
deficit; the growth of the public debt added a good deal to Egypt's foreign
debt, the cost of servicing it, and the further penetration of the country by
foreign investors and their local agents. The general cost for foreign loans
seems to have been somewhere between 30 and 40 percent of their face
value. (David Landes's *Bankers and Pashas* gives a detailed history of the
whole sordid yet amusing episode.)[113]

In addition to its deepening economic weakness and dependency on
European finance, Egypt under Ismail underwent an important series of
antithetical developments. At the same time that the population grew naturally, the size of foreign resident communities grew geometrically—to
90,000 by the early 1880s. The concentration of wealth in the viceregal family

and its retainers in turn established a pattern of virtual feudal landholding and urban privilege, which in turn hastened the development of a nationalist consciousness of resistance. Public opinion seems to have opposed Ismail as much because he was perceived to be handing Egypt over to foreigners as because those foreigners for their part appeared to take Egypt's quiescence and weakness for granted. It was noted angrily, says the Egyptian historian Sabry, that in Napoleon III's speech at the canal's opening, he mentioned France and *its* canal but never Egypt.[114] On the other side of the spectrum, Ismail was publicly attacked by pro-Ottoman journalists[115] for the folly of his exorbitantly expensive European trips (these are chronicled in almost sickening detail in Georges Douin, *Histoire du règne du Khedive Ismail,* vol. 2),[116] his pretence of independence from the Porte, his overtaxing of his subjects, his lavish invitations to European celebrities for the canal opening. The more Khedive Ismail wished to appear independent, the more his effrontery cost Egypt, the more the Ottomans resented his shows of independence, and the more his European creditors resolved to keep a closer hand on him. Ismail's "ambition and imagination startled his listeners. In the hot, straitened summer of 1864, he was thinking not only of canals and railroads, but of Paris-on-the-Nile and of Ismail, Emperor of Africa. Cairo would have its *grands boulevards,* Bourse, theatres, opera; Egypt would have a large army, a powerful fleet. Why? asked the French Consul. He might also have asked, How?"[117]

"How" was to proceed with the renovation of Cairo, which required the employment of many Europeans (among them Draneht) and the development of a new class of city-dwellers whose tastes and requirements portended the expansion of a local market geared to expensive imported goods. As Owen says, "where foreign imports were important . . . was in catering to the completely different consumption pattern of a large foreign population and those among the local Egyptian landowners and officials who had begun to live in European types of houses in the Europeanized section of Cairo and Alexandria where almost everything of importance was purchased from abroad—even building material."[118] And, we might add, operas, composers, singers, conductors, sets, and costumes. An important added benefit to such projects was to convince foreign creditors with visible evidence that their money was being put to good use.[119]

Unlike Alexandria, however, Cairo was an Arab and Islamic city, even in Ismail's heyday. Aside from the romance of the Giza archeological sites, Cairo's past did not communicate easily or well with Europe; here were no Hellenistic or Levantine associations, no gentle sea breezes, no bustling Mediterranean port life. Cairo's massive centrality to Africa, to Islam, to the Arab and Ottoman worlds seemed like an intransigent barrier to European investors, and the hope of making it more accessible and attractive to them surely prompted Ismail to support the city's modernization. This he did essentially by dividing Cairo. One can do no better than to quote from the best twentieth-century account of Cairo, *Cairo: 1001 Years of the City Victorious*, by the American urban historian Janet Abu-Lughod:

> Thus by the end of the nineteenth century Cairo consisted of two distinct physical communities, divided one from the other by barriers much broader than the little single street that marked their borders. The discontinuity between Egypt's past and future, which appeared as a small crack in the early nineteenth century, had widened into a gaping fissure by the end of that century. The city's physical duality was but a manifestation of the cultural cleavage.
>
> To the east lay the native city, still essentially pre-industrial in technology, social structure, and way of life; to the west lay the "colonial" city with its steam-powered techniques, its faster pace and wheeled traffic, and its European identification. To the east lay the labyrinth street pattern of yet unpaved *harat* and *durub*, although by then the gates had been dismantled and two new thoroughfares pierced the shade; to the west were broad straight streets of macadam flanked by wide walks and setbacks, militantly crossing one another at rigid right angles or converging here and there in a roundpoint or *maydan*. The quarters of the eastern city were still dependent upon itinerant water peddlars, although residents in the western city had their water delivered through a convenient network of conduits connected with the steam pumping station near the river. Eastern quarters were plunged into darkness at nightfall, while gaslights illuminated the thoroughfares to the west. Neither parks nor street trees relieved the sand and mud tones of the medieval city; yet the city to the west was elaborately adorned with French formal gardens, strips of decorative flower beds, or artificially shaped trees. One entered the old city by caravan and traversed it on foot or animal-back; one entered the new by railroad and proceeded via horse-drawn victoria. In short, on all critical points the two cities, despite their physical contiguity, were miles apart socially and centuries apart technologically.[120]

The Opera House built by Ismail for Verdi sat right at the center of the north-south axis, in the middle of a spacious square, facing the European city, which stretched westward to the banks of the Nile. To the north were the railroad station, Shepheards Hotel, and the Azbakiyah Gardens for which, Abu-Lughod adds, "Ismail imported the French landscape architect whose work he admired in the Bois de Boulogne and Champs de Mars and commissioned him to redesign Azbakiyah as a Parc Monceau, complete with the free form pool, grotto, bridges, and belvederes which instituted the inevitable clichés of a nineteenth-century French garden."[121] To the south lay Abdin Palace, redesigned by Ismail as his principal residence in 1874. Behind the Opera House lay the teeming quarters of Muski, Sayida Zeinab, 'Ataba al-Khadra, held back by the Opera House's imposing size and European authority.

Cairo was beginning to register the intellectual ferment of reform, some but by no means all of it under the influence of the European penetration, and this resulted, as Jacques Berque puts it, in a confusion of production.[122] This is beautifully evoked in perhaps the finest account of Ismailian Cairo, the *Khittat Tawfikiya* of Ali Pasha Mobarak, the prodigiously energetic minister of public works and education, an engineer, nationalist, modernizer, tireless historian, village son of a humble *faqih*, a man as fascinated by the West as he was compelled by the traditions and religion of the Islamic East. One has the impression that Cairo's changes in this period forced Ali Pasha to record the city's life in recognition that the dynamics of Cairo now required a new, modern attention to detail, detail which stimulated unprecedented discriminations and observations on the part of the native Cairene. Ali does not mention the Opera, although he speaks in detail of Ismail's lavish expenditure on his palaces, his gardens and zoos, and his displays for visiting dignitaries. Later Egyptian writers will, like Ali, note the ferment of this period, but will also note (e.g., Anwar Abdel-Malek) the Opera House and *Aida* as antinomian symbols of the country's artistic life *and* its imperialist subjugation. In 1971 the wooden Opera House burned down; it was never rebuilt there, and its site was occupied first by a parking lot, then by a multistoried garage. In 1988 a new cultural center was built on the Gezira Island with Japanese money; this center included an opera house.

Clearly we should conclude that Cairo could not long sustain *Aida* as an opera written for an occasion and a place it seemed to outlive, even as it triumphed on Western stages for many decades. *Aida*'s Egyptian identity was part of the city's European facade, its simplicity and rigor inscribed on those imaginary walls dividing the colonial city's native from its imperial quarters. *Aida* is an aesthetic of separation, and we cannot see in *Aida* the congruence between it and Cairo that Keats saw in both the frieze on the Grecian urn and what corresponded with it, the town and citadel "emptied of this folk, this pious morn." *Aida*, for most of Egypt, was an imperial *article de luxe* purchased by credit for a tiny clientele whose entertainment was incidental to their real purposes. Verdi thought of it as monument to his art; Ismail and Mariette, for diverse purposes, lavished on it their surplus energy and restless will. Despite its shortcomings, *Aida* can be enjoyed and interpreted as a kind of curatorial art, whose rigor and unbending frame recall, with relentlessly mortuary logic, a precise historical moment and a specifically dated aesthetic form, an imperial spectacle designed to alienate and impress an almost exclusively European audience.

Of course, this is very far from *Aida*'s position in the cultural repertory today. And certainly it is true that many great aesthetic objects of empire are remembered and admired without the baggage of domination that they carried through the process from gestation to production. Yet the empire remains, in inflection and traces, to be read, seen, and heard. And by not taking account of the imperialist structures of attitude and reference they suggest, even in works like *Aida*, which seem unrelated to the struggle for territory and control, we reduce those works to caricatures, elaborate ones perhaps, but caricatures nonetheless.

One must remember, too, that when one belongs to the more powerful side in the imperial and colonial encounter, it is quite possible to overlook, forget, or ignore the unpleasant aspects of what went on "out there." The cultural machinery—of spectacles like *Aida*, of the genuinely interesting books written by travellers, novelists, and scholars, of fascinating photographs and exotic paintings—has had an aesthetic as well as informative effect on European audiences. Things stay remarkably unchanged when such distancing and aestheticizing cultural practices are employed, for they split and then anesthetize the metropolitan consciousness. In 1865 the British Governor of Jamaica, E. J. Eyre, ordered a retaliatory massacre of Blacks for the killing of a few whites; this revealed to many English people the injustices and horrors of colonial life; the subsequent debate engaged famous public personalities both *for* Eyre's declaration of martial law and massacre of Jamaican Blacks (Ruskin, Carlyle, Arnold) and *against* him (Mill, Huxley, Lord Chief Justice Cockburn). In time, however, the case was forgotten, and other "administrative massacres" in the empire occurred. Yet, in the words of one historian, "Great Britain managed to maintain the distinction between domestic liberty and imperial authority [which he describes as "repression and terror"] abroad."[123]

Most modern readers of Matthew Arnold's anguished poetry, or of his celebrated theory in praise of culture, do not also know that Arnold connected the "administrative massacre" ordered by Eyre with tough British policies toward colonial *Eire* and strongly approved both; *Culture and Anarchy* is set plumb in the middle of the Hyde Park Riots of 1867, and what Arnold had to say about culture was specifically believed to be a deterrent to rampant disorder—colonial, Irish, domestic. Jamaicans, Irishmen, and women, and some historians bring up these massacres at "inappropriate" moments, but most Anglo-American readers of Arnold remain oblivious, see them—if they look at them at all—as irrelevant to the more important cultural theory that Arnold appears to be promoting for all the ages.

(As a small parenthesis, it is important to note that whatever its legal basis against Saddam Hussein's brutal occupation of Kuwait, Operation Desert Storm was also partly launched so as to lay the ghost of the "Vietnam syndrome," to assert that the United States could win a war, and win it quickly. To sustain this motive, one had to forget that two million Vietnamese were killed, and that sixteen years after the end of the war Southeast Asia is still devastated. Therefore making America strong and enhancing President Bush's image as a leader took precedence over destroying a distant society. And high technology and clever public relations were used to make the war seem exciting, clean, and virtuous. As Iraq underwent paroxysms of disintegration, counter-rebellion, and mass human suffering, American popular interest briefly cheered.)

For the European of the late nineteenth century, an interesting range of options are offered, all premised upon the subordination and victimization of the native. One is a self-forgetting delight in the use of power—the power to observe, rule, hold, and profit from distant territories and people. From these come voyages of discovery, lucrative trade, administration, annexation, learned expeditions and exhibitions, local spectacles, a new class of colonial rulers and experts. Another is an ideological rationale for reducing, then reconstituting the native as someone to be ruled and managed. There are styles of rule, as Thomas Hodgkin characterizes them in his *Nationalism in Colonial Africa*—French Cartesianism, British empiricism, Belgian Platonism.[124] And one finds them inscribed within the humanistic enterprise itself: the various colonial schools, colleges, and universities, the native elites created and manipulated throughout Africa and Asia. Third is the idea of Western salvation and redemption through its "civilizing mission." Supported jointly by the experts in ideas (missionaries, teachers, advisers, scholars) and in modern industry and communication, the imperial idea of westernizing the backward achieved permanent status world-wide, but, as Michael Adas and others have shown, it was always accompanied by domination.[125] Fourth is the security of a situation that permits the conqueror not to look into the truth of the violence he does. The idea of culture itself, as Arnold refined it, is designed to elevate practice to the level of theory, to liberate ideological coercion against rebellious elements—at home and abroad—from the mundane and historical to the abstract and general. "The best that is thought and done" is considered an unassailable position, at home and abroad. Fifth is the process by which, after the natives have been displaced from their historical location on their land, their history is rewritten as a function of the imperial one. This process uses narrative to dispel contradictory memories and occlude violence—the exotic replaces the impress of power with the blandishments of curiosity—with the imperial presence so dominating as to make impossible any effort to separate it from historical necessity. All these together create an amalgam of the arts of narrative and observation about the accumulated, dominated, and ruled territories whose inhabitants seem destined never to escape, to remain creatures of European will.

(v)

The Pleasures of Imperialism

*K*im is as unique in Rudyard Kipling's life and career as it is in English literature. It appeared in 1901, twelve years after Kipling had left India, the place of his birth and the country with which his name will always be associated. More interestingly, *Kim* was Kipling's only successfully sustained and mature piece of long fiction; although it can be read with enjoyment by adolescents, it can also be read with respect and interest years after adolescence, by the general reader and the critic alike. Kipling's other fiction consists either of short stories (or collections thereof, such as *The Jungle Books*), or deeply flawed longer works (like *Captains Courageous, The Light That Failed*, and *Stalky and Co.*, whose other interest is often overshadowed by failures of coherence, vision, or judgement). Only Conrad, another master stylist, can be considered along with Kipling, his slightly younger peer, to have rendered the experience of empire as the main subject of his work with such force; and even though the two artists are remarkably different in tone and style, they brought to a basically insular and provincial British audience the color, glamor, and romance of the British overseas enterprise, which was well-known to specialized sectors of the home society. Of the two, it is Kipling—less ironic, technically self-conscious, and equivocal than Conrad—who acquired a large audience early on. But both writers have remained a puzzle for scholars of English literature, who find them eccentric, often troubling, better treated with circumspection or even avoidance than absorbed into the canon and domesticated along with peers like Dickens and Hardy.

Conrad's major visions of imperialism concern Africa in *Heart of Darkness* (1899), the South Seas in *Lord Jim* (1900), and South America in *Nostromo*

(1904), but Kipling's greatest work concentrates on India, a territory Conrad never wrote about. And by the late nineteenth century India had become the greatest, most durable, and most profitable of all British, perhaps even European, colonial possessions. From the time the first British expedition arrived there in 1608 until the last British Viceroy departed in 1947, India had a massive influence on British life, in commerce and trade, industry and politics, ideology and war, culture and the life of imagination. In English literature and thought the list of great names who dealt with and wrote about India is astonishingly impressive, for it includes William Jones, Edmund Burke, William Makepeace Thackeray, Jeremy Bentham, James and John Stuart Mill, Lord Macaulay, Harriet Martineau, and, of course Rudyard Kipling, whose importance in the definition, the imagination, the formulation of what India was to the British empire in its mature phase, just before the whole edifice began to split and crack, is undeniable.

Kipling not only wrote about India, but was *of* it. His father, Lockwood, a refined scholar, teacher, and artist (the model for the kindly curator of the Lahore Museum in Chapter One of *Kim*), was a teacher in British India. Rudyard was born there in 1865, and during the first years of his life he spoke Hindustani and lived a life very much like Kim's, a Sahib in native clothes. At the age of six he and his sister were sent to England to begin school; appallingly traumatic, the experience of his first years in England (in the care of a Mrs. Holloway at Southsea) furnished Kipling with an enduring subject matter, the interaction between youth and unpleasant authority, which he rendered with great complexity and ambivalence throughout his life. Then Kipling went to one of the lesser public schools designed for children of the colonial service, the United Services College at Westward Ho! (the greatest of the schools was Haileybury, reserved for the upper echelons of the colonial elite); he returned to India in 1882. His family was still there, and so for seven years, as he tells of those events in his posthumously published autobiography *Something of Myself,* he worked as a journalist in the Punjab, first on *The Civil and Military Gazette,* later on *The Pioneer.*

His first stories came out of that experience, and were published locally; at that time he also began writing his poetry (what T. S. Eliot has called "verse"), first collected in *Departmental Ditties* (1886). Kipling left India in 1889, never again to reside there for any length of time, although for the rest of his life his art fed on the memories of his early Indian years. Subsequently, Kipling stayed for a while in the United States (and married an American woman) and South Africa, but settled in England after 1900: *Kim* was written at Bateman, the house he remained in till his death in 1936. He quickly won great fame and a large readership; in 1907 he was awarded the Nobel Prize. His friends were rich and powerful; they included his cousin Stanley Baldwin, King George V, Thomas Hardy; many prominent writers including Henry James and Conrad spoke respectfully of him. After World War One (in which his son John was killed) his vision darkened considerably. Although he remained a Tory imperialist, his bleak visionary stories of England and the future, together with his eccentric animal and quasi-theological stories, forecast also a change in his reputation. At his death, he was accorded the honor reserved by Britain for its greatest writers: he was buried in Westminster Abbey. He has remained an institution in English letters, albeit one always slightly apart from the great central strand, acknowledged but slighted, appreciated but never fully canonized.

Kipling's admirers and acolytes have often spoken of his representations of India as if the India he wrote about was a timeless, unchanging, and "essential" locale, a place almost as much poetic as it is actual in geographical concreteness. This, I think, is a radical misreading of his works. If Kipling's India has essential and unchanging qualities, this was because he deliberately saw India that way. After all, we do not assume that Kipling's late stories about England or his Boer War tales are about an essential England or an essential South Africa; rather, we surmise correctly that Kipling was responding to and in effect imaginatively reformulating his sense of these places at particular moments in their histories. The same is true of Kipling's India, which must be interpreted as a territory dominated by Britain for three hundred years, and only then beginning to experience the unrest that would culminate in decolonization and independence.

Two factors must be kept in mind as we interpret *Kim*. One is that, whether we like it or not, its author is writing not just from the dominating viewpoint of a white man in a colonial possession, but from the perspective of a massive colonial system whose economy, functioning, and history had acquired the status of a virtual fact of nature. Kipling assumes a basically uncontested empire. On one side of the colonial divide was a white Christian Europe whose various countries, principally Britain and France, but also Holland, Belgium, Germany, Italy, Russia, Portugal, and Spain, controlled most of the earth's surface. On the other side of the divide, there were an immense variety of territories and races, all of them considered lesser, inferior, dependent, subject. "White" colonies like Ireland and Australia too were considered made up of inferior humans; a famous Daumier drawing, for instance, explicitly connects Irish whites and Jamaican Blacks. Each of these lesser subjects was classified and placed in a scheme of peoples guaranteed scientifically by scholars and scientists like Georges Cuvier, Charles Darwin, and Robert Knox. The division between white and non-white, in India and elsewhere, was absolute, and is alluded to throughout *Kim* as well as the rest of Kipling's work; a Sahib is a Sahib, and no amount of friendship or camaraderie can change the rudiments of racial difference. Kipling would no more have questioned that difference, and the right of the white European to rule, than he would have argued with the Himalayas.

The second factor is that, no less than India itself, Kipling was a historical being as well as a major artist. *Kim* was written at a specific moment in his career, at a time when the relationship between the British and Indian people was changing. *Kim* is central to the quasi-official age of empire and in a way represents it. And even though Kipling resisted this reality, India was already well on its way toward a dynamic of outright opposition to British rule (the Indian National Congress was established in 1885), while among the dominant caste of British colonial officials, military as well as civilian, important changes in attitude were occurring as a result of the 1857 Rebellion. The British and Indians were both evolving, and together. They had a common interdependent history, in which opposition, animosity, and sympathy either kept them apart or brought them together. A remarkable, complex novel like *Kim* is a very illuminating part of that history, filled with emphases, inflections, deliberate inclusions and exclusions as any great work of art is, and made the more interesting because Kipling was not a neutral figure in the Anglo-Indian situation but a prominent actor in it.

Even though India gained its independence (and was partitioned) in 1947, the question of how to interpret Indian and British history in the period after decolonization is still, like all such dense and highly conflicted encounters, a matter of strenuous, if not always edifying, debate. There is the view, for example, that imperialism permanently scarred and distorted Indian life, so that even after decades of independence, the Indian economy, bled by British needs and practices, continues to suffer. Conversely, there are British intellectuals, political figures, and historians who believe that giving up the empire—whose symbols were Suez, Aden, and India—was bad for Britain and bad for "the natives," who both have declined in all sorts of ways ever since.[126]

When we read it today, Kipling's *Kim* can touch on many of these issues. Does Kipling portray the Indians as inferior, or as somehow equal but different? Obviously, an Indian reader will give an answer that focusses on some factors more than others (for example, Kipling's stereotypical views—some would call them racialist—on the Oriental character), whereas English and American readers will stress his affection for Indian life on the Grand Trunk Road. How then do we read *Kim* as a late-nineteenth-century novel, preceded by the works of Scott, Austen, Dickens, and Eliot? We must not forget that the book is after all a novel in a line of novels, that there is more than one history in it to be remembered, that the imperial experience while often regarded as exclusively political also entered into the cultural and aesthetic life of the metropolitan West as well.

A brief summary of the novel's plot may be rehearsed here. Kimball O'Hara is the orphaned son of a sergeant in the Indian army; his mother is also white. He has grown up as a child of the Lahore bazaars, carrying with him an amulet and some papers attesting to his origins. He meets up with a saintly Tibetan monk who is in search of the River where he supposes he will be cleansed of his sins. Kim becomes his chela, or disciple, and the two wander as adventurous mendicants through India, using some help from the English curator of the Lahore Museum. In the meantime Kim becomes involved in a British Secret Service plan to defeat a Russian-inspired conspiracy whose aim is to stir up insurrection in one of the northern Punjabi provinces. Kim is used as a messenger between Mahbub Ali, an Afghan horse dealer who works for the British, and Colonel Creighton, head of the Service, a scholarly enthnographer. Later Kim meets with the other members of Creighton's team in the Great Game, Lurgan Sahib and Hurree Babu, also an ethnographer. By the time that Kim meets Creighton, it is discovered that the boy is white (albeit Irish) and not a native, as he appears, and he is sent to school at St. Xavier's, where his education as a white boy is to be completed. The guru manages to get the money for Kim's tuition, and during the holidays the old man and his young disciple resume their peregrinations. Kim and the old man meet the Russian spies, from whom the boy somehow steals incriminating papers, but not before the "foreigners" strike the holy man. Although the plot has been found out and ended, both the chela and his mentor are disconsolate and ill. They are healed by Kim's restorative powers and a renewed contact with the earth; the old man understands that through Kim he has found the River. As the novel ends Kim returns to the Great Game, and in effect enters the British colonial service full-time.

Some features of *Kim* will strike every reader, regardless of politics and history. It is an overwhelmingly male novel, with two wonderfully attractive men at its center—a boy who grows into early manhood, and an old ascetic priest. Grouped around them are other men, some of them companions, others colleagues and friends; these make up the novel's major, defining reality. Mahbub Ali, Lurgan Sahib, the great Babu, as well as the old Indian soldier and his dashing horse-riding son, plus Colonel Creighton, Mr. Bennett, and Father Victor, to name only a few of the numerous characters in this teeming book: all of them speak the language that men speak among themselves. The women in the novel are remarkably few by comparison, and all of them are somehow debased or unsuitable for male attention—prostitutes, elderly widows, or importunate and lusty women like the widow of Shamlegh; to be "eternally pestered by women," says Kim, is to be hindered in playing the Great Game, which is best played by men alone. We are in a masculine world dominated by travel, trade, adventure, and intrigue, and it is a celibate world, in which the common romance of fiction and the enduring institution of marriage are circumvented, avoided, all but ignored. At best, women help things along: they buy you a ticket, they cook, they tend the ill, and . . . they molest men.

Kim himself, although he ages in the novel from thirteen until he is sixteen or seventeen, remains a boy, with a boy's passion for tricks, pranks, clever wordplay, resourcefulness. Kipling seems to have retained a life-long sympathy with himself as a boy beset by the adult world of domineering schoolmasters and priests (Mr. Bennett in *Kim* is an exceptionally unattractive specimen) whose authority must be always reckoned with—until another figure of authority, like Colonel Creighton, comes along and treats the young person with understanding, but no less authoritarian, compassion. The difference between St. Xavier's School, which Kim attends for a time, and service in the Great Game (British intelligence in India) does not lie in the greater freedom of the latter; quite the contrary, the demands of the Great Game are more exacting. The difference lies in the fact that the former imposes a useless authority, whereas the exigencies of the Secret Service demand from Kim an exciting and precise discipline, which he willingly accepts. From Creighton's point of view the Great Game is a sort of political economy of control, in which, as he once tells Kim, the greatest sin is ignorance, not to know. But for Kim the Great Game cannot be perceived in all its complex patterns, although it can be fully enjoyed as a sort of extended prank. The scenes where Kim banters, bargains, repartees with his elders, friendly and hostile alike, are indications of Kipling's seemingly inexhaustible fund of boyish enjoyment in the sheer momentary pleasure of playing a game, any sort of game.

We should not be mistaken about these boyish pleasures. They do not contradict the overall political purpose of British control over India and Britain's other overseas dominions: on the contrary, *pleasure*, whose steady presence in many forms of imperial-colonial writing as well as figurative and musical art is often left undiscussed, is an undeniable component of *Kim*. A different example of this mixture of fun and single-minded political seriousness is to be found in Lord Baden-Powell's conception of the Boy Scouts, founded and launched in 1907–8. An almost exact contemporary of Kipling, BP, as he was called, was greatly influenced by Kipling's boys generally and Mowgli in particular; BP's ideas about "boyology" fed those images directly into a grand scheme of imperial authority culminating in the great Boy

Scout structure "fortifying the wall of empire," which confirmed this inventive conjunction of fun and service in row after row of bright-eyed, eager, and resourceful little middle-class servants of empire.[127] Kim, after all, is both Irish and of an inferior social caste; in Kipling's eyes this enhances his candidacy for service. BP and Kipling concur on two other important points: that boys ultimately should conceive of life and empire as governed by unbreakable Laws, and that service is more enjoyable when thought of less like a story—linear, continuous, temporal—and more like a playing field—many-dimensional, discontinuous, spatial. A recent book by the historian J. A. Mangan sums it up nicely in its title: *The Games Ethic and Imperialism.*[128]

So large is his perspective and so strangely sensitive is Kipling to the range of human possibilities that he offsets this service ethic in *Kim* by giving full rein to another of his emotional predilections, expressed by the strange Tibetan lama and his relationship to the title character. Even though Kim is to be drafted into intelligence work, the gifted boy has already been charmed into becoming the lama's chela at the very outset of the novel. This almost idyllic relationship between two male companions has an interesting genealogy. Like a number of American novels (*Huckleberry Finn, Moby-Dick,* and *The Deerslayer* come quickly to mind), *Kim* celebrates the friendship of two men in a difficult, sometimes hostile environment. The American frontier and colonial India are quite different, but both bestow a higher priority on "male bonding" than on a domestic or amorous connection between the sexes. Some critics have speculated on a hidden homosexual motif in these relationships, but there is also the cultural motif long associated with picaresque tales in which a male adventurer (with wife or mother, if either exists, safely at home) and his male companions are engaged in the pursuit of a special dream—like Jason, Odysseus, or, even more compellingly, Don Quixote with Sancho Panza. In the field or on the open road, two men can travel together more easily, and they can come to each other's rescue more credibly than if a woman were along. So the long tradition of adventure stories, from Odysseus and his crew to the Lone Ranger and Tonto, Holmes and Watson, Batman and Robin, seems to hold.

Kim's saintly guru additionally belongs to the overtly religious mode of the pilgrimage or quest, common in all cultures. Kipling, we know, was an admirer of Chaucer's *Canterbury Tales* and Bunyan's *Pilgrim's Progress. Kim* is a good deal more like Chaucer's than like Bunyan's work. Kipling has the Middle English poet's eye for wayward detail, the odd character, the slice of life, the amused sense of human foibles and joys. Unlike either Chaucer or Bunyan, however, Kipling is less interested in religion for its own sake (although we never doubt the Abbot-Lama's piety) than in local color, scrupulous attention to exotic detail, and the all-enclosing realities of the Great Game. It is the greatness of his achievement that quite without selling the old man short or in any way diminishing the quaint sincerity of his Search, Kipling nevertheless firmly places him within the protective orbit of British rule in India. This is symbolized in Chapter 1, when the elderly British museum curator gives the Abbot his spectacles, thus adding to the man's spiritual prestige and authority, consolidating the justness and legitimacy of Britain's benevolent sway.

This view, in my opinion, has been misunderstood and even denied by many of Kipling's readers. But we must not forget that the lama depends on Kim for support and guidance, and that Kim's achievement is neither to have betrayed the lama's values nor to have let up in his work as junior spy. Throughout the novel Kipling is clear to show us that the lama, while a wise and good man, needs Kim's youth, his guidance, his wits; the lama even explicitly acknowledges his absolute, religious need for Kim when, in Benares, toward the end of Chapter 9, he tells the "Jataka," the parable of the young elephant ("The Lord Himself") freeing the old elephant (Ananda) imprisoned in a leg-iron. Clearly, the Abbot-Lama regards Kim as his savior. Later, after the fateful confrontation with the Russian agents who stir up insurrection against Britain, Kim helps (and is helped by) the lama, who in one of the most moving scenes in all Kipling's fiction says, "Child, I have lived on thy strength as an old tree lives on the lime of an old wall." Yet Kim, reciprocally moved by love for his guru, never abandons his duty in the Great Game, although he confesses to the old man that he needs him "for some other things."

Doubtless those "other things" are faith and unbending purpose. In one of its main narrative strands, *Kim* keeps returning to the quest, the lama's search for redemption from the Wheel of Life, a complex diagram of which he carries around in his pocket, and Kim's search for a secure place in colonial service. Kipling condescends to neither. He follows the lama wherever he goes in his wish to be freed from "the delusions of the Body," and it is surely part of our engagement in the novel's Oriental dimension, which Kipling renders with little false exoticism, that we can believe in the novelist's respect for this pilgrim. Indeed, the lama commands attention and esteem from nearly everyone. He honors his word to get the money for Kim's education; he meets Kim at the appointed times and places; he is listened to with veneration and devotion. In an especially nice touch in Chapter 14, Kipling has him tell "a fantastic piled narrative of bewitchment and miracles" about marvelous events in his native Tibetan mountains, events that the novelist courteously forbears from repeating, as if to say that this old saint has a life of his own that cannot be reproduced in sequential English prose.

The lama's search and Kim's illness at the end of the novel are resolved together. Readers of many of Kipling's other tales will be familiar with what the critic J.M.S. Tompkins has rightly called "the theme of healing."[129] Here too the narrative progresses inexorably toward a great crisis. In an unforgettable scene Kim attacks the lama's foreign and defiling assailants, the old man's talisman-like chart is rent, and the two forlorn pilgrims consequently wander through the hills bereft of calm and health. Kim waits to be relieved of his charge, the packet of papers he has stolen from the foreign spy; the lama is unbearably aware of how much longer he must now wait before he can achieve his spiritual goals. Into this heartrending situation, Kipling introduces one of the novel's two great fallen women (the other being the old widow of Kulu), the woman of Shamlegh, abandoned long ago by her "Kerlistian" Sahib, but strong, vital, and passionate nevertheless. (There is a memory here of one of Kipling's most affecting earlier short stories, "Lispeth," which treats the predicament of the native woman loved, but never married, by a departed white man.) The merest hint of a sexual charge between Kim and the lusty Shamlegh woman appears but is quickly dissipated, as Kim and the lama head off once again.

What is the healing process through which Kim and the old lama must pass before they can rest? This extremely complex and interesting question can only be answered slowly and deliberately, so carefully does Kipling *not* insist on the confining limits of a jingoistic imperial solution. Kipling will not abandon Kim and the old monk with impunity to the specious satisfactions of getting credit for a simple job well done. This caution is of course good novelistic practice, but there are other imperatives—emotional, cultural, aesthetic. Kim must be given a station in life commensurate with his stubbornly fought for identity. He has resisted Lurgan Sahib's illusionistic temptations and asserted the fact that *he is Kim;* he has maintained a Sahib's status even while remaining a graceful child of the bazaars and the rooftops; he has played the game well, fought for Britain at some risk to his life and occasionally with brilliance; he has fended off the woman of Shamlegh. Where should he be placed? And where the lovable old cleric?

Readers of Victor Turner's anthropological theories will recognize in Kim's displacements, disguises, and general (usually salutary) shiftiness the essential characteristics of what Turner calls the liminal. Some societies, Turner says, require a mediating character who can knit them together into community, turn them into something more than a collection of administrative or legal structures.

Liminal [or threshold] entities, such as neophytes in initiation or puberty rites, may be represented as possessing nothing. They may be disguised as monsters, wear only a strip of clothing, or even go naked, to demonstrate that they have no status, property, insignia. . . . It is as if they are being reduced or groomed down to a uniform condition to be fashioned anew and endowed with additional powers to enable them to cope with their new station in life.[130]

That Kim himself is both an Irish outcast boy and later an essential player in the British Secret Service Great Game suggests Kipling's uncanny understanding of the workings and managing control of societies. According to Turner, societies can be neither rigidly run by "structures" nor completely overrun by marginal, prophetic, and alienated figures, hippies or millenarians; there has to be alternation, so that the sway of one is enhanced or tempered by the inspiration of the other. The liminal *figure* helps to maintain societies, and it is this procedure that Kipling enacts in the climactic moment of the plot and the transformation of Kim's character.

To work out these matters, Kipling engineers Kim's illness and the lama's desolation. There is also the small practical device of having the irrepressible Babu—Herbert Spencer's improbable devotee, Kim's native and secular mentor in the Great Game—turn up to guarantee the success of Kim's exploits. The packet of incriminating papers that prove the Russo-French machinations and the rascally wiles of an Indian prince is safely taken from Kim. Then Kim begins to feel, in Othello's words, the loss of his occupation:

All that while he felt, though he could not put it into words, that his soul was out of gear with its surroundings—a cog-wheel unconnected with any machinery, just like the idle cog-wheel of a cheap Beheea sugar-crusher laid by in a corner. The breezes fanned over him, the parrots shrieked at him, the noises of the populated house behind— squabbles, orders, and reproofs—hit on dead ears.[131]

In effect Kim has died to this world, has, like the epic hero or the liminal personality, descended to a sort of underworld from which, if he is to emerge, he will arise stronger and more in command than before.

The breach between Kim and "this world" must now be healed. The next page may not be the summit of Kipling's art, but it is close to that. The passage is structured around a gradually dawning answer to Kim's question: "I am Kim. And what is Kim?" Here is what happens:

He did not want to cry—had never felt less like crying in his life—but of a sudden easy, stupid tears trickled down his nose, and with an almost audible click he felt the wheels of his being lock up anew on the world without. Things that rode meaningless on the eyeball an instant before slid into proper proportion. Roads were meant to be walked upon, houses to be lived in, cattle to be driven, fields to be tilled, and men and women to be talked to. They were all real and true—solidly planted upon the feet—perfectly comprehensible—clay of his clay, neither more nor less. . . .[132]

Slowly Kim begins to feel at one with himself and with the world. Kipling goes on:

There stood an empty bullock-cart on a little knoll half a mile away, with a young banian tree behind—a lookout, as it were, above some new-ploughed levels; and his eyelids, bathed in soft air, grew heavy as he neared it. The ground was good clean dust—not new herbage that, living, is half-way to death already, but the hopeful dust that holds the seed to all life. He felt it between his toes, patted it with his palms, and joint by joint, sighing luxuriously, laid him down full length along in the shadow of the wooden-pinned cart. And Mother Earth was as faithful as the Sahiba [the Widow of Kulu, who has been tending Kim]. She breathed through him to restore the poise he had lost lying so long on a cot cut off from her good currents. His head lay powerless upon her breast, and his opened hands surrendered to her strength. The many-rooted tree above him, and even the dead man-handled wood beside, knew what he sought, as he himself did not know. Hour upon hour he lay deeper than sleep.[133]

As Kim sleeps, the lama and Mahbub discuss the boy's fate; both men know he is healed, and so what remains is the disposition of his life. Mahbub wants him back in service; with that stupefying innocence of his, the lama suggests to Mahbub that he should join both chela and guru as pilgrims on the way of righteousness. The novel concludes with the lama revealing to Kim that all is now well, for having seen

"all Hind, from Ceylon in the sea to the hills, and my own Painted Rocks at Suchzen; I saw every camp and village, to the least, where we have rested. I saw them at one time and in one place; for they are within the Soul. By this I knew the Soul has passed beyond the illusion of Time and Space and of Things. By this I knew I was free."[134]

Some of this is mumbo jumbo, of course, but it should not all be dismissed. The lama's encyclopedic vision of freedom strikingly resembles Colonel

Creighton's Indian Survey, in which every camp and village is duly noted. The difference is that the positivistic inventory of places and peoples within the scope of British dominion becomes, in the lama's generous inclusiveness, a redemptive and, for Kim's sake, therapeutic vision. Everything is now held together. At its center resides Kim, the boy whose errant spirit has regrasped things "with an almost audible click." The mechanical metaphor of the soul being put back on the rails, so to speak, somewhat violates the elevated and edifying situation, but for an English writer situating a young white male coming back to earth in a vast country like India, the figure is apt. After all, the Indian railways were British-built and assured some greater hold than before over the place.

Other writers before Kipling have written this type of regrasping-of-life scene, most notably George Eliot in *Middlemarch* and Henry James in *The Portrait of a Lady*, the former influencing the latter. In both cases the heroine (Dorothea Brooke and Isabel Archer) is surprised, not to say shocked, by the sudden revelation of a lover's betrayal: Dorothea sees Will Ladislaw apparently flirting with Rosamond Vincy, and Isabel intuits the dalliance between her husband and Madame Merle. Both epiphanies are followed by long nights of anguish, not unlike Kim's illness. Then the women awake to a new awareness of themselves and the world. The scenes in both novels are remarkably similar, and Dorothea Brooke's experience can serve here to describe both. She looks out onto the world past "the narrow cell of her calamity," sees the

> fields beyond, outside the entrance-gates. On the road there was a man with a bundle on his back and a woman carrying a baby . . . she felt the largeness of the world and the manifold wakings of men to labour and endurance. She was a part of that involuntary palpitating life, and could neither look out on it from her luxurious shelter as a mere spectator, nor hide her eyes in selfish complaining.[135]

Eliot and James intend such scenes not only as moral reawakenings, but as moments in which the heroine gets past, indeed forgives, her tormentor by seeing herself in the larger scheme of things. Part of Eliot's strategy is to have Dorothea's earlier plans to help her friends be vindicated; the reawakening scene thus confirms the impulse to be in, engage with, the world. Much the same movement occurs in *Kim*, except that the world is defined as liable to a soul's locking up on it. The passage from *Kim* I quoted earlier has a kind of moral triumphalism carried in its accentuated inflections of purpose, will, voluntarism: things slide into proper proportion, roads are meant to be walked on, things are perfectly comprehensible, solidly planted on the feet, and so on. Above the passage are "the wheels" of Kim's being as they "lock up anew on the world without." And this series of motions is subsequently reinforced and consolidated by Mother Earth's blessing upon Kim as he reclines next to the cart: "she breathed through him to restore what had been lost." Kipling renders a powerful, almost instinctual desire to restore the child to its mother in a pre-conscious, undefiled, asexual relationship.

But whereas Dorothea and Isabel are described as inevitably being part of an "involuntary, palpitating life," Kim is portrayed as retaking voluntary hold of his life. The difference is, I think, capital. Kim's newly sharpened apprehension of mastery, of "locking up," of solidity, of moving from liminality to domination is to a very great extent a function of being a Sahib in colonial India: what Kipling has Kim go through is a ceremony of reappropriation, Britain (through a loyal Irish subject) taking hold once again of India. Nature, the involuntary rhythms of restored health, comes to Kim *after* the first, largely political-historical gesture is signalled by Kipling on his behalf. In contrast, for the European or American heroines in Europe, the world is there to be discovered anew; it requires no one in particular to direct it or exert sovereignty over it. This is not the case in British India, which would pass into chaos or insurrection unless roads were walked upon properly, houses lived in the right way, men and women talked to in the correct tones.

In one of the finest critical accounts of *Kim,* Mark Kinkead-Weekes suggests that *Kim* is unique in Kipling's *oeuvre* because what was clearly meant as a resolution for the novel does not really work. Instead, Kinkead-Weekes says, the artistic triumph transcends even the intentions of Kipling the author:

> [The novel] is the product of a peculiar tension between different ways of seeing: the affectionate fascination with the kaleidoscope of external reality for its own sake; the negative capability getting under the skin of attitudes different from one another and one's own; and finally, a product of this last, but at its most intense and creative, the triumphant achievement of an anti-self so powerful that it became a touchstone for everything else—the creation of the Lama. This involved imagining a point of view and a personality almost at the furthest point of view from Kipling himself; yet it is explored so lovingly that it could not but act as a catalyst towards some deeper synthesis. Out of this particular challenge—preventing self-obsession, probing deeper than a merely objective view of reality outside himself, enabling him now to see, think

and feel *beyond* himself—came the new vision of *Kim,* more inclusive, complex, humanised, and mature than that of any other work.[136]

However much we may agree with some of the insights in this rather subtle reading, it is, in my opinion, rather too ahistorical. Yes, the lama is a kind of anti-self, and, yes, Kipling can get into the skin of others with some sympathy. But no, Kipling never forgets that Kim is an irrefragable part of British India: the Great Game does go on, with Kim a part of it, no matter how many parables the lama fashions. We are naturally entitled to read *Kim* as a novel belonging to the world's greatest literature, free to some degree from its encumbering historical and political circumstances. Yet by the same token, we must not unilaterally abrogate the connections *in it,* and carefully observed by Kipling, to its contemporary actuality. Certainly Kim, Creighton, Mahbub, the Babu, and even the lama see India as Kipling saw it, as a part of the empire. And certainly Kipling minutely preserves the traces of this vision when he has Kim—a humble Irish boy, lower on the hierarchical scale than full-blooded Englishmen—reassert his British priorities well before the lama comes along to bless them.

Readers of Kipling's best work have regularly tried to save him from himself. Frequently this has had the effect of confirming Edmund Wilson's celebrated judgement about *Kim:*

Now what the reader tends to expect is that Kim will come eventually to realize that he is delivering into bondage to the British invaders those whom he has always considered his own people and that a struggle between allegiances will result. Kipling has established for the reader—and established with considerable dramatic effect—the contrast between the East, with its mysticism and sensuality, its extremes of saintliness and roguery, and the English, with their superior organization, their confidence in modern method, their instinct to brush away like cobwebs the native myths and beliefs. We have been shown two entirely different worlds existing side by side, with neither really understanding the other, and we have watched the oscillation of Kim, as he passes to and fro between them. But the parallel lines never meet; the alternating attractions felt by Kim never give rise to a genuine struggle. . . . The fiction of Kipling, then, does not dramatise any fundamental conflict because Kipling would never face one.[137]

There is an alternative to these two views, I believe, that is more accurate about and sensitive to the actualities of late-nineteenth-century British India as Kipling, and others, saw them. The conflict between Kim's colonial service and loyalty to his Indian companions is unresolved not because Kipling could not face it, but because for Kipling *there was no conflict;* one purpose of the novel is in fact to show the absence of conflict once Kim is cured of his doubts, the lama of his longing for the River, and India of a few upstarts and foreign agents. That there *might have been* a conflict had Kipling considered India as unhappily subservient to imperialism, we can have no doubt, but he did not: for him it was India's best destiny to be ruled by England. By an equal and opposite reductiveness, if one reads Kipling not simply as an "imperialist minstrel" (which he was not) but as someone who read Frantz Fanon, met Gandhi, absorbed their lessons, and remained stubbornly unconvinced by them, one seriously distorts his context, which he refines, elaborates, and illuminates. It is crucial to remember that there were no appreciable deterrents to the imperialist world-view Kipling held, any more than there were alternatives to imperialism for Conrad, however much he recognized its evils. Kipling was therefore untroubled by the notion of an independent India, although it is true to say that his fiction represents the empire and its conscious legitimizations, which in fiction (as opposed to discursive prose) incur ironies and problems of the kind encountered in Austen or Verdi and, we shall soon see, in Camus. My point in this contrapuntal reading is to emphasize and highlight the disjunctions, not to overlook or play them down.

Consider two episodes in *Kim*. Shortly after the lama and his chela leave Umballa, they meet the elderly, withered former soldier "who had served the Government in the days of the Mutiny." To a contemporary reader "the Mutiny" meant the single most important, well-known, and violent episode of the nineteenth-century Anglo-Indian relationship: the Great Mutiny of 1857, which began in Meerut on May 10 and led to the capture of Delhi. An enormous number of books (e.g., Christopher Hibbert's *The Great Mutiny*), British and Indian, cover the "Mutiny" (referred to as a "Rebellion" by Indian writers). What caused the "Mutiny"—here I shall use the ideologically British designation—was the suspicion of Hindu and Muslim soldiers in the Indian army that their bullets were greased with cow's fat (unclean to Hindus) and pig's fat (unclean to Muslims). In fact the causes of the Mutiny were constitutive to British imperialism itself, to an army largely staffed by natives and officered by Sahibs, to the anomalies of rule by the East India Company. In addition, there was a great deal of underlying resentment about white Christian rule in a country of many other races and cultures, all of whom most probably regarded their subservience to the British as degrading. It was lost on none of the mutineers that numerically they vastly outnumbered their superior officers.

In both Indian and British history, the Mutiny was a clear demarcation. Without going into the complex structure of actions, motives, events, and moralities debated endlessly during and since, we can say that to the British, who brutally and severely put the Mutiny down, all their actions were retaliatory; the mutineers murdered Europeans, they said, and such actions proved, as if proof were necessary, that Indians deserved subjugation by the higher civilization of European Britain; after 1857 the East India Company was replaced by the much more formal Government of India. For the Indians, the Mutiny was a nationalist uprising against British rule, which uncompromisingly reasserted itself despite abuses, exploitation, and seemingly unheeded native complaint. When in 1925 Edward Thompson published his powerful little tract *The Other Side of the Medal*—an impassioned statement against British rule and for Indian independence—he singled out the Mutiny as the great symbolic event by which the two sides, Indian and British, achieved their full and conscious opposition to each other. He dramatically showed that Indian and British history diverged most emphatically on representations of it. The Mutiny, in short, reinforced the difference between colonizer and colonized.

In such a situation of nationalist and self-justifying inflammation, to be an Indian would have meant to feel natural solidarity with the victims of British reprisal. To be British meant to feel repugnance and injury—to say nothing of righteous vindication—given the terrible displays of cruelty by "natives," who fulfilled the roles of savages cast for them. For an Indian, *not* to have had those feelings would have been to belong to a very small minority. It is therefore highly significant that Kipling's choice of an Indian to speak about the Mutiny is a loyalist soldier who views his countrymen's revolt as an act of madness. Not surprisingly, this man is respected by British "Deputy Commissioners" who, Kipling tells us, "turned aside from the main road to visit him." What Kipling eliminates is the likelihood that his compatriots regard him as (at very least) a traitor to his people. And when, a few pages later, the old veteran tells the lama and Kim about the Mutiny, his version of the events is highly charged with the British rationale for what happened:

A madness ate into all the Army, and they turned against their officers. That was the first evil, but not past remedy if they had then held their hands. But they chose to kill the Sahib's wives and children. Then came the Sahibs from over the sea and called them to most strict account.[138]

To reduce Indian resentment, Indian resistance (as it might have been called) to British insensitivity to "madness," to represent Indian actions as mainly the congenital choice of killing British women and children—these

are not merely innocent reductions of the nationalist Indian case but tendentious ones. And when Kipling has the old soldier describe the British
counter-revolt—with its horrendous reprisals by white men bent on "moral"
action—as "calling" the Indian mutineers "to strict account," we have left
the world of history and entered the world of imperialist polemic, in which
the native is naturally a delinquent, the white man a stern but moral parent
and judge. Thus Kipling gives us the extreme British view on the Mutiny,
and puts it in the mouth of an Indian, whose more likely nationalist and
aggrieved counterpart is never seen in the novel. (Similarly Mahbub Ali,
Creighton's faithful adjutant, belongs to the Pathan people, historically in a
state of unpacified insurrection against the British throughout the nineteenth
century, yet here represented as happy with British rule, even a collaborator
with it.) So far is Kipling from showing two worlds in conflict that he has
studiously given us only one, and eliminated any chance of conflict appearing altogether.

The second example confirms the first. Once again it is a small, significant
moment. Kim, the lama, and the Widow of Kulu are en route to Saharunpore
in Chapter 4. Kim has just been exuberantly described as being "in the
middle of it, more awake and more excited than anyone," the "it" of Kipling's description standing for "the world in real truth; this was life as he
would have it—bustling and shouting, the buckling of belts, the beating of
bullocks and creaking of wheels, lighting of fires and cooking of food, and
new sights at every turn of the approving eye."[139] We have already seen a
good deal of this side of India, with its color, excitement, and interest
exposed in all their variety for the English reader's benefit. Somehow,
though, Kipling needs to show some authority over India, perhaps because
only a few pages earlier he senses in the old soldier's minatory account of
the Mutiny the need to forestall any further "madness." After all India itself
is responsible for both the local vitality enjoyed by Kim and the threat to
Britain's empire. A District Superintendent of Police trots by, and his appearance occasions this reflection from the Old Widow:

> "These be the sort to oversee justice. They know the land and the
> customs of the land. The others, all new from Europe, suckled by white
> women and learning our tongue from books, are worse than the pesti-
> lence. They do harm to Kings."[140]

Doubtless some Indians believed that English police officials knew the
country better than the natives, and that such officials—rather than Indian
rulers—should hold the reins of power. But note that in *Kim* no one challenges British rule, and no one articulates any of the local Indian challenges

that must then have been greatly in evidence—even for someone as obdurate as Kipling. Instead we have one character explicitly saying that a colonial police official ought to rule India and adding that she prefers the older style of official who (like Kipling and his family) had lived among the natives and was therefore better than the newer, academically trained bureaucrats. This is a version of the argument of the so-called Orientalists in India, who believed that Indians should be ruled according to Oriental-Indian modes by India "hands," but in the process Kipling dismisses as academic all the philosophical or ideological approaches contending with Orientalism. Among those discredited styles of rule were Evangelicalism (the missionaries and reformers, parodied in Mr. Bennett), Utilitarianism and Spencerianism (parodied in the Babu), and of course the unnamed academics lampooned as "worse than the pestilence." It is interesting that, phrased the way it is, the widow's approval is wide enough to include police officers like the Superintendent, as well as a flexible educator like Father Victor, and the quietly authoritative figure of Colonel Creighton.

Having the widow express what is in effect a sort of uncontested normative judgement about India and its rulers is Kipling's way of demonstrating that natives accept colonial rule so long as it is the right kind. Historically this has always been how European imperialism made itself palatable to itself, for what could be better for its self-image than native subjects who express assent to the outsider's knowledge and power, implicitly accepting European judgement on the undeveloped, backward, or degenerate nature of their own society? If one reads *Kim* as a boy's adventure or as a rich and lovingly detailed panorama of Indian life, one is not reading the novel that Kipling in fact wrote, so carefully inscribed is it with these considered views, suppressions, and elisions. As Francis Hutchins puts it in *The Illusion of Permanence: British Imperialism in India*, by the late nineteenth century,

> An India of the imagination was created which contained no elements
> of either social change or political menace. Orientalization was the
> result of this effort to conceive of Indian society as devoid of elements
> hostile to the perpetualization of British rule, for it was on the basis of
> this presumptive India that Orientalizers sought to build a permanent
> rule.[141]

Kim is a major contribution to this Orientalized India of the imagination, as it is also to what historians have come to call "the invention of tradition."

There is still more to be noted. Dotting *Kim*'s fabric is a scattering of editorial asides on the immutable nature of the Oriental world as distinguished from the white world, no less immutable. Thus, for example, "Kim would lie like an Oriental"; or, a bit later, "all hours of the twenty-four are alike to Orientals"; or, when Kim pays for train tickets with the lama's money he keeps one anna per rupee for himself, which, Kipling says, is "the immemorial commission of Asia"; later still Kipling refers to "the huckster instinct of the East"; at a train platform, Mahbub's retainers "being natives" have not unloaded the trucks which they should have; Kim's ability to sleep as the trains roar is an instance of "the Oriental's indifference to mere noise"; as the camp breaks up, Kipling says that it is done "swiftly—as Orientals understand speed—with long explanations, with abuse and windy talk, carelessly, amid a hundred checks for little things forgotten"; Sikhs are characterized as having a special "love of money"; Hurree Babu equates being a Bengali with being fearful; when he hides the packet taken from the foreign agents, the Babu "stows the entire trove about his body, as only Orientals can."

None of this is unique to Kipling. The most cursory survey of late-nineteenth-century Western culture reveals an immense reservoir of popular wisdom of this sort, a good deal of which, alas, is still very much alive today. Furthermore, as John M. MacKenzie has shown in his valuable book *Propaganda and Empire*, manipulative devices from cigarette cards, postcards, sheet music, almanacs, and manuals to music-hall entertainments, toy soldiers, brass band concerts, and board games extolled the empire and stressed its necessity to England's strategic, moral, and economic well-being, at the same time characterizing the dark or inferior races as unregenerate, in need of suppression, severe rule, indefinite subjugation. The cult of the military personality was prominent, usually because such personalities had managed to bash a few dark heads. Different rationales for holding overseas territories were given; sometimes it was profit, other times strategy or competition with other imperial powers (as in *Kim:* in *The Strange Ride of Rudyard Kipling* Angus Wilson mentions that as early as age sixteen Kipling proposed at a school debate the motion that "the advance of Russia in Central Asia is hostile to British Power").[142] The one thing that remains constant is the subordination of the non-white.

Kim is a work of great aesthetic merit; it cannot be dismissed simply as the racist imagining of one disturbed and ultra-reactionary imperialist. George Orwell was certainly right to comment on Kipling's unique power to have added phrases and concepts to the language—East is East, and West is West; the White Man's Burden; somewhere East of Suez—and right also to say that Kipling's concerns are both vulgar and permanent, of urgent interest.[143] One reason for Kipling's power is that he was an artist of enormous gifts; what he did in his art was to elaborate ideas that would have had far less permanence, for all their vulgarity, without the art. But he was also supported by (and therefore could use) the authorized monuments of nine-teenth-century European culture, and the inferiority of non-white races, the necessity that they be ruled by a superior race, and their absolute unchang-ing essence was a more or less unquestioned axiom of modern life.

True, there were debates about how the colonies were to be ruled, or whether some of them should be given up. Yet no one with any power to influence public discussion or policy demurred as to the basic superiority of the white European male, who should always retain the upper hand. State-ments like "The Hindu is inherently untruthful and lacks moral courage" were expressions of wisdom from which very few, least of all the governors of Bengal, dissented; similarly, when a historian of India like Sir H. M. Elliot planned his work, central to it was the notion of Indian barbarity. Climate and geography dictated certain character traits in the Indian; Orientals, according to Lord Cromer, one of their most redoubtable rulers, could not learn to walk on sidewalks, could not tell the truth, could not use logic; the Malaysian native was essentially lazy, just as the north European was essen-tially energetic and resourceful. V. G. Kiernan's book *The Lords of Human Kind*, referred to earlier, gives a remarkable picture of how widespread these views were. As I suggested earlier, disciplines like colonial economics, anthropology, history, and sociology were built out of these dicta, with the result that almost to a man and woman the Europeans who dealt with colonies like India became insulated from the facts of change and national-ism. A whole experience—described in meticulous detail in Michael Ed-wardes's *The Sahibs and the Lotus*—with its own integral history, cuisine, dialect, values, and tropes more or less detached itself from the teeming, contradictory realities of India and perpetuated itself heedlessly. Even Karl Marx succumbed to thoughts of the changeless Asiatic village, or agricul-ture, or despotism.

A young Englishman sent to India to be a part of the "covenanted" civil service would belong to a class whose national dominance over each and every Indian, no matter how aristocratic and rich, was absolute. He would have heard the same stories, read the same books, learned the same lessons, joined the same clubs as all the other young colonial officials. Yet, Michael Edwardes says, "few really bothered to learn the language of the people they ruled with any fluency, and they were heavily dependent on their native clerks, who had taken the trouble to learn the language of their conquerors, and were, in many cases, not at all unwilling to use their masters' ignorance to their own advantage."[144] Ronny Heaslop in Forster's *A Passage to India* is an effective portrait of such an official.

All of this is relevant to *Kim*, whose main figure of worldly authority is Colonel Creighton. This ethnographer-scholar-soldier is no mere creature of invention, but almost certainly a figure drawn from Kipling's experiences in the Punjab, and he is most interestingly interpreted both as derived from earlier figures of authority in colonial India and as an original figure perfect for Kipling's new purposes. In the first place, although Creighton is seen infrequently and his character is not so fully drawn as Mahbub Ali's or the Babu's, he is nevertheless present as a point of reference for the action, a discreet director of events, a man whose power is worthy of respect. Yet he is no crude martinet. He takes over Kim's life by persuasion, not by imposition of his rank. He can be flexible when it seems reasonable—who could have wished for a better boss than Creighton during Kim's footloose holidays?—and stern when events require it.

In the second place, it is especially interesting that he is a colonial official and scholar. This union of power and knowledge is contemporary with Doyle's invention of Sherlock Holmes (whose faithful scribe, Dr. Watson, is a veteran of the Northwest Frontier), also a man whose approach to life includes a healthy respect for, and protection of, the law allied with a superior, specialized intellect inclining to science. In both instances, Kipling and Doyle represent for their readers men whose unorthodox style of operation is rationalized by new fields of experience turned into quasi-academic specialties. Colonial rule and crime detection almost gain the respectability and order of the classics or chemistry. When Mahbub Ali turns Kim in for his education, Creighton, overhearing their conversation, thinks "that the boy mustn't be wasted if he is as advertised." He sees the world from a totally systematic viewpoint. Everything about India interests Creighton, because everything in it is significant for his rule. The interchange between ethnography and colonial work in Creighton is fluent; he can study the talented boy both as a future spy and as an anthropological curiosity. Thus when Father Victor wonders whether it might not be too much for Creighton to attend to a bureaucratic detail concerning Kim's education, the colonel dismisses the scruple. "The transformation of a regimental badge like your Red Bull into a sort of fetish that the boy follows is very interesting."

Creighton as anthropologist is important for other reasons. Of all the modern social sciences, anthropology is the one historically most closely tied to colonialism, since it was often the case that anthropologists and ethnologists advised colonial rulers on the manners and mores of the native people. (Claude Levi-Strauss's allusion to anthropology as "the handmaiden of colonialism" recognizes this; the excellent collection of essays edited by Talal Asad, *Anthropology and the Colonial Encounter*, 1973, develops the connections still further; and in Robert Stone's novel on the United States in Latin American affairs, *A Flag for Sunrise*, 1981, the central character is Holliwell, an anthropologist with ambiguous ties to the CIA.) Kipling was one of the first novelists to portray this logical alliance between Western science and political power at work in the colonies.[145] And Kipling always takes Creighton seriously, which is one of the reasons the Babu is there. The native anthropologist, clearly a bright man whose reiterated ambitions to belong to the Royal Society are not unfounded, is almost always funny, or gauche, or somehow caricatural, not because he is incompetent or inept—on the contrary—but because he is not white; that is, he can never be a Creighton. Kipling is very careful about this. Just as he could not imagine an India in historical flux *out of* British control, he could not imagine Indians who could be effective and serious in what he and others of the time considered exclusively Western pursuits. Lovable and admirable as he may be, there remains in the Babu the grimacing stereotype of the ontologically funny native, hopelessly trying to be like "us."

I said that the figure of Creighton is the culmination of a change taking place over generations in the personification of British power in India. Behind Creighton are late-eighteenth-century adventurers and pioneers like Warren Hastings and Robert Clive, whose innovative rule and personal excesses required England to subdue the unrestricted authority of the Raj by law. What survives of Clive and Hastings in Creighton is their sense of freedom, their willingness to improvise, their preference for informality. After such ruthless pioneers came Thomas Munro and Mountstuart Elphinstone, reformers and synthesizers who were among the first senior scholar-administrators whose dominion reflected something resembling expert knowledge. There are also the great scholar figures for whom service in India was an opportunity to study an alien culture—men like Sir William ("Asiatic") Jones, Charles Wilkins, Nathaniel Halhed, Henry Colebrooke, Jonathan Duncan. These men belonged to principally commercial enterprises, and they seemed not to feel, as Creighton (and Kipling) did, that work in India was as patterned and economical (in the literal sense) as running a total system.

Creighton's norms are those of disinterested government, government based not upon whim or personal preference (as was the case for Clive), but upon laws, principles of order and control. Creighton embodies the notion that you cannot govern India unless you know India, and to know India means to understand the way it operates. The understanding developed during William Bentinck's rule as Governor-General and drew on Orientalist as well as Utilitarian principles for ruling the largest number of Indians with the greatest benefits (to Indians as well as the British),[146] but it was always enclosed by the unchanging fact of British imperial authority, which set the Governor apart from ordinary human beings, for whom questions of right and wrong, of virtue and harm are emotionally involving and important. To the government person representing Britain in India, the main thing is not whether something is good or evil, and therefore must be changed or kept, but whether it works or not, whether it helps or hinders in ruling the alien entity. Thus Creighton satisfies the Kipling who had imagined an ideal India, unchanging and attractive, as an eternally integral part of the empire. *This* was an authority one could give in to.

In a celebrated essay, "Kipling's Place in the History of Ideas," Noel Annan presents the notion that Kipling's vision of society was similar to that of the new sociologists—Durkheim, Weber, and Pareto—who

> saw society as a nexus of groups; and the pattern of behaviour which these groups unwittingly established, rather than men's wills or anything so vague as a class, cultural or national tradition, primarily determined men's actions. They asked how these groups promoted order or instability in society, whereas their predecessors had asked whether certain groups helped society to progress.[147]

Annan goes on to say that Kipling was similar to the founders of modern sociological discourse insofar as he believed efficient government in India depended upon "the forces of social control [religion, law, custom, convention, morality] which imposed upon individuals certain rules which they broke at their peril." It had become almost a commonplace of British imperial theory that the British empire was different from (and better than) the Roman Empire in that it was a rigorous system in which order and law prevailed, whereas the latter was mere robbery and profit. Cromer makes the point in *Ancient and Modern Imperialism,* and so does Marlow in *Heart of Darkness.*[148] Creighton understands this perfectly, which is why he works with Muslims, Bengalis, Afghans, Tibetans without appearing ever to belittle their beliefs or slight their differences. It was a natural insight for Kipling to have imagined Creighton as a scientist whose specialty includes the minute workings of a complex society, rather than as either a colonial bureaucrat or a rapacious profiteer. Creighton's Olympian humor, his affectionate but detached attitude to people, his eccentric bearing, are Kipling's embellishments on an ideal Indian official.

Creighton the organization man not only presides over the Great Game (whose ultimate beneficiary is of course the Kaiser-i-Hind, or Queen Empress, and her British people), but also works hand in hand with the novelist himself. If we can ascribe a consistent point of view to Kipling, we can find it in Creighton, more than anyone else. Like Kipling, Creighton respects the distinctions within Indian society. When Mahbub Ali tells Kim that he must never forget that he is a Sahib, he speaks as Creighton's trusted, experienced employee. Like Kipling, Creighton never tampers with the hierarchies, the priorities and privileges of caste, religion, ethnicity, and race; neither do the men and women who work for him. By the late nineteenth century the so-called Warrant of Precedence—which began, according to Geoffrey Moorhouse, by recognizing "fourteen different levels of status"—had expanded to "sixty-one, some reserved for one person, others shared by a number of people."[149] Moorhouse speculates that the love-hate relationship between British and Indians derived from the complex hierarchical attitudes present in both people. "Each grasped the other's basic social premise and not only understood it but subconsciously respected it as a curious variant of their own."[150] One sees this kind of thinking reproduced nearly everywhere in *Kim*—Kipling's patiently detailed register of India's different races and castes, the acceptance by everyone (even the lama) of the doctrine of racial separation, the lines and customs which cannot easily be traversed by outsiders. Everyone in *Kim* is equally an outsider to other groups and an insider in his.

Creighton's appreciation of Kim's abilities—his quickness, his capacity for disguise and for getting into a situation as if it were native to him—is like the novelist's interest in this complex and chameleon-like character, who darts in and out of adventure, intrigue, episode. The ultimate analogy is between the Great Game and the novel itself. To be able to see all India from the vantage of controlled observation: this is one great satisfaction. Another is to have at one's fingertips a character who can sportingly cross lines and invade territories, a little Friend of all the World—Kim O'Hara himself. It is as if by holding Kim at the center of the novel (just as Creighton the spy master holds the boy in the Great Game) Kipling can *have* and enjoy India in a way that even imperialism never dreamed of.

What does this mean in terms of so codified and organized a structure as the late-nineteenth-century realistic novel? Along with Conrad, Kipling is a writer of fiction whose heroes belong to a startlingly unusual world of foreign adventure and personal charisma. Kim, Lord Jim, and Kurtz, say, are creatures with flamboyant wills who presage later adventurers like T. E. Lawrence in *The Seven Pillars of Wisdom* and Malraux's Perken in *La Voie royale.* Conrad's heroes, afflicted as they may be by an unusual power of reflection and cosmic irony, remain in the memory as strong, often heedlessly daring men of action.

And although their fiction belongs to the genre of adventure-imperialism —along with the work of Rider Haggard, Doyle, Charles Reade, Vernon Fielding, G. A. Henty, and dozens of lesser writers—Kipling and Conrad claim serious aesthetic and critical attention.

But one way of grasping what is unusual about Kipling is to recall briefly who his contemporaries were. We have become so used to seeing him alongside Haggard and Buchan that we have forgotten that as an artist he can justifiably be compared with Hardy, Henry James, Meredith, Gissing, the later George Eliot, George Moore, or Samuel Butler. In France, his peers are Flaubert and Zola, even Proust and the early Gide. Yet the works of these writers are essentially novels of disillusion and disenchantment, whereas *Kim* is not. Almost without exception the protagonist of the late-nineteenth-century novel is someone who has realized that his or her life's project—the wish to be great, rich, or distinguished—is mere fancy, illusion, dream. Frédéric Moreau in Flaubert's *Sentimental Education,* or Isabel Archer in *The Portrait of a Lady,* or Ernest Pontifex in Butler's *The Way of All Flesh*—the figure is a young man or woman bitterly awakened from a fancy dream of accomplishment, action, or glory, forced instead to come to terms with a reduced status, betrayed love, and a hideously bourgeois world, crass and philistine.

This awakening is not to be found in *Kim*. Nothing brings the point home more powerfully than a comparison between Kim and his nearly exact contemporary Jude Fawley, the "hero" of Thomas Hardy's *Jude the Obscure* (1894). Both are eccentric orphans objectively at odds with their environment: Kim is an Irishman in India, Jude a minimally gifted rural English boy who is interested more in Greek than in farming. Both imagine lives of appealing attractiveness for themselves, and both try to achieve these lives through apprenticeship of some sort, Kim as chela to the wandering Abbot-Lama, Jude as a supplicant student at the university. But there the comparisons stop. Jude is ensnared by one circumstance after the other; he marries the ill-suited Arabella, falls in love disastrously with Sue Bridehead, conceives children who commit suicide, ends his days as a neglected man after years of pathetic wandering. Kim, by contrast, graduates from one brilliant success to another.

Yet it is important to insist again on the similarities between *Kim* and *Jude the Obscure*. Both boys, Kim and Jude, are singled out for their unusual pedigree; neither is like "normal" boys, whose parents and family assure a smooth passage through life. Central to their predicaments is the problem of identity—what to be, where to go, what to do. Since they cannot be like the others, who are they? They are restless seekers and wanderers, like the archetypal hero of the novel form itself, Don Quixote, who decisively marks off the world of the novel in its fallen, unhappy state, its "lost transcendence," as Lukacs puts it in *The Theory of the Novel,* from the happy, satisfied world of the epic. Every novelistic hero, Lukacs says, attempts to restore the lost world of his or her imagination, which in the late-nineteenth-century novel of disillusionment is an unrealizable dream.[151] Jude, like Frédéric Moreau, Dorothea Brooke, Isabel Archer, Ernest Pontifex, and all the others, is condemned to such a fate. The paradox of personal identity is that it is implicated in that unsuccessful dream. Jude would not be who he is were it not for his futile wish to become a scholar. Escape from being a social non-entity holds out the promise of relief, but that is impossible. The structural irony is precisely that conjunction: what you wish for is exactly what you cannot have. The poignancy and defeated hope at the end of *Jude the Obscure* have become synonymous with Jude's very identity.

Because he gets beyond this paralyzing, dispiriting impasse, Kim O'Hara is so remarkably optimistic a character. Like those of other heroes of imperial fiction, his actions result in victories not defeats. He restores India to health, as the invading foreign agents are apprehended and expelled. Part of his strength is his deep, almost instinctive knowledge of this difference from the Indians around him; he has a special amulet given him during infancy, and unlike the other boys he plays with—this is established at the novel's opening—he is endowed through natal prophecy with a unique fate of which he wishes to make everyone aware. Later he becomes explicitly aware of being a Sahib, a white man, and whenever he wavers there is someone to remind him that he is indeed a Sahib, with all the rights and privileges of that special rank. Kipling even makes the saintly guru affirm the difference between a white man and a non-white.

But that alone does not impart to the novel its curious sense of enjoyment and confidence. Compared with James or Conrad, Kipling was not an introspective writer, nor—from the evidence that we have—did he think of himself, like Joyce, as an Artist. The force of his best writing comes from ease and fluency, the seeming naturalness of his narration and characterization, while the sheer variousness of his creativity rivals that of Dickens and Shakespeare. Language for him was not, as it was for Conrad, a resistant medium; it was transparent, easily capable of many tones and inflections, all of them directly representative of the world he explored. And this language gives Kim his sprightliness and wit, his energy and attractiveness. In many ways Kim resembles a character who might have been drawn much earlier in the nineteenth century, by a writer like Stendhal, for example, whose vivid portrayals of Fabrice del Dongo and Julien Sorel have the same blend of adventure and wistfulness, which Stendhal called *espagnolisme*. For Kim, as for Stendhal's characters and unlike Hardy's Jude, the world is full of possibilities, much like Caliban's island, "full of noises, sounds, and sweet airs, that give delight and hurt not."

At times, that world is restful, even idyllic. So we get not only the bustle and vitality of the Grand Trunk Road, but also the welcoming, gentle pastoralism of the scene en route with the old soldier (Chapter 3) as the little group of travellers reposes peacefully:

> There was a drowsy buzz of small life in hot sunshine, a cooing of doves, and a sleepy drone of well-wheels across the fields. Slowly and impressively the lama began. At the end of ten minutes the old soldier slid from his pony, to hear better as he said, and sat with the reins round his wrist. The lama's voice faltered—the periods lengthened. Kim was busy watching a gray squirrel. When the little scolding bunch of fur, close pressed to the branch, disappeared, preacher and audience were fast asleep, the old officer's strong-cut head pillowed on his arm, the lama's thrown back against the tree bole, where it showed like yellow ivory. A naked child toddled up, stared, and moved by some quick impulse of reverence made a solemn little obeisance before the lama— only the child was so short and fat that it toppled over sideways, and Kim laughed at the sprawling, chubby legs. The child, scared and indignant, yelled aloud.[152]

On all sides of this Edenic composure is the "wonderful spectacle" of the Grand Trunk Road, where, as the old soldier puts it, " 'all castes and kinds of men move . . . Brahmins and chumars, bankers and tinkers, barbers and bunnias, pilgrims and potters—all the world coming and going. It is to me as a river from which I am withdrawn like a log after a flood.' "[153]

One fascinating index of Kim's way with this teeming, strangely hospitable world is his remarkable gift for disguise. We first see him perched on the ancient gun in a square in Lahore—where it still stands today—an Indian boy among other Indian boys. Kipling carefully differentiates the religions and backgrounds of each boy (the Muslim, the Hindu, the Irish) but is just as careful to show us that none of these identities, though they may hinder the other boys, is a hindrance to Kim. He can pass from one dialect, one set of values and beliefs, to the other. Throughout the book Kim takes on the dialects of numerous Indian communities; he speaks Urdu, English (Kipling does a superbly funny, gentle mockery of his stilted Anglo-Indian, finely distinguished from the Babu's orotund verbosity), Eurasian, Hindi, and Bengali; when Mahbub speaks Pashtu, Kim gets that too; when the lama speaks Chinese Tibetan, Kim understands that. As orchestrator of this Babel of tongues, this veritable Noah's Ark of Sansis, Kashmiris, Akalis, Sikhs, and many others, Kipling also manages Kim's chameleon-like progress dancing in and out of it all, like a great actor passing through many situations and at home in each.

How very different this all is from the lusterless world of the European bourgeoisie, whose ambiance as every novelist of importance renders it reconfirms the debasement of contemporary life, the extinction of all dreams of passion, success, and exotic adventure. Kipling's fiction offers an antithesis: his world, because it is set in an India dominated by Britain, holds nothing back from the expatriate European. *Kim* shows how a white Sahib can enjoy life in this lush complexity; and, I would argue, the absence of resistance to European intervention in it—symbolized by Kim's abilities to move relatively unscarred through India—is due to its imperialist vision. For what one cannot accomplish in one's own Western environment— where trying to live out the grand dream of a successful quest means coming up against one's own mediocrity and the world's corruption and degradation—one can do abroad. Isn't it possible in India to do everything? be anything? go anywhere with impunity?

Consider the pattern of Kim's wanderings as they affect the structure of the novel. Most of his voyages move within the Punjab, around the axis formed by Lahore and Umballa, a British garrison town on the frontier of the United Provinces. The Grand Trunk Road, built by the great Muslim ruler Sher Shan in the late sixteenth century, runs from Peshawar to Calcutta, although the lama never goes farther south and east than Benares. Kim makes excursions to Simla, to Lucknow, and later to the Kulu valley; with Mahbub he goes as far south as Bombay and as far west as Karachi. But the overall impression created by these voyages is of carefree meandering. Occasionally Kim's trips are punctuated by the requirements of the school year at St. Xavier's, but the only serious agendas, the only equivalents of temporal pressure on the characters, are (a) the Abbot-Lama's Search, which is fairly elastic, and (b) the pursuit and final expulsion of the foreign agents trying to stir up trouble on the Northwest Frontier. There are no scheming money-lenders here, no village prigs, no vicious gossips or unattractive and heartless *parvenus,* as there are in the novels of Kipling's major European contemporaries.

Now contrast *Kim*'s rather loose structure, based as it is on a luxurious geographical and spatial expansiveness, with the tight, relentlessly unforgiving temporal structure of the European novels contemporary with it. Time, says Lukacs in *The Theory of the Novel,* is the great ironist, almost a character in these novels, as it drives the protagonist further into illusion and derangement, and also reveals his or her illusions to be groundless, empty, bitterly futile.[154] In *Kim,* you have the impression that time is on your side, because the geography is yours to move about in more or less freely. Certainly Kim feels that, and so does Colonel Creighton, in his patience, and in the sporadic, even vague way he appears and disappears. The opulence of India's space, the commanding British presence there, the sense of freedom communicated by the interaction between these two factors add up to a wonderfully positive atmosphere irradiating the pages of *Kim*. This is not a driven world of hastening disaster, as in Flaubert or Zola.

The novel's ease of atmosphere also comes, I think, from Kipling's own recollected sense of being at home in India. In *Kim* representatives of the Raj seem to have no problem with being "abroad"; India for' them requires no self-conscious apologetic, no embarrassment or unease. The French-speaking Russian agents admit that in India, "we have nowhere left our mark yet,"[155] but the British know they have, so much so that Hurree, that self-confessed "Oriental," is agitated by the Russians' conspiracy on behalf of the Raj, not his own people. When the Russians attack the lama and rip apart his map, the defilement is metaphorically of India itself, and Kim corrects this defilement later. Kipling's mind plays over reconciliation, healing, and wholeness in the conclusion, and his means are geographical: the British repossessing India, in order once again to enjoy its spaciousness, to be at home in it again, and again.

There is a striking coincidence between Kipling's reassertion over the geography of India and Camus's in some of his Algerian stories written almost a half century later. Their gestures are symptomatic not of confidence, but of a lurking, often unacknowledged malaise, I believe. For if you belong in a place, you do not have to keep saying and showing it: you just are, like the silent Arabs in *L'Etranger* or the fuzzy-haired Blacks in *Heart of Darkness* or the various Indians in *Kim*. But colonial, i.e., geographical, appropriation requires such assertive inflections, and these emphases are the hallmark of the imperial culture reconfirming itself to and for itself.

Kipling's geographical and spatial governance of *Kim* rather than the temporal one of metropolitan European fiction, gains special eminence by political and historical factors; it expresses an irreducible political judgement on Kipling's part. It is as if he were saying, India is ours and therefore we can see it in this mostly uncontested, meandering, and fulfilling way. India is "other" and, importantly, for all its wonderful size and variety, it is safely held by Britain.

Kipling arranges another aesthetically satisfying coincidence, and it, too, must be taken into account. This is the confluence between Creighton's Great Game and Kim's inexhaustibly renewed capacity for disguises and adventure; Kipling keeps the two tightly connected. The first is a device of political surveillance and control; the second, at a deeper and interesting level, is a wish-fantasy of someone who would like to think that everything is possible, that one can go anywhere and be anything. T. E. Lawrence in *The Seven Pillars of Wisdom* expresses this fantasy over and over, as he reminds us how he—a blond, blue-eyed Englishman—moved among the desert Arabs as if he were one of them.

I call this a fantasy because, as both Kipling and Lawrence endlessly remind us, no one—least of all actual whites and non-whites in the colonies—ever forgets that "going native" or playing the Great Game depends on the rock-like foundations of European power. Was there ever a native fooled by the blue- or green-eyed Kims and T. E. Lawrences who passed among them as agent adventurers? I doubt it, just as I doubt that any white man or woman lived within the orbit of European imperialism who ever forgot that the discrepancy in power between the white rulers and the native subjects was absolute, intended to be unchanging, rooted in cultural, political, and economic reality.

Kim, the positive boy hero who travels in disguise all over India, across boundaries and rooftops, into tents and villages, is everlastingly responsible to British power, represented by Creighton's Great Game. The reason we can see that so clearly is that since *Kim* was written India *has* become independent, just as since the publication of Gide's *The Immoralist* and Camus's *The Stranger* Algeria has become independent of France. To read these major works of the imperial period retrospectively and heterophonically with other histories and traditions counterpointed against them, to read them in the light of decolonization, is neither to slight their great aesthetic force, nor to treat them reductively as imperialist propaganda. Still, it is a much graver mistake to read them stripped of their affiliations with the facts of power which informed and enabled them.

The device invented by Kipling by which British control over India (the Great Game) coincides in detail with Kim's disguise fantasy to be at one with India, and later to heal its defilements, obviously could not have occurred without British imperialism. We must read the novel as the realization of a great cumulative process, which in the closing years of the nineteenth century is reaching its last major moment before Indian independence: on the one hand, surveillance and control over India; on the other, love for and fascinated attention to its every detail. The overlap between the political hold of the one and the aesthetic and psychological pleasure of the other is made possible by British imperialism itself; Kipling understood this, yet many of his later readers refuse to accept this troubling, even embarrassing truth. And it was not just Kipling's recognition of British imperialism in general, but imperialism at that specific moment in its history, when it had almost lost sight of the unfolding dynamics of a human and secular truth: the truth that India had existed before the Europeans arrived, that control was seized by a European power, and that

Indian resistance to that power would inevitably struggle out from under British subjugation.

In reading *Kim* today we can watch a great artist in a sense blinded by his own insights about India, confusing the realities that he saw with such color and ingenuity, with the notion that they were permanent and essential. Kipling takes from the novel form qualities that he tries to bend to this basically obfuscatory end. But it is surely a great artistic irony that he does not truly succeed in this obfuscation, and his attempt to use the novel for this purpose reaffirms his aesthetic integrity. *Kim* most assuredly is *not* a political tract. Kipling's choice of the novel form and of his character Kim O'Hara to engage profoundly with an India that he loved but could not properly have—this is what we should keep resolutely as the book's central meaning. Then we can read *Kim* as a great document of its historical moment and, too, an aesthetic milestone along the way to midnight August 14–15, 1947, a moment whose children have done so much to revise our sense of the past's richness and its enduring problems.

(VI)

The Native Under Control

I have been trying, on the one hand, to focus on those aspects of an ongoing European culture that imperialism made use of as its successes accelerated and, on the other, to describe how it was that the imperial European would not or could not see that he or she was an imperialist and, ironically, how it was that the non-European in the same circumstances saw the European *only* as imperial. "For the native," Fanon says, such a European value as "objectivity is always directed against him."[156]

Even so, can one speak of imperialism as being so ingrained in nineteenth-century Europe as to have become indistinguishable from the culture as a whole? What is the meaning of a word like "imperialist" when it is used for Kipling's jingoist work as well for his subtler literary work, or for his contemporaries Tennyson and Ruskin? Is every cultural artefact theoretically implicated?

Two answers propose themselves. No, we must say, such concepts as "imperialism" have a generalized quality that masks with an unacceptable vagueness the interesting heterogeneity of Western metropolitan cultures. Discriminations must be made between one kind of cultural work and another when it comes to involvement in imperialism; so we can say, for example, that for all his illiberalism about India, John Stuart Mill was more complex and enlightened in his attitudes to the notion of empire than either Carlyle or Ruskin (Mill's behavior in the Eyre case was principled, even retrospectively admirable). The same is true of Conrad and Kipling as artists compared with Buchan or Haggard. Yet the objection that culture should not be considered a part of imperialism can become a tactic to prevent one from seriously connecting the two. By looking at culture and imperialism carefully, we may discern various forms in the relationship, and we shall see that we can profitably draw connections that enrich and sharpen our reading of major cultural texts. The paradoxical point, of course, is that European culture was no less complex, rich, or interesting for having supported most aspects of the imperial experience.

Let us look at Conrad and Flaubert, writers who worked in the second half of the nineteenth century, the former concerned explicitly with imperialism, the latter implicitly involved with it. Despite their differences both writers similarly emphasize characters whose capacity for isolating and surrounding themselves in structures they create takes the same form as the colonizer at the center of an empire he rules. Axel Heyst in *Victory* and St. Antoine in *La Tentation*—late works, both—are withdrawn into a place where, like guardians of a magic totality, they incorporate a hostile world purged of its troubling resistances to their control of it. These solitary withdrawals have a long history in Conrad's fiction—Almayer, Kurtz at the Inner Station, Jim at Patusan, and most memorably Charles Gould in Sulaco; in Flaubert they recur with increasing intensity after *Madame Bovary*. Yet unlike Robinson Crusoe on his island, these modern versions of the imperialist who attempts self-redemption are doomed ironically to suffer interruption and distraction, as what they had tried to exclude from their island worlds penetrates anyway. The covert influence of imperial control in Flaubert's imagery of solitary imperiousness is striking when juxtaposed with Conrad's overt representations.

Within the codes of European fiction, these interruptions of an imperial project are realistic reminders that no one can in fact withdraw from the world into a private version of reality. The link back to Don Quixote is obvious, as is the continuity with institutional aspects of the novel form itself, where the aberrant individual is usually disciplined and punished in the interests of a corporate identity. In Conrad's overtly colonial settings, the disruptions are occasioned by Europeans, and they are enfolded within a narrative structure that is retrospectively resubmitted to European scrutiny for interpretation and questioning. One sees this in both the early *Lord Jim* and the later *Victory:* as the idealistic or withdrawn white man (Jim, Heyst)

lives a life of somewhat Quixotic seclusion, his space is invaded by Mephis-
tophelian emanations, adventurers whose subsequent malfeasance is examined retrospectively by a narrating white man.

Heart of Darkness is another example. Marlow's audience is English, and
Marlow himself penetrates to Kurtz's private domain as an inquiring Western mind trying to make sense of an apocalyptic revelation. Most readings
rightly call attention to Conrad's skepticism about the colonial enterprise,
but they rarely remark that in telling the story of his African journey Marlow
repeats and confirms Kurtz's action: restoring Africa to European hegemony
by historicizing and narrating its strangeness. The savages, the wilderness,
even the surface folly of popping shells into a vast continent—all these
reaccentuate Marlow's need to place the colonies on the imperial map and
under the overarching temporality of narratable history, no matter how
complicated and circuitous the results.

Marlow's historical equivalents, to take two prominent examples, would
be Sir Henry Maine and Sir Roderick Murchison, men celebrated for their
massive cultural and scientific work—work unintelligible except in the
imperial context. Maine's great study Ancient Law (1861) explores the structure of law in a primitive patriarchal society that accorded privilege to fixed
"status" and could not become modern until the transformation to a "contractual" basis took place. Maine uncannily prefigures Foucault's history, in
Discipline and Punish, of the shift in Europe from "sovereign" to administrative surveillance. The difference is that for Maine the empire became a sort
of laboratory for proving his theory (Foucault treats the Benthamite Panop-
ticon in use at European correctional facilities as the proof of his): appointed
to the Viceroy's Council in India as legal member, Maine regarded his
sojourn in the East as an "extended field-trip." He fought the Utilitarians on
issues concerning the sweeping reform of Indian legislation (two hundred
pieces of which he wrote), and interpreted his task as the identification and
preservation of Indians who could be rescued from "status" and, as carefully
nurtured elites, brought over to the contractual basis of British policy. In
Village Communities (1871) and later in his Rede Lectures, Maine outlined a
theory amazingly like Marx's: that feudalism in India, challenged by British
colonialism, was a necessary development; in time, he argued, a feudal lord
would establish the basis for individual ownership and allow a prototype
bourgeoisie to emerge.

The equally striking Roderick Murchison was a soldier turned geologist,
geographer, and administrator of the Royal Geographical Society. As Robert
Stafford points out in a gripping account of Murchison's life and career,
given the man's military background, his peremptory conservatism, his

inordinate self-confidence and will, his tremendous scientific and acquisitive
zeal, it was inevitable that he approached his work as a geologist like an
all-conquering army whose campaigns added power and global reach to the
British empire.[157] Whether in Britain itself, Russia, Europe, or the An-
tipodes, Africa, or India, Murchison's work *was* empire. "Travelling and
colonizing are still as much the ruling passions of Englishmen as they were
in the days of Raleigh and Drake," he once said.[158]

Thus in his tales Conrad re-enacts the imperial gesture of pulling in
virtually the entire world, and he represents its gains while stressing its
irreducible ironies. His historicist vision overrides the other histories contained in the narrative sequence; its dynamic sanctions Africa, Kurtz, and
Marlow—despite their radical eccentricity—as objects of a superior Western (but admittedly problematic) *constitutive* understanding. Yet, as I have
said, much of Conrad's narrative is preoccupied with what eludes articulate
expression—the jungle, the desperate natives, the great river, Africa's magnificent, ineffable dark life. On the second of the two occasions when a native
utters an intelligible word, he thrusts an "insolent black head" through a
doorway to announce Kurtz's death, as if only a European pretext could
furnish an African with reason enough to speak coherently. Less the acknowledgement of an essential African difference, Marlow's narrative takes
the African experience as further acknowledgement of Europe's world significance; Africa recedes in integral meaning, as if with Kurtz's passing it had
once again become the blankness his imperial will had sought to overcome.

Conrad's readers of the time were not expected to ask about or concern
themselves with what became of the natives. What mattered to them was
how Marlow makes sense of everything, for without his deliberately fashioned narrative there is no history worth telling, no fiction worth entertaining, no authority worth consulting. This is a short step away from King
Leopold's account of his International Congo Association, "rendering lasting
and disinterested services to the cause of progress,"[159] and described by one
admirer in 1885 as the "noblest and most self-sacrificing scheme for African
development that has ever been or ever will be attempted."

Chinua Achebe's well-known criticism of Conrad (that he was a racist
who totally dehumanized Africa's native population) does not go far enough
in emphasizing what in Conrad's early fiction becomes more pronounced
and explicit in the late works, like *Nostromo* and *Victory,* that do not deal with
Africa.[160] In *Nostromo* the history of Costaguana is the merciless one of a
white family with grandiose schemes and suicidal bent. Neither the local
Indians nor the ruling-class Spaniards of Sulaco offer an alternative perspective: Conrad treats them with something of the same pitying contempt and

exoticism he reserves for African Blacks and Southeast Asian peasants. In the end, Conrad's audience was European, and his fiction had the effect not of challenging but of confirming that fact and consolidating consciousness of it, even though paradoxically his own corrosive skepticism was thereby released. A similar dynamic appears in Flaubert.

Despite their fineness and reticulation, then, the inclusive cultural forms dealing with peripheral non-European settings are markedly ideological and selective (even repressive) so far as "natives" are concerned, just as the picturesqueness of nineteenth-century colonial painting[161] is, despite its "realism," ideological and repressive: it effectively silences the Other, it reconstitutes difference as identity, it rules over and represents domains figured by occupying powers, not by inactive inhabitants. The interesting question is what, if anything, resisted such directly imperial narratives as Conrad's? Was the consolidated vision of Europe unbroken? or was it irresistible and unopposed within Europe?

European imperialism indeed developed European opposition—as A. P. Thornton, Porter, and Hobson demonstrate[162]—between the middle and the end of the century; certainly the Abolitionists, Anthony Trollope, and Goldwin Smith, for example, were relatively honorable figures among many individual and group movements. Still, people like Froude, Dilke, and Seeley represented the overwhelmingly more powerful and successful proimperial culture.[163] Missionaries, although they often functioned as agents of one or another imperial power throughout the nineteenth century, were sometimes able to curb the worst colonial excesses, as Stephen Neill argues in *Colonialism and Christian Missions*.[164] It is also true that Europeans brought modern technological change—steam engines, telegraphs, and even education—to some of the natives, benefits that persisted beyond the colonial period, although not without negative aspects. But the startling purity of the imperial quest in *Heart of Darkness*—when Marlow acknowledges that he always felt a passion to fill in the great blank spaces on the map—remains the overwhelming reality, a constitutive reality, in the culture of imperialism. In its impulsive power the gesture recalls *actual* explorers and imperialists like Rhodes, Murchison, and Stanley. There is no minimizing the discrepant power established by imperialism and prolonged in the colonial encounter. Conrad underscores that actuality not just in the content but also in the form of Kurtz's seventeen-page report to the Society for the Suppression of Savage Customs: the aim to civilize and bring light to dark places is both antithetical and logically equivalent to its effective end: the desire to "exterminate the brutes" who may not be cooperative or may entertain ideas about resistance. In Sulaco, Gould is both the mine's patron *and* the man who plans to blow up the enterprise. No connectives are necessary: the imperial vision enables the natives' life and death at the same time.

But of course the natives could not really *all* be made to disappear, and in fact they encroached more and more on the imperial consciousness. And what follow are schemes for separating the natives—Africans, Malays, Arabs, Berbers, Indians, Nepalese, Javanese, Filipinos—from the white man on racial and religious grounds, then for reconstituting them as people requiring a European presence, whether a colonial implantation or a master discourse in which they could be fitted and put to work. Thus, on the one hand, one has Kipling's fiction positing the Indian as a creature clearly needing British tutelage, one aspect of which is a narrative that encircles and then assimilates India, since without Britain India would disappear into its own corruption and underdevelopment. (Kipling here repeats the well-known views of James and John Stuart Mill and other Utilitarians during their tenure at India House.)[165]

Or, on the other hand, one has the shadowy discourse of colonial capitalism, with its roots in liberal free-trade policies (also deriving from evangelical literature), in which, for instance, the indolent native again figures as someone whose natural depravity and loose character necessitate a European overlord. We see this in the observations of colonial rulers like Galieni, Hubert Lyautey, Lord Cromer, Hugh Clifford, and John Bowring: "His hands are large, and the toes of his feet pliant, being exercised in climbing trees, and divers other active functions. . . . The impressions made upon him are transitory, and he retains a feeble memory of passing or past events. Ask him his age, he will not be able to answer: who were his ancestors? he neither knows nor cares. . . . His master vice is idleness, which is his felicity. The labour that necessity demands he gives grudgingly."[166] And we see it in the monographic rigors of scholarly colonial social scientists like the economic historian Clive Day, who in 1904 wrote, "In practice it has been found impossible to secure the services of the native [Javanese] population by any appeal to an ambition to better themselves and raise their standard. Nothing less than immediate material enjoyment will stir them from their indolent routine."[167] These descriptions commodified the natives and their labor and glossed over the actual historical conditions, spiriting away the facts of drudgery and resistance.[168]

But these accounts also spirited away, occluded, and elided the real power of the observer, who for reasons guaranteed only by power and by its alliance with the spirit of World History, could pronounce on the reality of native peoples as from an invisible point of super-objective perspective, using the protocols and jargon of new sciences to displace "the natives'" point of view. As Romila Thapar points out, for example,

> The history of India became one of the means of propagating those interests. Traditional Indian historical writing, with its emphasis on historical biographies and chronicles, was largely ignored. European writing on Indian history was an attempt to create a fresh historical tradition. The historiographical pattern of the Indian past which took shape during the colonial period in the eighteenth and nineteenth centuries was probably similar to the patterns which emerged in the histories of other colonial societies.[169]

Even oppositional thinkers like Marx and Engels were no less capable of such pronouncements than French and British governmental spokesmen; both political camps relied on colonial documents, the fully encoded discourse of Orientalism, for example, and Hegel's view of the Orient and Africa as static, despotic, and irrelevant to world history. When on September 17, 1857, Engels spoke of the Moors of Algeria as a "timid race" because they were repressed but "reserving nevertheless their cruelty and vindictiveness while in moral character they stand very low,"[170] he was merely echoing French colonial doctrine. Conrad similarly used colonial accounts of lazy natives, much as Marx and Engels spun out their theories of Oriental and African ignorance and superstition. This is a second aspect of the wordless imperial wish; for if the obdurately material natives are transformed from subservient beings into inferior humanity, then the colonizer is similarly transformed into an invisible scribe, whose writing reports on the Other and at the same time insists on its scientific disinterestedness and (as Katherine George has noted)[171] the steady improvement in the condition, character, and custom of primitives as a result of their contact with European civilization.[172]

At the apex of high imperialism early in this century, then, we have a conjunctural fusion between, on the one hand, the historicizing codes of discursive writing in Europe, positing a world universally available to transnational impersonal scrutiny, and, on the other hand, a massively colonized world. The object of this consolidated vision is always either a victim or a highly constrained character, permanently threatened with severe punishment, despite his or her many virtues, services, or achievements, excluded ontologically for having few of the merits of the conquering, surveying, and civilizing outsider. For the colonizer the incorporative apparatus requires unremitting effort to maintain. For the victim, imperialism offers these alternatives: serve or be destroyed.

(VII)

Camus and the French Imperial Experience

Yet not all empires were the same. France's empire, according to one of its most famous historians, though no less interested than Britain's in profit, plantations, and slaves, was energized by "prestige."[173] Its various domains acquired (and sometimes lost) over three centuries were presided over by its irradiating "genius," itself a function of France's *"vocation superieure,"* in the words of Delavigne and Charles André Julien, the compilers of a fascinating work, *Les Constructeurs de la France d'outre-mer.*[174] Their cast of characters begins with Champlain and Richelieu, includes such redoubtable proconsuls as Bugeaud, conqueror of Algeria; Brazza, the man who established the French Congo; Gallieni, the pacifier of Madagascar; and Lyautey, along with Cromer the greatest of European rulers of Muslim Arabs. One senses little equivalent of the British "departmental view," and much more the personal style of being French in a great assimilationist enterprise.

Whether this may only be a French self-perception does not really matter, since consistency and regularity of appeal were the driving forces in justifying territorial acquisition before, during, and after the fact. When Seeley (his famous book was translated into French in 1885, and much admired and commented upon) said of Britain's empire that it was acquired absentmindedly, he was only describing an attitude very different from that of contemporary French writers on empire.

As Agnes Murphy shows, the Franco-Prussian War of 1870 directly stimulated the increase in French geographical societies.[175] Geographical knowledge and exploration were thereafter tied to the discourse (and acquisition) of empire, and in the popular prominence of people like Eugene Etienne (founder of the Groupe Coloniale in 1892) one may plot the rise of French imperial theory to almost an exact science. After 1872 and for the first time, according to Girardet, a coherent political doctrine of colonial expansion developed at the head of the French state; between 1880 and 1895 French colonial possessions went from 1.0 to 9.5 million square kilometers, from five to fifty million native inhabitants.[176] At the Second International Congress of Geographical Sciences in 1875, attended by the President of the Republic, the Governor of Paris, the President of the Assembly, Admiral La Roucière–Le Noury's opening address revealed the attitude prevalent throughout the meeting: "Gentlemen, Providence has dictated to us the obligation of know-

ing the earth and making the conquest of it. This supreme command is one
of the imperious duties inscribed on our intelligences and on our activities.
Geography, that science which inspires such beautiful devotedness and in
whose name so many victims have been sacrificed, has become the philosophy of the earth."[177]

Sociology (inspired by Le Bon), psychology (inaugurated by Leopold de
Saussure), history, and of course anthropology flourished in the decades
after 1880, many of them culminating at International Colonial Congresses
(1889, 1894, etc.) or in specific groups (e.g., the 1890 International Congress of
Colonial Sociology or the 1902 Congress of Ethnographic Sciences in Paris).
Whole regions of the world were made the objects of learned *colonial* attention; Raymond Betts mentions that the *Revue internationale de sociologie* devoted annual surveys to Madagascar in 1900, Laos and Cambodia in 1908.[178]
The ideological theory of colonial assimilation begun under the Revolution
collapsed, as theories of racial types—Gustave Le Bon's primitive, inferior,
intermediate, and superior races; or Ernest Seillère's philosophy of pure
force; or Albert Sarraut's and Paul Leroy-Beaulieu's systematics of colonial
practice; or Jules Harmand's principle of domination[179]—guided French
imperial strategies. Natives and their lands were not to be treated as entities
that could be made French, but as possessions the immutable characteristics
of which required separation and subservience, even though this did not rule
out the *mission civilisatrice*. The influence of Fouillée, Clozel, and Giran
turned such ideas into a language and, in the imperial realms themselves, a
practice that closely resembled a science, a science of ruling inferiors whose
resources, lands, and destinies France was in charge of. At best, France's
relationship with Algeria, Senegal, Mauritania, Indochina was *association*
through "hierarchic partnership," as René Maunier argues in his book *The
Sociology of Colonies*,[180] but Betts rightly notes that nonetheless the theory of
"imperialism did not occur by invitation but by force, and in the long run,
all noble doctrines considered, was only successful so long as this *ultima ratio*
was apparent."[181]

To compare discussion of empire by and for the French with the actualities of imperial conquest is to be struck by many disparities and ironies.
Pragmatic considerations were always allowed for people like Lyautey,
Gallieni, Faidherbe, Bugeaud—generals, proconsuls, administrators—to act
with force and draconian dispatch. Politicians like Jules Ferry, who articulated imperial policy after (and during) the fact, reserved the right to
postulate goals that scanted the natives like "la gestion même et ... la defense
du patrimoine nationale."[182] For the lobbies and what today we call publicists—ranging from novelists and jingoists to mandarin philosophers—the

French empire was uniquely connected to the French national identity, its brilliance, civilizational energy, special geographical, social, and historical development. None of this was consistent or corresponded to daily life in Martinique, or Algeria, or Gabon, or Madagascar, and this was, to put it mildly, difficult for the natives. In addition, other empires—German, Dutch, British, Belgian, American—were jostling France, approaching all-out war (as at Fashoda) with it, negotiating with it (as in Arabia in 1917–18), threatening or emulating it.[183]

In Algeria, however inconsistent the policy of French governments since 1830, the inexorable process went on to make Algeria French. First the land was taken from the natives and their buildings were occupied; then French settlers gained control of the cork oak forests and mineral deposits. Then, as David Prochaska notes for Annaba (formerly named Bône), "they displaced the Algerians and peopled [places like] Bône with Europeans."[184] For several decades after 1830 "booty capital" ran the economy, the native population decreased, and settler groups increased. A dual economy came into being: "The European economy can be likened by and large to a firm-centered capitalist economy, while the Algerian economy can be compared to a bazaar-oriented, pre-capitalist economy."[185] So while "France reproduced itself in Algeria,"[186] Algerians were relegated to marginality and poverty. Prochaska compares a French *colon*'s account of the Bône story with one by an Algerian patriot, whose version of events in Annaba "is like reading the French historians of Bône turned upside down."[187]

> Over and above everything else, Arnaud trumpets the progress made by the French in Bône after the mess left by the Algerians. "It is not because the 'old city' is dirty" that it should be kept intact, but because "it alone permits the visitor . . . to understand better the grandeur and beauty of the task accomplished by the French in this country in this place previously deserted, barren and virtually without natural resources," this "small, ugly Arab village of scarcely 1,500 people."[188]

No wonder that H'sen Derdour's book on Annaba uses as a title for its chapter on the Algerian revolution of 1954–1962, "Algeria, prisoner in a universal concentration camp, bursts colonialism asunder and obtains its freedom."[189]

Next to Bône is the village of Mondovi, eighteen miles away, founded in 1849 by "red" laborers transported by the government from Paris (as a way of getting rid of politically troublesome elements) and endowed with land expropriated from Algerian natives. Prochaska's research shows how

Mondovi began as a wine-growing satellite of Bône, a place where in 1913 Albert Camus was born, the son of a "Spanish charwoman and a French cellerman."[190]

Camus is the one author of French Algeria who can with justification be considered of world status. As was Jane Austen a century earlier, Camus is a novelist from whose work the facts of imperial actuality, so clearly there to be noted, have dropped away; as in Austen a detachable *ethos* has remained, an ethos suggesting universality and humanism, deeply at odds with the descriptions of geographical locale plainly given in the fiction. Fanny holds both Mansfield Park and the Antigua plantation; France holds Algeria and, in the same narrative grasp, Meursault's astonishingly existential isolation.

Camus is particularly important in the ugly colonial turbulence of France's twentieth-century decolonizing travail. He is a very late imperial figure who not only survived the heyday of empire, but survives today as a "universalist" writer with roots in a now forgotten colonialism. His retrospective relationship with George Orwell is even more interesting. Like Orwell, Camus became a well-known writer around issues highlighted in the 1930s and 1940s: fascism, the Spanish Civil War, resistance to the fascist onslaught, issues of poverty and social injustice treated from within the discourse of socialism, the relationship between writers and politics, the role of the intellectual. Both were famous for the clarity and plainness of their style—we should recall Roland Barthes's description of Camus's style in *Le Degré zéro de l'écriture* (1953) as *écriture blanche*[191]—as well as the unaffected clarity of their political formulations. Both also made the transformation to the post-war years with less than happy results. Both, in short, are posthumously interesting because of narratives they wrote that now seem to be about a situation that on closer inspection appears quite different. Orwell's fictional examinations of British socialism have taken on a prophetic quality (if you like them; symptomatic if you do not) in the domain of Cold War polemic; Camus's narratives of resistance and existential confrontation, which had once seemed to be about withstanding or opposing both mortality and Nazism, can now be read as part of the debate about culture and imperialism.

Despite Raymond Williams's rather powerful critique of Orwell's social vision, Orwell is regularly claimed by intellectuals on the Left and Right.[192] Was he a neo-conservative in advance of his time, as Norman Podhoretz claims, or was he, as Christopher Hitchens more persuasively argues, a hero of the Left?[193] Camus is somewhat less available to Anglo-American concerns now, but he is cited as critic, political moralist, and admirable novelist in discussions of terrorism and colonialism.[194] The striking parallel between

Camus and Orwell is that both men have become exemplary figures in their respective cultures, figures whose significance derives from but nevertheless seems to transcend the immediate force of their native context. The note is perfectly struck in a description of Camus that comes near the end of Conor Cruise O'Brien's agile demystification of him in a book that in many ways resembles (and was written for the same series as) Raymond Williams's *Modern Masters* study of Orwell. O'Brien says:

> Probably no European writer of his time left so deep a mark on the imagination and, at the same time, on the moral and political consciousness of his own generation and of the next. He was intensely European because he belonged to the frontier of Europe and was aware of a threat. The threat also beckoned to him. He refused, but not without a struggle.
>
> No other writer, not even Conrad, is more representative of the Western consciousness and conscience in relation to the non-Western world. The inner drama of his work is the development of this relation, under increasing pressure and in increasing anguish.[195]

Having shrewdly and even mercilessly exposed the connections between Camus's most famous novels and the colonial situation in Algeria, O'Brien lets him off the hook. There is a subtle act of transcendence in O'Brien's notion of Camus as someone who belonged "to the frontier of Europe," when anyone who knows anything about France, Algeria, and Camus— O'Brien certainly knows a great deal—would not characterize the colonial tie as one between Europe and its frontier. Similarly Conrad and Camus are not merely representative of so relatively weightless a thing as "Western consciousness" but rather of Western *dominance* in the non-European world. Conrad makes this abstract point with unerring power in his essay "Geography and Some Explorers," where he celebrates British exploration of the Arctic and then concludes with an example of his own "militant geography," the way, he says, by "putting my finger on a spot in the very middle of the then white heart of Africa, I declared that some day I would go there."[196] Later of course he does go there, and rehabilitates the gesture in *Heart of Darkness*.

The Western colonialism that O'Brien and Conrad are at such pains to describe is first a penetration *beyond* the European frontier and *into* the heart of another geographical entity, and second, it is specific not to an ahistorical "Western consciousness . . . in relation to the non-Western world" (most African or Indian natives considered their burdens as having less to do with "Western consciousness" than with specific colonial practices like slavery, land expropriation, murderous armed force) but to a laboriously constructed relationship in which France and Britain called themselves "the West" vis-à-vis subservient, lesser peoples in a largely underdeveloped and inert "non-Western world."[197]

The elision and compression in O'Brien's otherwise tough-minded analysis of Camus come as he deals with Camus as individual artist, anguished over difficult choices. Unlike Sartre and Jeanson, for whom, according to O'Brien, the choice to oppose French policy during the Algerian War was fairly easy, Camus was born and brought up in French Algeria, his family remained there after he began to live in France, and his involvement in the struggle with the FLN was a matter of life and death. One can certainly agree with this much of O'Brien's claim. What is less easy to accept is how O'Brien elevates Camus's difficulties to the symbolic rank of "Western consciousness," a receptacle emptied of all but its capacity for sentience and reflection.

O'Brien further rescues Camus from the embarrassment he had put him in by stressing the privilege of his individual experience. With this tactic we are likely to have some sympathy, for whatever the unfortunate collective nature of French colon behavior in Algeria, there is no reason to burden Camus with it; his entirely French upbringing in Algeria (well described in Herbert Lottman's biography)[198] did not prevent him from producing a famous pre-war report on the miseries of the place, most of them due to French colonialism.[199] Here then is a moral man in an immoral situation. And what Camus focusses on is the individual in a social setting: this is as true of L'Etranger as it is of La Peste and La Chute. He prizes self-recognition, disillusioned maturity, and moral steadfastness in the midst of a bad situation.

But three methodological points need to be made. The first is to question and deconstruct Camus's choice of geographical setting for L'Etranger (1942), La Peste (1947), and his extremely interesting group of short stories collected under the title L'Exil et le royaume (1957). Why was Algeria a setting for narratives whose main reference (in the case of the first two) has always been construed as France generally and, more particularly, France under the Nazi Occupation? O'Brien goes further than most in noting that the choice is not innocent, that much in the tales (e.g., Meursault's trial) is either a surreptitious or unconscious justification of French rule or an ideological attempt to prettify it.[200] But in trying to establish a continuity between Camus as an individual artist and French colonialism in Algeria we must ask whether Camus's narratives themselves are connected to, and derive advantages from, earlier and more overtly imperial French narratives. In widening the historical perspective from Camus as an attractively solitary writer of the

1940s and 1950s to include the century-old French presence in Algeria, we can perhaps better understand not just the form and ideological meaning of his narratives, but also the degree to which his work inflects, refers to, consolidates, and renders more precise the nature of the French enterprise there.

A second methodological point concerns the type of evidence necessary for this wider optic, and the related question of who does the interpreting. A European critic of historical bent is likely to believe that Camus represents the tragically immobilized French consciousness of the *European* crisis near one of its great watersheds; although Camus seems to have regarded *colon* implantations as rescuable and extendable past 1960 (the year of his death), he was simply wrong historically, since the French ceded possession of and all claims on Algeria a mere two years later. Insofar as his work clearly alludes to contemporary Algeria, Camus's general concern is the actual state of Franco-Algerian affairs, not their history of dramatic changes in their long-term destiny. Except occasionally, he usually ignores or overlooks the history, which an Algerian for whom the French presence was a *daily* enactment of power would not do. To an Algerian, therefore, 1962 would more likely be seen as the end of a long, unhappy epoch in a history that began when the French arrived in 1830, and as the triumphant inauguration of a new phase. A correlative way of interpreting Camus's novels therefore would be as interventions in the history of French efforts in Algeria, making and keeping it French, not as novels that tell us about their author's state of mind. Camus's incorporations of and assumptions about Algerian history would have to be compared with histories written by Algerians *after* independence, in order to get a fuller sense of the contest between Algerian nationalism and French colonialism. And it would be correct to regard Camus's work as affiliated historically both with the French colonial venture itself (since he assumes it to be immutable) and with outright opposition to Algerian independence. This Algerian perspective may unblock and release aspects hidden, taken for granted, or denied by Camus.

Last, there is a crucial methodological value in detail, patience, insistence where Camus's highly compressed texts are concerned. The tendency is for readers to associate Camus's novels with French novels about France, not only because of their language and the forms they seem to take over from such illustrious antecedents as *Adolphe* and *Trois Contes*, but also because his choice of an Algerian locale seems incidental to the pressing moral issues at hand. Almost half a century after their first appearance, his novels are thus read as parables of the human condition. True, Meursault kills an Arab, but this Arab is not named and seems to be without a history, let alone a mother and father; true also, Arabs die of plague in Oran, but they are not named either, whereas Rieux and Tarrou are pushed forward in the action. One ought to read the texts for the richness of what is there, we are likely to say, not for what if anything has been excluded. But I want to insist that one finds in Camus's novels what they once were thought to have been cleared of—detail about that very distinctly French imperial conquest begun in 1830, continuing during Camus's life, and projecting into the composition of the texts.

This restorative interpretation is not meant vindictively. Nor do I intend after the fact to *blame* Camus for hiding things about Algeria in his fiction that, for example, in the various pieces collected in the *Chroniques algériennes* he was at pains to explain. What I want to do is to see Camus's fiction as an element in France's methodically constructed political geography of Algeria, which took many generations to complete, the better to see it as providing an arresting account of the political and interpretative contest to represent, inhabit, and possess the territory itself—at exactly the time that the British were leaving India. Camus's writing is informed by an extraordinarily belated, in some ways incapacitated colonial sensibility, which enacts an imperial gesture within and by means of a form, the realistic novel, well past its greatest achievements in Europe.

As *locus classicus* I shall use an episode near the end of "La Femme adultère" when Janine, the protagonist, leaves her husband's bedside during a sleepless night in a small hotel in the Algerian countryside. A formerly promising law student, he has become a travelling salesman; after a long and tiring bus journey the couple arrives at their destination, where he makes the rounds of his various Arab clients. During the trip Janine has been impressed with the silent passivity and incomprehensibility of the native Algerians; their presence seems like a barely evident natural fact, scarcely noticed by her in her emotional trouble. When she leaves the hotel and her sleeping husband, Janine encounters the night watchman, who speaks to her in Arabic, a language she appears not to understand. The climax of the story is a remarkable, almost pantheistic communion she has with the sky and the desert. Clearly, I think, Camus's intention is to present the relationship between woman and geography in sexual terms, as an alternative to her now nearly dead relationship with her husband; hence the adultery referred to in the story's title.

> She was turning with them [the drifting stars in a sky "moving in a sort of slow gyration"], and the apparently stationary progress little by little identified her with the core of her being, where cold and desire were now vying with each other. Before her the stars were falling one by one and being snuffed out among the stones of the desert, and each time

Janine opened a little more to the night. Breathing deeply, she forgot the cold, the dead weight of others, the craziness or stuffiness of life, the long anguish of living and dying [le poids des êtres, la vie dementé ou figée, la longue angoisse de vivre et de mourir]. After so many years of mad, aimless fleeing from fear, she had come to a stop at last. At the same time, she seemed to recover her roots and the sap again rose in her against the parapet as she strained toward the moving sky; she was merely waiting for her fluttering heart to calm down and establish silence within her. The last stars of the constellations dropped their clusters a little lower on the desert horizon and became still. Then, with unbearable gentleness, the water of night began to fill Janine, drowned the cold, rose gradually from the hidden core of her being, rising up even to her mouth full of moans [l'eau de la nuit . . . monta peu á peu du centre obscur de son être et deborda en flots ininterrompus jusqu'à sa bouche pleine de gemissements]. The next moment, the whole sky stretched over her, fallen on her back on the cold earth.[201]

The effect is that of a moment out of time in which Janine escapes the sordid narrative of her present life and enters the kingdom of the collection's title; or as Camus put it in a note he wanted to insert in subsequent editions of the collection, "au royaume . . . [qui] coincide avec une certaine vie libre et nue que nous avons à retrouver pour renaître enfin"[202] ("the kingdom . . . [which] coincides with a certain free and bare life and which it is up to us to re-find in order for us finally to be reborn"). Her past and present drop away from her, as does the actuality of other beings (*le poids des êtres*, symptomatically mistranslated as "the dead weight of other people" by Justin O'Brien). In this passage Janine "comes to a stop at last," motionless, fecund, ready for communion with this piece of sky and desert, where (echoing Camus's explanatory note, designed as a later elucidation of the six stories) the woman—*pied noir* and *colon*—discovers her roots. What her real identity is or may be is judged later in the passage when she achieves what is an unmistakably sexual climax: Camus speaks here of the "centre obscur de son être," which suggests both her own sense of obscurity and ignorance, and Camus's as well. Her specific history as a Frenchwoman in Algeria does not matter, for she has achieved a superveningly immediate and direct access to that particular earth and sky.

Each of the stories in *L'Exil et le royaume* (with one exception, a garrulous and unaffecting parable of Parisian artistic life) deals with the exile of people with a non-European history (four tales are set in Algeria, one each in Paris and in Brazil) that is deeply, even threateningly unpleasant, who are trying precariously to achieve a moment of rest, idyllic detachment, poetic self-realization. Only in "La Femme adultère" and in the story set in Brazil, where through sacrifice and commitment a European is received by natives into their circle of intimacy as a substitute for a dead native, is there any suggestion that Camus allowed himself to believe that Europeans might achieve sustained and satisfactory identification with the overseas territory. In "Le Renégat" a missionary is captured by an outcast southern Algerian tribe, has his tongue torn out (an eerie parallel with Paul Bowles's story "A Distant Episode"), and becomes a super-zealous partisan of the tribe, joining in an ambush of French forces. This is as if to say that going native can only be the result of mutilation, which produces a diseased, ultimately unacceptable loss of identity.

A matter of months separates this relatively late (1957) book of stories (the individual publication of each preceded and followed the appearance of *La Chute* in 1956) from the contents of the later pieces in Camus's *Chroniques algériennes,* published in 1958. Although passages in *L'Exil* go back to the earlier lyricism and controlled nostalgia of *Noces,* one of Camus's few atmospheric works about life in Algeria, the stories are filled with anxiety about the gathering crisis. We should bear in mind that the Algerian Revolution was officially announced and launched on November 1, 1954; the Sétif massacres by French troops of Algerian civilians had occurred in May 1945, and the years before that, when Camus was working on *L'Etranger,* were filled with numerous events punctuating Algerian nationalism's long and bloody resistance to the French. Even though Camus grew up in Algeria as a *French* youth, according to all his biographers, he was always surrounded by the signs of Franco-Algerian struggle, most of which he seems to have either evaded or, in his last years, openly translated into the language, imagery, and geographical apprehension of a singular French will contesting Algeria against its native Muslim inhabitants. In 1957 François Mitterrand's book *Presence française et abondon* stated flatly, "Sans Afrique, il n'y aura pas l'histoire de France au XXIe siècle."[203]

To situate Camus *contrapuntally* in most (as opposed to a small part) of his actual history, one must be alert to his true French antecedents, as well as the work of post-independence Algerian novelists, historians, sociologists, political scientists. There remains today a readily decipherable (and persistent) Eurocentric tradition of interpretatively blocking off what Camus (and Mitterrand) blocked off about Algeria, what he and his fictional characters blocked off. When in the last years of his life Camus publicly and even vehemently opposed the nationalist demands put forward for Algerian independence, he did so in the same way he had represented Algeria from the beginning of his artistic career, although now his words resonate depressingly with the accents of official Anglo-French Suez rhetoric. His comments

about "Colonel Nasser," about Arab and Muslim imperialism, are familiar
to us, but the one uncompromisingly severe political statement about Algeria he makes in the text appears as an unadorned political summary of his
previous writing:

> en ce qui concerne l'Algérie, l'independence nationale est une formule
> purement passionnelle. Il n'y a jamais eu encore de nation algérienne.
> Les Juifs, les Turcs, les Grecs, les Italiens, les Berbères, auraient autant
> de droit à reclamer la direction de cette nation virtuelle. Actuellement,
> les Arabes ne forment pas a eux seuls toute l'Algérie. L'importance et
> l'ancienneté du peuplement français, en particulier, suffisent à créer un
> problème qui ne peut se comparer à rien dans l'histoire. Les Français
> d'Algérie sont, eux aussie, et au sens fort du terme, des indigènes. Il faut
> ajouter qu'une Algérie purement arabe ne pourrait accéder a l'in-
> dependence economique sans laquelle l'independence politique n'est
> qu'un leurre. Si insuffisant que soit l'effort français, il est d'une telle
> envergure qu'aucun pays, à l'heure actuelle, ne consentirait à le pren-
> dre en charge."[204]

(As far as Algeria is concerned, national independence is a formula
driven by nothing other than passion. There has never yet been an
Algerian nation. The Jews, Turks, Greeks, Italians, or Berbers would be
as entitled to claim the leadership of this potential nation. As things
stand, the Arabs alone do not comprise the whole of Algeria. The size
and duration of the French settlement, in particular, are enough to
create a problem that cannot be compared to anything else in history.
The French of Algeria are also natives, in the strong sense of the word.
Moreover, a purely Arab Algeria could not achieve that economic
independence without which political independence is nothing but an
illusion. However inadequate the French effort has been, it is of such
proportions that no other country would today agree to take over the
responsibility.)

The irony is that wherever in his novels or descriptive pieces Camus tells
a story, the French presence in Algeria is rendered either as outside narrative, an essence subject to neither time nor interpretation (like Janine), or as
the only history worth being narrated *as history*. (How different in attitude
and tone is Pierre Bourdieu's *Sociologie de l'Algérie*, also published in 1958,
whose analysis refutes Camus's jejune formulae and speaks forthrightly of
colonial war as the result of *two* societies in conflict.) Camus's obduracy
accounts for the blankness and absence of background in the Arab killed by
Meursault; hence also the sense of devastation in Oran that is implicitly

meant to express not mainly the Arab deaths (which, after all, are the ones that matter demographically) but French consciousness.

It is accurate to say, therefore, that Camus's narratives lay severe and ontologically prior claims to Algeria's geography. For anyone who has even a cursory acquaintance with the extended French colonial venture there, these claims are as preposterously anomalous as the declaration in March 1938 by French Minster Chautemps that Arabic was "a foreign language" in Algeria. They are not Camus's alone, although he gave them a semi-transparent and lasting currency. He inherits and uncritically accepts them as conventions shaped in the long tradition of colonial writing on Algeria, forgotten today or unacknowledged by his readers and critics, most of whom find it easier to interpret his work as being about "the human condition."

An excellent index of how many assumptions about French colonies Camus's readers and critics share is given in a remarkable survey of French schoolbooks from World War One to the period right after World War Two by Manuela Semidei. Her findings show a steadily mounting insistence on France's colonial role after World War One, the "glorious episodes" in its history as "a world power," as well as lyrical descriptions of France's colonial achievements, its establishment of peace and prosperity, the various schools and hospitals benefitting the natives, and so forth; occasional references are made to the use of violence, but these are overshadowed by France's wonderful overall aim to eliminate slavery and despotism, replace them with peace and prosperity. North Africa figures prominently, but there is never any acknowledgement, according to Semidei, that the colonies might become independent; nationalistic movements of the 1930s are "difficulties" rather than serious challenges.

Semidei notes that these interwar school texts favorably contrast France's superior colonial rule with Britain's, suggesting that French dominions are ruled without the prejudice and racialism of their British counterparts. By the 1930s this motif is endlessly repeated. When references are made to violence in Algeria, for example, they are couched in such a way as to render French forces having to take such disagreeable measures because of the natives' "ardeur religieuse et par l'attrait du pillage."[205] Now, however, Algeria has become "a new France": prosperous, full of excellent schools, hospitals, and roads. Even after independence, France's colonial history is seen as essentially constructive, laying the foundation for "fraternal" links between it and its former colonies.

Just because only one side of a contest appears relevant to a French audience, or because the full dynamic of colonial implantation and native resistance embarrassingly detracts from the attractive humanism of a major European tradition is no reason to go along with this interpretative current, or to accept the constructions and ideological images. I would go so far as to say that *because* Camus's most famous fiction incorporates, intransigently recapitulates, and in many ways depends on a massive French discourse on Algeria, one that belongs to the language of French imperial attitudes and geographical reference, his work is *more,* not less interesting. His clean style, the anguished moral dilemmas he lays bare, the harrowing personal fates of his characters, which he treats with such fineness and regulated irony— all these draw on and in fact revive the history of French domination in Algeria, with a circumspect precision and a remarkable lack of remorse or compassion.

Once again the interrelationship between geography and the political contest must be reanimated exactly where, in the novels, Camus covers it with a superstructure celebrated by Sartre as providing "a climate of the absurd."[206] Both *L'Etranger* and *La Peste* are about the deaths of Arabs, deaths that highlight and silently inform the French characters' difficulties of conscience and reflection. Moreover, the structure of civil society so vividly presented—the municipality, the legal apparatus, hospitals, restaurants, clubs, entertainments, schools—is French, although in the main it administers the non-French population. The correspondence between how Camus writes about this and how the French schoolbooks do is arresting: the novels and short stories narrate the result of a victory won over a pacified, decimated Muslim population whose rights to the land have been severely curtailed. In thus confirming and consolidating French priority, Camus neither disputes nor dissents from the campaign for sovereignty waged against Algerian Muslims for over a hundred years.

At the center of the contest is the military struggle, whose first great protagonists are Marshall Theodore Bugeaud and the Emir Abdel Kader, the one a ferocious martinet whose patriarchal severity toward the Algerian natives begins in 1836 as an effort at discipline and ends a decade or so later with a policy of genocide and massive territorial expropriation; the other is a Sufi mystic and relentless guerilla fighter, endlessly regrouping, reforming, rededicating his troops against a stronger, more modern invading enemy. To read the documents of the time—whether Bugeaud's letters, proclamations, and dispatches (compiled and published at about the same time as *L'Etranger*), or a recent edition of Abdel Qader's Sufi poetry (edited and translated into French by Michel Chodkiewicz),[207] or a remarkable portrait of the psychology of the conquest reconstructed from French diaries and letters of the 1830s and 1840s by Mostafa Lacheraf, senior member of the FLN and post-independence professor at the University of Algiers[208]—is to perceive the dynamic that makes Camus's diminishment of the Arab presence inevitable.

The core of French military policy as Bugeaud and his officers articulated it was the *razzia,* or punitive raid on Algerians' villages, their homes, harvests, women and children. "The Arabs," said Bugeaud, "must be prevented from sowing, from harvesting, and from pasturing their flocks."[209] Lacheraf gives a sampling of the poetic exhilaration recorded time after time by the French officers at their work, their sense that here at last was an opportunity for *guerre à outrance* beyond all morality or need. General Changarnier, for instance, describes a pleasant distraction vouchsafed his troops in raiding peaceful villages; this type of activity is taught by the scriptures, he says, in which Joshua and other great leaders conducted "de bien terribles *razzias,*" and were blessed by God. Ruin, total destruction, uncompromising brutality are condoned not only because legitimized by God but because, in words echoed and re-echoed from Bugeaud to Salan, "les Arabes ne comprennent que la force brutale."[210]

Lacheraf comments that the French military effort in the first decades went well beyond its object—the suppression of Algerian resistance—and attained the absolute status of an ideal.[211] Its other side, as expressed with tireless zeal by Bugeaud himself, was colonization. Toward the end of his stay in Algeria, he is constantly exasperated by the way in which European civilian emigrants are using up the resources of Algeria without restraint or reason; leave colonization to the military, he writes in his letters, but to no avail.[212]

As it happens, one of the quiet themes running through French fiction from Balzac to Psichari and Loti is precisely this abuse of Algeria and the scandals deriving from shady financial schemes operated by unscrupulous individuals for whom the openness of the place permitted nearly every conceivable thing to be done if profit could be promised or expected. Unforgettable portraits of this state of affairs can be found in Daudet's *Tartarin de Tarascon* and Maupassant's *Bel-Ami* (both of which are referred to in Martine Loutfi's perspicacious *Littérature et colonialisme*).[213]

The destruction wrought upon Algeria by the French was systematic on the one hand, and constitutive of a new French polity on the other. About this no contemporary witness between 1840 and 1870 was in doubt. Some, like Tocqueville, who sternly criticized American policy toward Blacks and native Indians, believed that the advance of European civilization necessitated inflicting cruelties on the Muslim *indigènes:* in his view, total conquest became equivalent to French greatness. He considered Islam synonymous with "polygamy, the isolation of women, the absence of all political life, a tyrannical and omnipresent government which forces men to conceal themselves and to seek all their satisfactions in family life."[214] And because he thought the natives were nomadic, he believed "that all means of desolating these tribes ought to be used. I make an exception only in case of what is interdicted by international law and that of humanity." But, as Melvin Richter comments, Tocqueville said nothing "in 1846 when it was revealed that hundreds of Arabs had been smoked to death in the course of the *razzias* he had approved for their humane quality."[215] "Unfortunate necessities," Tocqueville thought, but nowhere near as important as the "good government" owed the "half-civilized" Muslims by French government.

To today's leading North African historian, Abdullah Laroui, French colonial policy intended nothing less than to destroy the Algerian state, such as it was. Clearly Camus's declaration that an Algerian nation never existed presumed that the ravages of French policy had wiped the slate clean. Nevertheless, as I have been saying, post-colonial events impose upon us both a longer narrative and a more inclusive and demystifying interpretation. Laroui says:

> The history of Algeria from 1830 to 1870 is made up of pretenses: the colons who allegedly wished to transform the Algerians into men like themselves, when in reality their only desire was to transform the soil of Algeria into French soil; the military, who supposedly respected the local traditions and way of life, whereas in reality their only interest was to govern with the least possible effort; the claim of Napoleon III that he was building an Arab kingdom, whereas his central ideas were the "Americanization" of the French economy and the French colonization of Algeria.[216]

When he arrives in Algeria in 1872, Daudet's Tartarin sees few traces of "the Orient" that had been promised him, and finds himself instead in an overseas copy of his native Tarascon. For writers like Segalen and Gide, Algeria is an exotic locale in which their own spiritual problems—like Janine's—can be addressed and therapeutically treated. Scant attention is paid to the natives, whose purpose is routinely to provide transient thrills or opportunities for exercises of will—not only Michel in *L'Immoraliste* but also Malraux's protagonist Perken in the Cambodian setting of *La Voie royale*. Differences in French representations of Algeria, whether they are the crude harem postcards studied so memorably by Malek Alloula,[217] or the sophisticated anthropological constructions unearthed by Fanny Colonna and Claude Brahimi,[218] or the impressive narrative structures of which Camus's works furnish so important an example, can all be traced back to the geographical *morte-main* of French colonial practice.

How deeply felt, consistently replenished, incorporated, and institutionalized an enterprise is French discourse we can further discover in early-twentieth-century works of geography and colonial thought. Albert Sarraut's *Grandeur et servitude coloniales* states no less a goal for colonialism than the biological unity of mankind, "la solidarité humaine." Races incapable of utilizing their resources (e.g., natives in France's overseas territories) are to be brought back to the human family; "c'est là pour le colonisateur, la contre-partie formelle de la prise de possession; elle enlève a son acte le caractère de spoliation; elle en fait une creation de droit humain"[219] ("Here, for the colonizer, is the formal counterpart of the act of possession; it removes from the act its character of plunder and makes it a creation of human law"). In his classic *La Politique coloniale et le partage du terre aux XIXe et XXe siècles,* Georges Hardy ventures to argue that the assimilation of colonies to France "a fait jaillir des sources d'inspiration et non seulement provoque l'apparition d'innombrables romans coloniaux, mais encore ouvert les esprits à la diversité des formes morales et mentales, incite les ecrivains à des genres inédits d'exploration psychologique"[220] ("caused inspiration to burst forth and not only led to the appearance of numerous colonial novels but also opened minds to the diversity of moral and mental forms, encouraging writers to adopt new modes of psychological exploration"). Hardy's book was published in 1937; Rector of the Academy of Algiers, he was also honorary director of the Ecole Coloniale and, in his uncannily declarative phrases, an immediate forerunner of Camus.

Camus's novels and stories thus very precisely distill the traditions, idioms, and discursive strategies of France's appropriation of Algeria. He gives its most exquisite articulation, its final evolution to this massive "structure of feeling." But to discern this structure, we must consider Camus's works as a metropolitan transfiguration of the colonial dilemma: they represent the *colon* writing for a French audience whose personal history is tied irrevocably to this southern department of France; a history taking place anywhere else is unintelligible. Yet the ceremonies of bonding with the territory— enacted by Meursault in Algiers, Tarrou and Rieux enfolded within the walls of Oran, Janine during a Saharan vigil—ironically stimulate queries in the reader about the need for such affirmations. When the violence of the French past is thus inadvertently recalled, these ceremonies become foreshortened, highly compressed commemorations of survival, that of a community with nowhere to go.

Meursault's predicament is more radical than the others'. For even if we assume that the falsely constituted law court (as Conor Cruise O'Brien rightly says, a most unlikely place to try a Frenchman for killing an Arab) has a continuing existence, Meursault himself understands the finality; at last he can experience relief and defiance together: "J'avais eu raison, j'avais encore raison, j'avais toujours raison. J'avais vécu de telle façon et j'aurais pu vivre de telle autre. J'avais fait ceci et je n'avais pas fait cela. Je n'avais pas fait cette autre. Et après? C'était comme si j'avais attendu pendant tout le temps cette minute et cette petite aube ou je serais justifié."[221] ("I had been right. I was again right, I was still right. I had lived like this and could have lived like that. I had done this and had not done that. I had not done that other thing. And so? It was as if I had all along been waiting for this moment and this daybreak when I would be vindicated.")

There are no choices left here, no alternatives, no humane substitutes. The *colon* embodies both the real human effort his community contributed and the obstacle of refusing to give up a systematically unjust political system. The deeply conflicted strength of Meursault's suicidal self-acknowledgement can have emerged only out of *that* specific history and in *that* specific community. At the end, he accepts what he is and yet also understands why his mother, confined to an old persons' home, has decided to remarry: "elle avait joué à recommencer.... Si près de la mort, maman devait s'y sentir libre et prête à tout revivre."[222] ("She had played at starting again. ... So close to death, Mother had to feel free and ready to live everything again.") We have done what we have done here, and so let us do it again. This tragically unsentimental obduracy turns into the unflinching human capacity for renewed generation and regeneration. Camus's readers have imputed to *L'Etranger* the universality of a liberated existential humanity facing cosmic indifference and human cruelty with impudent stoicism.

To resituate *L'Etranger* in the geographical nexus from which its narrative trajectory emerges is to interpret it as a heightened form of historical experience. Like Orwell's work and status in England, Camus's plain style and unadorned reporting of social situations conceal rivetingly complex contradictions, contradictions unresolvable by rendering, as critics have done, his feelings of loyalty to French Algeria as a parable of the human condition. This is what his social and literary reputation still depends on. Yet because there was always the more difficult and challenging alternative of first judging, then refusing France's territorial seizure and political sovereignty, blocking as it did a compassionate, shared understanding of Algerian nationalism, Camus's limitations seem unacceptably paralyzing. Counterpoised with the decolonizing literature of the time, whether French or Arab—Germaine Tillion, Kateb Yacine, Fanon, or Genet—Camus's narratives have a negative vitality, in which the tragic human seriousness of the colonial effort achieves its last great clarification before ruin overtakes it. They express a waste and sadness we have still not completely understood or recovered from.

(VIII)

A Note on Modernism

N o vision, any more than any social system, has total hegemony over
its domain. In studying cultural texts that happily co-existed with or
lent support to the global enterprises of European and American empire, one
is not indicting them wholesale or suggesting that they are less interesting
as art for being in complex ways part of the imperialist undertaking. My
account here speaks of *largely* unopposed and undeterred will to overseas
dominion, not of a *completely* unopposed one. We ought to be impressed with
how, by the end of the nineteenth century, colonial lobbies in Europe, for
instance, could whether by cabal or by popular support press the nation into
more scrambling for land and more natives being compelled into imperial
service, with little at home to stop or inhibit the process. Yet there are always
resistances, however ineffective. Imperialism not only is a relationship of
domination but also is committed to a specific ideology of expansion; as
Seeley to his credit recognized, expansion was more than an inclination, "it
is evidently the great fact of modern English history."[223] Admiral Mahan in
the United States and Leroy-Beaulieu in France made similar claims. And
expansion could occur with such stunning results only because there was
power—power military, economic, political, *and* cultural—enough for the
task in Europe and America.

Once the basic fact of European and Western control over the non-
Western world was taken as fact, as inevitable, much complex and, I would
add, antinomian cultural discussion began to occur with noticeably greater
frequency. This did not immediately disturb the sense of sovereign permanence and irreversible presence, but it did lead to an extremely important
mode of cultural practice in Western society, which played an interesting
part in the development of anti-imperialist resistance in the colonies.

Readers of Albert O. Hirschman's *The Passions and the Interests* will recall
that he describes the intellectual debate accompanying European economic
expansion as proceeding from—and then consolidating—the argument that
human *passion* should give way to *interests* as a method for governing the
world. When this argument had triumphed, by the late eighteenth century,
it became a target of opportunity for those Romantics who saw in an
interest-centered world a symbol for the dull, uninteresting, and selfish
situation they had inherited from prior generations.[224]

Let us extend Hirschman's method to the question of imperialism. By the late nineteenth century England's empire was pre-eminent in the world and the cultural argument for empire was triumphing. The empire was a real thing, after all, and, as Seeley told his audience, "We in Europe ... are pretty well agreed that the treasure of truth which forms the nucleus of the civilization of the West is incomparably more sterling not only than the Brahmanic mysticism with which it has to contend, but even than the Roman enlightenment which the old Empire transmitted to the nations of Europe."[225]

At the center of this remarkably confident statement are two somewhat recalcitrant realities that Seeley deftly incorporates and also dismisses: one is the contending native (the Brahmanic mystic himself), the second is the existence of other empires, past as well as present. In both, Seeley allusively records the paradoxical consequences of imperialism's triumphs and then passes on to other subjects. For once imperialism, like the doctrine of interests, had become the settled norm in political ideas about Europe's world-wide destiny, then, ironically, the allure of its opponents, the intransigence of its subjugated classes, the resistance to its irresistible sway were clarified and heightened. Seeley deals with these matters as a realist, not as a poet who might wish to make of the one a noble or romantic presence, or of the other a base and immoral competitor. Nor does he attempt a revisionist account in the manner of Hobson (whose book on imperialism is a dissenting counterpart).

Let me now jump abruptly back to the realistic novel with which I have been much concerned in this chapter. Its central theme by the late nineteenth century was disenchantment, or what Lukacs called ironic disillusion. Tragically or sometimes comically blocked protagonists are brusquely and often rudely awakened by the novel's action to the discrepancy between their illusory expectations and the social realities. Hardy's Jude, George Eliot's Dorothea, Flaubert's Frédéric, Zola's Nana, Butler's Ernest, James's Isabel, Gissing's Reardon, Meredith's Feverel—the list is very long. Into this narrative of loss and disablement is gradually interjected an alternative—not only the novel of frank exoticism and confident empire, but travel narratives, works of colonial exploration and scholarship, memoirs, experience and expertise. In Dr. Livingstone's personal narratives and Haggard's *She,* Kipling's Raj, Loti's *Le Roman d'un Spahi,* and most of Jules Verne's adventures, we discern a new narrative progression and triumphalism. Almost without exception these narratives, and literally hundreds like them based on the exhilaration and interest of adventure in the colonial world, far from casting doubt on the imperial undertaking, serve to confirm and celebrate its success. Explorers find what they are looking for, adventurers return home safe and wealthier, and even the chastened Kim is drafted into the Great Game.

As against this optimism, affirmation, and serene confidence, Conrad's narratives—to which I have so often referred because more than anyone else he tackled the subtle cultural reinforcements and manifestations of empire—radiate an extreme, unsettling anxiety: they react to the triumph of empire the way Hirschman says that romantics responded to the triumph of an interest-centered view of the world. Conrad's tales and novels in one sense reproduce the aggressive contours of the high imperialist undertaking, but in another sense they are infected with the easily recognizable, ironic awareness of the post-realist modernist sensibility. Conrad, Forster, Malraux, T. E. Lawrence take narrative from the triumphalist experience of imperialism into the extremes of self-consciousness, discontinuity, self-referentiality, and corrosive irony, whose formal patterns we have come to recognize as the hallmarks of modernist culture, a culture that also embraces the major work of Joyce, T. S. Eliot, Proust, Mann, and Yeats. I would like to suggest that many of the most prominent characteristics of modernist culture, which we have tended to derive from purely internal dynamics in Western society and culture, include a response to the external pressures on culture from the *imperium*. Certainly this is true of Conrad's entire *oeuvre*, and it is also true of Forster's, T. E. Lawrence's, Malraux's; in different ways, the impingements of empire on an Irish sensibility are registered in Yeats and Joyce, those on American expatriates in the work of Eliot and Pound.

In Mann's great fable of the alliance between creativity and disease— *Death in Venice*—the plague that infects Europe is Asiatic in origin; the combination of dread and promise, of degeneration and desire, so effectively rendered by Aschenbach's psychology is Mann's way of suggesting, I believe, that Europe, its art, mind, monuments, is no longer invulnerable, no longer able to ignore its ties to its overseas domains. Similarly Joyce, for whom the Irish nationalist and intellectual Stephen Dedalus is ironically fortified not by Irish Catholic comrades but by the wandering Jew Leopold Bloom, whose exoticism and cosmopolitan skills undercut the morbid solemnity of Stephen's rebellion. Like the fascinating inverts of Proust's novel, Bloom testifies to a new presence within Europe, a presence rather strikingly described in terms unmistakably taken from the exotic annals of overseas discovery, conquest, vision. Only now instead of being *out there*, they are *here*, as troubling as the primitive rhythms of the *Sacre du printemps* or the African icons in Picasso's art.

The formal dislocations and displacements in modernist culture, and most strikingly its pervasive irony, are influenced by precisely those two disturbing factors Seeley mentions as a consequence of imperialism: the contending native and the fact of other empires. Along with "the old men" who ruin and hijack his great adventure, Lawrence's Arabs in *The Seven Pillars of Wisdom* require his sad and dissatisfied acknowledgement, just as imperial France and Turkey do; in *A Passage to India*, it is Forster's great achievement to show with remarkable precision (and discomfort) how the moral drama of contemporary Indian mysticism and nationalism—Godbole and Aziz—unfolds against the older clash between the British and Mogul empires. In Loti's *L'Inde (sans les Anglais)* we read a travel narrative based on a journey across India in which the ruling English are deliberately, even spitefully, not once mentioned,[226] as if to suggest that *only* the natives are to be seen, whereas of course India was an exclusively British (and certainly not a French) possession.

I venture the suggestion that when European culture finally began to take due account of imperial "delusions and discoveries"—in Benita Parry's fine phrase for the Anglo-Indian cultural encounter[227]—it did so not oppositionally but ironically, and with a desperate attempt at a new inclusiveness. It was as if having for centuries comprehended empire as a fact of national destiny to be either taken for granted or celebrated, consolidated, and enhanced, members of the dominant European cultures now began to look abroad with the skepticism and confusion of people surprised, perhaps even shocked by what they saw. Cultural texts imported the foreign into Europe in ways that very clearly bear the mark of the imperial enterprise, of explorers and ethnographers, geologists and geographers, merchants and soldiers. At first they stimulated the interest of European audiences; by the beginning of the twentieth century, they were used to convey an ironic sense of how vulnerable Europe was, and how—in Conrad's great phrase—"this also has been one of the dark places on the earth."

To deal with this, a new encyclopedic form became necessary, one that had three distinctive features. First was a circularity of structure, inclusive and open at the same time: *Ulysses, Heart of Darkness, A la recherche, The Waste Land, Cantos, To the Lighthouse*. Second was a novelty based almost entirely on the reformulation of old, even outdated fragments drawn self-consciously from disparate locations, sources, cultures: the hallmark of modernist form is the strange juxtaposition of comic and tragic, high and low, commonplace and exotic, familiar and alien whose most ingenious resolution is Joyce's fusing of the *Odyssey* with the Wandering Jew, advertising and Virgil (or Dante), perfect symmetry and the salesman's catalogue. Third is the irony of a form that draws attention to itself as substituting art and its creations for the once-possible synthesis of the world empires. When you can no longer assume that Britannia will rule the waves forever, you have to reconceive reality as something that can be held together by you the artist, in history rather than in geography. Spatiality becomes, ironically, the characteristic of an aesthetic rather than of political domination, as more and more regions—from India to Africa to the Caribbean—challenge the classical empires and their cultures.

CHAPTER THREE

RESISTANCE AND OPPOSITION

lie moi de tes vastes bras à l'argile lumineuse

AIMÉ CÉSAIRE, *Cahier d'un retour au pays natal*

(I)

There Are Two Sides

A standard topic in the history of ideas and the study of cultures is that constellation of relationships that can be collected under the general heading of "influence." I began this book by invoking Eliot's famous essay "Tradition and the Individual Talent" as a way of introducing the matter of influence in its most basic, even abstract form: the connection between the present and the pastness (or not) of the past, a connection which as Eliot discusses it includes the relationship between an individual writer and the tradition of which he or she is a part. I suggested that studying the relationship between the "West" and its dominated cultural "others" is not just a way of understanding an unequal relationship between unequal interlocutors, but also a point of entry into studying the formation and meaning of Western cultural practices themselves. And the persistent disparity in power between the West and non-West must be taken into account if we are accurately to understand cultural forms like that of the novel, of ethnographic and historical discourse, certain kinds of poetry and opera, where allusions to and structures based on this disparity abound. I went on to argue that when supposedly otherwise neutral departments of culture like literature and critical theory converge upon the weaker or subordinate culture and interpret it with ideas of unchanging non-European and European essences, narratives about geographical possession, and images of legitimacy and redemption, the striking consequence has been to disguise the power situation and to conceal how much the experience of the stronger party overlaps with and, strangely, depends on the weaker.

An instance of this is found in Gide's *L'Immoraliste* (1902), usually read as the story of a man who comes to terms with his eccentric sexuality by allowing it to strip him not only of his wife, Marceline, and career, but paradoxically of his will. Michel is a philologist whose academic research into Europe's barbarian past reveals to him his own suppressed instincts, longings, proclivities. As with Thomas Mann's *Death in Venice,* the setting is representative of an exotic locale at or just beyond the boundaries of Europe; a major locale for the action of *L'Immoraliste* is French Algeria, a place of deserts, languorous oases, amoral native boys and girls. Michel's Nietzchean mentor, Ménalque, is straightforwardly described as a colonial official, and although he is straight out of an imperial world recognizable to readers of T. E. Lawrence or Malraux, his sybaritic and epicurean presence is quite Gidean. Ménalque (more than Michel) derives knowledge and also pleasure from his life of "obscure expeditions," sensual indulgence, and anti-domestic freedom. "La vie, le moindre geste de Ménalque," reflects Michel, as he compares his course of academic lectures with the flamboyant imperialist, "n'etait-il pas plus eloquent mille fois que mon cours?"[1]

What first connects the two men, however, is neither ideas nor life histories but the confessions of Moktir, a native boy in Biskra (to which Gide returned in book after book), who tells Ménalque how he watched Michel spying on him in the act of stealing Marceline's scissors. The homosexual complicity among the three is an unmistakably hierarchical relationship: Moktir, the African boy, gives a surreptitious thrill to Michel, his employer, which in turn is a step along the way to his self-knowledge, in which Ménalque's superior insights guide him. What Moktir thinks or feels (which seems congenitally, if not also racially, mischievous) is far less important than what Michel and Ménalque make of the experience. Gide explicitly connects Michel's self-knowledge with his experiences of Algeria, which are causally related to the death of his wife, his intellectual reorientation, and his final, rather pathetic bisexual forlornness.

Speaking of French North Africa—it is Tunisia he has in mind—Michel offers the following *aperçus:*

This land of pleasure satisfies without calming desire; indeed, every satisfaction merely exalts it.

A land liberated from works of art. I despise those who can acknowledge beauty only when it's already transcribed, interpreted. One thing admirable about the Arabs: they live their art, they sing and scatter it from day to day; they don't cling to it, they don't enbalm it in *works.*

Which is the cause and the effect of the absence of great artists.... Just as I was returning to the hotel, I remembered a group of Arabs I had noticed lying in the open air on the mats of a little café. I went and slept among them. I returned covered with vermin.[2]

The people of Africa, and especially those Arabs, are just there; they have no accumulating art or history that is sedimented into works. Were it not for the European observer who attests to its existence, it would not matter. To be among those people is pleasurable, but one needs to accept its risks (the vermin, for example).

L'Immoraliste has an additionally problematic dimension in that its first-person narration—Michel tells his own story—heavily depends on a number of inclusions he makes: through him come the North Africans, come his wife and Ménalque. Michel is a prosperous Normandy landowner, a scholar, and a Protestant—suggesting that Gide intends multiple sides of personality, able to negotiate the travails of both selfhood and worldliness. All of these aspects in the final analysis depend on what Michel discovers about himself in Africa, yet his self-discovery is limited by transitoriness and transparency, and unvalued. Once again, the narrative has a "structure of attitude and reference" that entitles the European authorial subject to hold on to an overseas territory, derive benefits from it, depend on it, but ultimately refuse it autonomy or independence.

Gide is a special case—treating in his North African works relatively restricted material: Islamic, Arab, homosexual. But although the instance of a highly individualistic artist, Gide's relationship to Africa belongs to a larger formation of European attitudes and practices toward the continent, out of which emerged what late-twentieth-century critics have called Africanism, or Africanist discourse, a systematic language for dealing with and studying Africa *for* the West.[3] Conceptions of primitivism are associated with it, as well as concepts deriving a special epistemological privilege from the African provenance, such as tribalism, vitalism, originality. We can see these obligingly serviceable concepts at work in Conrad and Isak Dinesen, as well as, later, in the audacious scholarship of Leo Frobenius, the German anthropologist who claimed to have discovered the perfect order of the African system, and Placide Tempels, the Belgian missionary whose book *Bantu Philosophy* proposed an essentialist (and reductive) vitality at the heart of African philosophy. So productive and adaptable was this notion of African identity that it could be used by Western missionaries, then anthropologists, then Marxist historians, then, antagonistically, even liberation movements, as V. Y. Mudimbe has shown in his remarkable *The Invention of Africa* (1988), the history of what he calls an African *gnosis*.[4]

The general cultural situation obtaining between the West and its overseas *imperium* until the modern period, especially the period around World
War One, conformed to this kind of pattern. Since my enormous topic can
best be dealt with at this stage by alternating general with very specific and
local studies, my purpose here is to sketch the interacting experience that
links imperializers with the imperialized. The study of the relationship
between culture and imperialism at this quite early stage of development
needs neither simple chronological nor simple anecdotal narrative (a fair
number of these already exist in separate fields), but an attempt at a globalized (not total) description. And of course any study of the connection
between culture and empire is itself an integral part of the topic, part of what
George Eliot in another connection called the same embroiled medium—
rather than a discourse written from a distant, and disengaged perspective.
The emergence of almost a hundred new decolonized post-colonial states
after 1945 is not a neutral fact, but one to which, in discussions of it, scholars,
historians, activists have been either for or against.

Exactly as in its triumphant period imperialism tended to license only a
cultural discourse that was formulated from within it, today post-imperial-
ism has permitted mainly a cultural discourse of suspicion on the part of
formerly colonized peoples, and of theoretical avoidance at most on the part
of metropolitan intellectuals. I find myself caught between the two, as many
of us are who were brought up during the period when the classical colonial
empires were dismantled. We belong to the period both of colonialism and
of resistance to it; yet we also belong to a period of surpassing theoretical
elaboration, of the universalizing techniques of deconstruction, structuralism, and Lukacsian and Althusserian Marxism. My homemade resolution of
the antitheses between involvement and theory has been a broad perspective
from which one could view both culture and imperialism and from which
the large historical dialectic between one and the other might be observed
even though its myriad details cannot be except occasionally. I shall proceed
on the assumption that whereas the whole of a culture is a disjunct one,
many important sectors of it can be apprehended as working *contrapuntally*
together.

Here I am especially concerned with the extraordinary, almost Coperni-
can change in the relationship between Western culture and the empire
during the early years of this century. It is useful to see this change as similar
in scope and significance to two earlier ones: the rediscovery of Greece
during the humanistic period of the European Renaissance; and the "Oriental Renaissance"—so called by its great modern historian Raymond
Schwab[5]—from the late eighteenth to the middle nineteenth century, when
the cultural riches of India, China, Japan, Persia, and Islam were firmly

deposited at the heart of European culture. The second, what Schwab calls Europe's magnificent appropriation of the Orient—the discoveries of Sanskrit by German and French grammarians, of the great Indian national epics by English, German, and French poets and artists, of Persian imagery and Sufi philosophy by many European and even American thinkers from Goethe to Emerson—was one of the most splendid episodes in the history of the human adventure, and a subject sufficient unto itself.

The missing dimension in Schwab's narrative is the political one, much sadder and less edifying than the cultural one. As I have argued in *Orientalism,* the net effect of cultural exchange between partners conscious of inequality is that the people suffer. The Greek classics served the Italian, French, and English humanists without the troublesome interposition of actual Greeks. Texts by dead people were read, appreciated, and appropriated by people who imagined an ideal commonwealth. This is one reason that scholars rarely speak suspiciously or disparagingly of the Renaissance. In modern times, however, thinking about cultural exchange involves thinking about domination and forcible appropriation: someone loses, someone gains. Today, for example, discussions of American history are increasingly interrogations of that history for what it did to native peoples, immigrant populations, oppressed minorities.

But only recently have Westerners become aware that what they have to say about the history and the cultures of "subordinate" peoples is challengeable by the people themselves, people who a few years back were simply incorporated, culture, land, history, and all, into the great Western empires, and their disciplinary discourses. (This is not to denigrate the accomplishments of many Western scholars, historians, artists, philosophers, musicians, and missionaries, whose corporate and individual efforts in making known the world beyond Europe are a stunning achievement.)

An immense wave of anti-colonial and ultimately anti-imperial activity, thought, and revision has overtaken the massive edifice of Western empire, challenging it, to use Gramsci's vivid metaphor, in a mutual siege. For the first time Westerners have been required to confront themselves not simply as the Raj but as representatives of a culture and even of races accused of crimes—crimes of violence, crimes of suppression, crimes of conscience. "Today," says Fanon in *The Wretched of the Earth* (1961), "the Third World . . . faces Europe like a colossal mass whose aim should be to try to resolve the problems to which Europe has not been able to find the answers."[6] Such accusations had of course been made before, even by such intrepid Europeans as Samuel Johnson and W. S. Blunt. Right across the non-European world there had been earlier colonial uprisings, from the San Domingo revolution and the Abdul Kader insurrection to the 1857 Rebellion, the Orabi

Revolt, and the Boxer Rebellion. There had been reprisals, changes of regime, *causes célèbres,* debates, reforms, and reappraisals. All along, though, the empires increased in size and profit. The new situation was a sustained confrontation of, and systematic resistance to, the Empire *as West.* Long-simmering resentments against the white man from the Pacific to the Atlantic sprang into fully fledged independence movements. Pan-African and Pan-Asian militants emerged who could not be stopped.

The militant groups between the two world wars were not clearly or completely anti-West. Some believed that relief from colonialism could come by working with Christianity; others believed that westernization was the solution. In Africa these between-the-wars efforts were represented, according to Basil Davidson, by such people as Herbert Macaulay, Leopold Senghor, J. H. Casely Hayford, Samuel Ahuma;[7] in the Arab world during this period Saad Zaghloul, Nuri as-Said, Bishara al-Khoury were counterparts. Even later revolutionary leaders—Ho Chi Minh in Vietnam, for example—originally held the view that aspects of Western culture could be helpful in ending colonialism. But their efforts and ideas received little response in the metropole, and in time their resistance was transformed.

For if colonialism was a system, as Sartre was to say in one of his post-war essays, then resistance began to feel systematic too.[8] Someone like Sartre could say, in the opening sentences of his preface to Fanon's *The Wretched of the Earth* (1961), that the world was really two warring factions, "five hundred million men and one thousand five hundred million natives. The former had the Word; the others had the use of it.... In the colonies the truth stood naked, but the citizens of the mother country preferred it with clothes on."[9] Davidson puts the case for the new African response with his usual eloquent perspicacity:

> History ... is not a calculating machine. It unfolds in the mind and the imagination and takes body in the multifarious responses of a people's culture itself the infinitely subtle mediation of material realities, of underpinning economic facts, of gritty objectivities. African cultural responses after 1945 were as varied as one might expect from so many peoples and perceived interests. But they were above all inspired by a vivid hope of change, scarcely present before, certainly never before felt with any such intensity or wide appeal; and they were spoken by men and women whose hearts beat to a brave music. These were the responses that moved African history into a new course.[10]

The sense for Europeans of a tremendous and disorienting change in perspective in the West–non-West relationship was entirely new, experienced neither in the European Renaissance nor in the "discovery" of the Orient three centuries later. Think of the differences between Poliziano's recovery and editing of Greek classics in the 1460s, or Bopp and Schlegel reading Sanskrit grammarians in the 1810s, and a French political theorist or Orientalist reading Fanon during the Algerian War in 1961, or Césaire's *Discours sur le colonialisme* when it appeared in 1955 just after the French defeat at Dien Bien Phu. Not only is this last unfortunate fellow addressed by natives while his army is engaged by them, as neither of his predecessors were, but he is reading a text in the language of Bossuet and Chateaubriand, using concepts of Hegel, Marx, and Freud to incriminate the very civilization producing all of them. Fanon goes still further when he reverses the hitherto accepted paradigm by which Europe gave the colonies their modernity and argues instead that not only were "the well-being and the progress of Europe . . . built up with the sweat and the dead bodies of Negroes, Arabs, Indians, and the yellow races"[11] but "Europe is literally the creation of the Third World,"[12] a charge to be made again and again by Walter Rodney, Chinweizu, and others. Concluding this preposterous reordering of things, we find Sartre echoing Fanon (instead of the other way around) when he says, "There is nothing more consistent than a racist humanism, since the European has only been able to become a man through creating slaves and monsters."[13]

World War One did nothing to lessen the Western hold on colonial territories, because the West needed those territories to furnish Europe with manpower and resources for a war of little direct concern for Africans and Asians.[14] Yet the processes that resulted in independence after World War Two were already under way. The question of dating the resistance to imperialism in subject territories is crucial to both sides in how imperialism is seen. For the successful nationalist parties that led the struggle against the European powers, legitimacy and cultural primacy depend on their asserting an unbroken continuity leading to the first warriors who stood against the intrusive white man. Thus the Algerian National Liberation Front which inaugurated its insurrection against France in 1954 traced its ancestry to the Emir Abdel Kader, who fought the French occupation during the 1830s and 1840s. In Guinea and Mali resistance against the French is traced back generations to Samory and Hajji Omar.[15] But only occasionally did scribes of empire recognize the validity of these resistances; as we saw in our discussion of Kipling, numerous attenuating rationalizations of the native presence ("they" were really happy until roused by troublemakers, for example) were preferred to the rather more simple reason for dissatisfaction, that the natives wished for relief from the European presence in their land.

The debate continues until today among historians in Europe and the

United States. Were those early "prophets of rebellion," as Michael Adas has called them, backward-looking, romantic, and unrealistic people who acted negatively against the "modernizing" Europeans,[16] or are we to take seriously the statements of their modern heirs—for example, Julius Nyerere and Nelson Mandela—as to the continuing significance of their early, usually doomed efforts? Terence Ranger has shown that these are matters not simply of academic speculation, but of urgent political moment. Many of the resistance movements, for instance, "shaped the environment in which later politics developed; . . . resistance had profound effects upon white policies and attitudes; . . . during the course of the resistances, or some of them, types of political organization or inspiration emerged which looked in important ways to the future; which in some cases are directly and in others indirectly linked with later manifestations of African opposition [to European imperialism]."[17] Ranger demonstrates that the intellectual and moral battle over the continuity and coherence of nationalist resistance to imperialism went on for dozens of years, and became an organic part of the imperial experience. If, as an African or Arab, you choose to remember the Ndebele-Shona and Orabi uprisings of 1896–97 and 1882, respectively, you honor nationalist leaderships whose *failures* enabled later success; it is likely that Europeans will interpret these uprisings more disparagingly, as the work of cliques, or of crazy millenarians, and so forth.

Then, stunningly, by and large the entire world was decolonized after World War Two. Grimal's study includes a map of the British empire at its height: it is compelling evidence both of how vast its possessions were and of how more or less completely it lost them in a matter of years after war's end in 1945. John Strachey's well-known book *The End of Empire* (1959), commemorates the loss definitively. From London, British statesmen, soldiers, merchants, scholars, educators, missionaries, bureaucrats, and spies had decisive responsibility for Australia, New Zealand, Hong Kong, New Guinea, Ceylon, Malaya, all of the Asian subcontinent, most of the Middle East, all of East Africa from Egypt to South Africa, a big chunk of Central West Africa (including Nigeria), Guiana, some of the Caribbean islands, Ireland, and Canada.

Decidedly smaller than Britain's, France's empire comprised a mass of islands in the Pacific and Indian oceans as well as the Caribbean (Madagascar, New Caledonia, Tahiti, Guadeloupe, etc.), Guiana, and all of Indochina (Annan, Cambodia, Cochin China, Laos, and Tonkin); in Africa, France seriously vied with Britain for supremacy—most of the western half of the continent from the Mediterranean to the Equator was in French hands, as well as French Somaliland. In addition, there were Syria and Lebanon, which, like so many of France's African and Asian colonies, encroached on

British routes and territories. Lord Cromer, one of the most famously redoubtable of British imperial proconsuls (as he once rather haughtily put it, "We do not govern Egypt, we only govern the governors of Egypt"),[18] who had distinguished service in India before he ruled Egypt almost single-handedly between 1883 and 1907, often spoke irritatedly of the "flighty" French influence in British colonies.

For these immense territories (and those of Belgium, Holland, Spain, Portugal, Germany) the metropolitan Western cultures devised huge investments and strategies. Very few people in Britain or France seemed to think that anything would change. I have tried to show that most cultural formations presumed the permanent primacy of the imperial power. Still, an alternative view to imperialism arose, persisted, and eventually prevailed.

By 1950 Indonesia had won its freedom from Holland. In 1947 Britain handed over India to the Congress Party, and Pakistan immediately split off, guided by Jinnah's Muslim League. Malaysia, Ceylon, and Burma became independent, as did the nations of "French" Southeast Asia. All through East, West, and North Africa, British, French, and Belgian occupations were terminated, sometimes (as in Algeria) with enormous losses of life and property. Forty-nine new African states came into existence by 1990. But none of these struggles took place in a vacuum. As Grimal points out, the internationalized relationship between colonizer and colonized was spurred by global forces—churches, the United Nations, Marxism, the Soviet Union and the United States. The anti-imperial struggle, as so many Pan-African, Pan-Arab, Pan-Asian congresses testified, was universalized, and the rift between Western (white, European, advanced) and non-Western (colored, native, underdeveloped) cultures and peoples was dramatized.

Because this redrawing of the world's map was so dramatic, we have lost (and perhaps have been encouraged to lose) an accurate historical, let alone moral sense that even in the contentiousness of struggle, imperialism and its opponents fought over the same terrain, contested the same history. Certainly they overlapped where French-educated Algerians or Vietnamese, British-educated East or West Indians, Arabs, and Africans confronted their imperial masters. Opposition to empire in London and Paris was affected by resistance offered in Delhi and Algiers. Although it was not the struggle of same with same (a standard imperialist misrepresentation has it that exclusively Western ideas of freedom led the fight against colonial rule, which mischievously overlooks the reserves in Indian and Arab culture that *always* resisted imperialism, and claims the fight against imperialism as one of imperialism's major triumphs), opponents on the same cultural ground had fascinating encounters. Without metropolitan doubts and opposition, the characters, idiom, and very structure of native resistance to imperialism would have been different. Here, too, culture is in advance of politics, military history, or economic process.

This overlapping is not a small or negligible point. Just as culture may predispose and actively prepare one society for the overseas domination of another, it may also prepare that society to relinquish or modify the idea of overseas domination. These changes cannot occur without the willingness of men and women to resist the pressures of colonial rule, to take up arms, to project ideas of liberation, and to imagine (as Benedict Anderson has it) a new national community, to take the final plunge. Nor can they occur unless either economic or political exhaustion with empire sets in at home, unless the idea of empire and the cost of colonial rule are challenged publicly, unless the representations of imperialism begin to lose their justification and legitimacy, and, finally, unless the rebellious "natives" impress upon the metropolitan culture the independence and integrity of their own culture, free from colonial encroachment. But having noted all these prerequisites, we should acknowledge that, at both ends of the redrawn map, opposition and resistance to imperialism are articulated together on a largely common although disputed terrain provided by culture.

What are the cultural grounds on which both natives and liberal Europeans lived and understood each other? How much could they grant each other? How, within the circle of imperial domination, could they deal with each other before radical change occurred? Consider first E. M. Forster's *A Passage to India*, a novel that surely expresses the author's affection (sometimes petulant and mystified) for the place. I have always felt that the most interesting thing about *A Passage to India* is Forster's using India to represent material that according to the canons of the novel form cannot in fact be represented—vastness, incomprehensible creeds, secret motions, histories, and social forms. Mrs. Moore especially and Fielding too are clearly meant to be understood as Europeans who go beyond the anthropomorphic norm in remaining in that (to them) terrifying new element—in Fielding's case, experiencing India's complexity but then returning to familiar humanism (following the trial he comes home through Suez and Italy to England, after having had a shattering presentiment of what India *could* do to one's sense of time and place).

But Forster is too scrupulous an observer of the reality that contains him to leave it at that. The novel returns to a traditional sense of social propriety in its last section, where the author deliberately and affirmatively imports into India the habitual novelistic domestic resolution (marriage and property): Fielding marries Mrs. Moore's daughter. Yet he and Aziz—a Muslim nationalist—ride together *and* remain apart: " 'They didn't want it,' they said

in their hundred voices, 'No, not yet,' and the sky said, 'No, not here.' "
There is resolution and union, but neither is complete.[19]

If present-day India is neither the place nor the time (Forster's directions
are careful) for identity, convergence, merger, then for what? The novel
indicates that the political origins of this issue lie in the British presence, yet
it also allows one to experience various aspects of this impasse with a feeling
that the political conflict will simply be resolved in the future. Godbole's and
Aziz's diametrically different resistances to empire are acknowledged—Aziz
the Muslim nationalist, Godbole the almost surrealistic Hindu—and so is
Fielding's inherent opposition, though he cannot put his objections to the
iniquities of British rule in political or philosophical terms, and only makes
local objections to local abuses. Benita Parry's interesting argument in *Delusions and Discoveries* that Forster resolves the novel positively hinges on
"evanescent hints" given by Forster despite "the total text":[20] it is more exact
to say that he intended the gulf between India and Britain to stand, but
allowed intermittent crossings back and forth. Be that as it may, we are
entitled to associate the Indian animosity against British rule that is displayed during Aziz's trial with the emergence of a visible Indian resistance,
which Fielding comes reluctantly to perceive in Aziz, one of whose nationalist models is Japan. The British club members whose snubs force Fielding
to resign are nervous and downright nasty, and they consider Aziz's infraction to be such that any sign of "weakness" is an attack on British rule itself:
these too are indications of a hopeless atmosphere.

Almost by virtue of its liberal, humane espousal of Fielding's views and
attitudes, *A Passage to India* is at a loss, partly because Forster's commitment
to the novel form exposes him to difficulties in India he cannot deal with.
Like Conrad's Africa, Forster's India is a locale frequently described as
unapprehendable and too large. Once, when Ronny and Adela are together
early in the novel, they watch a bird disappear into a tree, yet they cannot
identify it since, as Forster adds for their benefit and ours, "nothing in India
is identifiable, the mere asking of a question causes it to disappear or to
merge in something else."[21] The crux of the novel is therefore the sustained
encounter between the English colonials—"well-developed bodies, fairly
developed minds, and undeveloped hearts"—and India.

As Adela approaches the Marabar Caves, she notes that the train's
"pomper, pomper," which accompanied her musing, had a message she
could not fathom.

How could the mind take hold of such a country? Generations of
invaders have tried, but they remain in exile. The important towns they

build are only retreats, their quarrels the malaise of men who cannot
find their way home. India knows of their trouble. She knows of the
whole world's trouble to its uttermost depth. She calls "Come" through
her hundred mouths, through objects ridiculous and august. But come
to what? She has never defined. She is not a promise, only an appeal.[22]

Yet Forster shows how British "officialism" tries to impose sense on India.
There are orders of precedence, clubs with rules, restrictions, military hierarchies, and, standing above and informing it all, British power. India "is not
a tea-party," says Ronny Heaslop. "I have never known anything but disaster
result when English people and Indians attempt to be intimate socially.
Intercourse, yes. Courtesy, by all means. Intimacy—never, never."[23] No
wonder that Dr. Aziz is so surprised when Mrs. Moore takes off her shoes
to enter a mosque, a gesture that suggests deference and establishes friendship in a manner forbidden by the code.

Fielding is also untypical: truly intelligent and sensitive, happiest in the
give-and-take of a private conversation. Yet his capacities for understanding
and sympathy fail before India's massive incomprehensibility; he would
have been a perfect hero in Forster's earlier fictions, but here he is defeated.
At least Fielding can "connect" with a character like Aziz, half of Forster's
ploy for dealing with India in a British novel by dividing it into two parts,
one Islamic, the other Hindu. In 1857, Harriet Martineau had remarked,
"The unprepared mind, whether Hindu or Mussulman, developed under
Asiatic conditions, cannot be in sympathy, more or less, intellectually or
morally, with the Christianized European mind."[24] Forster emphasizes the
Muslims, compared with whom the Hindus (including Godbole) are peripheral, as if they were not amenable to novelistic treatment. Islam was closer
to Western culture, standing in a median position to the English and the
Hindus in Forster's Chandrapore. Forster is slightly nearer Islam than Hin-
duism in *A Passage to India*, but the final lack of sympathy is obvious.

Hindus, according to the novel, believe that all is muddle, all connected,
God is one, is not, was not, was. By contrast, Islam, as represented by Aziz,
apprehends order and a specific God. ("The comparatively simple mind of
the Mohammedan,"[25] says Forster ambiguously, as if to imply both that Aziz
has a comparatively simple mind, and that "the Mohammedan," generally
speaking, does also.) To Fielding, Aziz is quasi-Italian, although his exaggerated view of the Mogul past, his passion for poetry, his odd *pudeur* with
the pictures of his wife that he carries around, suggest an exotic un-Mediter-
ranean being. Despite Fielding's wonderful Bloomsbury qualities, his ability
to judge charitably and lovingly, his passionate intelligence based on human
norms, he is finally rejected by India itself, to whose disorienting heart only

Mrs. Moore penetrates, but she is ultimately killed by her vision. Dr. Aziz becomes a nationalist, but I think Forster is disappointed by him for what only seem his posturings; he cannot connect him to the larger, coherent movement for Indian independence. According to Francis Hutchins, in the late nineteenth century and early twentieth "the nationalist movement, to an astonishing extent, drew no response from the British imagination in India."[26]

When they travelled through India in 1912, Beatrice and Sidney Webb noted the difficulty British employers were having with Indian laborers working for the Raj, either because laziness was a form of resistance (very common elsewhere in Asia, as S. H. Alatas has shown)[27] or because of the so-called "drain theory" of Dadabhai Naoroji, who had argued to the satisfaction of nationalist parties that India's wealth was being drained off by the British. The Webbs blame "those old standing European inhabitants of India [who] have not acquired the art of managing the Indians." Then they add:

> What is equally clear is that the Indian is sometimes an extraordinarily difficult worker *to sweat*. He does not care enough for his earnings. He prefers to waste away in semi-starvation than overwork himself. However low his standard of life, his standard of work is lower—at any rate when he is working for an employer he does not like. And his irregularities are baffling.[28]

This hardly suggests a contest between two warring nations; similarly, in *A Passage to India* Forster finds India difficult because it is so strange and unidentifiable, or because people like Aziz will let themselves be seduced by jejune nationalist sentiment, or because if one tries to come to terms with it, as Mrs. Moore does, one cannot recover from the encounter.

To the Westerners Mrs. Moore is a nuisance, as she is to herself after her sojourn in the Caves. To the Indians roused momentarily to a sort of nationalist coherence during the court scene, Mrs. Moore is less a person than a mobilizing phrase, a funny Indianized principle of protest and community: "Esmiss Esmoor." She has an experience of India that she does not understand, whereas Fielding superficially understands but does not have the deep experience. The novel's helplessness neither goes all the way and condemns (or defends) British colonialism, nor condemns or defends Indian nationalism. True, Forster's ironies undercut everyone from the blimpish Turtons and Burtons to the posturing, comic Indians, but one cannot help feeling that in view of the political realities of the 1910s and 1920s even such a remarkable novel as *A Passage to India* nevertheless founders on the undodgeable facts of Indian nationalism. Forster identifies the course of the narrative with a Britisher, Fielding, who can understand only that India is too vast and baffling, and that a Muslim like Aziz can be befriended only up to a point, since his antagonism to colonialism is so unacceptably silly. The sense that India and Britain are opposed nations (though their positions overlap), is played down, muffled, frittered away.

These are the prerogatives of a novel that deals with personal, not official or national, histories. Kipling, in contrast, directly acknowledged the political reality as more than a source of novelistic irony, however threatened, tragic, or violent the history of Britain in India may have been for him. Indians are a various lot, they need to be known and understood, British power has to reckon with Indians in India: such are Kipling's coordinates, politically speaking. Forster is evasive and more patronizing; there is truth to Parry's comment that *"A Passage to India* is the triumphant expression of the British imagination exploring India,"[29] but it is also true that Forster's India is so affectionately personal and so remorselessly metaphysical that his view of Indians as a nation contending for sovereignty with Britain is not politically very serious, or even respectful. Consider the following:

> Hamidullah had called in on his way to a worrying committee of notables, nationalist in tendency, where Hindus, Moslems, two Sikhs, two Parsis, a Jain, and Native Christian tried to like one another more than came natural to them. As long as someone abused the English, all went well, but nothing constructive had been achieved, and if the English were to leave India, the committee would vanish also. He was glad that Aziz, whom he loved and whose family was connected with his own, took no interest in politics, which ruin the character and career, yet nothing can be achieved without them. He thought of Cambridge—sadly, as of another poem that had ended. How happy he had been there, twenty years ago! Politics had not mattered in Mr. and Mrs. Bannister's rectory. There, games, work, and pleasant society had interwoven, and appeared to be sufficient substructure for a national life. Here all was wire-pulling and fear.[30]

This registers a change in political climate: what was once possible in the Bannister rectory or in Cambridge is no longer appropriate in the age of strident nationalism. But Forster sees Indians with imperial eyes when he says that it is "natural" for sects to dislike one another or when he dismisses the power of nationalist committees to last beyond the English presence, or when nationalism, humdrum and modest though it may have been, is only "wire-pulling and fear." His presumption is that *he* can get past the puerile nationalist put-ons to the essential India; when it comes to ruling India—

which is what Hamidullah and the others are agitating about—the English had better go on doing it, despite their mistakes: "they" are not yet ready for self-rule.

This view goes back to Mill, of course, and surprisingly resembles the position of Bulwer-Lytton, who as Viceroy in 1878 and 1879 had this to say:

> Already great mischief has been done by the deplorable tendency of second-rate Indian officials, and superficial English philanthropists to ignore the essential and insurmountable distinctions of race qualities, which are fundamental to our position in India; and thus, unintentionally, to pamper the conceit and the vanity of half-educated natives, to the serious detriment of commonsense, and of the wholesome recognition of realities.[31]

On another occasion he said that "the Baboodom of Lower Bengal, though disloyal is fortunately cowardly and its only revolver is its ink bottle; which though dirty, is not dangerous."[32] In *The Emergence of Indian Nationalism*, where these passages are cited, Anil Seal notes that Bulwer-Lytton missed the main trend in Indian politics, a trend perceived by an alert District Commissioner who wrote that

> twenty years ago . . . we had to take account of local nationalities and particular races. The resentment of the Mahratta did not involve that of the Bengalee. . . . Now . . . we have changed all that, and are beginning to find ourselves face to face, not with the population of individual provinces, but with 200 millions of people united by sympathies and intercourse which we have ourselves created and fostered.[33]

Of course Forster was a novelist, not a political officer or theorist or prophet. Yet he found a way to use the mechanism of the novel to elaborate on the already existing structure of attitude and reference without changing it. This structure permitted one to feel affection for and even intimacy with some Indians and India generally, but made one see Indian politics as the charge of the British, and culturally refused a privilege to Indian nationalism (which, by the way, it gave willingly to Greeks and Italians). Anil Seal again:

> In Egypt, as in India, activities inconvenient to the British were judged to be self-interested machinations rather than genuine nationalisms. The Gladstone government saw Arabi's revolt in Egypt as a few army officers on the make, abetted by some Egyptian intellectuals who had taken to reading the works of Lamartine—a comforting conclusion for

it justified Gladstonians in negating their own principles. After all, there were no Garibaldis in Cairo. And neither were there in Calcutta or Bombay.[34]

How a resisting nationalism can be represented by a British writer who views it sympathetically is a problem Forster does not himself explicitly take on in his own work. It is, however, very affectingly studied by the crusading opponent of British policy in India, Edward Thompson, in his *The Other Side of the Medal*, published in 1926, two years after *A Passage to India*. Thompson's subject is misrepresentation. Indians, he says, see the English entirely through the experience of British brutality during the 1857 "Mutiny." The English, with the pompous, cold-blooded religiosity of the Raj at its worst, see Indians and their history as barbaric, uncivilized, inhuman. Thompson notes the imbalance between the two misrepresentations, that one misrepresentation has all the power of modern technology and diffusion to back it—from the army to the *Oxford History of India*—whereas the other relies on the pamphlet and the mobilizing rejectionist sentiments of an oppressed people. Still, Thompson says, we must recognize the fact that Indian

> hatred exists—savage, set hatred—is certain; and the sooner we recognize it, and search for its reasons, the better. The discontent with our rule is growing universal, and there must be first, widespread popular memories to account for that discontent being able to spread; and, secondly, blazing hatred at its heart, to have caused it to gather such rapid momentum.[35]

Hence, he says, we must ask for "a new orientation in the histories of India," we must express "atonement" for what we have done, and above all, we should recognize that Indian men and women "want their self-respect given back to them. Make them free again, and enable them to look us and everyone in the eyes, and they will behave like free people and cease to lie."[36]

Thompson's powerful and admirable book is deeply symptomatic in two ways. He admits the paramount importance of culture in consolidating imperial feeling: the writing of history, he says over and over, is tied to the extension of empire. His is one of the earliest and most persuasive metropolitan attempts to understand imperialism as a cultural affliction for colonizer as well as colonized. But he is bound to the notion that there is "a truth" to events involving both sides that transcends them. Indians "lie" because they are not free, whereas he (and other oppositional figures like him) can see the truth because they *are* free and because they are English. No more than

Forster could Thompson grasp that—as Fanon argued—the empire never gives anything away out of goodwill.[37] It cannot *give* Indians their freedom, but must be forced to yield it as the result of a protracted political, cultural, and sometimes military struggle that becomes more, not less adversarial as time goes on. Similarly the British, who in holding on to empire are part of the same dynamic; their attitudes can only be defended until they are defeated.

The battle between native and white man had to be visibly joined, as it had been by 1926, for Thompson to see himself as being on "the other side." There are now two sides, two nations, in combat, not merely the voice of the white master answered antiphonally—reactively—by the colonial up-start. Fanon calls this in a theatrical passage the "alterity of rupture, of conflict, of battle."[38] Thompson accepts this more fully than Forster, for whom the novel's nineteenth-century legacy of seeing the natives as subordinate and dependent is still powerful.

In France, there was no one who, like Kipling, even as he celebrated the empire warned of its impending cataclysmic demise, and no one like Forster, either. France was culturally attached to what Raoul Girardet calls a double movement of pride and worry—pride taken in work accomplished in the colonies, fear about the colonies' destiny.[39] But as in England, the French reaction to Asian and African nationalism scarcely amounted to a lifted eyebrow, except when the Communist Party, in line with the Third International, supported anti-colonial revolution and resistance against empire. Girardet remarks that two important works by Gide in the years after *L'Immoraliste,* his *Voyage au Congo* (1927) and *Retour du Tchad* (1928), raise doubts about French colonialism in sub-Saharan Africa, but he adds shrewdly, Gide nowhere questions "le principe elle-même de la colonisation."[40]

The pattern is, alas, always the same: critics of colonialism like Gide and Tocqueville attack abuses in places and by powers that do not greatly touch them and either condone abuses of power in French territories they care about or, failing to make a general case against *all* repression or imperial hegemony, say nothing.

During the 1930s a serious ethnographic literature lovingly and painstakingly discussed native societies in the French *imperium.* Works by Maurice Delafosse, Charles André Julien, Labouret, Marcel Griaule, Michel Leiris gave substantive and careful thought to distant, often obscure cultures, and gave them an esteem otherwise denied within the strictures of political imperialism.[41]

Something of that special mix of learned attention and the imperial enclosure is to be found in Malraux's *La Voie royale* (1930), one of the least known and discussed of his works. Malraux was himself both adventurer and amateur ethnographer-archeologist; in his background were Leo Frobenius, the Conrad of *Heart of Darkness*, T. E. Lawrence, Rimbaud, Nietzsche, and, I am convinced, Gide's character Ménalque. *La Voie royale* enacts a voyage into "the interior," in this case French Indochina (a fact scarcely noted by Malraux's major critics, for whom, as with Camus and *his* critics, the only setting worth talking about is European). Perken and Claude (the narrator) on the one hand, and the French authorities on the other contest for domination and loot: Perken wants the Cambodian bas-reliefs, the bureaucrats look on his quest with suspicion and dislike. When the adventurers find Grabot, a Kurtz figure, who has been captured, blinded, and tortured, they try to get him back from the natives who have him, but his spirit has been broken. After Perken is wounded and his diseased leg is seen to be destroying him, the indomitable egoist (like Kurtz in his final agony) pronounces his defiant message to the grieving Claude (like Marlow):

> "il n'y a pas . . . de mort . . . Il y a seulement . . . *moi* . . . Un doigt se crispa sur la cuisse. . . . *moi . . . qui vais mourir.*"[42]

The jungle and tribes of Indochina are represented in *La Voie royale* with a combination of fear and inviting allure. Grabot is held by Mois tribespeople; Perken has ruled the Stieng people for a long period and, like a devoted anthropologist, tries in vain to protect them from encroaching modernization (in the form of a colonial railroad). Yet despite the menace and disquiet of the novel's imperial setting, little suggests the *political* menace, or that the cosmic doom engulfing Claude, Perken, and Grabot is anything more historically concrete than a generalized malevolence against which one must exert one's will. Yes, one can negotiate small deals in the alien world of the *indigènes* (Perken does this with the Mois, for example), but his overall hatred for Cambodia suggests, rather melodramatically, the metaphysical gulf separating East from West.

I attach so much importance to *La Voie royale* because, as the work of an extraordinary European talent, it testifies so conclusively to the inability of the Western humanistic conscience to confront the political challenge of the imperial domains. For both Forster in the 1920s and Malraux in 1930, men genuinely familiar with the non-European world, a grander destiny confronts the West than one of mere national self-determination—self-consciousness, will, or even the deep issues of taste and discrimination. Perhaps the novel form itself dulls their perceptions, with its structure of attitude and reference held over from the previous century. If one compares Malraux with the celebrated French expert on Indochinese culture Paul

Mus, whose book *Viet-Nam: Sociologie d'une guerre* appeared twenty years later, on the eve of Dien Bien Phu, and who saw, as Edward Thompson did, the profound political crisis that separated France from Indochina, the difference is striking. In a remarkable chapter entitled "Sur la route Viet-namienne" (perhaps echoing *La Voie royale*), Mus speaks plainly of the French institutional system and its secular violation of Vietnamese sacred values; the Chinese, he says, understood Vietnam better than France, with its railroads, schools, and "administration laique." Without religious mandate, with little knowledge of Vietnamese traditional morality, and even less attention to local nativism and sensibility, the French were merely inattentive conquerors.[43]

Like Thompson, Mus sees Europeans and Asiatics bound together, and, again like Thompson, he opposes continuing the colonial system. He proposes independence for Vietnam, despite the Soviet and Chinese menace, yet wants a French-Vietnamese pact that would give France certain privileges in Vietnamese reconstruction (this is the burden of the book's final chapter, "Que faire?"). This is a very far cry from Malraux, but only a small mutation in the European concept of tutelage—albeit enlightened tutelage—for the non-European. And it falls short of recognizing the full strength of what so far as Western imperialism was concerned became the Third World's antinomian nationalism, which expressed not cooperation but antagonism.

(11)

Themes of Resistance Culture

The slow and often bitterly disputed recovery of geographical territory which is at the heart of decolonization is preceded—as empire had been—by the charting of cultural territory. After the period of "primary resistance," literally fighting against outside intrusion, there comes the period of secondary, that is, ideological resistance, when efforts are made to reconstitute a "shattered community, to save or restore the sense and fact of community against all the pressures of the colonial system,"[44] as Basil Davidson puts it. This in turn makes possible the establishment of new and independent stakes. It is important to note that we are not mainly talking here about utopian regions—idyllic meadows, so to speak—discovered in their private past by the intellectuals, poets, prophets, leaders, and historians of resistance. Davidson speaks of the "otherworldly" promises made by some in their early phase, for example, rejecting Christianity and the wearing of Western clothes. But all of them respond to the humiliations of colonialism, and lead to "the principal teaching of nationalism: the need to find the ideological basis for a wider unity than any known before."[45]

This basis is found, I believe, in the rediscovery and repatriation of what had been suppressed in the natives' past by the processes of imperialism. Thus we can understand Fanon's insistence on rereading Hegel's master-slave dialectic in light of the colonial situation, a situation in which Fanon remarks on how the master in imperialism "differs basically from the master described by Hegel. For Hegel there is reciprocity; here the master laughs at the consciousness of the slave. What he wants from the slave is not recognition but work."[46] To achieve recognition is to rechart and then occupy the place in imperial cultural forms reserved for subordination, to occupy it self-consciously, fighting for it on the very same territory once ruled by a consciousness that assumed the subordination of a designated inferior Other. Hence, *reinscription*. The irony is that Hegel's dialectic is Hegel's, after all: he was there first, just as the Marxist dialectic of subject and object had been there before the Fanon of *Les Damnés* used it to explain the struggle between colonizer and colonized.

That is the partial tragedy of resistance, that it must to a certain degree work to recover forms already established or at least influenced or infiltrated by the culture of empire. This is another instance of what I have called overlapping territories: the struggle over Africa in the twentieth century, for example, is over territories designed and redesigned by explorers from Europe for generations, a process memorably and painstakingly conveyed in Philip Curtin's *The Image of Africa*.[47] Just as the Europeans saw Africa polemically as a blank place when they took it, or assumed its supinely yielding availability when they plotted to partition it at the 1884–85 Berlin Congress, decolonizing Africans found it necessary to reimagine an Africa stripped of its imperial past.

Take as a specific instance of this battle over projections and ideological images the so-called quest or voyage motif, which appears in much European literature and especially literature about the non-European world. In all the great explorers' narratives of the late Renaissance (Daniel Defert has aptly called them the collection of the world [la collecte du monde])[48] and those of the nineteenth-century explorers and ethnographers, not to mention Conrad's voyage up the Congo, there is the *topos* of the voyage south as Mary Louise Pratt has called it, referring to Gide and Camus,[49] in which the motif of control and authority has "sounded uninterruptedly." For the native who begins to see and hear that persisting note, it sounds "the note of crisis, of banishment, banishment from the heart, banishment from home." This is how Stephen Dedalus memorably states it in the Library episode of *Ulysses;*[50] the decolonizing native writer—such as Joyce, the Irish writer colonized by the British—re-experiences the quest-voyage motif from which he had been banished by means of the same trope carried over from the imperial into the new culture and adopted, reused, relived.

The River Between, by James Ngugi (later Ngugi wa Thiongo), redoes *Heart of Darkness* by inducing life into Conrad's river on the very first page. "The river was called Honia, which meant cure, or bring-back-to-life. Honia river never dried: it seemed to possess a strong will to live, scorning droughts and weather changes. And it went on in the very same way, never hurrying, never hesitating. People saw this and were happy."[51] Conrad's images of river, exploration, and mysterious setting are never far from our awareness as we read, yet they are quite differently weighted, differently—even jarringly—experienced in a deliberately understated, self-consciously unidiomatic and austere language. In Ngugi the white man recedes in importance—he is compressed into a single missionary figure emblematically called Livingstone—although his influence is felt in the divisions that separate the villages, the riverbanks, and the people from one another. In the internal conflict ravaging Waiyaki's life, Ngugi powerfully conveys the unresolved tensions that will continue well after the novel ends and that the novel makes no effort to contain. A new pattern, suppressed in *Heart of Darkness,* appears, out of which Ngugi generates a new mythos, whose tenuous course and final obscurity suggest a return to an African Africa.

And in Tayeb Salih's *Season of Migration to the North,* Conrad's river is now the Nile, whose waters rejuvenate its peoples, and Conrad's first-person British narrative style and European protagonists are in a sense reversed, first through the use of Arabic; second in that Salih's novel concerns the northward voyage of a Sudanese to Europe; and third, because the narrator speaks from a Sudanese village. A voyage into the heart of darkness is thus converted into a sacralized *hegira* from the Sudanese countryside, still weighted down with its colonial legacy, into the heart of Europe, where Mostapha Said, a mirror image of Kurtz, unleashes ritual violence on himself, on European women, on the narrator's understanding. The *hegira* concludes with Said's return to and suicide in his native village. So deliberate are Salih's mimetic reversals of Conrad that even Kurtz's skull-topped fence is repeated and distorted in the inventory of European books stacked in Said's secret library. The interventions and crossings from north to south, and from south to north, enlarge and complicate the back-and-forth colonial trajectory mapped by Conrad; what results is not simply a reclamation of the fictive territory, but an articulation of some of the discrepancies and their imagined consequences muffled by Conrad's majestic prose.

> Over there is like here, neither better nor worse. But I am from here, just as the date palm standing in the courtyard of our house has grown in *our* house and not in anyone else's. The fact that they came to our land I know not why, does that mean that we should poison our present and our future? Sooner or later they will leave our country, just as many people throughout history left many countries. The railways, ships, hospitals, factories, and schools will be ours and we'll speak their language without either a sense of guilt or a sense of gratitude. Once again we shall be as we were—ordinary people—and if we are lies we shall be lies of our own making.[52]

The post-imperial writers of the Third World therefore bear their past within them—as scars of humiliating wounds, as instigation for different practices, as potentially revised visions of the past tending toward a post-colonial future, as urgently reinterpretable and redeployable experiences, in which the formerly silent native speaks and acts on territory reclaimed as part of a general movement of resistance, from the colonist.

Another motif emerges in the culture of resistance. Consider the stunning cultural effort to claim a restored and invigorated authority over a region in the many modern Latin American and Caribbean versions of Shakespeare's *The Tempest*. This fable is one of several that stand guard over the imagination of the New World; other stories are the adventures and discoveries of Columbus, Robinson Crusoe, John Smith and Pocahontas, and the adventures of Inkle and Yariko. (A brilliant study, *Colonial Encounters* by Peter Hulme, surveys them all in some detail.)[53] It is a measure of how embattled this matter of "inaugural figures" has become that it is now virtually impossible to say anything simple about any of them. To call this reinterpretative zeal merely simpleminded, vindictive, or assaultive is wrong, I think. In a totally new way in Western culture, the interventions of non-European artists and scholars cannot be dismissed or silenced, and these interventions are not only an integral part of a political movement, but in many ways the movement's *successfully* guiding imagination, intellectual and figurative energy reseeing and rethinking the terrain common to whites and non-whites. For natives to want to lay claim to that terrain is, for many Westerners, an intolerable effrontery, for them actually to repossess it unthinkable.

The core of Aimé Césaire's Caribbean *Une Tempête* is not *ressentiment*, but an affectionate contention with Shakespeare for the right to represent the

Caribbean. That impulse to contend is part of a grander effort to discover the bases of an integral identity different from the formerly dependent, derivative one. Caliban, according to George Lamming, "is the excluded, that which is eternally below possibility.... He is seen as an occasion, a state of existence which can be appropriated and exploited to the purposes of another's own development."[54] If that is so, then Caliban must be shown to have a history that can be perceived on its own, as the result of Caliban's own effort. One must, according to Lamming, "explode Prospero's old myth" by christening "language afresh"; but this cannot occur "until we show language as the product of human endeavor; until we make available to all the result of certain enterprises undertaken by men who are still regarded as the unfortunate descendants of languageless and deformed slaves."[55]

Lamming's point is that, while identity is crucial, just to assert a different identity is never enough. The main thing is to be able to see that Caliban has a history capable of development, as part of the process of work, growth, and maturity to which only Europeans had seemed entitled. Each new American reinscription of *The Tempest* is therefore a local version of the old grand story, invigorated and inflected by the pressures of an unfolding political and cultural history. The Cuban critic Roberto Fernández Retamar makes the significant point that for modern Latin Americans and Caribbeans, it is Caliban himself, and not Ariel, who is the main symbol of hybridity, with his strange and unpredictable mixture of attributes. This is truer to the Creole, or *mestizo* composite of the new America.[56]

Retamar's choice of Caliban over Ariel signals a profoundly important ideological debate at the heart of the cultural effort to decolonize, an effort at the restoration of community and repossession of culture that goes on long after the political establishment of independent nation-states. Resistance and decolonization as I talk about them here persist well after successful nationalism has come to a stop. This debate is symbolized in Ngugi's *Decolonising the Mind* (1986), which records his farewell to English as well as his attempt to further the cause of liberation by exploring African language and literature more deeply.[57] A similar effort is embodied in Barbara Harlow's important book, *Resistance Literature* (1987), whose purpose is to employ the tools of recent literary theory to give a place to "the literary output of geopolitical areas which stand in opposition to the very social and political organization within which the theories are located and to which they respond."[58]

The basic form of the debate is best immediately translated into a set of alternatives that we can derive from the Ariel-Caliban choice, whose history in Latin America is a special and unusual one but useful for other areas as well. The Latin American discussion (to which Retamar is a well-known recent contributor: others were José Enrique Rodó and José Martí) is really a response to the question How does a culture seeking to become independent of imperialism imagine its own past? One choice is to do it as Ariel does, that is, as a willing servant of Prospero; Ariel does what he is told obligingly, and, when he gains his freedom, he returns to his native element, a sort of bourgeois native untroubled by his collaboration with Prospero. A second choice is to do it like Caliban, aware of and accepting his mongrel past but not disabled for future development. A third choice is to be a Caliban who sheds his current servitude and physical disfigurements in the process of discovering his essential, pre-colonial self. *This* Caliban is behind the nativist and radical nationalisms that produced concepts of *négritude*, Islamic fundamentalism, Arabism, and the like.

Both Calibans nourish and require each other. Every subjugated community in Europe, Australia, Africa, Asia, and the Americas has played the sorely tried and oppressed Caliban to some outside master like Prospero. To become aware of one's self as belonging to a subject people is the founding insight of anti-imperialist nationalism. From that insight came literatures, innumerable political parties, a host of other struggles for minority and women's rights, and, much of the time, newly independent states. Yet, as Fanon rightly observes, nationalist consciousness can very easily lead to frozen rigidity; merely to replace white officers and bureaucrats with colored equivalents, he says, is no guarantee that the nationalist functionaries will not replicate the old dispensation. The dangers of chauvinism and xenophobia ("Africa for the Africans") are very real. It is best when Caliban sees his own history as an aspect of the history of *all* subjugated men and women, and comprehends the complex truth of his own social and historical situation.

We must not minimize the shattering importance of that initial insight—peoples being conscious of themselves as prisoners in their own land—for it returns again and again in the literature of the imperialized world. The history of empire—punctuated by uprisings throughout most of the nineteenth century—in India; in German, French, Belgian, and British Africa; in Haiti, Madagascar, North Africa, Burma, the Philippines, Egypt, and elsewhere—seems incoherent unless one recognizes that sense of beleaguered imprisonment infused with a passion for community that grounds antiimperial resistance in cultural effort. Aimé Césaire:

> *Ce qui est à moi aussi: une petite*
> *cellule dans le Jura,*
> *une petite cellule, la neige la double de barreaux blancs*
> *la neige est un gêolier blanc qui monte*
> *la garde devant une prison*

Ce qui est à moi:
c'est un homme seul emprisonné de
blanc
c'est un homme seul qui défie les cris
blancs de la morte blanche
(TOUSSAINT, TOUSSAINT L'OUVERTURE)[59]

Most often, the concept of race itself gives the prison its *raison d'être;* and it turns up nearly everywhere in the culture of resistance. Tagore speaks of it in his great lectures called *Nationalism,* published in 1917. "The Nation" is for Tagore a tight and unforgiving receptacle of power for producing conformity, whether British, Chinese, Indian, or Japanese. India's answer, he said, must be to provide not a competing nationalism, but a creative solution to the divisiveness produced by racial consciousness.[60] A similar insight is at the heart of W.E.B. Du Bois's *The Souls of Black Folk* (1903): "How does it feel to be a problem? ... Why did God make me an outcast and a stranger in mine own house?"[61] Both Tagore and Du Bois, however, warn against a wholesale, indiscriminate attack on white or Western culture. It is not Western culture that is to blame, says Tagore, but "the judicious niggardliness of the Nation that has taken upon itself the white man's burden of criticizing the East."[62]

Three great topics emerge in decolonizing cultural resistance, separated for analytical purposes, but all related. One, of course, is the insistence on the right to see the community's history whole, coherently, integrally. Restore the imprisoned nation to itself. (Benedict Anderson connects this in Europe to "print-capitalism," which "gave a new fixity to language" and "created unified fields of exchange and communications below Latin and above the spoken vernaculars.")[63] The concept of the national language is central, but without the practice of a national culture—from slogans to pamphlets and newspapers, from folktales and heroes to epic poetry, novels, and drama—the language is inert; national culture organizes and sustains communal memory, as when early defeats in African resistance stories are resumed ("they took our weapons in 1903; now we are taking them back"); it reinhabits the landscape using restored ways of life, heroes, heroines, and exploits; it formulates expressions and emotions of pride as well as defiance, which in turn form the backbone of the principal national independence parties. Local slave narratives, spiritual autobiographies, prison memoirs form a counterpoint to the Western powers' monumental histories, official discourses, and panoptic quasi-scientific viewpoint. In Egypt, for example, the historical novels of Girgi Zaydan bring together for the first time a specifically Arab narrative (rather the way Walter Scott did a century before). In Spanish America, according to Anderson, *creole* communities "produced creoles who consciously redefined these [mixed] populations as fellow nationals."[64] Both Anderson and Hannah Arendt note the widespread global movement to "achieve solidarities on an essentially imagined basis."[65]

Second is the idea that resistance, far from being merely a reaction to imperialism, is an alternative way of conceiving human history. It is particularly important to see how much this alternative reconception is based on breaking down the barriers between cultures. Certainly, as the title of a fascinating book has it, *writing back* to the metropolitan cultures, disrupting the European narratives of the Orient and Africa, replacing them with either a more playful or a more powerful new narrative style is a major component in the process.[66] Salman Rushdie's novel *Midnight's Children* is a brilliant work based on the liberating imagination of independence itself, with all its anomalies and contradictions working themselves out. The conscious effort to enter into the discourse of Europe and the West, to mix with it, transform it, to make it acknowledge marginalized or suppressed or forgotten histories is of particular interest in Rushdie's work, and in an earlier generation of resistance writing. This kind of work was carried out by dozens of scholars, critics, and intellectuals in the peripheral world; I call this effort *the voyage in.*

Third is a noticeable pull away from separatist nationalism toward a more integrative view of human community and human liberation. I want to be very clear about this. No one needs to be reminded that throughout the imperial world during the decolonizing period, protest, resistance, and independence movements were fuelled by one or another nationalism. Debates today about Third World nationalism have been increasing in volume and interest, not least because to many scholars and observers in the West, this reappearance of nationalism revived several anachronistic attitudes; Elie Kedourie, for example, considers non-Western nationalism essentially condemnable, a negative reaction to a demonstrated cultural and social inferiority, an imitation of "Western" political behavior that brought little that was good; others, like Eric Hobsbawm and Ernest Gellner, consider nationalism as a form of political behavior that has been gradually superseded by new trans-national realities of modern economies, electronic communications, and superpower military projection.[67] In all these views, I believe, there is a marked (and, in my opinion, ahistorical) discomfort with non-Western societies acquiring national independence, which is believed to be "foreign" to their ethos. Hence the repeated insistence on the *Western* provenance of nationalist philosophies that are therefore ill-suited to, and likely to be abused by Arabs, Zulus, Indonesians, Irish, or Jamaicans.

This, I think, is a criticism of newly independent peoples that carries with it a broadly *cultural* opposition (from the Left as well as from the Right) to the proposition that the formerly subject peoples are entitled to the same kind of nationalism as, say, the more developed, hence more deserving, Germans or Italians. A confused and limiting notion of priority allows that only the original proponents of an idea can understand and use it. But the history of all cultures is the history of cultural borrowings. Cultures are not impermeable; just as Western science borrowed from Arabs, they had borrowed from India and Greece. Culture is never just a matter of ownership, of borrowing and lending with absolute debtors and creditors, but rather of appropriations, common experiences, and interdependencies of all kinds among different cultures. This is a universal norm. Who has yet determined how much the domination of others contributed to the enormous wealth of the English and French states?

A more interesting critique of non-Western nationalism comes from the Indian scholar and theoretician Partha Chatterjee (a member of the *Subaltern Studies* group). Much nationalist thought in India, he says, depends upon the realities of colonial power, either in totally opposing it or in affirming a patriotic consciousness. This "leads inevitably to an elitism of the intelligentsia, rooted in the vision of a radical regeneration of national culture."[68] To *restore* the nation in such a situation is basically to dream a romantically utopian ideal, which is undercut by the political reality. According to Chatterjee, the radical milestone in nationalism was reached in Gandhi's opposition to modern civilization entirely: influenced by anti-modern thinkers like Ruskin and Tolstoi, Gandhi stands epistemically outside the thematic of post-Enlightenment thought.[69] Nehru's accomplishment was to take the Indian nation as liberated from modernity by Gandhi and deposit it entirely within the concept of the state. "The world of the concrete, the world of differences, of conflict, of the struggle between classes, of history and politics, now finds its unity in the life of the state."[70]

Chatterjee shows that successful anti-imperialist nationalism has a history of evasion and avoidance, and that nationalism can become a panacea for *not* dealing with economic disparities, social injustice, and the capture of the newly independent state by a nationalist elite. But he does not emphasize enough, I think, that the culture's contribution to statism is often the result of a separatist, even chauvinist and authoritarian conception of nationalism. There is also, however, a consistent intellectual trend within the nationalist consensus that is vitally critical, that refuses the short-term blandishments of separatist and triumphalist slogans in favor of the larger, more generous human realities of community *among* cultures, peoples, and societies. This community is the real human liberation portended by the resistance to imperialism. Basil Davidson makes roughly the same point in his magisterial book *Africa in Modern History: The Search for a New Society*.[71]

I do not want to be misunderstood as advocating a simple anti-nationalist position. It is historical fact that nationalism—restoration of community, assertion of identity, emergence of new cultural practices—as a mobilized political force instigated and then advanced the struggle against Western domination everywhere in the non-European world. It is no more useful to oppose that than to oppose Newton's discovery of gravity. Whether it was the Philippines, or any number of African territories, or the Indian subcontinent, the Arab world, or the Caribbean and much of Latin America, China or Japan, natives banded together in independence and nationalist groupings that were based on a sense of identity which was ethnic, religious, or communal, and was opposed to further Western encroachment. That happened from the beginning. It became a global reality in the twentieth century because it was so widespread a reaction to the Western incursion, which had also become extraordinarily widespread; with few exceptions people banded together in asserting their resistance to what they perceived was an unjust practice against them, mainly for being what they were, i.e., non-Western. Certainly it was the case that these groupings were at times fiercely exclusivist, as many historians of nationalism have shown. But we must also focus on the intellectual and cultural argument within the nationalist resistance that once independence was gained new and imaginative reconceptions of society and culture were required in order to avoid the old orthodoxies and injustices.

The women's movement is central here. For as primary resistance gets under way, to be followed by fully fledged nationalist parties, unfair male practices like concubinage, polygamy, foot-binding, *sati*, and virtual enslavement become the focal points of women's resistance. In Egypt, Turkey, Indonesia, China, and Ceylon the early-twentieth-century struggle for the emancipation of women is organically related to nationalist agitation. Raja Ramuhan Roy, an early-nineteenth-century nationalist influenced by Mary Wollstonecraft, mobilized the early campaign for Indian women's rights, a common pattern in the colonized world, where the first intellectual stirrings against injustice included attention to the abused rights of all oppressed classes. Later women writers and intellectuals—often from privileged classes and often in alliance with Western apostles of women's rights like Annie Besant—came to the forefront of agitation for women's education. Kumari Jayawardena's central work *Feminism and Nationalism in the Third World* describes the efforts of Indian reformers like Tora Dutt, D. K. Karve, and Cornelia Sorabjee, and of militants such as Pundita Ramabai. Their counterparts in the Philippines, Egypt (Huda Shaarawi), Indonesia (Raden Kartini) broadened the stream of what became feminism, which after independence became one of the main liberationist tendencies.[72]

This larger search for liberation was most in evidence where the nationalist accomplishment had been either checked or greatly delayed—in Algeria, Guinea, Palestine, sections of the Islamic and Arab world, and South Africa. Students of post-colonial politics have not, I think, looked enough at the ideas that minimize orthodoxy and authoritarian or patriarchal thought, that take a severe view of the coercive nature of identity politics. Perhaps this is because the Idi Amins and Saddam Husseins of the Third World have hijacked nationalism so completely and in so ghastly a manner. That many nationalists are sometimes more coercive or more intellectually self-critical than others is clear, but my own thesis is that, at its best, nationalist resistance to imperialism was always critical of itself. An attentive reading of towering figures within the nationalist ranks—writers like C.L.R. James, Neruda, Tagore himself, Fanon, Cabral, and others—discriminates among the various forces vying for ascendancy within the anti-imperialist, nationalist camp. James is a perfect case in point. Long a champion of Black nationalism, he always tempered his advocacy with disclaimers and reminders that assertions of ethnic particularity were not enough, just as solidarity without criticism was not enough. There is a great deal of hope to be derived from this if only because, far from being at the end of history, we are in a position to do something about our own present and future history, whether we live inside or outside the metropolitan world.

In sum, decolonization is a very complex battle over the course of different political destinies, different histories and geographies, and it is replete with works of the imagination, scholarship and counter-scholarship. The struggle took the form of strikes, marches, violent attack, retribution and counter-retribution. Its fabric is also made up of novelists and colonial officials writing about the nature of the Indian mentality, for example, of the land rent schemes of Bengal, of the structure of Indian society; and, in response, of Indians writing novels about a greater share in their rule, intellectuals and orators appealing to the masses for greater commitments to and mobilization for independence.

One cannot put timetables or fixed dates on this. India followed one course, Burma another, West Africa another, Algeria still another, Egypt, Syria, and Senegal still others. But in all cases one sees the gradually more and more perceptible divisions between the massive national blocks: the West—France, Britain, Holland, Belgium, Germany, etc.—on one side, most of the natives on the other. Generally speaking therefore anti-imperialist resistance builds gradually from sporadic and often unsuccessful revolts until after World War One it erupts variously in major parties, movements, and personalities all over the empire; for three decades after World War Two, it becomes more militantly independence-minded and yields up the new states in Africa and Asia. In the process it permanently changes the internal situation of the Western powers, which divided into opponents and supporters of the imperial policy.

(III)

Yeats and Decolonization

William Butler Yeats has now been almost completely assimilated into the canon as well as into the discourses of modern English literature and European high modernism. Both these reckon with him as a great modern Irish poet, deeply affiliated and interacting with his native traditions, the historical and political context of his times, and the complex situation of being a poet writing in English in a turbulently nationalist Ireland. Despite Yeats's obvious and, I would say, settled presence in Ireland, in British culture and literature, and in European modernism, he does present another fascinating aspect: that of the indisputably great *national* poet who during a period of anti-imperialist resistance articulates the experiences, the aspirations, and the restorative vision of a people suffering under the dominion of an offshore power.

From this perspective Yeats is a poet who belongs in a tradition not usually considered his, that of the colonial world ruled by European imperialism during a climactic insurrectionary stage. If this is not a customary way of interpreting Yeats, then we need to say that he also belongs naturally to the cultural domain, his by virtue of Ireland's colonial status, which it shares with a host of non-European regions: cultural dependency and antagonism together.

The high age of imperialism is said to have begun in the late 1870s, but in English-speaking realms, it began well over seven hundred years before, as Angus Calder's gripping book *Revolutionary Empire* demonstrates so well. Ireland was ceded by the Pope to Henry II of England in the 1150s; he himself came to Ireland in 1171. From that time on an amazingly persistent cultural attitude existed toward Ireland as a place whose inhabitants were a barbarian and degenerate race. Recent critics and historians—Seamus Deane, Nicholas Canny, Joseph Leerson, and R. N. Lebow among others—have studied and documented this history, to whose formation such impressive figures as Edmund Spenser and David Hume contributed in very large measure.

Thus India, North Africa, the Caribbean, Central and South America, many parts of Africa, China and Japan, the Pacific archipelago, Malaysia, Australia, New Zealand, North America, and of course Ireland belong in a group together, although most of the time they are treated separately. All of them were sites of contention well before 1870, either between various local resistance groups, or between the European powers themselves; in some cases, India and Africa, for instance, the two struggles against outside domination were going on simultaneously long before 1857, and long before the various European congresses on Africa at the end of the century.

The point here is that no matter how one wishes to demarcate high imperialism—that period when nearly everyone in Europe and America believed him or herself to be serving the high civilizational and commercial cause of empire—imperialism itself had already been a continuous process for several centuries of overseas conquest, rapacity, and scientific exploration. For an Indian, or Irishman, or Algerian, the land was and had been dominated by an alien power, whether liberal, monarchical, or revolutionary.

But modern European imperialism was a constitutively, radically different type of overseas domination from all earlier forms. Scale and scope were only part of the difference, though certainly not Byzantium, or Rome, or Athens, or Baghdad, or Spain and Portugal during the fifteenth and sixteenth centuries controlled anything like the size of the territories controlled by Britain and France in the nineteenth century. The more important differences are first the sustained longevity of the disparity in power, and second, the massive organization of the power, which affected the details and not just the large outlines of life. By the early nineteenth century, Europe had begun the industrial transformation of its economies—Britain leading the way; feudal and traditional landholding structures were changing; new mercantilist patterns of overseas trade, naval power, and colonialist settlement were being established; the bourgeois revolution was entering its triumphant stage. All these developments gave Europe a further ascendancy over its offshore possessions, a profile of imposing and even daunting power. By the beginning of World War One, Europe and America held most of the earth's surface in some sort of colonial subjugation.

This came about for many reasons, which a whole library of systematic studies (beginning with those by critics of imperialism during its most aggressive phase such as Hobson, Rosa Luxemburg, and Lenin) has ascribed to largely economic and somewhat ambiguously characterized political processes (in the case of Joseph Schumpeter, psychologically aggressive ones as well). The theory I advance in this book is that culture played a very important, indeed indispensable role. At the heart of European culture during the many decades of imperial expansion lay an undeterred and unrelenting Eurocentrism. This accumulated experiences, territories, peoples, histories; it studied them, it classified them, it verified them, and as Calder says, it allowed "European men of business" the power "to scheme grandly";[73] but above all, it subordinated them by banishing their identities, except as a lower order of being, from the culture and indeed the very idea of white Christian Europe. This cultural process has to be seen as a vital, informing, and invigorating counterpoint to the economic and political machinery at the material center of imperialism. This Eurocentric culture relentlessly codified and observed everything about the non-European or peripheral world, and so thoroughly and in so detailed a manner as to leave few items untouched, few cultures unstudied, few peoples and spots of land unclaimed.

From these views there was hardly any significant divergence from the Renaissance on, and if it is embarrassing for us to remark that those elements of a society we have long considered to be progressive were, so far as empire was concerned, uniformly retrograde, we still must not be afraid to say it. Advanced writers and artists, the working class, and women—groups marginal in the West—showed an imperialist fervor that increased in intensity and perfervid enthusiasm as the competition among various European and American powers increased in brutality and senseless, even profitless, control. Eurocentrism penetrated to the core of the workers' movement, the women's movement, the avant-garde arts movement, leaving no one of significance untouched.

As imperialism increased in scope and in depth, so too, in the colonies themselves, the resistance mounted. Just as in Europe the global accumulation that gathered the colonial domains into the world market economy was supported and enabled by a culture giving empire ideological license, so in the overseas *imperium* the massive political, economic, and military resistance was carried forward and informed by an actively provocative and challenging culture of resistance. This was a culture with a long tradition of integrity and power in its own right, not simply a belated reactive response to Western imperialism.

In Ireland, Calder says, the idea of murdering Gaels was from the start "as part of a royal army or with royal approval, [considered] patriotic, heroic and just."[74] The idea of English racial superiority became ingrained; so humane a poet and gentleman as Edmund Spenser in his *View of the Present State of Ireland* (1596) was boldly proposing that since the Irish were barbarian Scythians, most of them should be exterminated. Revolts against the English naturally began early, and by the eighteenth century under Wolfe Tone and Grattan the opposition had acquired an identity of its own, with organizations, idioms, rules. "Patriotism was coming into vogue"[75] during mid-century, Calder continues, which, with the extraordinary talents of Swift, Goldsmith, and Burke, gave Irish resistance a discourse entirely its own.

Much but by no means all the resistance to imperialism was conducted in the broad context of nationalism. "Nationalism" is a word that still signifies all sorts of undifferentiated things, but it serves me quite adequately to identify the mobilizing force that coalesced into resistance against an alien and occupying empire on the part of peoples possessing a common history, religion, and language. Yet for all its success—indeed because of its success— in ridding many territories of colonial overlords, nationalism has remained a deeply problematic enterprise. When it got people out on the streets to march against the white master, nationalism was often led by lawyers, doctors, and writers who were partly formed and to some degree produced by the colonial power. The national bourgeoisies and their specialized elites, of which Fanon speaks so ominously, in effect tended to replace the colonial force with a new class-based and ultimately exploitative one, which replicated the old colonial structures in new terms. There are states all across the formerly colonized world that have bred pathologies of power, as Eqbal Ahmad has called them.[76] Also, the cultural horizons of a nationalism may be fatally limited by the common history it presumes of colonizer and colonized. Imperialism after all was a cooperative venture, and a salient trait of its modern form is that it was (or claimed to be) an educational movement; it set out quite consciously to modernize, develop, instruct, and civilize. The annals of schools, missions, universities, scholarly societies, hospitals in Asia, Africa, Latin America, Europe, and America are filled with this history, which over time established so-called modernizing trends as much as it muted the harsher aspects of imperialist domination. But at its center it preserved the nineteenth-century divide between native and Westerner.

The great colonial schools, for example, taught generations of the native bourgeoisie important truths about history, science, culture. Out of that learning process millions grasped the fundamentals of modern life, yet remained subordinate dependents of an authority based elsewhere than in their lives. Since one of the purposes of colonial education was to promote the history of France or Britain, that same education also demoted the native history. Thus for the native, there were always the Englands, Frances, Germanys, Hollands as distant repositories of the Word, despite the affinities developed between native and "white man" during the years of productive collaboration. Joyce's Stephen Dedalus as he faces his English director of studies is a famous example of someone who discovers this with unusual force:

> The language we are speaking is his before it is mine. How different are the words *home, Christ, ale, master,* on his lips and on mine! I cannot speak

or write these words without unrest of spirit. His language, so familiar and so foreign, will always be for me an acquired speech. I have not made or accepted its words. My voice holds them at bay. My soul frets in the shadow of his language.[77]

Nationalism in Ireland, India, and Egypt, for example, was rooted in the long-standing struggle for native rights and independence by nationalist parties like the Sinn Fein, Congress, and Wafd. Similar processes occurred in other parts of Africa and Asia. Nehru, Nasser, Sukarno, Nyerere, Nkrumah: the pantheon of Bandung flourished, in all its suffering and greatness, because of the nationalist dynamic, which was culturally embodied in the inspirational autobiographies, instructional manuals, and philosophical meditations of these great nationalist leaders. An unmistakable patriarchal cast can be discerned everywhere in classical nationalism, with delays and distortions in women's and minority rights (to say nothing of democratic freedoms) that are still perceptible today. Crucial works like Panikar's *Asia and Western Dominance,* George Antonius's *The Arab Awakening,* and the various works of the Irish Revival were also produced out of classical nationalism.

Within the nationalist revival, in Ireland and elsewhere, there were two distinct political moments, each with its own imaginative culture, the second unthinkable without the first. The first was a pronounced awareness of European and Western culture *as* imperialism; this reflexive moment of consciousness enabled the African, Caribbean, Irish, Latin American, or Asian citizen to assert the end of Europe's cultural claim to guide and/or instruct the non-European or non-mainland individual. Often this was first done, as Thomas Hodgkin has argued, by "prophets and priests,"[78] among them poets and visionaries, versions perhaps of Hobsbawm's "primitive rebels." The second more openly liberationist moment occurred during the dramatically prolonged Western imperial mission after World War Two in various colonial regions, principally Algeria, Vietnam, Palestine, Ireland, Guinea, and Cuba. Whether in the Indian constitution, or in statements of Pan-Arabism and Pan-Africanism, or in its particularist forms such as Pearse's Gaelic or Senghor's *négritude,* conventional nationalism was revealed to be both insufficient and crucial, but only as a first step. Out of this paradox comes the idea of liberation, a strong new post-nationalist theme that had been implicit in the works of Connolly, Garvey, Martí, Mariategi, Cabral, and Du Bois, for instance, but required the propulsive infusion of theory and even of armed, insurrectionary militancy to bring it forward clearly.

Let us look again at the literature of the first of these moments, that of anti-imperialist resistance. If there is anything that radically distinguishes the imagination of anti-imperialism, it is the primacy of the geographical element. Imperialism after all is an act of geographical violence through which virtually every space in the world is explored, charted, and finally brought under control. For the native, the history of colonial servitude is inaugurated by loss of the locality to the outsider; its geographical identity must thereafter be searched for and somehow restored. Because of the presence of the colonizing outsider, the land is recoverable at first only through the imagination.

Let me give three examples of how imperialism's complex yet firm geographical *morte main* moves from the general to the specific. The most general is presented in Crosby's *Ecological Imperialism*. Crosby says that wherever they went Europeans immediately began to change the local habitat; their conscious aim was to transform territories into images of what they had left behind. This process was never-ending, as a huge number of plants, animals, and crops as well as building methods gradually turned the colony into a new place, complete with new diseases, environmental imbalances, and traumatic dislocations for the overpowered natives.[79] A changed ecology also introduced a changed political system. In the eyes of the later nationalist poet or visionary, this alienated the people from their authentic traditions, ways of life, and political organizations. A great deal of romantic mythmaking went into these nationalist versions of how imperialism alienated the land, but we must not doubt the extent of the actual changes wrought.

A second example is the rationalizing projects of long-standing territorial possession, which seek routinely to make land profitable and at the same time to integrate it with an external rule. In his book *Uneven Development* the geographer Neil Smith brilliantly formulates how capitalism historically has produced a particular kind of nature and space, an unequally developed landscape that integrates poverty with wealth, industrial urbanization with agricultural diminishment. The culmination of this process is imperialism, which dominates, classifies, and universally commodifies all space under the aegis of the metropolitan center. Its cultural analogue is late-nineteenth-century commercial geography, whose perspectives (for example in the work of Mackinder and Chisolm) justified imperialism as the result of "natural" fertility or infertility, available sea-lanes, permanently differentiated zones, territories, climates, and peoples.[80] Thus is accomplished "the universality of capitalism," which is "the differentiation of national space according to the territorial division of labor."[81]

Following Hegel, Marx, and Lukacs, Smith calls the production of this scientifically "natural" world a *second* nature. To the anti-imperialist imagination, our space at home in the peripheries has been usurped and put to use by outsiders for their purpose. It is therefore necessary to seek out, to map, to invent, or to discover a *third* nature, not pristine and pre-historical ("Romantic Ireland's dead and gone," says Yeats) but deriving from the deprivations of the present. The impulse is cartographic, and among its most striking examples are Yeats's early poems collected in "The Rose," Neruda's various poems charting the Chilean landscape, Césaire on the Antilles, Faiz on Pakistan, and Darwish on Palestine—

> *Restore to me the color of face*
> *And the warmth of body,*
> *The light of heart and eye,*
> *The salt of bread and earth . . . the Motherland.*[82]

But—a third example—colonial space must be transformed sufficiently so as no longer to appear foreign to the imperial eye. More than any other of its colonies, Britain's Ireland was subjected to innumerable metamorphoses through repeated settling projects and, in culmination, its virtual incorporation in 1801 through the Act of Union. Thereafter an Ordnance Survey of Ireland was ordered in 1824 whose goal was to anglicize the names, redraw the land boundaries to permit valuation of property (and further expropriation of land in favor of English and "seignorial" families), and permanently subjugate the population. The survey was carried out almost entirely by English personnel, which, as Mary Hamer has cogently argued, had the "immediate effect of defining the Irish as incompetent [and] . . . depress[ing] their] national achievement."[83] One of Brian Friel's most powerful plays, *Translations* (1980), deals with the shattering effect of the Ordnance Survey on the indigenous inhabitants. "In such a process," Hamer continues, "the colonized is typically [supposed to be] passive and spoken for, does not control its own representation but is represented in accordance with a hegemonic impulse by which it is constructed as a stable and unitary entity."[84] And what was done in Ireland was also done in Bengal or, by the French, in Algeria.

One of the first tasks of the culture of resistance was to reclaim, rename, and reinhabit the land. And with that came a whole set of further assertions, recoveries, and identifications, all of them quite literally grounded on this poetically projected base. The search for authenticity, for a more congenial national origin than that provided by colonial history, for a new pantheon of heroes and (occasionally) heroines, myths, and religions—these too are made possible by a sense of the land reappropriated by its people. And along with these nationalistic adumbrations of the decolonized identity, there always goes an almost magically inspired, quasi-alchemical redevelopment of the native language.

Yeats is especially interesting here. With Caribbean and some African writers he expresses the predicament of sharing a language with the colonial overlord, and of course he belongs in many important ways to the Protestant Ascendancy, whose Irish loyalties were confused, to put it mildly, if not in his case quite contradictory. There is a fairly logical progression from Yeats's early Gaelicism, with its Celtic preoccupations and themes, to his later systematic mythologies as set down in programmatic poems like "Ego Dominus Tuus" and in the treatise *A Vision*. For Yeats the overlapping he knew existed of his Irish nationalism with the English cultural heritage, which both dominated and empowered him, was bound to cause tension, and one may speculate that it was the pressure of this urgently political and secular tension that caused him to try to resolve it on a "higher," that is, non-political level. The deeply eccentric and aestheticized histories he produced in *A Vision* and the later quasi-religious poems elevate the tension to an extra-worldly level, as if Ireland were best taken over, so to speak, at a level above that of the ground.

Seamus Deane, in *Celtic Revivals*, the most interesting and brilliant account of Yeats's super-terrestrial idea of revolution, has suggested that Yeats's early and invented Ireland was "amenable to his imagination . . . [whereas] he ended by finding an Ireland recalcitrant to it." Whenever Yeats tried to reconcile his occultist views with an actual Ireland—as in "The Statues"—the results are strained, Deane says correctly.[85] Because Yeats's Ireland was a revolutionary country, he could use its backwardness as a source for a radically disturbing, disruptive return to spiritual ideals lost in an over-developed modern Europe. In such dramatic realities as the Easter 1916 uprising, Yeats also saw the breaking of a cycle of endless, perhaps finally meaningless recurrence, as symbolized by the apparently limitless travails of Cuchulain. Deane's theory is that the birth of an Irish national identity coincides for Yeats with the breaking of the cycle, although it also under-scores, and reinforces in Yeats himself, the colonialist British attitude of a specific Irish national character. Thus Yeats's return to mysticism and his recourse to fascism, Deane says perceptively, underline the colonial predica-ment also expressed, for example, in V. S. Naipaul's representations of India, that of a culture indebted to the mother country for its own self and for a sense of "Englishness" and yet turning toward the colony: "such a search for a national signature becomes colonial, on account of the different histories of the two islands. The greatest flowering of such a search has been Yeats's poetry."[86] Far from representing an outdated nationalism, Yeats's wilful mysticism and incoherence embody a revolutionary potential, and the poet insists "that Ireland should retain its culture by keeping awake its consciousness of metaphysical questions," as Deane puts it.[87] In a world from which the harsh strains of capitalism have removed thought and reflection, a poet who can stimulate a sense of the eternal and of death into consciousness is the true rebel, a figure whose colonial diminishments spur him to a negative apprehension of his society and of "civilized" modernity.

This rather Adorno-esque formulation of Yeats's quandary is of course powerfully attractive. Yet perhaps it is weakened by its wanting to render Yeats more heroic than a crudely political reading would have suggested, and excuse his unacceptable and indigestible reactionary politics—his outright fascism, his fantasies of old homes and families, his incoherently occult divagations—by translating them into an instance of Adorno's "negative dialectic." As a small corrective, we might more accurately see Yeats as an exacerbated example of the *nativist* phenomenon which flourished elsewhere (e.g., *négritude*) as a result of the colonial encounter.

True, the physical, geographical connections are closer between England and Ireland than between England and India, or between France and Algeria or Senegal. But the imperial relationship is there in all cases. Irish people can never be English any more than Cambodians or Algerians can be French. This it seems to me was always the case in every colonial relationship, because it is the first principle that a clear-cut and absolute hierarchical distinction should remain constant between ruler and ruled, whether or not the latter is white. Nativism, alas, reinforces the distinction even while revaluating the weaker or subservient partner. And it has often led to compelling but demagogic assertions about a native past, narrative or actuality that stands free from worldly time itself. One sees this in such enterprises as Senghor's *négritude*, or in the Rastafarian movement, or in the Garveyite back to Africa project for American Blacks, or in the rediscoveries of various unsullied, pre-colonial Muslim essences.

The tremendous *ressentiment* in nativism aside (for example, in Jalal Ali Ahmad's *Occidentosis*, an influential Iranian tract published in 1978 that blames the West for most evils in the world), there are two reasons for rejecting, or at least reconceiving, the nativist enterprise. To say, as Deane does, that it is incoherent and yet, by its negation of politics and history, also heroically revolutionary seems to me is to fall into the nativist position as if it were the only choice for a resisting, decolonizing nationalism. But we have evidence of its ravages: to accept nativism is to accept the consequences of imperialism, the racial, religious, and political divisions imposed by imperialism itself. To leave the historical world for the metaphysics of essences like *négritude*, Irishness, Islam, or Catholicism is to abandon history for essentializations that have the power to turn human beings against each other; often this abandonment of the secular world has led to a sort of millenarianism if the movement has had a mass base, or it has degenerated into small-scale private craziness, or into an unthinking acceptance of stereotypes, myths, animosities, and traditions encouraged by imperialism. Such programs are hardly what great resistance movements had imagined as their goals.

A useful way of getting a better hold of this analytically is to look at an analysis of the same problem done in the African context: Wole Soyinka's withering critique of *négritude* published in 1976. Soyinka notes that the concept of *négritude* is the second, inferior term in an opposition—European versus African—that "accepted the dialectical structure of European ideological confrontations but borrowed from the very components of its racist syllogism."[88] Thus Europeans are analytical, Africans "incapable of analytical thought. Therefore the African is not highly developed" whereas the European is. The result is, according to Soyinka, that

> *négritude* trapped itself in what was primarily a defensive role, even though its accents were strident, its syntax hyperbolic and its strategy aggressive. . . . *Négritude* stayed within a pre-set system of Eurocentric intellectual analysis of both man and his society, and tried to re-define the African and his society in those externalized terms.[89]

We are left with the paradox that Soyinka himself articulates, that (he has Fanon in mind) adoring the Negro is as "sick" as abominating him. And while it is impossible to avoid the combative, assertive early stages in the nativist identity—they *always* occur: Yeats's early poetry is not only about Ireland, but about Irishness—there is a good deal of promise in getting beyond them, not remaining trapped in the emotional self-indulgence of celebrating one's own identity. There is first of all the possibility of discovering a world *not* constructed out of warring essences. Second, there is the possibility of a universalism that is not limited or coercive, which believing that all people have only one single identity is—that all the Irish are only Irish, Indians Indians, Africans Africans, and so on *ad nauseam*. Third, and most important, moving beyond nativism does not mean abandoning nationality, but it does mean thinking of local identity as not exhaustive, and therefore not being anxious to confine oneself to one's own sphere, with its ceremonies of belonging, its built-in chauvinism, and its limiting sense of security.

Nationality, nationalism, nativism: the progression is, I believe, more and more constraining. In countries like Algeria and Kenya one can watch the heroic resistance of a community partly formed out of colonial degradations, leading to a protracted armed and cultural conflict with the imperial powers, in turn giving way to a one-party state with dictatorial rule and, in the case of Algeria, an uncompromising Islamic fundamentalist opposition. The debilitating despotism of the Moi regime in Kenya can scarcely be said to complete the liberationist currents of the Mau Mau uprising. No transformation of social consciousness here, but only an appalling pathology of power duplicated elsewhere—in the Philippines, Indonesia, Pakistan, Zaire, Morocco, Iran.

In any case nativism is *not* the only alternative. There is the possibility of a more generous and pluralistic vision of the world, in which imperialism courses on, as it were, belatedly in different forms (the North-South polarity of our own time is one), and the relationship of domination continues, but the opportunities for liberation are open. Even though there was an Irish Free State by the end of his life in 1939, Yeats partially belonged to this second moment, as shown by his sustained anti-British sentiment and the anger and gaiety of his anarchically disturbing last poetry. In this phase *liberation,* and not nationalist independence, is the new alternative, liberation which by its very nature involves, in Fanon's words, a transformation of social consciousness beyond national consciousness.[90]

Looking at it from this perspective, then, Yeats's slide into incoherence and mysticism during the 1920s, his rejection of politics, and his arrogant if charming espousal of fascism (or authoritarianism of an Italian or South American kind) are not to be excused, not too quickly to be dialecticized into the negative utopian mode. For one can quite easily situate and criticize those unacceptable attitudes of Yeats without changing one's view of Yeats as a poet of decolonization.

This way beyond nativism is figured in the great turn at the climax of Césaire's *Cahier d'un retour* when the poet realizes that, after rediscovering and re-experiencing his past, after re-entering the passions, horrors, and circumstances of his history as a Black, after feeling and then emptying himself of his anger, after accepting—

> *J'accepte . . . j'accepte . . . entièrement, sans reserve*
> *ma race qu'aucune ablution d'hypsope et de lys melés ne pourrait purifier*
> *ma race rongée de macule*
> *ma race raisin mur pour pieds ivres*[91]

> *(I accept . . . I accept . . . totally, without reservation*
> *my race that no ablution of hyssop mixed with lilies could purify*
> *my race pitted with blemishes*
> *my race a ripe grape for drunken feet)*

—after all this he is suddenly assailed by strength and life "comme un taureau," and begins to understand that

> *il n'est point vrai que l'oeuvre de l'homme est finie*
> *que nous n'avons rien à faire au monde*
> *que nous parasitons le monde*
> *qu'il suffit que nous nous mettions au pas du monde*
> *mais l'oeuvre de l'homme vient seulment de commencer*
> *et il reste à l'homme à conquérir toute interdiction*
> *immobilisée aux coins de sa ferveur et aucune race*
> *ne possède le monopole de la beauté, de l'intelligence, de la force*
>
> *et il est place pour tous au rendez-vous de la conquête*
> *et nous savons maintenant que le soleil tourne*
> *autour de notre terre éclairant la parcelle qu'a fixé*
> *notre volonté seule et que toute étoile chute de ciel*
> *en terre à notre commandement sans limite.*[92]
>
> *(for it is not true that the work of man is done*
> *that we have no business being on earth*
> *that we parasite the world*
> *that it is enough for us to heel to the world*
> *whereas the work has only begun*
> *and man still must overcome all the interdictions*
> *wedged in the recesses of his fervor and no race has a*
> *monopoly on beauty, on intelligence, on strength*
>
> *and there is room for everyone at the convocation of*
> *conquest and we know now that the sun turns around our*
> *earth lighting the parcel designated by our will alone*
> *and that every star falls from sky to earth at our*
> *omnipotent command.)*

The striking phrases are "à conquérir toute interdiction immobilisée aux coins de sa ferveur" and "le soleil . . . éclairant la parcelle qu'a fixé notre volonté seule." You don't give in to the rigidity and interdictions of self-imposed limitations that come with race, moment, or milieu; instead you move through them to an animated and expanded sense of "[le] rendez-vous de la conquête," which necessarily involves more than your Ireland, your Martinique, your Pakistan.

I don't mean to use Césaire *against* Yeats (or Seamus Deane's Yeats), but rather more fully to associate a major strand in Yeats's poetry both with the poetry of decolonization and resistance, and with the historical alternatives to the nativist impasse. In many other ways Yeats is like other poets resisting imperialism—in his insistence on a new narrative for his people, his anger at England's schemes for Irish partition (and enthusiasm for wholeness), the celebration and commemoration of violence in bringing about a new order, and the sinuous interweaving of loyalty and betrayal in the nationalist setting. Yeats's direct association with Parnell and O'Leary, with the Abbey Theatre, with the Easter Uprising, bring to his poetry what R. P. Blackmur, borrowing from Jung, calls "the terrible ambiguity of an immediate experience."[93] Yeats's work of the early 1920s has an uncanny resemblance to the engagement and ambiguities of Darwish's Palestinian poetry half a century later, in its renderings of violence, of the overwhelming suddenness and surprises of historical events, of politics and poetry as opposed to violence and guns (see his marvelous lyric "The Rose and The Dictionary"),[94] of the search for respites after the last border has been crossed, the last sky flown in. "The holy centaurs of the hills are vanished," says Yeats, "I have nothing but the embittered sun."

One feels in reading the great poems of that climactic period after the Easter Uprising of 1916, like "Nineteen Hundred and Nineteen" or "Easter 1916," and "September 1913," not just the disappointments of life commanded by "the greasy till" or the violence of roads and horses, of "weasels fighting in a hole," or the rituals of what has been called Blood Sacrifice poetry, but also a terrible new beauty that changes the old political and moral landscape. Like all poets of decolonization, Yeats struggles to announce the contours of an imagined or ideal community, crystallized by its sense not only of itself but also of its enemy. "Imagined community" is apt here, so long as we are not obliged also to accept Benedict Anderson's mistakenly linear periodizations. In the cultural discourses of decolonization, a great many languages, histories, forms circulate. As Barbara Harlow has shown in *Resistance Literature*, the instability of time, which has to be made and remade by the people and its leaders, is a theme one sees in all the genres—spiritual autobiographies, poems of protest, prison memoirs, didactic dramas of deliverance. The shifts in Yeats's accounts of his great cycles invoke this instability, as does the easy commerce in his poetry between popular and formal speech, folk-tale and learned writing. The disquiet of what T. S. Eliot calls the "cunning history [and] contrived corridors" of time—the wrong turns, the overlap, the senseless repetition, the occasionally glorious moment—furnishes Yeats, as it does all the poets and men of letters of decolonization—Tagore, Senghor, Césaire—with stern martial accents, heroism, and the grinding persistence of "the uncontrollable mystery on the bestial floor." Thus the writer rises out of his national environment and gains universal significance.

In the first volume of his memoirs, Pablo Neruda speaks of a writers' congress in Madrid held in 1937 in defense of the Republic. "Priceless replies" to the invitations "poured in from all over. One was from Yeats, Ireland's national poet; another, from Selma Lagerlöf, the notable Swedish writer. They were both too old to travel to a beleaguered city like Madrid, which was steadily being pounded by bombs, but they rallied to the defense of the Spanish Republic."[95] Just as Neruda saw no difficulty in thinking of himself as a poet who dealt both with internal colonialism in Chile and with external imperialism throughout Latin America, we should think of Yeats, I believe, as an Irish poet with more than strictly local Irish meaning and applications. Neruda accepted him as a national poet representing the Irish nation in its war against tyranny and, according to Neruda, Yeats responded positively to that unmistakably anti-fascist call, despite his frequently cited dispositions toward European fascism.

The resemblance between Neruda's justly famous poem "El Pueblo" (in the 1962 collection *Plenos Poderes,* translated by Alastair Reid, whose version I have used, as *Fully Empowered*) and Yeats's "The Fisherman" is striking: in both poems the central figure is an anonymous man of the people, who in his strength and loneliness is a mute expression *of* the people, a quality that inspires the poet in his work. Yeats:

> *It's long since I began*
> *To call up to the eyes*
> *This wise and simple man.*
> *All day I'd look in the face*
> *What I had hoped 'twould be*
> *To write for my own race*
> *And the reality.*[96]

Neruda:

> *I knew that man, and when I could*
> *when I still had eyes in my head,*
> *when I still had a voice in my throat,*
> *I sought him among the tombs and I said to him,*
> *pressing his arm that still was not dust:*
> *"Everything will pass, you will still be living.*
> *You set fire to life.*

You made what is yours."
So let no one be perturbed when
I seem to be alone and am not alone;
I am not without company and I speak for all.
Someone is hearing me without knowing it,
But those I sing of, those who know,
go on being born and will overflow the world.[97]

The poetic calling develops out of a pact made between people and poet; hence the power of such invocations to an actual poem as those provided by the figures both men seem to require.

The chain does not stop there, since Neruda goes on (in "Deber del Poeta") to claim that "through me, freedom and the sea/will call in answer to the shrouded heart," and Yeats in "The Tower" speaks of sending imagination forth "and call[ing] images and memories/From ruin or from ancient trees."[98] Because such protocols of exhortation and expansiveness are announced from under the shadow of domination, we may connect them with the narrative of liberation depicted so memorably in Fanon's *Wretched of the Earth.* For whereas the divisions and separations of the colonial order freeze the population's captivity into a sullen torpor, "new outlets . . . engender aims for the violence of colonized peoples."[99] Fanon specifies the declarations of rights, clamors for free speech and trades union demands; later, an entirely new history unfolds as a revolutionary class of militants, drawn from the ranks of the urban poor, outcasts, criminals, and *déclassés,* takes to the countryside, there slowly to form cells of armed activists, who return to the city for the final stages of the insurgency.

The extraordinary power of Fanon's writing is that it is presented as a surreptitious counter-narrative to the above-ground force of the colonial regime, which in the teleology of Fanon's narrative is certain to be defeated. The difference between Fanon and Yeats is that Fanon's theoretical and perhaps even metaphysical narrative of anti-imperialist decolonization is marked throughout with the accents and inflections of liberation: this is far more than a reactive native defensiveness, whose main problem (as Soyinka analyzed it) is that it implicitly accepts, and does not go beyond, the basic European versus non-European oppositions. Fanon's is a discourse of that anticipated triumph, liberation, that marks the second moment of decolonization. Yeats's early work, by contrast, sounds the nationalist note and stands at a threshold it cannot cross, although he sets a trajectory in common with that of other poets of decolonization, like Neruda and Darwish, which he could not complete, even though perhaps they could go further than he. One might at least give him credit for adumbrating the liberationist and utopian revolutionism in his poetry that was belied and even cancelled out by his later reactionary politics.

Yeats has often been cited in recent years as someone whose poetry warned of nationalist excesses. He is quoted without attribution, for example, in Gary Sick's book on the Carter administration's handling of the Iranian hostage crisis 1979–1981 *(All Fall Down)*;[100] and *The New York Times* correspondent in Beirut in 1975–77, the late James Markham, quoted the same passages from "The Second Coming" in an article on the onset of the Lebanese civil war in 1976. "Things fall apart; the centre cannot hold" is one phrase. The other is "The best lack all conviction, while the worst/Are full of passionate intensity." Sick and Markham both write as American liberals alarmed at the revolutionary tide sweeping through a Third World once contained by Western power. Their use of Yeats is minatory: remain orderly, or you're doomed to a frenzy you cannot control. As to how, in an inflamed colonial situation, the colonized are supposed to hold the center, neither Sick nor Markham tells us, but their presumption is that Yeats, in any event, would oppose the anarchy of civil war. It is as if both men had not thought to take the disorder back to the colonial intervention in the first place—which is what Chinua Achebe did in 1959 in his great novel *Things Fall Apart*.[101]

The point is that Yeats is at his most powerful precisely as he imagines and renders that very moment. It is helpful to remember that "the Anglo-Irish conflict" with which Yeats's poetic *oeuvre* is saturated was a "model of twentieth-century wars of liberation."[102] His greatest decolonizing works concern the birth of violence, or the violent birth of change, as in "Leda and the Swan," instants when a blinding flash of simultaneity is presented to his colonial eyes—the girl's rape, and alongside that, the question "Did she put on his knowledge with his power/Before the indifferent beak could let her drop?"[103] Yeats situates himself at that juncture where the violence of change is unarguable but where the results of the violence beseech necessary, if not always sufficient, reason. His greatest theme, in the poetry that culminates in *The Tower* (1928), is how to reconcile the inevitable violence of the colonial conflict with the everyday politics of an ongoing national struggle, and also how to square the power of the various parties in the conflict with the discourse of reason, persuasion, organization, and the requirements of poetry. Yeats's prophetic perception that at some point violence cannot be enough and that the strategies of politics and reason must come into play is, to my knowledge, the first important announcement in the context of decolonization of the need to balance violent force with an exigent political and organizational process. Fanon's assertion that liberation cannot be accomplished simply by seizing power (though "Even the wisest man grows tense/With some sort of violence")[104] comes almost half a century later. That neither Yeats nor Fanon offers a prescription for making a transition *after* decolonization to a period when a new political order achieves moral hegemony is symptomatic of the difficulty that millions of people live with today.

It is an amazing thing that the problem of Irish liberation not only has continued longer than other comparable struggles, but is so often not regarded as being an imperial or nationalist issue; instead it is comprehended as an aberration within the British dominions. Yet the facts conclusively reveal otherwise. Since Spenser's 1596 tract on Ireland, a whole tradition of British and European thought has considered the Irish to be a separate and inferior race, usually unregenerately barbarian, often delinquent and primitive. Irish nationalism for at least the last two hundred years is marked by internecine struggles involving the land question, the Church, the nature of parties and leaders. But dominating the movement is the attempt to regain control of the land where, in the words of the 1916 proclamation that founded the Irish Republic, "the right of the people of Ireland to the ownership of Ireland, and to the unfettered control of Irish destinies, [is] to be sovereign and indefeasible."[105]

Yeats cannot be severed from this quest. Regardless of his astounding genius, he contributed, as Thomas Flanagan puts it, "in Irish terms, and of course in a singularly powerful and compelling manner, that process of simultaneous abstraction and reification that, defiant of logic, is the heart of nationalism."[106] And to this work several generations of lesser writers also contributed, articulating the expression of Irish identity as it attaches to the land, to its Celtic origins, to a growing body of nationalist experiences and leaders (Wolfe Tone, Connolly, Mitchel, Isaac Butt, O'Connell, the United Irishmen, the Home Rule movement, and so on), and to a specifically national literature.[107] Literary nationalism also retrospectively includes many forerunners: Thomas Moore, early literary historians like the Abbe McGeoghehan and Samuel Ferguson, James Clarence Mangan, the Orange–Young Ireland movement, Standish O'Grady. In the poetic, dramatic, and scholarly work of today's Field Day Company (Seamus Heaney, Brian Friel, Seamus Deane, Tom Paulin) and of the literary historians Declan Kiberd and W. J. McCormack, these "revivals" of the Irish national experience are brilliantly reimagined and take the nationalist adventure to new forms of verbal expression.[108]

The essential Yeatsian themes sound through the earlier and later literary work: the problem of assuring the marriage of knowledge to power, of understanding violence; interestingly they are also sounded in Gramsci's roughly contemporary work, undertaken and elaborated in a different context. In the Irish colonial setting, Yeats seems best able to pose and re-pose the question provocatively, using his poetry, Blackmur says, as a technique of trouble.[109] And he goes further in the great poems of summation and vision like "Among School Children," "The Tower," "A Prayer for My Daughter," "Under Ben Bulben," and "The Circus Animals' Desertion." These are poems of genealogy and recapitulation, of course: telling and retelling the story of his life from early nationalist turbulence to the status of a senator walking through a classroom and thinking of how Leda figured in all their pasts, or a loving father thinking about his child, or a senior artist trying to achieve equanimity of vision, or finally, as a long-time craftsman somehow surviving the loss (desertion) of his powers, Yeats reconstructs his own life poetically as an epitome of the national life.

These poems reverse the reductive and slanderous encapsulation of Irish actualities which, according to Joseph Leerssen's learned book *Mere Irish and Fior-Ghael*, had been the fate of the Irish at the hands of English writers for eight centuries, displacing ahistorical rubrics like "potato-eaters," or "bog-dwellers," or "shanty people."[110] Yeats's poetry joins his people to its history, the more imperatively in that as father, or as "sixty-year-old smiling public man," or as son and husband, the poet assumes that the narrative and the density of personal experience are equivalent to the experience of his people. The references in the closing strophes of "Among School Children" suggest that Yeats was reminding his audience that history and the nation are not separable, any more than a dancer is separate from the dance.

The drama of Yeats's accomplishment in restoring a suppressed history and rejoining the nation to it is expressed well by Fanon's description of the situation Yeats had to overcome: "Colonialism is not satisfied merely with holding a people in its grip and emptying the native's brain of all form and content. By a kind of perverted logic, it turns to the past of the people, and distorts, disfigures and destroys it."[111] Yeats rises from the level of personal and folk experience to that of national archetype without losing the immediacy of the former or the stature of the latter. And his unerring choice of genealogical fables and figures speaks to another aspect of colonialism as Fanon described it: its capacity for separating the individual from his or her own instinctual life, breaking the generative lineaments of the national identity:

On the unconscious plane, colonialism therefore did not seek to be considered by the native as a gently loving mother who protects her child from a hostile environment, but rather as a mother who unceasingly restrains her fundamentally perverse offspring from managing to commit suicide and from giving free rein to its evil instincts. The colonial mother protects her child from itself, from its ego, and from its physiology, its biology, and its own unhappiness which is its very essence.

In such a situation the claims of the native intellectual [and poet] are not a luxury but a necessity in any coherent program. The native intellectual who takes up arms to defend his nation's legitimacy, who is willing to strip himself naked to study the history of his body, is obliged to dissect the heart of his people.[112]

No wonder that Yeats instructed Irish poets to

> *Scorn the sort now growing up*
> *All out of shape from toe to top,*
> *Their unremembering hearts and heads*
> *Base-born products of base beds.*[113]

That in the process Yeats ended up creating not individuals but types that "cannot quite overcome the abstractions from which they sprang," again according to Blackmur,[114] is true insofar as the decolonizing program and its background in the history of Ireland's subjugation are ignored, as Blackmur was wont to do; his interpretations are masterful yet ahistorical. When the colonial realities are taken into account, we get insight and experience, and not merely "the allegorical simulacrum churned with action."[115]

Yeats's full system of cycles, pernes, and gyres seems important only as it symbolizes his efforts to lay hold of a distant and yet orderly reality as a refuge from the turbulence of his immediate experience. When in the Byzantium poems he asks to be gathered into the artifice of eternity, the need for respite from age and from what he would later call "the struggle of the fly in marmalade" is even more starkly at work. Otherwise it is difficult to read most of his poetry and not feel that Swift's devastating anger and genius were harnessed by Yeats to lift the burdens of Ireland's colonial afflictions. True, he stopped short of imagining full political liberation, but he gave us a major international achievement in cultural decolonization nonetheless.

(IV)

The Voyage In and the Emergence of Opposition

The Irish experience and other colonial histories in other parts of the contemporary world testify to a new phenomenon: a spiral away and extrapolation from Europe and the West. I am not saying that only native writers are part of this transformation, but the process begins most productively in peripheral, off-center work that gradually enters the West and then requires acknowledgement.

As recently as thirty years ago, few European or American universities devoted curricular attention to African literature. Now a healthy interest is taken in the works of Bessie Head, Alex La Guma, Wole Soyinka, Nadine Gordimer, J. M. Coetzee as literature that speaks independently of an African experience. Similarly it is no longer possible to ignore the work of Anta Diop, Paulin Hountondjii, V. Y. Mudimbe, Ali Mazrui in even the most cursory survey of African history, politics, and philosophy. True, an ambiance of polemic surrounds this work, but that is only because one cannot look at African writing except as embedded in its political circumstances, of which the history of imperialism and resistance to it is surely one of the most important. This is not to say that African culture is any less cultural than, say, French or British culture, but that it is harder to render invisible the politics of African culture. "Africa" is still a site of contention, as we can tell when we note that its scholars, like those of the Middle East, are put into categories based on the old imperialist politics—pro-liberation, anti-*apartheid,* and so on. A set of alliances, or intellectual formations, thus connects the English work of Basil Davidson with the politics of Amílcar Cabral, for example, to produce oppositional and independent scholarship.

Nevertheless, many constituent parts of the West's major cultural formations, of which this "peripheral" work is one, have been historically hidden in and by imperialism's consolidating vision. One is reminded of Maupassant enjoying a daily lunch at the Eiffel Tower because it was the only place in Paris where he did not have to look at the imposing structure. Even now, since most accounts of European cultural history take little notice of the empire, and the great novelists especially are analyzed as if they were completely aloof from it, today's scholar and critic is accustomed to accept without noticing their imperial attitudes and references along with their authoritative centrality.

Yet it bears repeating that no matter how apparently complete the dominance of an ideology or social system, there are always going to be parts of the social experience that it does not cover and control. From these parts very frequently comes opposition, both self-conscious and dialectical. This is not as complicated as it sounds. Opposition to a dominant structure arises out of a perceived, perhaps even militant awareness on the part of individuals and groups outside and inside it that, for example, certain of its policies are wrong. As the major studies of Gordon K. Lewis *(Slavery, Imperialism, and Freedom)* and Robin Blackburn *(The Overthrow of Colonial Slavery, 1776–1848)* show,[116] an extraordinary amalgam of metropolitan individuals and movements—millenarians, revivalists, do-gooders, political radicals, cynical planters, and canny politicians—contributed to the decline and end of the slave trade by the 1840s. And far from there being a single unopposed British colonial interest running directly from, say, the Hanoverians to Queen Victoria, historical research that might be called revisionist or oppositional has shown a variegated contest of interests. Scholars like Lewis, Blackburn, Basil Davidson, Terence Ranger, and E. P. Thompson among others premised their work on the paradigm given by the cultural and political resistance *within* imperialism. Thus British historians of colonial India and Africa, for example, came to write oppositional histories of those territories in sympathetic alliance with local forces there, cultural as well as political, who were considered nationalist and anti-imperialist. As Thomas Hodgkin notes, having explained the rise and subsequent effects of imperialism, these intellectuals tried to show "how this entire system of relationships, and the attitudes arising therefrom, can be abolished or transformed."[117]

A distinction between anti-colonialism and anti-imperialism needs quickly to be made. There was a lively European debate dating from at least the mid–eighteenth century on the merits and demerits of holding colonies. Behind it were the earlier positions of Bartolomé de las Casas, Francisco de Vitoria, Francisco Suarez, Camöens, and the Vatican, on the rights of native peoples and European abuses. Most French Enlightenment thinkers, among them Diderot and Montesquieu, subscribed to the Abbé Raynal's opposition to slavery and colonialism; similar views were expressed by Johnson, Cowper, and Burke, as well as by Voltaire, Rousseau, and Bernardin de St. Pierre. (A useful compilation of their thoughts is in Marcel Merle, *L'Anticolonialisme Européen de Las Casas à Karl Marx.*)[118] During the nineteenth century, if we exclude rare exceptions like the Dutch writer Multatuli, debate over colonies usually turned on their profitability, their management and mismanagement, and on theoretical questions such as whether and how colonialism might be squared with *laissez-faire* or tariff policies; an *imperialist* and Eurocentric framework is implicitly accepted. Much of the discussion is both obscure, and, as Harry Bracken and others have shown, ambiguous, even contradictory on the deeper questions concerning the ontological status, as it were, of European domination of non-Europeans.[119] Liberal anti-colonialists, in other words, take the humane position that colonies and slaves ought not too severely to be ruled or held, but—in the case of Enlightenment philosophers—do not dispute the fundamental superiority of Western man or, in some cases, of the white race.

This view insinuated itself into the heart of the nineteenth-century disciplines and discourses dependent on knowledge observed and collected within the colonial setting.[120] But the period of decolonization is different. It is a matter of a changing cultural situation rather than completely distinct periods: just as nationalist or anti-imperial resistance in the colonies gradually becomes more and more noticeable, so too do a wildly contradictory number of anti-imperialist forces. One of the earliest and perhaps the most famous of the systematic European critiques—J. A. Hobson's *Imperialism: A Study* (1902)—attacks imperialism for its heartless economics, its export of capital, its alliance with ruthless forces, and its facade of well-meaning "civilizing" pretexts. Yet the book offers no critique of the notion of the "lower races," an idea Hobson finds acceptable.[121] Similar views were advanced by Ramsay MacDonald, certainly a critic of British imperialist practices but not opposed to imperialism as such.

No one has studied the anti-imperialist movement in Britain and France better than A. P. Thornton *(The Imperial Idea and Its Enemies)*, Bernard Porter *(Critics of Empire)*, and Raoul Girardet in his *L'Idée coloniale en France*. Two main characteristics mark their summaries: certainly there were late-nineteenth-century intellectuals (Wilfrid Scawen Blunt and William Morris) who were totally opposed to imperialism, but they were far from influential; many of those who were, like Mary Kingsley and the Liverpool school, were self-described imperialists and jingoists yet remorselessly severe about the abuses and cruelties of the system. In other words, there was no overall condemnation of imperialism until—and this is my point—*after* native uprisings were too far gone to be ignored or defeated.

(A footnote to this is worth registering: like Tocqueville on Algeria, European intellectuals were prone to attack the abuses of rival empires, while either mitigating or excusing the practices of their own.[122] This is the reason why I insist both on how modern empires replicate one another, despite their disclaimers about being different, and on the necessity of a rigorously anti-imperialist position. The United States was routinely turned to by many nationalist parties and leaders in the Third World because, through World War Two, it was openly anti-imperialist. As late as the 1950s and early 1960s, U.S. policy on Algeria shifted such as to alter the cordiality of Franco-American relations quite considerably, all because the United States disapproved of French colonialism. Yet in general the United States after World War Two considered itself responsible for many parts of the Third World which the British and French had evacuated [Vietnam, of course, is the main instance],[123] and, because of an exceptional history based on the legitimacy of an anti-colonial revolution, largely exempt from the charge that in its own way it began to resemble Britain and France. Doctrines of cultural exceptionalism are altogether too abundant.)

The second characteristic, especially brought out in Girardet, is that only after nationalists first took the lead in the imperial territories, then expatriate intellectuals and activists, did there develop a significant anti-colonial movement in the metropolis. To Girardet writers like Aimé Césaire and then Fanon represent a somewhat suspicious "revolutionary messianism," but they did spur Sartre and other Europeans openly to oppose French colonial policy in Algeria and Indochina during the 1950s.[124] From those initiatives came others: humanist opposition to colonial practices like torture and deportation, a new awareness of the global end-of-empire era and, with it, redefinitions of national purpose, and, not least in the Cold War years, various defenses of the "Free World" that entailed winning over postcolonial natives via cultural journals, trips, and seminars. A far from negligible part was played by the Soviet Union and by the United Nations, not always in good faith, and in the case of the former not for altruistic reasons; nearly every successful Third World liberation movement after World War Two was helped by the Soviet Union's counter-balancing influence against the United States, Britain, France, Portugal, and Holland.

Most histories of European aesthetic modernism leave out the massive infusions of non-European cultures into the metropolitan heartland during the early years of this century, despite the patently important influence they had on modernist artists like Picasso, Stravinsky, and Matisse, and on the very fabric of a society that largely believed itself to be homogenously white and Western. In the interwar period students from India, Senegal, Vietnam, and the Caribbean flocked to London and Paris;[125] journals, reviews, and political associations formed—one thinks of the pan-African congresses in England, magazines like *Cri des nègres*, parties like the Union des Travailleurs Nègres established by expatriates, dissidents, exiles, and refugees, who paradoxically work better in the heart of the empire than in its far-flung domains, or of the invigoration provided African movements by the Harlem Renaissance.[126] A common anti-imperialist experience was felt, with new associations between Europeans, Americans, and non-Europeans, and they transformed disciplines and gave voice to new ideas that unalterably changed that structure of attitude and reference which had endured for generations within European culture. The cross-fertilization between African nationalism as represented by George Padmore, Nkrumah, C.L.R. James on the one hand, and, on the other the emergence of a new literary style in the works of Césaire, Senghor, poets of the Harlem Renaissance like Claude McKay and Langston Hughes, is a central part of the global history of modernism.

A huge and remarkable adjustment in perspective and understanding is required to take account of the contribution to modernism of decolonization, resistance culture, and the literature of opposition to imperialism. Although, as I said, the adjustment has still not fully taken place, there are good reasons for thinking that it has started. Many defenses of the West today are in fact defensive, as if to acknowledge that the old imperial ideas have been seriously challenged by the works, traditions, and cultures to which poets, scholars, political leaders from Africa, Asia, and the Caribbean have contributed so greatly. Moreover, what Foucault has called subjugated knowledges have erupted across the field once controlled, so to speak, by the Judeo-Christian tradition; and those of us who live in the West have been deeply affected by the remarkable outpouring of first-rate literature and scholarship emanating from the post-colonial world, a locale no longer "one of the dark places of the earth" in Conrad's famous description, but once again the site of vigorous cultural effort. To speak today of Gabriel García Márquez, Salman Rushdie, Carlos Fuentes, Chinua Achebe, Wole Soyinka, Faiz Ahmad Faiz, and many others like them is to speak of a fairly novel emergent culture unthinkable without the earlier work of partisans like C.L.R. James, George Antonius, Edward Wilmot Blyden, W.E.B. Du Bois, José Martí.

I want to discuss one fairly discrete aspect of this powerful impingement—that is, the work of intellectuals from the colonial or peripheral regions who wrote in an "imperial" language, who felt themselves organically related to the mass resistance to empire, and who set themselves the revisionist, critical task of dealing frontally with the metropolitan culture, using the techniques, discourses, and weapons of scholarship and criticism once reserved exclusively for the European. Their work is, on its merits, only apparently dependent (and by no means parasitic) on mainstream Western discourses; the result of its originality and creativity has been the transformation of the very terrain of the disciplines.

A general, quasi-theoretical account of the phenomenon I shall be discussing occurs in Raymond Williams's *Culture* (1981). In the chapter on what he calls "Formations," Williams begins by discussing guilds, professions, clubs, and movements, and then proceeds to the more complex issues of schools, factions, dissidents, and rebels. All these, he says, "relate to developments within a single national social order." In the twentieth century, however, new international or para-national formations occur, and they have tended to be avant-garde in the metropolitan center. To some extent these para-formations—Paris 1890–1930, New York 1940–1970—are the result of newly effective market forces that internationalize culture—for instance, "Western music," twentieth-century art, European literature. But more interestingly "contributors to avant-garde movements were immigrants to such a metropolis, not only from outlying national regions but from other and smaller national cultures, now seen as culturally provincial in relation to the metropolis." Williams's example is Apollinaire, although he writes of "the sociology of metropolitan encounters and associations between immigrants" and mainstream groups, which "create especially favorable supportive conditions for dissident groups."[127]

Williams concludes by saying that it is still not certain whether such encounters produce effects of "sharp and even violent breaks with traditional practices (a dissidence or revolt rather than a literal avant-garde)" or whether they are absorbed into and become a part of the "dominant culture of a succeeding metropolitan and paranational period." Yet if we historicize and politicize Williams's argument at the outset and then put it into the historical setting of imperialism and anti-imperialism, a number of factors become clear. First, anti-imperialist intellectual and scholarly work done by writers from the peripheries who have immigrated to or are visiting the metropolis is usually an extension into the metropolis of large-scale mass movements. One vivid expression of this occurred during the Algerian war, when the FLN called France the Seventh Wilaya, the other six constituting Algeria proper,[128] thus moving the contest over decolonization from the peripheries to the center. Second, these incursions concern the same areas of experience, culture, history, and tradition hitherto commanded unilaterally by the metropolitan center. When Fanon wrote his books, he intended to talk about the experience of colonialism as seen by a Frenchman, from within a French space hitherto inviolable and now invaded and re-examined critically by a dissenting native. There is thus an overlap and interdependence that cannot theoretically be described as only the reactive assertion of a separate colonial or native identity. Last, these *voyages in* represent, I believe, a still unresolved contradiction or discrepancy within metropolitan culture, which through co-optation, dilution, and avoidance partly acknowledges and partly refuses the effort.

The voyage in, then, constitutes an especially interesting variety of hybrid cultural work. And that it exists at all is a sign of adversarial internationalization in an age of continued imperial structures. No longer does the logos dwell exclusively, as it were, in London and Paris. No longer does history run unilaterally, as Hegel believed, from east to west, or from south to north, becoming more sophisticated and developed, less primitive and backward as it goes. Instead, the weapons of criticism have become part of the historical legacy of empire, in which the separations and exclusions of "divide and rule" are erased and surprising new configurations spring up.

Each of the four texts I want to discuss belongs specifically to a particular historical moment: the first two are C.L.R. James's *The Black Jacobins,* published in 1938, and, appearing at almost the same time, George Antonius's *The Arab Awakening.* The first is about a late-eighteenth-century Black Caribbean insurrection, the other about a recent Arab one; both deal with events in the past in whose pattern, protagonist, and antagonist the writer is concerned to detect a native or colonial reality that was ignored or betrayed by Europe. Both writers are brilliant stylists, remarkable men (and in the case of James a sportsman), whose early formation in British colonial schools brought forth a wonderful appreciation of English culture as well as serious disagreements with it. Both books now seem remarkably prescient, James forecasting an unbroken history of agonized and still profoundly unsettled Caribbean life, Antonius just as precisely forecasting today's front-page stories and shocking televised scenes from the Middle East, as the situation in Palestine-Israel remains fraught, having already resolved itself adversely from the Arab point of view with the establishment of Israel in 1948, an eventuality predicted with dire forebodings by Antonius ten years before the fact.

Whereas the James and Antonius books were intended as serious works of scholarship and advocacy addressed from within a national movement for independence to a general audience, my other two works, Ranajit Guha's *A Rule of Property for Bengal* (1963) and S. H. Alatas's *The Myth of the Lazy Native* (1977), are post-colonial and specialist, addressing a smaller audience about more specific issues. Both these books, the former by a Bengali political economist, the latter by a Malaysian Muslim historian and social theorist, show their authors' assiduous archival research and scrupulously up-to-date documentation, argument, and generalization.

Guha's book is, in a manner that later post-structuralist writers (including Guha himself) recognize, an archeological and deconstructive study of how the 1826 Act of Permanent Settlement for Bengal—according to which the British regulated rents and revenues in Bengal with unvarying precision—derived from a complex background of Physiocratic and Ideological thought in Europe that had been pressed into service in Bengal in the late eighteenth century by Philip Francis. Alatas's book, as startlingly original in its own way as Guha's, also details how European colonialism created an object, in this case the lazy native, who performed a crucial function in the calculations and advocacies of what Alatas calls colonial capitalism. This native, subjected to astringent rules and an exacting discipline, was meant, in the words of Sinbaldo de Mas, a Spanish official who in 1843 was entrusted with keeping the Philippines as a Spanish colony, to be sustained "in an intellectual and moral state that despite their numerical superiority they may weigh less politically than a bar of gold";[129] this native was talked about, analyzed, abused, and worked, fed with bad food and with opium, separated from his or her natural environment, covered with a discourse whose purpose was to keep him industrious and subordinate. Thus, says Alatas, "Gambling, opium, inhuman labour conditions, one-sided legislation, acquisition of tenancy rights belonging to the people, forced labour, were all in one way or another woven into the fabric of colonial ideology and given an aura of respectability. Those outside it were derided."[130]

The contrast between James and Antonius on the one hand and Guha and Alatas on the other is not only that the earlier writers were more immediately involved in contemporary politics, whereas the later two care a great deal about scholarly disputes in post-colonial India and Malaysia, but that post-colonial history itself has changed the terms, indeed the very nature of the argument. For James and Antonius the world of discourse inhabited by natives in the Caribbean and the Arab Orient during the 1930s was honorably dependent upon the West. Toussaint L'Ouverture, says James, could not have argued the way he did were it not for the Abbé Raynal, other Encyclopedists, and the great Revolution itself:

> in the hour of danger Toussaint, uninstructed as he was, could find the language and accent of Diderot, Rousseau and Raynal, of Mirabeau, Robespierre and Danton. And in one respect he excelled them all. For even these masters of the spoken and written word, owing to the class complications of their society, too often had to pause, to hesitate, to qualify. Toussaint could defend the freedom of the blacks without reservation, and this gave to his declaration a strength and a single-mindedness rare in the great documents of the time. The French bourgeoisie could not understand it. Rivers of blood were to flow before they understood that elevated as was his tone Toussaint had written neither bombast nor rhetoric but the simple and sober truth.[131]

In this wonderful description of a man completely internalizing the literal truth of the universalist sentiments propounded by the European Enlightenment, James shows Toussaint's sincerity and also his latent flaw, his willingness to trust European declarations, to see them as literal intentions rather than class and history-determined remarks of interests and groups.

Antonius developed much the same theme; his chronicle of the Arab awakening, nurtured by Britain early in our own century, focuses on how the Arabs, after liberating themselves from the Ottomans in 1917 and 1918, took British promises for Arab independence as the literal truth. Antonius's account of Sherif Hussein's correspondence with Sir Henry McMahon, in which the British official promised his people independence and sovereignty, corresponds to James's description of how Toussaint grasped and acted upon the Declarations of the Rights of Man. Yet for Antonius, who writes as a partisan of both the Arabs and the British—a classic case of interdependence if there ever was one—it is deliberate subterfuge, ascribed neither to classes nor to history but to dishonor, which for him has the force of catastrophe.

> There is little doubt that the verdict of history will substantially endorse the Arab view. Whatever else may be said of the San Remo decisions [of spring 1920, in which "the whole of the Arab Rectangle lying between the Mediterranean and the Persian frontier was to be placed under mandatory rule"] they did violate the general principles proclaimed and the specific promises made by the Allies, and more particularly by Great Britain. The purport of the pledges given in secret is now known: what with that and the assurances made publicly, the student has all the relevant material for a judgement. It was on the strength of those promises that the Arabs had come into the War and made their contribution and their sacrifices; and that fact alone sufficed to turn the corresponding obligation into a debt of honour. What the San Remo conference did was, in effect, to ignore the debt and come to decisions which, on all the essential points, ran counter to the wishes of the peoples concerned.[132]

It would be wrong to downplay the differences between James and Antonius, separated as they are not only by ideology and race, but by temperament and education. Still, the same sadness, disappointment, and unrequited hope linger unmistakably in their prose, and both men belonged to, and were shaped by, the politics of decolonization. James belonged to the lower middle class in Trinidad; he was an autodidact, athlete, and ever—as I was able to see for myself when I visited him, then aged eighty-six, in Brixton in June 1987—the precocious schoolboy, with the revolutionary's interest in history, politics, and theory, and the intellectual's attentiveness to ideas, contradictions, and the sheer sporty adventurousness of good literature, music, and conversation. Antonius, as Albert Hourani has memorably described him,[133] belonged to an older, more worldly class of Levantine Syrians resident for a time in Egypt (where he attended Victoria College, a school I myself attended); he was graduated from Cambridge University. When he wrote *The Arab Awakening*, Antonius was in his forties (he died in 1942, aged about fifty); James was a full decade younger. Whereas Antonius had had a rich career as a confidant of high British officers, as adviser to major Arab leaders and elites from Hussein and Faysal to Faris Nimr and Haj Amin al-Husayni, as heir to decades of Arab nationalist thought and activity, and was a worldly man addressing other worldly men in positions of power, James, newly arrived in England, worked as a cricket correspondent; he was a Black, a Marxist, a great public speaker and organizer; above all he was a revolutionary steeped in African, Caribbean, and Black nationalism. *The Black Jacobins* was first presented not as a book but as an acting vehicle in London for Paul Robeson; during the performances of the play, Robeson and James alternated the parts of Toussaint and Dessalines.[134]

Despite the differences between the indigent and itinerant West Indian Black Marxist historian and the more conservative, highly educated, and brilliantly well-connected Arab, both addressed their work to a world they considered their own, even if that very European world of power and colonial domination excluded, to some degree subjugated, and deeply disappointed them. They addressed that world from within it, and on cultural grounds they disputed and challenged its authority by presenting alternative versions of it, dramatically, argumentatively, and intimately. There is no sense in their work of their standing outside the Western cultural tradition, however much they articulate the adversarial experience of colonial and/or non-Western peoples. Well after *négritude*, Black nationalism, and the nativism of the 1960s and 1970s, James stubbornly supported the Western heritage at the same time that he belonged to the insurrectionary anti-imperialist moment which he shared with Fanon, Cabral, and Rodney. In an interview he said:

> How am I to return to non-European roots? If it means that Caribbean writers today should be aware that there are emphases in their writing that we owe to non-European, non-Shakespearean roots, and the past in music that is not Beethoven, that I agree. But I don't like them posed there in the way they have been posed *either-or*. I don't think so. I think *both* of them. And fundamentally we are a people whose literacy and aesthetic past is rooted in Western European civilisation.[135]

And if in his masterful account of the rise of Arab nationalism Antonius stresses the capital importance of the rediscovery of the Arabic language and the classical Islamic heritage (most often through the work of Christian thinkers like himself, an emphasis that subsequent historians have criticized as exaggerated), he also insists that the Arabic tradition is in no essential way in conflict with the Western one. There is instead parturition and filiation between them, as, for example, he explains in the following important passage:

> The educational activities of the American missionaries in that early period [the 1850s and 1860s] had, among many virtues, one outstanding merit; they gave the pride of place to Arabic, and, once they had committed themselves to teaching in it, put their shoulders with vigour to the task of providing an adequate literature. In that, they were the pioneers; and because of that, the intellectual effervescence which marked the first stirrings of the Arab revival owes most to their labours.[136]

No such harmonious coincidence between the West and its overseas colonies is observed in the work of Guha and Alatas. The colonial wars and the protracted political and military conflicts thereafter have intervened. And if direct political control has disappeared, economic, political, and sometimes military domination, accompanied by cultural hegemony—the force of ruling and, as Gramsci calls them, directive *(dirigente)* ideas— emanating from the West and exerting power over the peripheral world, has sustained it. One of the sharpest attacks in Alatas's *The Myth of the Lazy Native* is against those Malaysians who continue to reproduce in their own thinking the colonial ideology that created and sustained the "lazy native" idea. In passages that recall Fanon's strictures against the nationalist bourgeoisie, Alatas shows how residues of colonial capitalism remain in the thought of the newly autonomous Malays, confining them—those, that is, who have not become self-conscious in methodology and aware of the class affiliations that affect thought—to the categories of "colonial capitalist thought." Thus, he continues,

> The false consciousness distorts the reality. The Malay ruling party inherited the rule from the British without a struggle for independence such as that which took place in Indonesia, India and the Philippines. As such there was also no ideological struggle. There was no intellectual break with British ideological thinking at the deeper level of thought. The leadership of this party were recruited from the top hierarchy of the civil service trained by the British, and middle class Malay school teachers and civil servants. The few professionals associated with it did not set the pattern.[137]

Guha is no less concerned with the problematic of continuity and discontinuity, but for him the issue has autobiographical resonances, given his own profoundly self-conscious methodological preoccupations. How is one to study the Indian past as radically affected by British power not in the abstract but concretely when one is a modern Indian whose origin, upbringing, and family reality historically depended on that power? How can one see that relationship after Indian independence when one had been of, rather than outside, it? Guha's predicament is resolved in an intellectual strategy that dramatizes the strict otherness of British rule, which gave rise not only to the Act of Permanent Settlement but also to his own class:

In his early youth the author, like many others of his generation in Bengal, grew up in the shadow of the Permanent Settlement: his livelihood, like that of his family, was derived from remote estates they had never visited; his education was orientated by the needs of a colonial bureaucracy recruiting its cadre from among the scions of Lord Cornwallis's beneficiaries; his world of culture was strictly circumscribed by the values of a middle class living off the fat of the land and divorced from the indigenous culture of its peasant masses. He had therefore learnt to regard the Permanent Settlement as a charter of social and economic stagnation. Subsequently, as a post-graduate student of Calcutta University he read about the anti-feudal ideas of Philip Francis and was at once faced with a question which the text-books and the academics could not answer for him. How was it that the quasi-feudal land settlement of 1793 had originated from the ideas of a man who was a great admirer of the French Revolution? One could not know from the history books that such a contradiction existed and had to be explained. The manuals were satisfied that the good work England had done in India represented a series of successful experiments which had little to do with the ideas and prejudices inherited by the rulers from their European background. This view of British policy as a "rootless blossom" is not confirmed by the history of the land law that had the longest life under the raj. The author hopes that he has been able to locate the origins of the Permanent Settlement in that confluence of ideas where the two mainstreams of English and French thought merged in the second half of the eighteenth century.[138]

An act of separation repeats the basic gesture of decolonization. By understanding that the ideology that produced Permanent Settlement in India derived historically from French and British sources, and by seeing that his own class heritage stemmed not from the land but from the structure of colonial power, Guha can thereafter detach himself intellectually. As it is for Alatas, history for Guha is critique, not the dutiful replication of colonialist objects, ideologies, and arguments. In subsequent work, both men concentrate on trying to rescue the suppressed native voice from colonial history, and to derive new historiographical insights not only into the past but into the very weaknesses in native society that made it for so long vulnerable to schemes like the Act of Permanent Settlement.

In the introductory essay to *Subaltern Studies,* a series of collective volumes by like-minded colleagues launched under his aegis in 1982, Guha remarks that the "unhistorical historiography" of colonial India left out "the politics of the people" in favor of the nationalist elites created by the British. Hence "the historic failure of the nation to come into its own," which makes "the study of this failure [what] constitutes the central problematic of the historiography of colonial India."[139]

Metropolitan culture, in short, can now be seen to have suppressed the authentic elements in colonized society. It is not simply that Alatas and Guha are academic specialists, but that, after several decades of independence, the relationship between cultures is perceived as radically antithetical. One sign of this new post-war perception is the gradual disappearance of narrative. The subjects of *The Arab Awakening* and *The Black Jacobins* are mass movements led by extraordinary leaders. There are gripping, even noble stories here, of the rise of popular resistance movements—the slave revolt in Santo Domingo, the Arab revolt—grand narratives, in Jean-François Lyotard's terms, of enlightenment and emancipation. No such stories animate the pages of Alatas and Guha.

One strikingly similar aspect of both the earlier books is that they are meant to enlarge the awareness of Western readers, for whom the narrated events were previously recounted by metropolitan witnesses. James's task is to produce a narrative of the French Revolution that incorporates events in France and overseas, and so for him Toussaint and Napoleon are the two great figures produced by the Revolution. *The Arab Awakening* is, in all sorts of fascinating ways, designed to restrict and counteract the very famous account of the Arab Revolt written and much vaunted by T. E. Lawrence in *The Seven Pillars of Wisdom.* Here at last, Antonius seems to be saying, the Arabs, their leaders and warriors and thinkers, can tell their own story. It is an aspect of their generous historical vision that both James and Antonius offer an alternative narrative that can be read as part of a story already well-known to European audiences, but not until now well-known from a native point of view. And of course both men write from the standpoint of an ongoing mass political struggle—"Negro revolution" in James's case, Arab nationalism in Antonius's. The enemy is still the same, Europe and the West.

One problem with Antonius's book is that because he is principally focussed on the political events in which he himself was so involved, he either scants or does not adequately assess the vast cultural revival in the Arab and Islamic world that preceded his own period. Later historians—A. L. Tibawi, Albert Hourani, Hisham Sharabi, Bassam Tibi, Mohammad Abed al-Jabry—offer a more precise and wider account of this revival, and of its awareness (already present in Jabarti) of Western imperial impingement on Islam.[140] Writers like the Egyptian Tahtawi or the Tunisian Khayr al-Din, or the crucial late-nineteenth-century religious pamphleteers and reformers who include Jamal al-Din al-Afghani and Muhammad Abduh, emphasize the importance of developing a revitalized independent culture to resist the West, to match it technologically, to be able to develop a coherently indigenous Arab-Islamic identity. Such an important study as A. A. Duri's *The Historical Formation of the Arab Nation* (1984)[141] carries that story into the classical Arab nationalist narrative of an integral nation, pursuing its own development in spite of such obstacles as imperialism, internal stagnation, economic underdevelopment, political despotism.

In all these works, including Antonius's, the narrative progresses from dependence and inferiority to nationalist revival, independent state formation, and cultural autonomy in anxious partnership with the West. This is very far from a triumphalist story. Lodged at its heart, so to speak, is a complex of hope, betrayal, and bitter disappointment; the discourse of Arab nationalism today carries this complex along with it. The result is an unfulfilled and incomplete culture, expressing itself in a fragmented language of torment, angry insistence, often uncritical condemnation of outside (usually Western) enemies. Post-colonial Arab states thus have two choices: many, like Syria and Iraq, retain the pan-Arab inflection, using it to justify a one-party national security state that has swallowed up civil society almost completely; others, like Saudi Arabia, Egypt, Morocco, while retaining aspects of the first alternative, have devolved into a regional or local nationalism whose political culture has not, I believe, developed beyond dependence on the metropolitan West. Both alternatives, implicit in *The Arab Awakening,* are at odds with Antonius's own preference for dignified and integral autonomy.

In James's case, *The Black Jacobins* bridges an important cultural and political gap between Caribbean, specifically Black, history on the one hand, and European history on the other. Yet it too is fed by more currents and flows in a wider stream than even its rich narrative may suggest. At about the same time James composed *A History of Negro Revolt* (1938), whose purpose was "to give historical depth to the process of resistance itself," in Walter Rodney's brilliant description of the work.[142] Rodney notes that James acknowledged the long-standing (if usually unsuccessful) resistance to colonialism in Africa and the Caribbean that went unrecognized by colonial historians. Again like that of Antonius, his work was an adjunct to his engagement with and commitment to African and West Indian political struggle, a commitment that took him to the United States, to Africa (where his life-long friendship with George Padmore and a mature association with Nkrumah were crucial to the formation of politics in Ghana, as is clear from his highly critical study *Nkrumah and the Ghana Revolution*), then to the West Indies again, and finally to England.

Although James was an anti-Stalinist dialectician, like Antonius's, his critical attitude to the West as imperial center never kept him from understanding its cultural achievements, or from criticizing failings of the Black partisans (like Nkrumah) he supported. He lived longer than Antonius of course, but, as his opinions expanded and changed, as he added more areas of experience to his liberationist concerns, as he entered and exited from polemics and controversies, he kept a steady focus on (the phrase keeps turning up) *the story*. He saw the central pattern of politics and history in linear terms—"from Du Bois to Fanon," "from Toussaint to Castro"—and his basic metaphor is that of a voyage taken by ideas and people; those who were slaves and subservient classes could first become the immigrants and then the principal intellectuals of a diverse new society.

In the work of Guha and Alatas, that narrative sense of the human adventure is replaced with irony. Both men bring to light the unattractive strategies that went along with the pretensions of imperialism, its now completely discredited ideology of ennoblement and pedagogic improvement. Consider first Guha's minute reconstruction of the ways in which British East India Company officials married empiricism and anti-feudalism to French Physiocratic philosophy (whose basis was the ideology of land revenue) in order to achieve a permanence of British dominion, to use the phrase employed by Guha's protagonist Philip Francis.[143] Guha's masterful account of Francis—a "young Alcibiades" who was a friend of Burke, contemporary of Warren Hastings, anti-monarchist, abolitionist, consummate political animal—and his idea of permanent settlement is told as a montage, with various cuts and splices, not as a heroic story. Guha shows how Francis's ideas about land and their gradual acceptance well after his years of service occur along with the refurbishing of the image of Hastings, and help to enhance, enrich, and buttress the idea of Empire, which, to quote Guha, was already fast outstripping in importance the individual record of its architects and as an abstraction assuming the independence of a firm's goodwill with respect to the personality of its founder.[144]

Guha's theme is therefore the way abstraction requires and appropriates not only people but geography. The central notion is that as imperialists the British felt their task in India was to solve "the problem of sovereignty in Bengal"[145] in favor, naturally enough, of the British crown. And Francis's real achievement in decreeing the scheme whereby all the land rents in Bengal were to be permanently settled according to mathematical formulae was that he succeeded in "forming or restoring the constitution of an Empire."[146]

Guha's work is intended to demonstrate one way to dismantle imperial historiography—undergirded by the British charting of Indian territory—not in India so much as in Europe, the original site of its greatest security, longevity, and authority. The irony is that a native does the job, mastering not only sources and methods, but the overpowering abstractions whose traces in the minds of imperialists themselves were scarcely discernible when they originated.

The same dramatic achievement occurs in Alatas's book. Whereas Guha's characters are literally ideologists, concerned with asserting authority over India in philosophically coherent ways, no such program is claimed for the Portuguese, Spanish, and British colonialists analyzed by Alatas. They are in the Southeast Pacific to get treasure (rubber and metals) and cheap labor, in the pursuit of economic profit. Requiring service from the natives, they devise various schemes for lucrative colonial economies, destroying local middle-level traders in the process, subjugating and virtually enslaving the natives, setting off internecine ethnic wars among Chinese, Javanese, and Malaysian communities the better to rule and to keep the natives divided as well as weak. Out of this welter emerges the mythical figure of the lazy native, from whose existence as an essential and unchanging constant in Eastern society, a number of basic truths supposedly flow. Alatas patiently documents how these descriptions—all of them based on the "false consciousness" of colonialists unwilling to accept that the natives' refusal to work was one of the earliest forms of resistance to the European incursion—steadily acquire consistency, authority, and the irrefutable immediacy of objective reality. Observers such as Raffles then construct a rationale for further subjugating and punishing the natives, since the decline in native character had already occurred, as colonialist administrators saw it, and was irreversible.

Alatas supplies us with an alternative argument about the meaning of the lazy native, or rather, he supplies us with an argument for why the Europeans succeeded in holding on to the myth for as long as they did. Indeed, he also demonstrates how the myth lives on, how, in Eric Williams's words quoted earlier, "an outworn interest, whose bankruptcy smells to heaven in historical perspective, can exercise an obstructionist and disruptive effect which can only be explained by the powerful services it had previously rendered and the entrenchment previously gained."[147] The myth of the lazy native is synonymous with domination, and domination is at bottom power. Many scholars have become so accustomed to regard power only as a discursive effect that Alatas's description of how the colonialists systematically destroyed the commercial coastal states on Sumatra and along the Malay coast, how territorial conquest led to the elimination of native classes like fishermen and weapons craftsmen, and how, above all, foreign overlords did things that no indigenous class ever would, is likely to shock us with its plainness:

> Power falling into Dutch hands was different from power falling into the hands of an indigenous successor. An indigenous power was generally more liberal in trade. It did not destroy its own trading class throughout the whole area, and continued to use the products of its own industry. It built its own boats, and last but not least was incapable of imposing a monopoly throughout the major part of Indonesia. It promoted the abilities of its own people even though a tyrant was on the throne.[148]

Control of the sort described here by Alatas and by Guha in his book is almost total and in devastating, continuous conflict with the colonized society. To tell the narrative of how a continuity is established between Europe and its peripheral colonies is therefore impossible, whether from the European or the colonial side; what seems most appropriate for the decolonizing scholar is instead a hermeneutics of suspicion. Nevertheless, though the grand, nourishingly optimistic narratives of emancipatory nationalism no longer serve to confirm a community of culture as they did for James and Antonius in the 1930s, a new community of method—more difficult and astringent in its demands—arises instead. Guha's work has stimulated an important cooperative enterprise, *Subaltern Studies,* which in turn has led Guha and his colleagues into remarkable further researches on the problems of power, historiography, and people's history. Alatas's work has had two aims: to establish a foundation for a post-colonial methodology of South Asian history and society, and to further the demystifying and deconstructive work suggested in *The Myth of the Lazy Native.*

I do not mean to suggest either that the enthusiasm and passionately narrated works of the two pre-war intellectuals have been rejected and found wanting by later generations, or that the more technical and demanding work by Alatas and Guha shows a more narrowly professional and, alas, less culturally generous view of the metropolitan Western audience. Rather, it seems to me that James and Antonius speak for movements already launched toward self-determination, albeit of a partial and ultimately very unsatisfactory sort, whereas Guha and Alatas, in their discussion of issues raised by the post-colonial predicament, take earlier successes (such as national independence) for granted while also underlining the imperfections of the decolonizations, the freedoms and self-identity gained hitherto. Also, Guha and Alatas address themselves equally to Western scholars and to compatriots, native scholars still held in thrall by colonialist conceptions of their own past.

The question of constituency raises the more general question of audiences; as the many general readers of *The Black Jacobins* or *The Arab Awakening* can quickly testify, the audience has shrunk for the later, more disciplinary and rarefied books. James and Antonius assume that what they have to say is of major political and aesthetic import. James draws Toussaint as an appealingly admirable man, non-vindictive, immensely intelligent, subtle, and responsive to the sufferings of his fellow Haitians. "Great men make history," says James, "but only such history as it is possible for them to make."[149] Toussaint rarely took his people into his confidence and he misjudged his antagonists. James makes no such mistake, sustains no illusions. In *The Black Jacobins* he clinically reconstructs the imperialist context of self-interest and moral scruple out of which British Abolitionism and the well-intentioned Wilberforce arose; but as France and the Haitian Blacks were locked in bloody war, the British government manipulated philanthropic feeling to advance British Caribbean power at the expense of France and her antagonists. James is excoriating about imperialism's never giving anything away. Yet he retains his faith in the persuasive powers of a narrative whose main ingredients are the struggle for freedom common to France and to Haiti, and the wish to know and act; this underpins his writing as a Black historian for a contesting Black as well as a metropolitan white audience.

Is this *voyage in* retributive, the repressed colonial object coming to haunt and dog the footsteps of the modern European, for whom the misshapen legacy of Toussaint in the Duvaliers and Trujillos of this world confirms the idea of the savage non-European? James does not fall into the trap of being mainly reactive, preferring instead, in his 1962 preface, to show how Toussaint's revolutionary ideas have re-emerged in successful liberation struggles and, with equal force, in the birth of newly self-conscious and confident national cultures, aware of the colonial past yet pushing toward "the ultimate stage of a Caribbean quest for national identity."[150] Not for nothing has James been considered by so many writers—George Lamming, V. S. Naipaul, Eric Williams, Wilson Harris—the grand patriarch of contemporary West Indian culture.

Similarly for Antonius, the Allies' betrayal of the Arabs does not diminish the grand retrospective sweep of his narrative, in which the Arabs are moved by ideas of freedom shared with Europeans. Just as *The Black Jacobins* grounded the study of modern "Negro Revolt" (James's phrase), so also did *The Arab Awakening* inaugurate the academic investigation of Arab nationalism, which has gradually become a discipline not only in the Arab world but also in the West. Here too the affiliation with an ongoing politics is especially moving. Taking his case and expressing the unfulfilled self-determination of the Arabs to the same jury of Western politicians and thinkers who had thwarted a movement of history, Antonius is very much like James speaking both to his own people and to a resistant white audience for whom the emancipation of non-whites had become a marginal issue. The appeal made is not to fairness or compassion, but to the often startling and supervening realities of history itself. How remarkable then to read Antonius's comments contained in a lecture at Princeton in 1935, while he was working on *The Arab Awakening:*

> It often happens in the history of nations that a conflict of opposing forces which seems destined inevitably to end in the triumph of the stronger party is given an unspecified twist by the emergence of new forces which owe their emergence to that very triumph.[151]

Uncannily, it seems to me, Antonius was seeing from the depths of present disappointment through to the explosion of that very mass insurrection he seems in his book implicitly to be arguing for. (The Palestinian *intifada*, one of the great anti-colonial uprisings of our times, continues the struggle over historical Palestine, one of the principal themes of *The Arab Awakening.*)

And that observation returns us brusquely to the general subject of scholarship and politics. Each of the scholars I have discussed is firmly rooted in a local situation, with its histories, traditions, and affiliations inflecting both the choice of topic and its treatment. Antonius's book, for example, solicits our attention today as a history of early-twentieth-century Arab nationalism and as the poignant document of a class of notables superseded after the 1930s and '40s by more radical, popular, and nativist writers in Arabic; no longer could, or need, Western policymakers be addressed at all, much less addressed from within a common universe of discourse. Guha emerges in the 1960s as an exile, profoundly at odds with Indian politics, controlled as they were by those whom Tariq Ali has called "the Nehrus and the Gandhis."[152]

Politics—and the frankly political impulse behind their work—naturally affects the scholarship and research that all four men present. An explicit political or human urgency in the tone and the import of their books contrasts noticeably with what in the modern West has come to represent the norm for scholarship. (How that norm, with its supposed detachment, its protestations of objectivity and impartiality, its code of politesse and ritual calmness, came about is a problem for the sociology of taste and knowledge.) Each of these four Third World intellectuals writes out of and within a political situation whose pressures are constant, not momentary annoyances or minor empirical concerns to be brushed aside in the interests of a higher goal. The unresolved political situation is very near the surface, and it infects the rhetoric, or skews the accents of that scholarship, because the authors write from a position, it is true, of knowledge and authoritative learning, but also from the position of people whose message of resistance and contestation is the historical result of subjugation. As Adorno says of the apparent mutilation of the language used in such circumstances, "The language of the subjected, on the other hand, domination alone has stamped, so robbing them further of the justice promised by the unmutilated, autonomous word to all those free enough to pronounce it without rancor."[153]

I do not mean to suggest that oppositional scholarship must be shrill and unpleasantly insistent, or that Antonius and James (or Guha and Alatas for that matter) punctuate their discourse with insults and accusations. I am only saying that scholarship and politics are more openly connected in these books because these writers think of themselves as emissaries to Western culture representing a political freedom and accomplishment as yet unfulfilled, blocked, postponed. To misinterpret the historical force of their statements, discourses, and interventions, to impugn them (as Conor Cruise O'Brien once did)[154] as wailing for sympathy, to dismiss them as emotional and subjective *cris de cœur* of strenuous activists and partisan politicians is to attenuate their force, to misrepresent their value, to dismiss their enormous contribution to knowledge. No wonder Fanon said that "for the native, objectivity is always directed against him."[155]

The temptation for metropolitan audiences has usually been to rule that these books, and others like them, are merely evidence of native literature written by "native informants," rather than coeval contributions to knowledge. The authority in the West even of works like Antonius's and James's has been marginalized because to Western professional scholars they seem to be written from outside looking in. Perhaps that is one reason why Guha and Alatas, a generation later, choose to focus on rhetoric, ideas, and language rather than upon history *tout court*, preferring to analyze the verbal symptoms of power rather than its brute exercise, its processes and tactics rather than its sources, its intellectual methods and enunciative techniques rather than its morality—to deconstruct rather than to destroy.

To rejoin experience and culture is of course to read texts from the metropolitan center and from the peripheries contrapuntally, according neither the privilege of "objectivity" to "our side" nor the encumbrance of "subjectivity" to "theirs."[156] The question is a matter of knowing *how* to read, as the deconstructors say, and not detaching this from the issue of knowing *what* to read. Texts are not finished objects. They are, as Williams once said, notations and cultural practices. And texts create not only their own precedents, as Borges said of Kafka, but their successors. The great imperial experience of the past two hundred years is global and universal; it has implicated every corner of the globe, the colonizer and the colonized together. Because the West acquired world dominance, and because it seems to have completed its trajectory by bringing about "the end of history" as Francis Fukuyama has called it, Westerners have assumed the integrity and the inviolability of their cultural masterpieces, their scholarship, their worlds of discourse; the rest of the world stands petitioning for attention at our windowsill. Yet I believe it is a radical falsification of culture to strip it of its affiliations with its setting, or to pry it away from the terrain it contested or—more to the point of an oppositional strand within Western culture—to deny its real influence. Jane Austen's *Mansfield Park* is about England *and* about Antigua, and the connection is made explicitly by Austen; it is therefore about order at home and slavery abroad, and can—indeed ought—to be read that way, with Eric Williams and C.L.R. James alongside the book. Similarly Camus and Gide write about precisely the same Algeria written about by Fanon and Kateb Yacine.

If these ideas of counterpoint, intertwining, and integration have anything more to them than a blandly uplifting suggestion for catholicity of vision, it is that they reaffirm the historical experience of imperialism as a matter first of interdependent histories, overlapping domains, second of something requiring intellectual and political choices. If, for example, French and Algerian or Vietnamese history, Caribbean or African or Indian and British history are studied separately rather than together, then the experiences of domination and being dominated remain artificially, and falsely, separated. And to consider imperial domination and resistance to it as a dual process evolving toward decolonization, then independence, is largely to align oneself with the process, and to interpret both sides of the contest not only hermeneutically but also politically.

Such books as *The Black Jacobins, The Arab Awakening, A Rule of Property,* and *The Myth of the Lazy Native* belong squarely in the contest itself. They make the interpretative choice clearer, harder to avoid.

Consider the contemporary history of the Arab world as an instance of a history of continuing stress. Antonius's achievement was to establish that the interaction between Arab nationalism and the West (or its regional surrogates) was something to be studied and something to be either supported or fought. Subsequent to *The Arab Awakening,* especially in the United States, France, and Britain, the emergence of an academic field called "Middle Eastern studies" in anthropology, history, sociology, political science, economics, and literature is related to the political tensions in the area and to the position of the two former colonial powers and the present superpower. Ever since the Second World War it has been impossible to evade either the Arab-Israeli conflict or the study of individual societies in academic "Middle Eastern studies." Thus to write about the Palestinian issue at all required one to decide whether the Palestinians were a people (or national community), which in turn implied supporting or opposing their right to self-determination. For both sides, scholarship leads back to Antonius—accepting his views on the Western betrayal or, conversely, the West's right to have promised Palestine to the Zionist movement given the greater cultural importance of Zionism.[157]

And this choice opens up others. On the one hand, can one with any other than a political or ideological justification speak of the modern "Arab mind," with its alleged propensity to violence, its culture of shame, the historical overdetermination of Islam, its political semantics, its degeneration *vis-à-vis* Judaism and Christianity? These notions produce such tendentious works as Raphael Patai's *The Arab Mind,* David Pryce-Jones's *The Closed Circle,* Bernard Lewis's *The Political Language of Islam,* Patricia Crone and Michael Cook's *Hagarism.*[158] They wear the clothing of scholarship, but none of these works moves outside the arena of struggle as first defined in the West by Antonius; none can be described as being free from hostility to the Arabs' collective aspiration to break out of the historical determinism developed in colonial perspectives.

On the other hand, the critical and anti-Orientalist discourse of an older generation of scholars like Anwar Abdel-Malek and Maxime Rodinson continues with a younger generation that comprises Timothy Mitchell, Judith Tucker, Peter Gran, Rashid al-Khalidi, and their counterparts in Europe. During the 1980s the formerly conservative Middle East Studies Association underwent an important ideological transformation that these people helped to bring about. Formerly aligned with and often staffed by mainline academics, oil company executives, governmental consultants and

employees, MESA openly took up issues of contemporary political significance in its large annual meetings: the Iranian Revolution, the Gulf War, the
Palestinian *intifada*, the Lebanese Civil War, the Camp David Accords, the
relationship between Middle East scholarship and political ideology—issues
that had formerly been occluded or minimized in the studies of individuals
like Lewis, Patai, plus more recently Walter Laqueur, Emmanuel Sivan,
and Daniel Pipes. Academic work that advocated a policy line opposed to
native Arab or Islamic nationalism had dominated professional and even
journalistic discussion (as in such best-selling works of journalism-as-
instant-scholarship as Thomas Friedman's *From Beirut to Jerusalem* and David
Shipler's *Arab and Jew*), but that began to change.

At the core of the "old" line was an essentialization of Arabs as basically,
irrecusably, and congenitally "Other," and it took on racist overtones in its
elaborations of an "Arab" anti-democratic, violent, and regressive attitude to
the world. Central to this attitude was another factor, Israel, also a contributor to the polarity that was set up between democratic Israel and a homogenously non-democratic Arab world, in which the Palestinians, dispossessed
and exiled by Israel, came to represent "terrorism" and little beyond it. But
now it was the precisely differentiated histories of various Arab peoples,
societies, and formations that younger anti-Orientalist scholars put forward;
in respecting the history of and developments within the Arab world, they
restored to it a dynamic sense of the unfulfilled march toward independence,
of human rights (especially those of women and disadvantaged minorities),
and freedom from outside (often imperialist) interference and internal corruption or collaboration.

What happened in the Middle East Studies Association therefore was a
metropolitan story of cultural opposition to Western domination. It was
matched by similar important changes in African, Indian, Caribbean, and
Latin American studies. No longer were these fields commanded by ex-
colonial officers or a platoon of academics speaking the appropriate language. Instead a new receptivity to both liberation movements and
post-colonial criticism, and newly conscious opposition groups (the civil
rights movements in America, the immigrant rights movement in the United
Kingdom) effectively took away the monopoly of discourse held by Eurocentric intellectuals and politicians. Here Basil Davidson, Terence Ranger,
Johannes Fabian, Thomas Hodgkin, Gordon K. Lewis, Ali Mazrui, Stuart
Hall were essential, their scholarship a catalyst for other scholars. And for
all these people the inaugural work of the four scholars I have discussed
here—their voyage in—was fundamental to the cultural coalition now being
built between anti-imperialist resistance in the peripheries and oppositional
culture of Europe and the United States.

(v)

Collaboration, Independence, and Liberation

A t a 1969–70 seminar on imperialism held at Oxford, Ronald Robinson's
paper "Non-European Foundations of European Imperialism" was
among the most interesting contributions. Along with Thomas Hodgkin's
"African and Third World Theories of Imperialism," Robinson's "suggestion" for theoretical and empirical study showed the influence of the many
post-colonial developments I have been mentioning:

> Any new theory must recognize that imperialism was as much a func-
> tion of its victims' collaboration or non-collaboration—of their indige-
> nous politics, as it was of European expansion. . . . Nor [without the
> voluntary or enforced cooperation of their governing elites and] with-
> out indigenous collaboration, when the time came for it, could Euro-
> peans have conquered and ruled their non-European empires. From
> the outset that rule was continuously resisted; just as continuously
> native mediation was needed to avert resistance or hold it down.[159]

Robinson goes on to explore how in Egypt before 1882 the pashas and the
Khedive collaborated in permitting European penetration, after which, with
the dramatic overshadowing of that sector by the Orabi nationalist rebellion,
the British occupied the country militarily. He might have added, although
he does not, that many of the classes and individuals collaborating with
imperialism began by trying to emulate modern European ways, to modernize according to what was perceived of as European advancement. During
the first two decades of the nineteenth century, Muhammad Ali sent missions to Europe, three decades before Japanese missions came to the United
States and Europe for the same purpose. Within the French colonial orbit,
gifted students were brought to France to be educated until as late as the
1920s and 1930s, although some of them, like Senghor and Césaire and many
Indochinese intellectuals, turned into vigorous opponents of empire.

The primary purpose of these early missions to the West was to learn the
ways of the advanced white man, translate his works, pick up his habits.
Recent studies of the subject by Masao Miyoshi *(As We Saw Them)* and
Ibrahim Abu-Lughod *(The Arab Rediscovery of Europe)*[160] show how the impe-

rial hierarchy was imparted to eager students from the East along with information, useful texts, and profitable habits.[161]

Out of this particular dynamic of dependency came the first long reactive experience of nativist anti-imperialism, typified in the exchange published in 1883 between Afghani and Ernest Renan in the *Revue de deux mondes,* in which the native, using terms defined in advance by Renan, tries to "disprove" the European's racist and culturally arrogant assumptions about his inferiority. Whereas Renan speaks of Islam's status as lower than that of Judaism and Christianity, Afghani asserts that Islam is "better," and claims that the West improved itself by borrowing from the Muslims. Afghani also argues that Islamic development in science occurred earlier than its Western counterpart, and, if there was anything regressive about the religion, it came from something common to all religions, an irreconcilability with science.[162]

Afghani's tone is amiable, even though he clearly opposes Renan. In contrast to later resisters of imperialism—for whom liberation is the key theme—Afghani, like Indian lawyers in the 1880s, belongs to a stratum of people who while fighting for their communities try to find a place for themselves within the cultural framework they share with the West. They are the elites who in leading the various nationalist independence movements have authority handed on to them by the colonial power: thus Mountbatten to Nehru, or de Gaulle to the FLN. To this sort of antagonistic collaboration belong such different configurations of cultural dependency as Western advisers whose work helped native peoples or nations to "rise" (one aspect has been well chronicled in Jonathan Spence's book on Western advisers, *To Change China*), and those Western champions of the oppressed— Mrs. Jellyby is an early caricature, members of the Liverpool School a later example—who represented their own versions of the natives' interest. Another example is in the competition between T. E. Lawrence and Louis Massignon immediately after World War One, described with great subtlety in an essay by Albert Hourani.[163] Each man had a genuine empathy with the Arabs who fought against the Ottomans during the war (indeed, Massignon made empathy with Islam the very center of his theory of the monotheistic community, the Abrahamic succession), yet out of imperial conviction each acted his part in the partitioning of the Arab world between France and Britain: Lawrence served Britain, Massignon France, *for* the Arabs.

An entire massive chapter in cultural history across five continents grows out of this kind of collaboration between natives on the one hand and conventional as well as eccentric and contradictory representatives of imperialism on the other. In paying respect to it, acknowledging the shared and combined experiences that produced many of us, we must at the same time note how at its center it nevertheless preserved the nineteenth-century imperial divide between native and Westerner. The many colonial schools in the Far East, India, the Arab world, East and West Africa, for example, taught generations of the native bourgeoisie important truths about history, science, culture. And out of that learning process millions grasped the fundamentals of modern life, yet remained subordinate dependents of a foreign imperial authority.

The culmination of this dynamic of dependence is the nationalism that finally produced independent states in the once colonial countries across the globe. Two political factors whose importance had already been registered in culture now marked off the end of the period of nationalist anti-imperialism and inaugurated the era of liberationist anti-imperialist resistance. One was a pronounced awareness of culture *as* imperialism, the reflexive moment of consciousness that enabled the newly independent citizen to assert the end of Europe's cultural claim to guide and/or instruct the non-European. The second was the dramatically prolonged Western imperial mission in various regions that I have already mentioned, principally Algeria, Vietnam, Palestine, Guinea, and Cuba. But liberation, as distinguished from nationalist independence, became the strong new theme, a theme already implicit in earlier works by people like Marcus Garvey, José Martí, and W.E.B. Du Bois, for instance, but now requiring the propulsive infusion of theory and sometimes armed, insurrectionary militancy.

The national identity struggling to free itself from imperialist domination found itself lodged in, and apparently fulfilled by, the state. Armies, flags, legislatures, schemes of national education, and dominant (if not single) political parties resulted and usually in ways that gave the nationalist elites the places once occupied by the British or the French. Basil Davidson's important distinction between mass mobilization (the huge Indian crowds who demonstrated in the streets of Calcutta, for example) and mass *participation* highlights the distinction between the nationalist elite and the rural and urban masses who were briefly an organic part of the nationalist project. What Yeats does in Ireland is to help create a sense of restored community—an Ireland regaled by "a company that sang, to sweeten Ireland's wrong, Ballad and story, rann and song"[164]—but at its center stands a select group of men and women.

When the new national state gets established, argues Partha Chatterjee, it is ruled not by prophets and romantic rebels but, in India's case, by Nehru, "a state-builder, pragmatic and self-conscious."[165] To him the peasants and the urban poor are ruled by passions, not reason; they can be mobilized by poets like Tagore and charismatic presences like Gandhi, but after independence this large number of people ought to be absorbed into the state, to be made functional in its development. Yet Chatterjee makes the interesting point that by transforming nationalism into a new regional or state ideology, post-colonial countries subjected themselves to a global process of rationalization based on external norms, a process governed in the post-war years of modernization and development by the logic of a world system whose type is global capitalism, commanded at the top by the handful of leading industrial countries.

Chatterjee is correct to say that "no matter how skillfully employed, modern statecraft and the application of modern technology cannot effectively suppress the very real tensions which remain unresolved."[166] The new pathology of power, in Eqbal Ahmad's phrase, gives rise to national security states, to dictatorships, oligarchies, one-party systems. In V. S. Naipaul's novel *A Bend in the River* (1979) an unnamed African country is ruled by a Big Man, neither named nor present, who manipulates European consultants, Indian and Muslim minorities, and his own tribespeople in and out of rigid nativist doctrine (this is like the cult of Qaddafi's Green Book or Mobutu's invented tribal traditions); by the end of the book many of his subjects have been mercilessly killed; the one or two who survive the onslaught and realize what is happening—like Salim, the protagonist—decide that the situation is hopeless and yet another emigration is required. (From an East African Muslim Indian family, Salim drifts into the interior ruled by the Big Man, then leaves the place forlorn and completely dejected.) Naipaul's ideological point is that the triumph of nationalism in the Third World not only "suppresses the very real tensions . . . unresolved" in the post-colonial state, but also eliminates the last hope of resistance against it, as well as the last civilizing traces of Western influence.

Naipaul, a remarkably gifted travel writer and novelist, successfully dramatizes an ideological position in the West from which it is possible to indict the post-colonial states for having succeeded unconditionally in gaining independence. His attack on the post-colonial world for its religious fanaticism (in *Among the Believers*), degenerate politics (in *Guerrillas*), and fundamental inferiority (in his first two books on India)[167] is a part of a disenchantment with the Third World that overtook many people during the 1970s and 1980s, among them several prominent Western proponents of Third World nationalism, like Conor Cruise O'Brien, Pascal Bruckner *(The Tears of the White Man)*, and Gérard Chaliand. In an interesting semi-documentary history of the earlier French support for Third World resistance, *Aux Origines des tiers-mondismes: Colonisés et anti-colonialistes en France (1919–1939)*, Claude Liauzu ventures the thesis that by 1975 an anti-imperialist block no longer existed as it had earlier.[168] The disappearance of a domestic opposition to imperialism is a plausible argument about mainstream France and perhaps also the Atlantic West generally, but it is not helpful about persisting sites of contention, whether in the new states or in less prominent sectors of metropolitan culture. Questions of power and authority once directed at the classical empires of Britain and France are now thrown at despotic successor regimes, and against the idea that African or Asian countries should remain in thrall and dependency.

The evidence for this is dramatic. The struggle in behalf of human and democratic rights continues in, to name only a few places, Kenya, Haiti, Nigeria, Morocco, Pakistan, Egypt, Burma, Tunisia, and El Salvador. Also, the increasing significance of the women's movement has put more pressures on oligarchical statism and military (or one-party) rule. In addition the oppositional culture still maintains links between the Western and the non-European world: one first sees evidence of the connection in, for instance, Césaire's affiliations with Marxism and surrealism, and later in the connection between *Subaltern Studies* and Gramsci and Barthes. Many intellectuals in the formerly colonized world have refused to settle for the unhappy fate of Naipaul's Indar, once a promising young provincial who is sought out by foundations in the United States, but now a discarded and hopeless person with no place to go.

> From time to time that is all he knows, that it is time for him to go home. There is some dream village in his head. In between he does the lowest kind of job. He knows he is equipped for better things, but he doesn't want to do them. I believe he enjoys being told he can do better. We've given up now. He doesn't want to risk anything again.[169]

Indar is one of the "new men," a Third World intellectual who springs to undeserved prominence when fickle enthusiasts in the First World are in the mood to support insurgent nationalist movements, but loses out when they become less enthusiastic.

Is that an accurate representation of what resistance politics and culture were all about? Was the radical energy that propelled Algerians and Indians into mass insurrection finally contained and extinguished by independence? No, because nationalism was only one of the aspects of resistance, and not the most interesting or enduring one.

Indeed, that we can see and judge nationalist history so severely is a testament to the radically new perspective offered on the entire experience of historical imperialism by a deeper opposition; it comes positively from the decentering doctrines of Freud, Marx, and Nietzsche, and negatively from the insufficiencies of nationalist ideology. It infuses Aimé Césaire's *Discourse on Colonialism,* in which the ideologies of colonial dependency and Black racial inferiority are shown to have been incorporated surreptitiously into the modern jargon of psychiatry, which in turn permits Césaire to use *its* underlying deconstructive theoretical force to undermine its own imperial authority. Nationalist culture has been sometimes dramatically outpaced by a fertile culture of resistance whose core is energetic insurgency, a "technique of trouble," directed against the authority and the discourse of imperialism.

Yet this does not happen all or even most of the time, alas. All nationalist cultures depend heavily on the concept of national identity, and nationalist politics is a politics of identity: Egypt for the Egyptians, Africa for the Africans, India for the Indians, and so on. What Basil Davidson calls nationalism's "ambiguous fertility"[170] creates not only the assertion of a once incomplete and suppressed but finally restored identity through national systems of education, but also the inculcation of new authority. This is equally true in the United States, where the tonic force of African-American, women's and minority expression has here and there been turned into doctrine, as if the wish to criticize the myth of white America also meant the need to supplant that myth with dogmatic new ones.

In Algeria, for example, the French forbade Arabic as a formal language of instruction or administration; after 1962 the FLN made it understandably the only such language, and set in place a new system of Arab-Islamic education. The FLN then proceeded politically to absorb the whole of Algerian civil society: within three decades this alignment of state and party authority with a restored identity caused not only the monopolization of most political practices by one party and the almost complete erosion of democratic life, but, on the right wing, the challenging appearance of an Islamic opposition, favoring a militantly Muslim Algerian identity based on Koranic *(shari'ah)* principles. By the 1990s the country was in a state of crisis, whose result has been a deeply impoverishing face-off between government, which abrogated the results of the election as well as most free political activity, and the Islamic movement, which appeals to the past and orthodoxy for its authority. Both sides claim the right to rule Algeria.

In his chapter on "the pitfalls of nationalist consciousness" in *The Wretched of the Earth*, Fanon foresaw this turn of events. His notion was that unless national consciousness at its moment of success was somehow changed into a social consciousness, the future would hold not liberation but an extension of imperialism. His theory of violence is not meant to answer the appeals of a native chafing under the paternalistic surveillance of a European policeman and, in a sense, preferring the services of a native officer in his place. On the contrary, it first represents colonialism as a totalizing system nourished in the same way—Fanon's implicit analogy is devastating—that human behavior is informed by unconscious desires. In a second, quasi-Hegelian move, a Manichean opposite appears, the insurrectionary native, tired of the logic that reduces him, the geography that segregates him, the ontology that dehumanizes him, the epistemology that strips him down to an unregenerate essence. "The violence of the colonial regime and counter-violence of the native balance each other and respond to each other in an extraordinary reciprocal homogeneity."[171] The struggle must be lifted to a new level of contest, a synthesis represented by a war of liberation, for which an entirely new post-nationalist theoretical culture is required.

If I have so often cited Fanon, it is because more dramatically and decisively than anyone, I believe, he expresses the immense cultural shift from the terrain of nationalist independence to the theoretical domain of liberation. This shift takes place mainly where imperialism lingers on in Africa after most other colonial states have gained independence, e.g., Algeria and Guinea-Bissau. In any case Fanon is unintelligible without grasping that his work is a response to theoretical elaborations produced by the culture of late Western capitalism, received by the Third World native intellectual as a culture of oppression and colonial enslavement. The whole of Fanon's *oeuvre* is his attempt to overcome the obduracy of those very same theoretical elaborations by an act of political will, to turn them back against their authors so as to be able, in the phrase he borrows from Césaire, to invent new souls.

Fanon penetratingly links the settler's conquest of history with imperialism's regime of truth, over which the great myths of Western culture preside:

> The settler makes history; his life is an epoch, an Odyssey. He is the absolute beginning. "This land was created by us"; he is the unceasing cause: "If we leave all is lost, and the country will go back to the Middle Ages." Over against him torpid creatures, wasted by fevers, obsessed by ancestral customs, form an almost inorganic background for the innovating dynamism of colonial mercantilism.[172]

As Freud excavated the subterranean foundations of the edifice of Western reason, as Marx and Nietzsche interpreted the reified data of bourgeois society by translating them back into primitive but productive impulses toward dominance and accumulation, so Fanon reads Western humanism by transporting the large hectoring bolus of "the Greco-Latin pedestal" bodily to the colonial wasteland, where "this artificial sentinel is turned into dust."[173] It cannot survive juxtaposition with its quotidian debasement by European settlers. In the subversive gestures of Fanon's writing is a highly conscious man deliberately as well as ironically repeating the tactics of the culture he believes has oppressed him. The difference between Freud, Marx, and Nietzsche on the one hand and Fanon's "native intellectual" on the other is that the belated colonial thinker fixes his predecessors geographically—they are *of* the West—the better to liberate their energies from the oppressing cultural matrix that produced them. By seeing them antithetically as intrinsic to the colonial system and at the same time potentially at war with it, Fanon performs an act of closure on the empire and announces a new era. National consciousness, he says, "must now be enriched and deepened by a very rapid transformation into a consciousness of social and political needs, in other words, into [real] humanism."[174]

How odd the word "humanism" sounds in this context, where it is free from the narcissistic individualism, divisiveness, and colonialist egoism of the imperialism that justified the white man's rule. Like Césaire's in his *Retour*, Fanon's reconceived imperialism is in its positive dimension a collective act reanimating and redirecting an inert mass of silent natives into a new inclusive conception of history.

> This huge task, which consists of re-introducing mankind into the world, the whole of mankind, will be carried out with the indispensable help of the European peoples, who themselves must realize that in the past they have often joined the ranks of our common masters where colonial questions are concerned. To achieve this, the European peoples must first decide to wake up and shake themselves, use their brains, and stop playing the stupid faun of the Sleeping Beauty.[175]

How this can be enacted takes us from the apparent exhortations and prescriptions to the extraordinarily interesting structure and method of *The Wretched of the Earth*. Fanon's achievement in this his last work (published in 1961, a few months after his death) is first to represent colonialism and nationalism in their Manichean contest, then to enact the birth of an independence movement, finally to transfigure that movement into what is in effect a trans-personal and trans-national force. The visionary and innovative quality of Fanon's final work derives from the remarkable subtlety with which he forcibly *deforms* imperialist culture and its nationalist antagonist in the process of looking beyond both toward liberation. Like Césaire before him, Fanon impugns imperialism for what it has created by acts of powerful rhetorical and structured summary. These make clear imperialism's long cultural history, and—more tellingly—allow Fanon to formulate new strategies and goals for liberation.

The Wretched of the Earth is a hybrid work—part essay, part imaginative

story, part philosophical analysis, part psychological case history, part nationalist allegory, part visionary transcendence of history. It begins with a
territorial sketch of the colonial space, separated into the clean, well-lighted
European city and the dark, fetid, ill-lit casbah. From this Manichean and
physically grounded stalemate Fanon's entire work follows, set in motion, so
to speak, by the native's violence, a force intended to bridge the gap between
white and non-white. For Fanon violence, as I said earlier, is the synthesis
that overcomes the reification of white man as subject, Black man as object.
My conjecture is that while he was writing the work Fanon read Lukacs's
History and Class Consciousness, which had just appeared in Paris in French
translation in 1960. Lukacs shows that the effects of capitalism are fragmentation and reification: in such a dispensation, every human being becomes an
object, or commodity, the product of human work is alienated from its
maker, the image of whole or of community disappears entirely. Most
important to the insurgent and heretical Marxism put forward by Lukacs
(shortly after publication in 1923 the book was removed from circulation by
Lukacs himself) was the separation of subjective consciousness from the
world of objects. This, he says, could be overcome by an act of mental will,
by which one lonely mind could join another by imagining the common
bond between them, breaking the enforced rigidity that kept human beings
as slaves to tyrannical outside forces. Hence reconciliation and synthesis
between subject and object.

Fanon's violence, by which the native overcomes the division between
whites and natives, corresponds very closely to Lukacs's thesis about over-
coming fragmentation by an act of will; Lukacs calls this "no single, unrepeatable tearing of the veil that masks the process but the unbroken
alternation of ossification, contradiction and movement."[176] Thus the sub-
ject-object reification in its prison-like immobility is destroyed. Fanon
adopts much of this extremely audacious thesis, which is oppositional even
within oppositional Marxism, in passages like the following, where the
settler's consciousness functions like that of a capitalist, turning human
workers into inhuman and non-conscious objects:

> The settler makes history and is conscious of making it. And because
> he constantly refers to the history of his mother country, he clearly
> indicates that he himself is the extension of that mother country. Thus
> the history which he writes is not the history of the country which he
> plunders but the history of his own nation in regard to all that she skins
> off, all that she violates and starves.
> The immobility [later he speaks of *apartheid* as one of the forms of
> "division into compartments": "The native," he adds, "is being hemmed

in. . . . The first thing which a native learns is to stay in his place"][177]
to which the native is condemned can only be called in question if the
native decides to put an end to the history of colonization—the history
of pillage—and to bring into existence the history of the nation—the
history of decolonization.[178]

In Fanon's world change can come about only when the native, like
Lukacs's alienated worker, decides that colonization must end—in other
words, there must be an epistemological revolution. Only then can there be
movement. At this point enters violence, "a cleansing force," which pits
colonizer against colonized directly:

> The violence of the colonial regime and the counter-violence of the
> native balance each other and respond to each other in an extraordi-
> nary reciprocal homogeneity. . . . The settler's work is to make even
> dreams of liberty impossible for the native. The native's work is to
> imagine all possible methods for destroying the settler. On the logical
> plane, the Manicheanism of the settler produces a Manicheanism of the
> natives, to the theory of the "absolute evil of the native" the theory of
> the "absolute evil of the settler" replies.[179]

Here Fanon is not only reshaping colonial experience in terms suggested
by Lukacs, but also characterizing the emergent cultural and political antagonist to imperialism. His imagery for this emergence is biological:

> The appearance of the settler has meant in the terms of syncretism
> the death of the aboriginal society, cultural lethargy, and the petrifica-
> tion of individuals. For the native, life can only spring up again out of
> the rotting corpse of the settler. . . . But it so happens that for the
> colonized people this violence, because it constitutes their only work,
> invests their character with positive and creative qualities. The practice
> of violence binds them together as a whole, since each individual forms
> a violent link in the great chain, a part of the great organism of
> violence.[180]

Certainly Fanon depends here on the earlier language of French colonialism, in which publicists like Jules Harmand and Leroy-Beaulieu used the
biological imagery of birth, parturition, and genealogy to describe the parental relationship of France to its colonial children. Fanon reverses things,
using that language for the birth of a new nation, and the language of death
for the colonial settler-state. Even this antagonism, however, does not cover

all the differences that spring up once revolt begins and "life [appears to be] an unending contest."[181] There are the major divisions between legal and illegal nationalism, between the politics of nationalist reform and simple decolonization on the one hand, and the illicit politics of liberation on the other.

These divisions are just as important as the one between colonized and colonizer (whose motif is taken up, altogether more simply, by Albert Memmi.)[182] Indeed the true prophetic genius of *The Wretched of the Earth* is located precisely here: Fanon senses the divide between the nationalist bourgeoisie in Algeria and the FLN's liberationist tendencies, and he also establishes conflicting narrative and historical patterns. Once the insurrection gets under way, the nationalist elites try to establish parity with France: demands for human rights, self-rule, labor unions, and so on. And since French imperialism called itself "assimilationist," the official nationalist parties are trapped into becoming co-opted agents of the ruling authorities. (Such, for example, was the sad fate of Farhat Abbas, who as he gained in official French approval lost any hope of winning mass support.) Thus official bourgeois nationalists simply drop into the narrative pattern of the Europeans, hoping to become mimic men, in Naipaul's phrase, mere native correspondences of their imperial masters.

Fanon's brilliant analysis of the liberationist tendency opens Chapter 2, "Spontaneity: Its Strength and Weakness," the basis of which is a time lag and rhythm difference *(décalage)* "between the leaders of a nationalist party and the mass of the people."[183] As the nationalists copy their methods from Western political parties, all sorts of tensions develop within the nationalist camp—between country and city, between leader and rank-and-file, between bourgeoisie and peasants, between feudal and political leaders—all of them exploited by the imperialists. The core problem is that, although official nationalists want to break colonialism, "another quite different will [becomes apparent]: that of coming to a friendly agreement with it."[184] Thereafter an illegal group asks questions about this policy, and it is quickly isolated, often imprisoned.

> So we can observe the process whereby the rupture runs between the illegal and legal tendencies within the party . . . and an underground party, an offshoot of the legal party, will be the result.[185]

Fanon's method for showing the effect of this underground party is to dramatize its existence as a counter-narrative, an underground narrative, set in motion by fugitives, outcasts, hounded intellectuals who flee to the countryside and in their work and organization clarify and also undermine the weaknesses of the official narrative of nationalism. Far from leading

> the colonized people to supreme sovereignty at one fell swoop, that certainty which you had that all portions of the nation would be carried along with you at the same speed and led onward by the same light, that strength which gave you hope: all now are seen in the light of experience to be symptoms of a very great weakness.[186]

Precisely that power to convey "the light of experience" is located in the illegal tendency animating the liberationist party. This party shows to all that racialism and revenge "cannot sustain a war of liberation"; hence the native makes "the discovery" that in "breaking down colonial oppression he is automatically building up yet another system of exploitation," this time giving it "a black face or an Arab one," so long as the mimic men lead.

"History teaches clearly," remarks Fanon at this point, "that the battle against colonialism does not run straight away along the lines of nationalism."[187] In the image of the "lines of nationalism," Fanon understands that conventional narrative is, as we noted in Conrad's work, central to imperialism's appropriative and dominative attributes. Narrative itself is the representation of power, and its teleology is associated with the global role of the West. Fanon was the first major theorist of anti-imperialism to realize that orthodox nationalism followed along the same track hewn out by imperialism, which while it appeared to be conceding authority to the nationalist bourgeoisie was really extending its hegemony. To tell a simple national story therefore is to repeat, extend, and also to engender new forms of imperialism. Left to itself, nationalism after independence will "crumble into regionalisms inside the hollow shell of nationalism itself."[188] The old conflicts between regions are now repeated, privileges are monopolized by one people over another, and the hierarchies and divisions constituted by imperialism are reinstated, only now they are presided over by Algerians, Senegalese, Indians, and so forth.

Unless, Fanon says a little later, "a rapid step ... [is] taken from national consciousness to political and social consciousness."[189] He means first of all that needs based on identitarian (i.e., nationalist) consciousness must be overridden. New and general collectivities—African, Arab, Islamic—should have precedence over particularist ones, thus setting up lateral, non-narrative connections among people whom imperialism separated into autonomous tribes, narratives, cultures. Second—here Fanon follows some of Lukacs's ideas—the center (capital city, official culture, appointed leader) must be deconsecrated and demystified. A new system of mobile relationships must replace the hierarchies inherited from imperialism. In passages of an incandescent power, Fanon resorts to poetry and drama, to René Char and Keita Fodeba. Liberation is consciousness of self, "not the closing of a door to communication"[190] but a never-ending process of "discovery and encouragement" leading to true national self-liberation and to universalism.

One has the impression in reading the final pages of *The Wretched of the Earth* that having committed himself to combat both imperialism and orthodox nationalism by a counter-narrative of great deconstructive power, Fanon could not make the complexity and anti-identitarian force of that counter-narrative explicit. But in the obscurity and difficulty of Fanon's prose, there are enough poetic and visionary suggestions to make the case for liberation as a *process* and not as a goal contained automatically by the newly independent nations. Throughout *The Wretched of the Earth* (written in French), Fanon wants somehow to bind the European as well as the native together in a new non-adversarial community of awareness and anti-imperialism.

In Fanon's imprecations against and solicitations of European attention, we find much the same cultural energy that we see in the fiction of Ngugi, Achebe, and Salih. Its messages are we must strive to liberate all mankind from imperialism; we must all write our histories and cultures rescriptively in a new way; we share the same history, even though for some of us that history has enslaved. This, in short, is writing from the colonies coterminous with the real potential of post-colonial liberation. Algeria was liberated, as were Kenya and the Sudan. The important connections with the former imperial powers remain, as does a newly clarified sense of what can and cannot be relied on or salvaged from that former relationship. Once again it is culture and cultural effort that presage the course of things to come—well in advance of the cultural politics of the post-colonial period dominated by the United States, the surviving superpower.

Since much of the literature of resistance was written in the thick of battle, there is an understandable tendency to concentrate on its combative, often strident assertiveness. Or to see in it a blueprint for the horrors of the Pol Pot regime. On the one hand, a recent spate of articles on Fanon has looked at him strictly as a preacher calling the oppressed to violence, and violence only. Little is said about French colonial violence; according to the strident polemics of Sidney Hook, Fanon is nothing more than an irrational, finally stupid enemy of "the West." On the other hand, it is hard to miss in Amílcar Cabral's remarkable speeches and tracts the extraordinary intensity of the man's mobilizing force, his animosity and violence, the way *ressentiment* and hate keep turning up—all the more evident against the particularly ugly backdrop of Portuguese colonialism. Yet one would seriously misread such texts as "The Weapons of Theory" or "National Liberation and Culture" if one missed Cabral's enabling utopianism and theoretical generosity, just as it is a misreading of Fanon not to see in him something considerably beyond a celebration of violent conflict. For both Cabral and Fanon, the emphasis on "armed struggle" is at most tactical. For Cabral the liberation gained by violence, organization, and militancy is required because imperialism has sequestered the non-European away from experiences that have been permitted only to the white man. But, says Cabral, "the time is past when, in an attempt to perpetuate the domination of peoples, culture was regarded as an attribute of privileged peoples or nations and when, out of ignorance or bad faith, culture was confused with technical skill, if not with the colour of one's skin or the shape of one's eyes."[191] To end those barriers is to admit the non-European to the whole range of human experience; at least all humankind can have a destiny and, more important, a history.

Certainly, as I said earlier, cultural resistance to imperialism has often taken the form of what we can call nativism used as a private refuge. One finds this not only in Jabarti, but in the great early hero of Algerian resistance, the Emir Abdel Kader, a nineteenth-century warrior who, while fighting the French armies of occupation, also cultivated a cloistral spiritual apprenticeship to the thirteenth-century Sufi master Ibn Arabi.[192] To fight against the distortions inflicted on your identity in this way is to return to a pre-imperial period to locate a "pure" native culture. This is quite a different thing from revisionist interpretations, such as those of Guha or Chomsky, whose purpose is to demystify the interests at work in establishment scholars who specialize in "backward" cultures, and to appreciate the complexity of the interpretative process. In a way, the nativist argues that one can get past all interpretation to the pure phenomenon, a literal fact beseeching assent and confirmation, rather than debate and investigation. Something of this passionate intensity is found in blanket condemnations of "the West" such as Jalal Ali Ahmad's *Occidentosis: A Plague from the West* (1961–62)[193] or in Wole Soyinka implying the existence of a pure native African (as in his unfortunate attack on Islam and the Arabs as defacing the African experience);[194] one can see that intensity put more interestingly and productively to use in Anwar Abdel-Malek's proposal about "civilizational projects" and the theory of endogamous cultures.[195]

I am not particularly interested in spending much time discussing the altogether obvious unhappy cultural consequences of nationalism in Iraq, Uganda, Zaire, Libya, the Philippines, Iran, and throughout Latin America. Nationalism's disabling capacities have been lingered over and caricatured quite long enough by a large army of commentators, expert and amateur alike, for whom the non-Western world after the whites left it seems to have become little more than a nasty mix of tribal chieftains, despotic barbarians, and mindless fundamentalists. A more interesting commentary on the nativist tendency—and the rather naive foundationalist ideology that makes it possible—is provided in such accounts of creole or *mestizo* culture as in Rodó's *Ariel* and by those Latin American fabulists whose texts demonstrate the manifest *impurity,* the fascinating mixture of real and surreal in all experience. As one reads "magic realists" like Carpentier, who first describes it, Borges, García Márquez, and Fuentes, one vividly apprehends the dense interwoven strands of a history that mocks linear narrative, easily recuperated "essences," and the dogmatic mimesis of "pure" representation.

At its best, the culture of opposition and resistance suggests a theoretical alternative and a practical method for reconceiving human experience in non-imperialist terms. I say the tentative "suggests" rather than the more confident "provides" for reasons that will, I hope, become evident.

Let me quickly recapitulate the main points of my argument first. The ideological and cultural war against imperialism occurs in the form of resistance in the colonies, and later, as resistance spills over into Europe and the United States, in the form of opposition or dissent in the metropolis. The first phase of this dynamic produces nationalist independence movements, the second, later, and more acute phase produces liberation struggles. The basic premise of this analysis is that although the imperial divide in fact separates metropolis from peripheries, and although each cultural discourse unfolds according to different agendas, rhetorics, and images, they are in fact connected, if not always in perfect correspondence. The Raj required Babus, just as later the Nehrus and the Gandhis took over the India set up by the British. The connection is made on the cultural level since, I have been saying, like all cultural practices the imperialist experience is an intertwined and overlapping one. Not only did the colonizers emulate as well as compete with one another, but so also did the colonized, who often went from the same general type of "primary resistance" to similar nationalist parties seeking sovereignty and independence.

But is that all imperialism and its enemies have brought forward, a ceaseless round of impositions and counter-impositions, or is a new horizon opened up?

There can be little doubt that were they alive today Fanon and Cabral, for example, would be hugely disappointed at the results of their efforts. I make that speculation considering their work as a theory not just of resistance and decolonization, but of liberation. In all sorts of ways, the somewhat inchoate historical forces, confusing antitheses, unsynchronized events that their work tried to articulate were not fully controlled or rendered by it.

Fanon turned out to be right about the rapacity and divisiveness of national bourgeoisies, but he did not and could not furnish an institutional, or even theoretical, antidote for its ravages.

But it is not as state builders or, as the awful expression has it, founding fathers that the greatest resistance writers like Fanon and Cabral should be read and interpreted. Although the struggle for national liberation is continuous with national independence, it is not—and in my opinion never was—culturally continuous with it. To read Fanon and Cabral, or C.L.R. James and George Lamming, or Basil Davidson and Thomas Hodgkin merely as so many John the Baptists of any number of ruling parties or foreign-office experts is a travesty. Something else was going on, and it sharply disrupts, then abruptly veers away from the unity forged between imperialism and culture. Why is this difficult to perceive?

For one, the theory and theoretical structures suggested by writers on liberation are rarely given the commanding authority—I mean the phrase quite literally—or blithe universalism of their contemporary, mostly Western counterparts. There are many reasons for this, not the least being the one I mentioned in my previous chapter, that very much like the narrative devices in *Heart of Darkness,* many cultural theories pretending to universalism assume and incorporate the inequality of races, the subordination of inferior cultures, the acquiescence of those who, in Marx's words, cannot represent themselves and therefore must be represented by others. "Hence," says the Moroccan scholar Abdullah Laroui, "the Third World intelligentsia's condemnations of cultural imperialism. Sometimes people are puzzled by the ill-treatment meted out to the old liberal paternalism, to Marx's Europocentrism, and to structuralist anti-racism (Levi-Strauss). This is because they are unwilling to see how these can form part of the same hegemonic system."[196] Or, as Chinua Achebe puts it, when remarking that Western critics often fault African writing for lacking "universality":

> Does it ever occur to these universalists to try out their game of changing names of characters and places in an American novel, say, a Philip Roth or an Updike, and slotting in African names just to see how it works? But of course it would not occur to them to doubt the universality of their own literature. In the nature of things the work of a Western writer is automatically informed by universality. It is only others who must strain to achieve it. So-and-so's work is universal: he has truly arrived! As though universality were some distant bend in the road which you may take if you travel out far enough in the direction of Europe or America, if you put adequate distance between yourself and your home.[197]

As an instructive reminder of this unfortunate state of affairs, consider the roughly contemporary work of Michel Foucault and Frantz Fanon, both of whom stress the unavoidable problematic of immobilization and confinement at the center of the Western system of knowledge and discipline. Fanon's work programmatically seeks to treat colonial and metropolitan societies together, as discrepant but related entities, while Foucault's work moves further and further away from serious consideration of social wholes, focussing instead upon the individual as dissolved in an ineluctably advancing "microphysics of power"[198] that it is hopeless to resist. Fanon represents the interests of a double constituency, native and Western, moving from confinement to liberation; ignoring the imperial context of his own theories, Foucault seems actually to represent an irresistible colonizing movement that paradoxically fortifies the prestige of both the lonely individual scholar and the system that contains him. Both Fanon and Foucault have Hegel, Marx, Freud, Nietzsche, Canguihelm, and Sartre in their heritage, yet only Fanon presses that formidable arsenal into anti-authoritarian service. Foucault, perhaps because of his disenchantment with both the insurrections of the 1960s and the Iranian Revolution, swerves away from politics entirely.[199]

Much of Western Marxism, in its aesthetic and cultural departments, is similarly blinded to the matter of imperialism. Frankfurt School critical theory, despite its seminal insights into the relationships between domination, modern society, and the opportunities for redemption through art as critique, is stunningly silent on racist theory, anti-imperialist resistance, and oppositional practice in the empire. And lest that silence be interpreted as an oversight, we have today's leading Frankfurt theorist, Jürgen Habermas, explaining in an interview (originally published in *The New Left Review*) that the silence is deliberate abstention: no, he says, we have nothing to say to "anti-imperialist and anti-capitalist struggles in the Third World," even if, he adds, "I am aware of the fact that this is a eurocentrically limited view."[200] All the major French theoreticians except Deleuze, Todorov, and Derrida have been similarly unheeding, which has not prevented their ateliers from churning out theories of Marxism, language, psychoanalysis, and history with an implied applicability to the whole world. Much the same thing can be said of most Anglo-Saxon cultural theory, with the important exception of feminism, and a small handful of work by young critics influenced by Raymond Williams and Stuart Hall.

So if European theory and Western Marxism as cultural co-efficients of liberation haven't in the main proved themselves to be reliable allies in the resistance to imperialism—on the contrary, one may suspect that they are part of the same invidious "universalism" that connected culture with imperialism for centuries—how has the liberationist anti-imperialism tried to break this shackling unity? First, by a new integrative or contrapuntal orientation in history that sees Western and non-Western experiences as belonging together because they are connected by imperialism. Second, by an imaginative, even utopian vision which reconceives emancipatory (as opposed to confining) theory and performance. Third, by an investment neither in new authorities, doctrines, and encoded orthodoxies, nor in established institutions and causes, but in a particular sort of nomadic, migratory, and anti-narrative energy.

Let me illustrate my points by looking at a wonderful passage in C.L.R. James's *The Black Jacobins*. Twenty-odd years after his book appeared in 1938, James appended a further chapter, "From Toussaint L'Ouverture to Fidel Castro." Although James is a highly original figure, as I said, it takes nothing away from his contribution to associate his work with that of various metropolitan historians and journalists—Basil Davidson, Thomas Hodgkin, Malcolm Caldwell among others in Britain, Maxime Rodinson, Jacques Chesnaux, Charles-Robert Argeron among others in France—who labored at the intersection of imperialism with culture, and who went the range from journalism to fiction to scholarship. That is, there was a conscious attempt not only to write history saturated in, taking maximum account of, the struggle between imperial Europe and the peripheries, but to write it in terms both of subject matter and of treatment or method, from the standpoint of and as part of the struggle against imperial domination. For all of them, the history of the Third World had to overcome the assumptions, attitudes, and values implicit in colonial narratives. If this meant, as it usually did, adopting a partisan position of advocacy, then so be it; it was impossible to write of liberation and nationalism, however allusively, without also declaring oneself for or against them. They were correct, I believe, in presuming that in so globalizing a world-view as that of imperialism, there could be no neutrality: one either was on the side of empire or against it, and, since they themselves had lived the empire (as native or as white), there was no getting away from it.

James's *Black Jacobins* treats the Santo Domingo slave uprising as a process unfolding within the same history as that of the French Revolution, and Napoleon and Toussaint are the two great figures who dominate those turbulent years. Events in France and in Haiti crisscross and refer to one another like voices in a fugue. James's narrative is broken up as a history dispersed in geography, in archival sources, in emphases both Black and French. Moreover James writes of Toussaint as someone who takes up the struggle for human freedom—a struggle also going on in the metropolis to which culturally he owes his language and many of his moral allegiances—with a determination rare among subordinates, rarer still among slaves. He appropriates the principles of the Revolution not as a Black man but as a human, and he does so with a dense historical awareness of how in finding the language of Diderot, Rousseau, and Robespierre one follows predecessors creatively, using the same words, employing inflections that transformed rhetoric into actuality.

Toussaint's life ended terribly, as a prisoner of Napoleon, confined in France. Yet the subject of James's book properly speaking is not contained in Toussaint's biography any more than the history of the French Revolution would be adequately represented if the Haitian insurgency were left out. The process continues into the present—hence James's 1962 appendix, "from Toussaint to Castro"—and the predicament remains. How can a non- or post-imperial history be written that is not naively utopian or hopelessly pessimistic, given the continuing embroiled actuality of domination in the Third World? This is a methodological and meta-historical aporia, and James's swift resolution of it is brilliantly imaginative.

In digressing briefly to reinterpret Aimé Césaire's *Cahier d'un retour au pays natal,* James discovers the poet's movement through the deprivations of West Indian life, through "the blue steel rigidities" and "vainglorious conquests" of "the white world," to the West Indies again, where in wishing to be free from the hate he once felt toward his oppressors, the poet declares his commitment "to be the cultivator of this unique race." In other words, Césaire finds that the continuation of imperialism means that there is some need to think of "man" (the exclusively masculine emphasis is quite striking) as something more than "a parasite in the world." "To keep in step with the world" is not the only obligation:

> *but the work of man is only just beginning*
> *and it remains to man to conquer all*
> *the violence entrenched in the recesses of his passion.*

> *And no race possesses the monopoly of beauty,*
> *of intelligence, of force, and there*
> *is a place for all at the rendezvous*
> *of victory.*[201] *(James's translation)*

This, says James, is the very center of Césaire's poem, precisely as Césaire discovers that the defensive assertion of one's identity, *négritude,* is not enough. *Négritude* is just one contribution to "the rendezvous of victory." "The vision of the poet," James adds, "is not economics or politics, it is poetic, *sui generis,* true unto itself and needing no other truth. But it would be the most vulgar racism not to see here a poetic incarnation of Marx's famous sentence, 'The real history of humanity will begin.' "[202]

At this moment James accomplishes another contrapuntal, non-narrative turn. Instead of following Césaire back to West Indian or Third World history, instead of showing his immediate poetic, ideological, or political antecedents, James sets him next to his great Anglo-Saxon contemporary T. S. Eliot, whose conclusion is "Incarnation":

> *Here the impossible union*
> *Of spheres of existence is actual,*
> *Here the past and the future*
> *Are conquered, and reconciled,*
> *Where action were otherwise movement*
> *Of that which is only moved*
> *And has in it no source of movement.*[203]

By moving so unexpectedly from Césaire to Eliot's "Dry Salvages," verses by a poet who, one might think, belongs to a totally different sphere, James rides the poetic force of Césaire's "truth unto itself" as a vehicle for crossing over from the provincialism of one strand of history into an apprehension of other histories, all of them animated by and actualized in an "impossible union." This is a literal instance of Marx's stipulated beginning of human history, and it gives to his prose the dimension of a social community as actual as the history of a people, as general as the vision of the poet.

Neither an abstract, packaged theory, nor a disheartening collection of narratable facts, this moment in James's book embodies (and does not merely represent or deliver) the energies of anti-imperialist liberation. I doubt that anyone can take from it some repeatable doctrine, reusable theory, or memorable story, much less the bureaucracy of a future state. One might perhaps say that it is the history and politics of imperialism, of slavery, conquest, and domination freed by poetry, for a vision bearing on, if not delivering, true liberation. Insofar as it can be approximated in other beginnings then, like *The Black Jacobins,* it is a part of what in human history can move us from the history of domination toward the actuality of liberation. This movement resists the already charted and controlled narrative lanes and skirts the systems of theory, doctrine, and orthodoxy. But, as James's whole work attests, it does not abandon the social principles of community, critical vigilance, and theoretical orientation. And in contemporary Europe and the United States, such a movement, with its audacity and generosity of spirit, is particularly needed, as we advance into the twenty-first century.

CHAPTER FOUR

FREEDOM FROM DOMINATION IN THE FUTURE

The new men of Empire are the ones who believe in fresh starts, new chapters,
new pages; I struggle on with the old story, hoping that before it is finished it
will reveal to me why it was that I thought it worth the trouble.

J. M. COETZEE, *Waiting for the Barbarians*

(I)

American Ascendancy: The Public Space at War

Imperialism did not end, did not suddenly become "past," once decolonization had set in motion the dismantling of the classical empires. A legacy
of connections still binds countries like Algeria and India to France and
Britain respectively. A vast new population of Muslims, Africans, and West
Indians from former colonial territories now resides in metropolitan Europe;
even Italy, Germany, and Scandinavia today must deal with these dislocations, which are to a large degree the result of imperialism and decolonization as well as expanding European population. Also, the end of the Cold
War and of the Soviet Union has definitively changed the world map. The
triumph of the United States as the last superpower suggests that a new set
of force lines will structure the world, and they were already beginning to
be apparent in the 1960s and '70s.

Michael Barratt-Brown, in a preface to the 1970 second edition of his *After
Imperialism* (1963), argues "that imperialism is still without question a most
powerful force in the economic, political and military relations by which the
less economically developed lands are subjected to the more economically
developed. We may still look forward to its ending."[1] It is ironic that

descriptions of the new form of imperialism have regularly employed idioms of gigantism and apocalypse that could not have as easily been applied to the classical empires during their heyday. Some of these descriptions have an extraordinarily dispiriting inevitability, a kind of galloping, engulfing, impersonal, and deterministic quality. Accumulation on a world scale; the world capitalist system; the development of underdevelopment; imperialism and dependency, or the structure of dependence; poverty and imperialism: the repertory is well-known in economics, political science, history, and sociology, and it has been identified less with the New World Order than with members of a controversial Left school of thought. Nevertheless the cultural implications of such phrases and concepts are discernible—despite their oft-debated and far from settled nature—and, alas, they are undeniably depressing to even the most untutored eye.

What are the salient features of the re-presentation of the old imperial inequities, the persistence, in Arno Mayer's telling phrase, of the old regime?[2] One certainly is the immense economic rift between poor and rich states, whose basically quite simple topography was drawn in the starkest terms by the so-called Brandt Report, *North-South: A Program for Survival* (1980).[3] Its conclusions are couched in the language of crisis and emergency: the poorest nations of the Southern Hemisphere must have their "priority needs" addressed, hunger must be abolished, commodity earnings strengthened; manufacturing in the Northern Hemisphere should permit genuine growth in Southern manufacturing centers, trans-national corporations should be "restricted" in their practices, the global monetary system should be reformed, development finance should be changed to eliminate what has been accurately described as "the debt trap."[4] The crux of the matter is, as the report's phrase has it, power-sharing, that is, giving the Southern countries a more equitable share in "power and decision-making within monetary and financial institutions."[5]

It is difficult to disagree with the report's diagnosis, which is made more credible by its balanced tone and its silent picture of the untrammelled rapacity, greed, and immorality of the North, or even with its recommendations. But how will the changes come about? The post-war classifications of all the nations into three "worlds"—coined by a French journalist—has largely been abandoned.[6] Willy Brandt and his colleagues implicitly concede that the United Nations, an admirable organization in principle, has not been adequate to the innumerable regional and global conflicts that occur with increasing frequency. With the exception of the work of small groups (e.g., the World Order Models Project), global thinking tends to reproduce the superpower, Cold War, regional, ideological, or ethnic contests of old, even more dangerous in the nuclear and post-nuclear era, as the horrors of

Yugoslavia attest. The powerful are likely to get more powerful and richer, the weak less powerful and poorer; the gap between the two overrides the former distinctions between socialist and capitalist regimes that, in Europe at least, have become less significant.

In 1982 Noam Chomsky concluded that during the 1980s

> the "North-South" conflict will not subside, and new forms of domination will have to be devised to ensure that privileged segments of Western industrial society maintain substantial control over global resources, human and material, and benefit disproportionately from this control. Thus it comes as no surprise that the reconstitution of ideology in the United States finds echoes throughout the industrial world. . . . But it is an absolute requirement for the Western system of ideology that a vast gulf be established between the civilized West, with its traditional commitment to human dignity, liberty, and self-determination, and the barbaric brutality of those who for some reason— perhaps defective genes—fail to appreciate the depth of this historic commitment, so well revealed by America's Asian wars, for example.[7]

Chomsky's move from the North-South dilemma to American, and Western, dominance is, I think, basically correct, although the decrease in American economic power; the urban, economic, and cultural crisis in the United States; the ascendancy of Pacific Rim states; and the confusions of a multipolar world have muted the stridency of the Reagan period. For one it underlines the continuity of the ideological need to consolidate and justify domination in cultural terms that has been the case in the West since the nineteenth century, and even earlier. Second, it accurately picks up the theme based on repeated projections and theorizations of American power, sounded in often very insecure and therefore overstated ways, that we live today in a period of American ascendancy.

Studies during the past decade of major personalities of the mid-twentieth century illustrate what I mean. Ronald Steel's *Walter Lippmann and the American Century* represents the mind-set of that ascendancy as inscribed in the career of the most famous American journalist—the one with the most prestige and power—of this century. The extraordinary thing about Lippmann's career as it emerges from Steel's book is not that Lippmann was correct or especially perspicacious with regard to his reporting or his predictions about world events (he was not), but rather that from an "insider's" position (the term is his) he articulated American global dominance without demurral, except for Vietnam, and that he saw his role as pundit to be that of helping his compatriots to make "an adjustment to reality," the reality of unrivalled American power in the world, which he made more acceptable by stressing its moralism, realism, altruism with "a remarkable skill for not straying too far from the thrust of public opinion."[8]

A similar view, albeit differently expressed as a mandarin's more austere and elite understanding of the American global role, is found in George Kennan's influential writing. The author of the containment policy that guided United States official thinking for much of the Cold War period, Kennan believed his country to be the guardian of Western civilization. For him such a destiny in the non-European world implied no effort to be expended on making the United States popular ("rotarian idealism" he called it scornfully) but rather depended on "straight power concepts." And since no formerly colonized people or state had the wherewithal to challenge the United States militarily or economically, he cautioned restraint. Yet in a memo written in 1948 for the Policy Planning Staff, he approved of recolonizing Africa and also, in something he wrote in 1971, of *apartheid* (not of its abuses however), although he disapproved of the American intervention in Vietnam and generally of "a purely American kind of informal imperial system."[9] There was no doubt in his mind that Europe and America were uniquely positioned to lead the world, a view that caused him to regard his own country as a sort of "adolescent" growing into the role once played by the British empire.

Other forces shaped post-war United States foreign policy besides men like Lippmann and Kennan—both lonely men alienated from the mass society they lived in, who hated jingoism and the cruder forms of aggressive American behavior. They knew that isolationism, interventionism, anti-colonialism, free-trade imperialism were related to the domestic characteristics of American political life described by Richard Hofstadter as "anti-intellectual" and "paranoid": these produced the inconsistencies, advances, and retreats of United States foreign policy before the end of World War Two. Yet the idea of American leadership and exceptionalism is never absent; no matter what the United States does, these authorities often do not want it to be an imperial power like the others it followed, preferring instead the notion of "world responsibility" as a rationale for what it does. Earlier rationales—the Monroe Doctrine, Manifest Destiny, and so forth—lead to "world responsibility," which exactly corresponds to the growth in the United States' global interests after World War Two and to the conception of its enormous power as formulated by the foreign policy and intellectual elite.

In a persuasively clear account of what damage this has done, Richard Barnet notes that a United States military intervention in the Third World had occurred every year between 1945 and 1967 (when he stopped counting).

Since that time, the United States has been impressively active, most notably during the Gulf War of 1991, when 650,000 troops were dispatched 6,000 miles to turn back an Iraqi invasion of a United States ally. Such interventions, Barnet says in *The Roots of War*, have "all the elements of a powerful imperial creed . . . : a sense of mission, historical necessity, and evangelical fervor." He continues:

> The imperial creed rests on a theory of law-making. According to the strident globalists, like [Lyndon Baines] Johnson, and the muted globalists, like Nixon, the goal of U.S. foreign policy is to bring about a world increasingly subject to the rule of law. But it is the United States which must "organize the peace," to use Secretary of State Rusk's words. The United States imposes the "international interest" by setting the ground rules for economic development and military deployment across the planet. Thus the United States sets rules for Soviet behavior in Cuba, Brazilian behavior in Brazil, Vietnamese behavior in Vietnam. Cold War policy is expressed by a series of directives on such extraterritorial matters as whether Britain may trade with Cuba or whether the government of British Guiana may have a Marxist dentist to run it. Cicero's definition of the early Roman empire was remarkably similar. It was the domain over which Rome enjoyed the legal right to enforce the law. Today America's self-appointed writ runs throughout the world, including the Soviet Union and China, over whose territory the U.S. government has asserted the right to fly military aircraft. The United States, uniquely blessed with surpassing riches and an exceptional history, stands above the international system, not within it. Supreme among nations, she stands ready to be the bearer of the Law.[10]

Although these words were published in 1972, they even *more* accurately describe the United States during the invasion of Panama and the Gulf War, a country which continues to try to dictate its views about law and peace all over the world. The amazing thing about this is not that it is attempted, but that it is done with so much consensus and near unanimity in a public sphere constructed as a kind of cultural space expressly to represent and explain it. In periods of great internal crisis (e.g., a year or so after the Gulf War) this sort of moralistic triumphalism is suspended, put aside. Yet while it lasts the media play an extraordinary role in "manufacturing consent" as Chomsky calls it, in making the average American feel that it is up to "us" to right the wrongs of the world, and the devil with contradictions and inconsistencies. The Gulf intervention was preceded by a string of interventions (Panama,

Grenada, Libya), all of them widely discussed, most of them approved, or at least undeterred, as belonging to "us" by right. As Kiernan puts it: "America loved to think that whatever it wanted was just what the human race wanted."[11]

For years the United States government has had an active policy of direct and announced intervention in the affairs of Central and South America: Cuba, Nicaragua, Panama, Chile, Guatemala, Salvador, Grenada have had attacks made on their sovereignty ranging from outright war to coups and proclaimed subversion, from assassination attempts to the financing of "contra" armies. In East Asia the United States fought two large wars, sponsored massive military drives that caused hundreds of thousands of deaths at the hands of a "friendly" government (Indonesia in East Timor), overturned governments (Iran in 1953), and supported states in lawless activity, flouting United Nations resolutions, contravening stated policy (Turkey, Israel). The official line most of the time is that the United States is defending its interests, maintaining order, bringing justice to bear upon injustice and misbehavior. Yet, in the case of Iraq, the United States used the United Nations Security Council to push through resolutions for war, at the same time that in numerous other instances (Israel's chief among them) United Nations resolutions supported by the United States were unenforced or ignored, and the United States had unpaid dues to the United Nations of several hundred million dollars.

Dissenting literature has always survived in the United States alongside the authorized public space; this literature can be described as oppositional to the overall national and official performance. There are revisionist historians such as William Appleman Williams, Gabriel Kolko, and Howard Zinn, powerful public critics like Noam Chomsky, Richard Barnet, Richard Falk, and many others, all of them prominent not only as individual voices but as members of a fairly substantial alternative and anti-imperial current within the country. With them go such Left-liberal journals as *The Nation, The Progressive,* and, when its author was alive, *I. F. Stone's Weekly.* How much of a following there is for such views as represented by the opposition is very difficult to say; there has always been an opposition—one thinks of anti-imperialists like Mark Twain, William James, and Randolph Bourne—but the depressing truth is that its *deterrent* power has not been effective. Such views as opposed the United States attack on Iraq did nothing at all to stop, postpone, or lessen its horrendous force. What prevailed was an extraordinary mainstream consensus in which the rhetoric of the government, the policymakers, the military, think tanks, media, and academic centers converged on the necessity of United States force and the ultimate justice of its projection, for which a long history of theorists and apologists from Andrew Jackson through Theodore Roosevelt to Henry Kissinger and Robert W. Tucker furnished the preparation.

A correspondence is evident, but frequently disguised or forgotten, between the nineteenth-century doctrine of Manifest Destiny (the title of an 1890 book by John Fiske), the territorial expansion of the United States, the enormous literature of justification (historical mission, moral regeneration, the expansion of freedom: all of these studied in Albert K. Weinberg's massively documented 1958 work *Manifest Destiny*),[12] and the ceaselessly repeated formulae about the need for an American intervention against this or that aggression since World War Two. The correspondence is rarely made explicit, and indeed disappears when the public drums of war are sounded and hundreds of thousands of tons of bombs are dropped on a distant and mostly unknown enemy. The intellectual blotting-out of what "we" do in the process interests me, since it is obvious that no imperial mission or scheme can ever ultimately succeed in maintaining overseas control forever; history also teaches us that domination breeds resistance, and that the violence inherent in the imperial contest—for all its occasional profit or pleasure—is an impoverishment for both sides. These truths hold in an era saturated with the memory of past imperialisms. There are far too many politicized people on earth today for any nation readily to accept the finality of America's historical mission to lead the world.

Enough work has been done by American cultural historians for us to understand the sources of the drive to domination on a world scale as well as the way that drive is represented and made acceptable. Richard Slotkin argues, in *Regeneration Through Violence*, that the shaping experience of American history was the extended wars with the native American Indians; this in turn produced an image of Americans not as plain killers (as D. H. Lawrence said of them) but as "a new race of people, independent of the sin-darkened heritage of man, seeking a totally new and original relationship to pure nature as hunters, explorers, pioneers and seekers."[13] Such imagery keeps recurring in nineteenth-century literature, most memorably in Melville's *Moby-Dick*, where, as C.L.R. James and V. G. Kiernan have argued from a non-American perspective, Captain Ahab is an allegorical representation of the American world quest; he is obsessed, compelling, unstoppable, completely wrapped up in his own rhetorical justification and his sense of cosmic symbolism.[14]

No one would want to reduce Melville's great work to a mere literary decoration of events in the real world; besides, Melville himself was very critical of what Ahab was up to as an American. Yet the fact is that during the nineteenth century the United States *did* expand territorially, most often at the expense of native peoples, and in time came to gain hegemony over the North American continent and the territories and seas adjacent to it. Nineteenth-century offshore experiences ranged from the North African coast to the Philippines, China, Hawaii, and of course throughout the Caribbean and Central America. The broad tendency was to expand and extend control farther, and not to spend much time reflecting on the integrity and independence of Others, for whom the American presence was at very best a mixed blessing.

An extraordinary, but nevertheless typical, example of American wilfulness is at hand in the relationship between Haiti and the United States. As J. Michael Dash reads it in *Haiti and the United States: National Stereotypes and the Literary Imagination,* almost from the moment Haiti gained its independence as a Black republic in 1803 Americans tended to imagine it as a void into which they could pour their own ideas. Abolitionists, says Dash, thought of Haiti not as a place with its own integrity and people but as a convenient site for relocating freed slaves. Later the island and its people came to represent degeneracy and of course racial inferiority. The United States occupied the island in 1915 (and Nicaragua in 1916) and set in place a native tyranny that exacerbated an already desperate state of affairs.[15] And when in 1991 and 1992 thousands of Haitian refugees tried to gain entry into Florida, most were forcibly returned.

Few Americans have agonized over places like Haiti or Iraq once the crisis or their country's actual intervention was over. Strangely, and despite both its intercontinental range and its genuinely various elements, American domination is insular. The foreign-policy elite has no long-standing tradition of direct rule overseas, as was the case with the British or the French, so American attention works in spurts; great masses of rhetoric and huge resources are lavished somewhere (Vietnam, Libya, Iraq, Panama), followed by virtual silence. Again Kiernan: "More multifarious than the British empire, the new hegemony was even less capable of finding any coherent programme of action other than of bullheaded negation. Hence its readiness to let plans be made for it, by company directors or secret agents."[16]

Granted that American expansionism is principally economic, it is still highly dependent and moves together with, upon, cultural ideas and ideologies about America itself, ceaselessly reiterated in public. "An economic system," Kiernan rightly reminds us, "like a nation or a religion, lives not by bread alone, but by beliefs, visions, daydreams as well, and these may be no less vital to it for being erroneous."[17] There is a kind of monotony to the regularity of schemes, phrases, or theories produced by successive generations to justify the serious responsibilities of American global reach. Recent scholarship by Americans paints a bleak picture of how most of these attitudes and the policies they gave rise to were based on almost petulant misinterpretations and ignorance, unrelieved except by a desire for mastery and domination, itself stamped by ideas of American exceptionalism. The relationship between America and its Pacific or Far Eastern interlocutors— China, Japan, Korea, Indochina—is informed by racial prejudice, sudden and relatively unprepared rushes of attention followed by enormous pressure applied thousands of miles away, geographically and intellectually distant from the lives of most Americans. Taking into account the scholarly revelations of Akiri Iriye, Masao Miyoshi, John Dower, and Marilyn Young, we see that there was a great deal of misunderstanding of the United States by these Asian countries, but, with the complicated exception of Japan, they did not actually penetrate the American continent.

One can see this extraordinary asymmetry full blown with the emergence in the United States of the discourse (and the policies) of Development and Modernization, an actuality treated in Graham Greene's novel *The Quiet American,* and with somewhat less comprehending skill in Lederer and Burdick's *The Ugly American.* A truly amazing conceptual arsenal—theories of economic phases, social types, traditional societies, systems transfers, pacification, social mobilization, and so on—was deployed throughout the world; universities and think tanks received huge government subsidies to pursue these ideas, many of which commanded the attention of strategic planners and policy experts in (or close to) the United States government. Not until the great popular disquiet at the Vietnamese war did critical scholars pay attention to this, but then, almost for the first time, the criticism was heard not just of United States policy in Indochina but of the imperialist premises of United States attitudes to Asia. A persuasive account of the Development and Modernization discourse that takes advantage of the anti-war critique is Irene Gendzier's volume, *Managing Political Change.*[18] She shows how the unexamined drive to global reach had the effect of depoliticizing, reducing, and sometimes even eliminating the integrity of overseas societies that seemed in need of modernizing and of what Walt Whitman Rostow called "economic take-off."

Although these characterizations are not exhaustive, they do, I think, accurately describe a general policy with considerable social authority, which created what D.C.M. Platt called in the British context a "departmental view." The leading academic figures analyzed by Gendzier—Huntington, Pye, Verba, Lerner, Lasswell—determined the intellectual agenda and the perspectives of influential sectors of the government and academy. Subversion, radical nationalism, native arguments for independence: all these phenomena of decolonization and the aftermath of classical imperialism were seen within the guidelines provided by the Cold War. They had to be subverted or co-opted; in the case of Korea, China, Vietnam they required a renewed commitment to expensive military campaigns. The apparent challenge to American authority in the almost laughable case of post-Batista Cuba suggests that what was at stake was hardly security but rather a sense that within its self-defined domain (the hemisphere) the United States would not accept any infringements or sustained ideological challenges to what it considered to be "freedom."

This twinning of power and legitimacy, one force obtaining in the world of direct domination, the other in the cultural sphere, is a characteristic of classical imperial hegemony. Where it differs in the American century is the quantum leap in the reach of cultural authority, thanks in large measure to the unprecedented growth in the apparatus for the diffusion and control of information. As we shall see, the media are central to the domestic culture. Whereas a century ago European culture was associated with a white man's presence, indeed with his directly domineering (and hence resistible) physical presence, we now have in addition an international media presence that insinuates itself, frequently at a level below conscious awareness, over a fantastically wide range. The phrase "cultural imperialism," made current and even fashionable by Jacques Lang, loses some of its meaning when applied to the presence of television serials like *Dynasty* and *Dallas* in, say France or Japan, but becomes pertinent again when viewed in a global perspective.

The closest thing to such a perspective was offered in the report published by the International Commission for the Study of Communication Problems convened at the behest of UNESCO and chaired by Sean McBride: *Many Voices, One World* (1980), which addressed the so-called New World Information Order.[19] A great many often irrelevant words of angry analysis and attack have been heaped upon this report, most of them from American journalists and all-purpose sages who upbraid "the Communists" and "the Third World" for trying to curtail press democracy, the free flow of ideas, the market forces that shape telecommunications, the press and computer industries. But even the most cursory glance at the McBride Report will reveal that far from recommending simpleminded solutions like censorship, there was considerable doubt among most of the commission members that anything very much could be done to bring balance and equity in the anarchic world information order. Even not entirely sympathetic writers, for instance, Anthony Smith in *The Geopolitics of Information*, concede the seriousness of the issues:

> The threat to independence in the late twentieth century from the new electronics could be greater than was colonialism itself. We are begin-

ning to learn that de-colonization and the growth of supra-nationalism were not the termination of imperial relationships but merely the extending of a geo-political web which has been spinning since the Renaissance. The new media have the power to penetrate more deeply into a "receiving" culture than any previous manifestation of Western technology. The results could be immense havoc, an intensification of the social contradictions within developing societies today.[20]

No one has denied that the holder of greatest power in this configuration is the United States, whether because a handful of American trans-national corporations control the manufacture, distribution, and above all selection of news relied on by most of the world (even Saddam Hussein seems to have relied on CNN for his news), or because the effectively unopposed expansion of various forms of cultural control that emanate from the United States has created a new mechanism of incorporation and dependence by which to subordinate and compel not only a domestic American constituency but also weaker and smaller cultures. Some of the work done by critical theorists—in particular, Herbert Marcuse's notion of one-dimensional society, Adorno and Enzensberger's consciousness industry—has clarified the nature of the mix of repression and tolerance used as instruments of social pacification in Western societies (issues debated a generation ago by George Orwell, Aldous Huxley, and James Burnham); the influence of Western, and particularly American media imperialism on the rest of the world reinforces the findings of the McBride Commission, as do also the highly important findings by Herbert Schiller and Armand Mattelart about the ownership of the means of producing and circulating images, news, and representations.[21]

Yet before the media go abroad so to speak, they are effective in representing strange and threatening foreign cultures for the home audience, rarely with more success in creating an appetite for hostility and violence against these cultural "Others" than during the Gulf crisis and war of 1990–91. Nineteenth-century Britain and France used to send expeditionary forces to bomb natives—"it appears," Conrad's Marlow says as he gets to Africa, "that the French had one of their wars going on thereabouts. . . . In the empty immensity of earth, sky, and water, there she [a French man-of-war] was, incomprehensible, firing into a continent. Pop, would go one of the six-inch guns"—now the United States does it. Consider now how the Gulf War was made acceptable: in mid-December 1990 a small-scale debate occurred on the pages of *The Wall Street Journal* and *The New York Times:* Karen Elliott House of the former versus Anthony Lewis of the latter. House's thesis was that the United States should not wait for sanctions to work, but ought to attack Iraq, making Saddam Hussein a clear loser. Lewis's rebuttal displayed his usual measure of reasonableness and liberal good faith, qualities that have distinguished him among prominent American columnists. A supporter of George Bush's initial response to Iraq's invasion of Kuwait, Lewis now felt that the prospects of an early war were high, and ought to be resisted. He was impressed by the arguments of people like the super-hawk Paul Nitze, who had been saying that a large assortment of disasters would occur if an American ground offensive was undertaken in the Gulf. The United States should wait, increase economic and diplomatic pressure, then the case for a much later war *might* be plausible. A couple of weeks later the two antagonists appeared on the *MacNeil/Lehrer NewsHour*, a nightly national program that permits lengthy discussion and analysis, to dramatize their earlier positions. To watch the debate was to see opposed philosophies engaged in earnest discussion at a sensitive moment in the national experience. The United States seemed poised for war: here were the pros and cons eloquently put within the sanctioned public space, a national nightly news program.

As realists both House and Lewis accepted the principle that "we"—this pronoun, almost more than any other word, fortifies the somewhat illusory sense that all Americans, as co-owners of the public space, participate in the decisions to commit America to its far-flung foreign interventions—ought *to be in* the Gulf, regulating the behavior of states, armies, and peoples several thousand miles away. National survival was not an issue and never came up. But there was much talk of principles, morality, and right; both spoke of military force as something more or less at their disposal, to deploy, use, and withdraw appropriately, and in all this the United Nations seemed at best an extension of United States policy. This particular debate was depressing because both antagonists were considerable people, neither predictable hawks (like Henry Kissinger, who never tired of "surgical strikes") nor national security experts (like Zbigniew Brzezinski, who energetically opposed the war on solidly geo-political grounds).

For both House and Lewis, "our" actions were part of the assumed heritage of American actions in the world at large, where America has intervened for two centuries with often devastating, but routinely forgotten, results. Rarely in the debate was there mention of the Arabs as having something to do with the war, as its victims, for instance, or (equally convincingly) its instigators. One had the impression that the crisis was entirely to be dealt with *in petto*, as an internal issue for Americans. The impending conflagration, with its unconcealed and certain likelihood of terrible destruction, was distant, and once again, except for the (very few) arriving body bags and bereaved families, Americans were largely spared. The abstract quality imparted coldness and cruelty to the situation.

As an American and Arab who lived in both worlds, I found all this particularly troubling, not least because the confrontation appeared so total, so globally all-encompassing; there was no way of *not* being involved. Never had nouns designating the Arab world or its components been so bandied about; never had they had so strangely abstract and diminished a meaning, and rarely did any regard or care accompany them, even though the United States was not at war with *all* the Arabs. The Arab world compelled fascination and interest and yet withheld affection or enthusiastic and particular knowledge. No major cultural group, for example, was (and still is) as little known: if one were to ask an American *au courant* with recent fiction or poetry for the name of an Arab writer, probably the only one to come up would still be Kahlil Gibran. How could there be so much interaction on one level, and so little actuality on the other?

From the Arab point of view, the picture is just as skewed. There is still hardly any literature in Arabic that portrays Americans; the most interesting exception is Abdelrahman el Munif's massive series of novels *Cities of Salt*,[22] but his books are banned in several countries, and his native Saudi Arabia has stripped him of his citizenship. To my knowledge there is still no institute or major academic department in the Arab world whose main purpose is the study of America, although the United States is by far the largest, most significant outside force in the contemporary Arab world. Some Arab leaders who spend their lives denouncing American interests also expend considerable energies getting their children into American universities and arranging for green cards. It is still difficult to explain even to well-educated and experienced fellow Arabs that United States foreign policy is not in fact run by the CIA, or a conspiracy, or a shadowy network of key "contacts"; nearly everyone that I know believes the United States plans virtually every event of significance in the Middle East including even, in a mind-boggling suggestion made to me once, the Palestinian *intifada*.

This fairly stable mix of long familiarity (well described in James Field's *America and the Mediterranean World*),[23] hostility, and ignorance pertains on both sides of a complex, uneven, and relatively recent cultural encounter. The overriding sense one had at the time of Operation Desert Storm was inevitability, as if President Bush's declared need "to get down there" and (in his own sporty argot) "kick ass" *had* to run up against Saddam Hussein's sternly brutal expression of the post-colonial Arab need to confront, talk back to, stand unblinkingly before the United States. The public rhetoric, in other words, was undeterred, uncomplicated by considerations of detail, realism, cause or effect. For at least a decade movies about American commandos pitted a hulking Rambo or technically whiz-like Delta Force against

Arab/Muslim terrorist-desperadoes; in 1991 it was as if an almost metaphysical intention to rout Iraq had sprung into being, not because Iraq's offense, though great, was cataclysmic, but because a small non-white country had disturbed or rankled a suddenly energized super-nation imbued with a fervor that could only be satisfied with compliance or subservience from "sheikhs," dictators, and camel-jockeys. The truly acceptable Arabs would be those who like Anwar Sadat seemed purified almost completely of their bothersome national selfhood and might become folksy talk-show guests.

Historically the American, and perhaps generally the Western, media have been sensory extensions of the main cultural context. Arabs are only an attenuated recent example of Others who have incurred the wrath of a stern White Man, a kind of Puritan superego whose errand into the wilderness knows few boundaries and who will go to great lengths indeed to make his points. Yet of course the word "imperialism" was a conspicuously missing ingredient in American discussions about the Gulf. "In the United States," according to historian Richard W. Van Alstyne in *The Rising American Empire,* "it is almost heresy to describe the nation as an empire."[24] Yet he shows that the early founders of the Republic, including George Washington, characterized the country as an empire, with a subsequent foreign policy that renounced revolution and promoted imperial growth. He quotes one statesman after another arguing, as Reinhold Niebuhr put it caustically, that the country was "God's American Israel," whose "mission" was to be "trustee under God of the civilization of the world." It was therefore difficult not to hear echoes of that same grandiose self-endowment at the time of the Gulf War. And as the Iraqi infraction seemed actually to grow before the collective eyes of the nation, Saddam became Hitler, the butcher of Baghdad, the madman (as described by Senator Alan Simpson) who was to be brought low.

Anyone who has read *Moby-Dick* may have found it irresistible to extrapolate from that great novel to the real world, to see the American empire preparing once again, like Ahab, to take after an imputed evil. First comes the unexamined moral mission, then, in the media, its military-geo-strategic extension. The most disheartening thing about the media—aside from their sheepishly following the government policy model, mobilizing for war right from the start—was their trafficking in "expert" Middle East lore, supposedly well-informed about Arabs. All roads lead to the bazaar; Arabs only understand force; brutality and violence are part of Arab civilization; Islam is an intolerant, segregationist, "medieval," fanatic, cruel, anti-woman religion. The context, framework, setting of any discussion was limited, indeed frozen, by these ideas. There seemed considerable but inexplicable enjoyment to be had in the prospect that at last "the Arabs" as represented by

Saddam were going to get their comeuppance. Many scores would be settled against various old enemies of the West: Palestinians, Arab nationalism, Islamic civilization.

What got left out was enormous. Little was reported on oil company profits, or how the surge in oil prices had little to do with supply; oil continued to be overproduced. The Iraqi case against Kuwait, or even the nature of Kuwait itself—liberal in some ways, illiberal in others—received next to no hearing. Little was said or analyzed about the complicity and hypocrisy of the Gulf states, the United States, Europe, and Iraq together during the Iran-Iraq War. Opinion on such issues circulated well after the war, for example, in an essay by Theodore Draper in *The New York Review of Books* (January 16, 1992), which suggested that some acknowledgement of Iraq's claim against Kuwait might have staved off a war. There *were* efforts made by a small handful of scholars to analyze the popular rallying of some Arabs to Saddam, despite the unattractiveness of his rule, but these efforts were not integrated into, or allowed equal time with the peculiar inflections of American policy, which for a time promoted Saddam, then demonized him, then learned how to live with him all over again.

It is curious and profoundly symptomatic of the Gulf conflict that one word that was tediously pronounced and repronounced and yet left unanalyzed was "linkage," an ugly solecism that seems to have been invented as a symbol of the unexamined American right to ignore or include whole geographical sections of the globe in its considerations. During the Gulf crisis, "linkage" meant not that there was, but that there was *no* connection between things that in fact belonged together by common association, sense, geography, history. These were sundered, left apart for convenience's sake and for the benefit of imperious United States policymakers, military strategists, and area experts. Every one his own carver, said Jonathan Swift. That the Middle East was linked internally by all sorts of ties—*that* was irrelevant. That Arabs might see a connection between Saddam in Kuwait and, say, Turkey in Cyprus—that too was pointless. That United States policy itself was a linkage was a forbidden topic, most of all for pundits whose role was to manage popular consent for a war though it never actually emerged.

The entire premise was colonial: that a small Third World dictatorship, nurtured and supported by the West, did not have the right to challenge America, which was white and superior. Britain bombed Iraqi troops in the 1920s for daring to resist colonial rule; seventy years later the United States did it but with a more moralistic tone, which did little to conceal the thesis that Middle East oil reserves were an *American* trust. Such practices are anachronistic and supremely mischievous, since they not only make wars continuously possible and attractive, but also prevent a secure knowledge of history, diplomacy, and politics from having the importance it should.

An article that appeared in the Winter 1990–91 issue of *Foreign Affairs,* entitled "The Summer of Arab Discontent," opens with the following passage, which perfectly encapsulates the sorry state of knowledge and power that gave rise to Operation Desert Storm:

> No sooner had the Arab/Muslim world said farewell to the wrath and passion of the Ayatollah Khomeini's crusade than another contender rose in Baghdad. The new claimant was made of material different from the turbaned saviour from Qum: Saddam Hussein was not a writer of treatises in Islamic government nor a product of high learning in religious seminaries. Not for him were the drawn-out ideological struggles for the hearts and minds of the faithful. He came from a brittle land, a frontier country between Persia and Arabia, with little claim to culture and books and grand ideas. The new contender was a despot, a ruthless and skilled warden who had tamed his domain and turned it into a large prison.[25]

Yet even schoolchildren know that Iraq was the seat of Abbasid civilization, the highest flowering of Arab culture between the ninth and twelfth centuries, which produced works of literature still read today as Shakespeare, Dante, and Dickens are still read, and that, as a capital city, Baghdad is also one of the great monuments of Islamic art.[26] In addition, it is where, along with Cairo and Damascus, the nineteenth- and twentieth-century revival of Arab art and literature took place. Baghdad produced at least five of the greatest twentieth-century Arab poets and without any question most of its leading artists, architects, and sculptors. Even though Saddam was a Takrīlī, to imply that Iraq and its citizens had no relation to books and ideas is to be amnesiac about Sumer, Babylon, Nineveh, Hammurabi, Assyria, and all the great monuments of ancient Mesopotamian (and world) civilization, whose cradle Iraq is. To say in so unqualified a way that Iraq was a "brittle" land, with the suggestion of overall aridity and emptiness, is also to show an ignorance that an elementary schoolchild would be embarrassed to reveal. What happened to the verdant valleys of the Tigris and the Euphrates? What happened to the ancient truth that, of all the countries in the Middle East, Iraq has been by far the most fertile?

The author sings the praises of contemporary Saudi Arabia, more brittle and out of touch with books, ideas, and culture than Iraq ever was. My point is not to belittle Saudi Arabia, which is an important country and has much to contribute. But such writing as this is symptomatic of the intellectual will to please power in public, to tell it what it wants to hear, to say to it that it could go ahead and kill, bomb, and destroy, since what would be being attacked was really negligible, brittle, with no relationship to books, ideas, cultures, and no relation either, it gently suggests, to real people. With such information about Iraq, what forgiveness, what humanity, what chance for humane argument? Very little, alas. Hence the rather sodden and uneuphoric commemoration of Operation Desert Storm a year after it, with even right-wing columnists and intellectuals bewailing President Bush's "imperial presidency" and the inconclusiveness of a war that merely prolonged the country's many crises.

The world cannot long afford so heady a mixture of patriotism, relative solipsism, social authority, unchecked aggressiveness, and defensiveness toward others. Today the United States is triumphalist internationally, and seems in a febrile way eager to prove that it is number one, perhaps to offset the recession, the endemic problems posed by the cities, poverty, health, education, production, and the Euro-Japanese challenge. Although an American, I grew up in a cultural framework suffused with the idea that Arab nationalism was all-important, also that it was an aggrieved and unfulfilled nationalism, beset with conspiracies, enemies both internal and external, obstacles to overcome for which no price was too high.

My Arab environment had been largely colonial, but as I was growing up you could travel overland from Lebanon and Syria through Palestine to Egypt and points west. Today that is impossible. Each country places formidable obstacles at the borders. (And for Palestinians, crossing is an especially horrible experience, since often the countries who support Palestine loudly treat actual Palestinians the worst.) Arab nationalism has not died, but has all too often resolved itself into smaller and smaller units. Here too linkage comes last in the Arab setting. The past wasn't better, but it was more healthily interlinked, so to speak; people were actually connected to one another, rather than staring at one another over fortified frontiers. In many schools you would encounter Arabs from everywhere, Muslims and Christians, plus Armenians, Jews, Greeks, Italians, Indians, Iranians, all mixed up, all under one or another colonial regime, but interacting as if it were natural to do so. Today state nationalisms fracture into clan or sectarian ones. Lebanon and Israel are perfect examples of what has happened: the desirability of rigid cantonization in one form or another is present nearly everywhere as a group feeling if not practice, and is subsidized by the state, with its bureaucracies and secret polices. Rulers are clans, families, cliques, closed circles of aging oligarchs, almost mythologically immune, like García Márquez's autumnal patriarch, to new blood or change.

The effort to homogenize and isolate populations in the name of nationalism (*not* liberation) has led to colossal sacrifices and failures. In most parts of the Arab world, civil society (universities, the media, and culture broadly speaking) has been swallowed up by political society, whose main form is the state. One of the great achievements of the early post-war Arab nationalist governments was mass literacy: in Egypt the results were dramatically beneficial almost beyond imagining. Yet the mixture of accelerated literacy and tub-thumping ideology exactly bears out Fanon's fears. My impression is that more effort is spent in sustaining the connection, bolstering the idea that to be Syrian, Iraqi, Egyptian, or Saudi is a sufficient end, rather than in thinking critically, even audaciously, about the national program itself. Identity, always identity, over and above knowing about others.

In this lopsided state of affairs, militarism gained far too many privileges in the Arab world's moral economy. Much of the reason has to do with the sense of being unjustly treated, for which Palestine was not only a metaphor but a reality. But was the only answer military force, huge armies, brassy slogans, bloody promises, and, along with that, endless concrete instances of militarism, starting with catastrophically lost wars at the top and working down to physical punishment and menacing gestures at the bottom? I do not know a single Arab who would demur in private, or who would not readily agree that the state's monopoly on coercion has almost completely eliminated democracy in the Arab world, introduced immense hostility between rulers and ruled, placed much too high value on conformity, opportunism, flattery, and getting along rather than on risking new ideas, criticism, or dissent.

Taken far enough this produces exterminism, the notion that if you do not get your way or something displeases you it is possible simply to blot it out. That notion was surely in some way behind Iraq's aggression against Kuwait. What sort of muddled and anachronistic idea of Bismarckian "integration" was it to wipe out a country and smash its society with "Arab unity" as the goal? The most disheartening thing was that so many people, many of them victims of the same brutal logic, appear to have supported the action and sympathized not at all with Kuwait. Even if one grants that Kuwaitis were unpopular (does one have to be popular not to be exterminated?) and even if Iraq claimed to champion Palestine in standing up to Israel and the United States, surely the very idea that a nation should be obliterated along the way is a murderous proposition, unfit for a great civilization. It is a measure of the dreadful state of political culture in the Arab world today that such exterminism is current.

Oil, however much it may have brought development and prosperity—it did—where it was associated with violence, ideological refinement, political defensiveness, and cultural dependency on the United States created more rifts and social problems than it healed. For anyone who thinks of the Arab world as possessing a plausible sort of internal cohesion, the general air of mediocrity and corruption that hangs over this region that is limitlessly wealthy, superbly endowed culturally and historically, and amply blessed with gifted individuals is an immense puzzle and of course disappointment.

Democracy in any real sense of the word is nowhere to be found in the still "nationalistic" Middle East: there are either privileged oligarchies or privileged ethnic groups. The large mass of people is crushed beneath dictatorship or unyielding, unresponsive, unpopular government. But the notion that the United States is a virtuous innocent in this dreadful state of affairs is unacceptable, as is the proposition that the Gulf War was not a war between George Bush and Saddam Hussein—it most certainly was—and that the United States acted solely and principally in the interests of the United Nations. At bottom it was a personalized struggle between, on the one hand, a Third World dictator of the kind that the United States has long dealt with (Haile Selassie, Somoza, Syngman Rhee, the Shah of Iran, Pinochet, Marcos, Noriega, etc.), whose rule it encouraged, whose favors it long enjoyed, and, on the other, the president of a country which has taken on the mantle of empire inherited from Britain and France and was determined to remain in the Middle East for its oil and for reasons of geo-strategic and political advantage.

For two generations the United States has sided in the Middle East mostly with tyranny and injustice. No struggle for democracy, or women's rights, or secularism and the rights of minorities has the United States officially supported. Instead one administration after another has propped up compliant and unpopular clients, and turned away from the efforts of small peoples to liberate themselves from military occupation, while subsidizing their enemies. The United States has prompted unlimited militarism and (along with France, Britain, China, Germany, and others) engaged in vast arms sales everywhere in the region, mostly to governments which were driven to more and more extreme positions as a result of the United States' obsession with, and exaggeration of the power of Saddam Hussein. To conceive of a post-war Arab world dominated by the rulers of Egypt, Saudi Arabia, and Syria, all of them working in a new Pax Americana as part of the New World Order is neither intellectually nor morally credible.

There has not yet developed a discourse in the American public space that does anything more than identify with power, despite the dangers of that power in a world which has shrunk so small and has become so impressively interconnected. The United States cannot belligerently presume the right, with 6 percent of the world's population, to consume 30 percent of the world's energy, for example. But that is not all. For decades in America there has been a cultural war against the Arabs and Islam: appalling racist caricatures of Arabs and Muslims suggest that they are all either terrorists or sheikhs, and that the region is a large arid slum, fit only for profit or war. The very notion that there might be a history, a culture, a society—indeed many societies—has not held the stage for more than a moment or two, not even during the chorus of voices proclaiming the virtues of "multiculturalism." A flow of trivial instant books by journalists flooded the market and gained currency for a handful of dehumanizing stereotypes, all of them rendering the Arabs essentially as one or another variant of Saddam. As to the unfortunate Kurdish and Shi'ite insurgents, who were first encouraged by the United States to rise up against Saddam, then abandoned to his merciless revenge, they are scarcely remembered, much less mentioned.

After the sudden disappearance of Ambassador April Glaspie, who had long experience in the Middle East, the American administration had hardly any highly placed professional with any real knowledge or experience of the Middle East, its languages or its peoples. And after the systematic attack on its civilian infrastructure, Iraq is still being destroyed—by starvation, disease, and desperation—not because of its aggression against Kuwait, but because the United States wants a physical presence in the Gulf and an excuse to be there, wants to have direct leverage on oil to affect Europe and Japan, because it wishes to set the world agenda, because Iraq is still perceived as a threat to Israel.

Loyalty and patriotism should be based on a critical sense of what the facts are, and what, as residents of this shrinking and depleted planet, Americans owe their neighbors and the rest of mankind. Uncritical solidarity with the policy of the moment, especially when it is so unimaginably costly, cannot be allowed to rule.

Desert Storm was ultimately an imperial war against the Iraqi people, an effort to break and kill them as part of an effort to break and kill Saddam Hussein. Yet this anachronistic and singularly bloody aspect was largely kept from the American television audience, as a way of maintaining its image as a painless Nintendo exercise, and the image of Americans as virtuous, clean warriors. It might have made a difference even to Americans who are not normally interested in history to know that the last time Baghdad was destroyed was in 1258 by the Mongols, although the British furnish a more recent precedent for violent behavior against Arabs.

The absence of any significant domestic deterrent to this extraordinary example of an almost unimaginable collective violence unleashed by the United States against a distant non-white enemy is illuminated when we read Kiernan's account of why American intellectuals except for individuals and groups, as opposed to "enough numbers to give them [the criticisms] practical weight," were so uncritical of the country's behavior during the 1970s. Kiernan concedes that "the country's longstanding pride in itself as a new civilization" was real, but that it "lent itself perilously to perversion by demagogues" was also real. There was a danger that that sense of self-pride was becoming too much like Bismarckian *Kultur*, "with 'culture' hardening into technological 'know-how.' " In addition, and "like Britain's former sense of superiority, that of Americans was buttressed by a high degree of insulation from and ignorance of the rest of the world." Finally:

> This remoteness has helped to give the American intelligentsia in modern times an analogous remoteness from life, or historical reality. It was not easy for dissidents to break the barrier. There was a certain shallowness, a failure to rise much above the level of journalism, in the literature of protest in the inter-war years. . . . It lacked the imaginative depth or resonance which can only be derived from a responsive environment. . . . From the World War onward, intellectuals were drawn increasingly into public activities whose ultimate dynamo was the military-industrial complex. They took part in strategic planning, and the development of scientific warfare and counter-insurgency, were flatteringly invited to the White House, and rewarded presidents with the incense due to royalty. All through the Cold War, scholars engaged in Latin American studies, underwrote the ideology of "good neighborship," of the harmony of interests between the U.S. and the rest of the world. Chomsky had good reason to speak of the "overwhelming urgency" of the need to counteract "the effects of a generation of indoctrination and a long history of self-adulation"; he appealed to intellectuals to open their eyes to the "tradition of naivete and self-righteousness that disfigures our intellectual history."[27]

This applies with great force to the Gulf War of 1991. Americans watched the war on television with a relatively unquestioned certainty that they were seeing the reality, whereas what they saw was the most covered and the least reported war in history. The images and the prints were controlled by the government, and the major American media copied one another, and were in turn copied or shown (like CNN) all over the world. Hardly any attention to speak of was paid to the damage done to the enemy at the same time that some intellectuals were silent and felt helpless, or contributed to the "public" discussion in terms that were accommodated uncritically to the imperial desire to go to war.

So pervasive has the professionalization of intellectual life become that the sense of vocation, as Julien Benda described it for the intellectual, has been almost swallowed up. Policy-oriented intellectuals have internalized the norms of the state, which when it understandably calls them to the capital, in effect becomes their patron. The critical sense is often conveniently jettisoned. As for intellectuals whose charge includes values and principles—literary, philosophical, historical specialists—the American university, with its munificence, utopian sanctuary, and remarkable diversity, has defanged them. Jargons of an almost unimaginable rebarbativeness dominate their styles. Cults like post-modernism, discourse analysis, New Historicism, deconstruction, neo-pragmatism transport them into the country of the blue; an astonishing sense of weightlessness with regard to the gravity of history and individual responsibility fritters away attention to public matters, and to public discourse. The result is a kind of floundering about that is most dispiriting to witness, even as the society as a whole drifts without direction or coherence. Racism, poverty, ecological ravages, disease, and an appallingly widespread ignorance: these are left to the media and the odd political candidate during an election campaign.

(11)

Challenging Orthodoxy and Authority

Not that we have wanted for extremely loud reminders of Chomsky's "reconstitution of ideology," whose elements include notions about Western Judeo-Christian triumphalism, the inherent backwardness of the non-Western world, the dangers of various foreign creeds, the proliferation of "anti-democratic" conspiracies, the celebration and recuperation of canonical works, authors, and ideas. Inversely, other cultures are more and more looked at through the perspectives of pathology and/or therapy. However accurate and serious as scholarship, reflection, and analysis, books appearing in London, Paris, or New York with titles like *The African Condition* or *The Arab Predicament* or *The Republic of Fear* or *The Latin American Syndrome* are consumed in what Kenneth Burke calls "frameworks of acceptance" whose conditions are quite peculiar.

On the one hand, no one in the dominant public space had paid much attention to Iraq as society, culture, or history until August 1991; then the outpouring of quick-fix books and television programs could hardly be stopped. Typically *The Republic of Fear* appeared in 1989, unnoticed. Its author later became a celebrity not because his book makes a scholarly contribution—he does not pretend otherwise—but because its obsessive and monochromatic "portrait" of Iraq perfectly suits the need for dehumanized, ahistorical, and demonological representation of a country as the embodiment of an Arab Hitler. To be non-Western (the reifying labels are themselves symptomatic) is ontologically thus to be unfortunate in nearly every way, before the facts, to be at worst a maniac, and at best a follower, a lazy consumer who, as Naipaul says somewhere, can use but could never have invented the telephone.

On the other hand, the demystification of all cultural constructs, "ours" as well as "theirs," is a new fact that scholars, critics, and artists have put before us. We cannot speak of history today without, for instance, making room in our statements about it for Hayden White's theses in *Metahistory*, that all historical writing *is* writing and delivers figural language and representational tropes, be they in the codes of metonymy, metaphor, allegory, or irony. From the work of Lukacs, Fredric Jameson, Foucault, Derrida, Sartre, Adorno, and Benjamin—to mention only some of the obvious names—we have a vivid apprehension of the processes of regulation and force by which cultural hegemony reproduces itself, pressing even poetry and spirit into administration and the commodity form.

Yet, in the main, the breach between these consequential metropolitan theorists and either the ongoing or the historical imperial experience is truly vast. The contributions of empire to the arts of observation, description, disciplinary formation, and theoretical discourse have been ignored; and with fastidious discretion, perhaps squeamishness, these new theoretical discoveries have routinely bypassed the confluences between their findings and the liberationist energies released by resistance cultures in the Third World. Very rarely do we encounter direct applications from one realm to the other, as we do when, for a lonely example, Arnold Krupat turns the resources of post-structuralist theory on that sad panorama produced by genocide and cultural amnesia which is beginning to be known as "native American literature," in order to interpret the configurations of power and authentic experience contained in its texts.[28]

We can and indeed must speculate as to why there has been a practice of self-confinement of the libertarian theoretical capital produced in the West, and why at the same time, in the formerly colonial world, the prospect for a culture with strongly liberationist components has rarely seemed dimmer.

Let me give an example. Asked in 1985 by a national university in one of the Persian Gulf States to visit there for a week, I found that my mission was to evaluate its English program and perhaps offer some recommendations for its improvement. I was flabbergasted to discover that in sheer numerical terms English attracted the largest number of young people of any department in the university, but disheartened to find that the curriculum was divided about equally between what was called linguistics (that is, grammar and phonetic structure) and literature. The literary courses were, I thought, rigorously orthodox, a pattern followed even in older and more distinguished Arab universities like those of Cairo and Ain Shams. Young Arabs dutifully read Milton, Shakespeare, Wordsworth, Austen, and Dickens as they might have studied Sanskrit or medieval heraldry; no emphasis was placed on the relationship between English and the colonial processes that brought the language and its literature to the Arab world. I could not detect much interest, except in private discussions with a few faculty members, in the new English-language literatures of the Caribbean, Africa, or Asia. It was an anachronistic and odd confluence of rote learning, uncritical teaching, and (to put it kindly) haphazard results.

Still, I learned two facts that interested me as a secular intellectual and critic. The reason for the large numbers of students taking English was given frankly by a somewhat disaffected instructor: many of the students proposed to end up working for airlines, or banks, in which English was the world-wide *lingua franca*. This all but terminally consigned English to the level of a technical language stripped of expressive and aesthetic characteristics and denuded of any critical or self-conscious dimension. You learned English to use computers, respond to orders, transmit telexes, decipher manifests, and so forth. That was all. The other thing I discovered, to my alarm, was that English such as it was existed in what seemed to be a seething caldron of Islamic revivalism. Everywhere I turned, Islamic slogans relating to elections for the university senate were plastered all over the wall (I later found out that the various Islamic candidates won a handsome, if not crushing, plurality). In Egypt, in 1989, after having lectured to the English Faculty of Cairo University for an hour about nationalism, independence, and liberation as alternative cultural practices to imperialism, I was asked about "the theocratic alternative." I had mistakenly supposed the questioner was asking about "the Socratic alternative" and was put right very quickly. She was a well-spoken young woman whose head was covered by a veil; I had overlooked her concerns in my anti-clerical and secular zeal. (I nevertheless proceeded boldly to my attack!)

Thus using the very same English of people who aspire to literary accomplishments of a very high order, who allow a critical use of the language to permit a decolonizing of the mind, as Ngugi wa Thiongo puts it, co-exists with very different new communities in a less appealing new configuration. In places where English was once the language of ruler and administrator, it is a much diminished presence, either a technical language with wholly instrumental characteristics and features, or a foreign language with various implicit connections to the larger English-speaking world, but its presence competes with the impressively formidable emergent reality of organized religious fervor. Since the language of Islam is Arabic, a language with considerable literary community and hieratic force, English has sunk to a low, uninteresting, and attenuated level.

To gauge this new subordination in an era when in other contexts English has acquired remarkable prominence and many interesting new communities of literary, critical, and philosophical practice, we need only briefly recall the stunning acquiescence of the Islamic world to the prohibitions, proscriptions, and threats pronounced by Islam's clerical and secular authorities against Salman Rushdie because of his novel *The Satanic Verses*. I do not mean that the entire Islamic world acquiesced, but that its official agencies and spokespeople either blindly rejected or vehemently refused to engage with a book which the enormous majority of people never read. (Khomeini's *fatwa* of course went a good deal further than mere rejection, but the Iranian position was a relatively isolated one.) That it dealt with Islam in English for what was believed to be a largely Western audience was its main offense. But, equally important, two factors marked the English-speaking world's reaction to the events surrounding *The Satanic Verses*. One was the virtual unanimity of cautious and timid condemnations of Islam, marshalled in a cause that appeared to most of the metropolitan writers and intellectuals both safe and politically correct. As for the many writers who had been murdered, imprisoned, or banned in nations that were either American allies (Morocco, Pakistan, Israel) or anti-American so-called "terrorist" states (Libya, Iran, Syria), very little was said. And second, once the ritual phrases in support of Rushdie and denunciatory of Islam were pronounced, there seemed to be not much further interest either in the Islamic world as a whole or in conditions of authorship there. Greater enthusiasm and energy might have been expended in dialogue with those considerable literary and intellectual figures from the Islamic world (Mahfouz, Darwish, Munif, among others) who occasionally defended (and attacked) Rushdie in more trying circumstances than those obtaining in Greenwich Village or Hampstead.

There are highly significant *deformations* within the new communities and states that now exist alongside and partially within the world-English group dominated by the United States, a group that includes the heterogenous voices, various languages, and hybrid forms that give Anglophonic writing its distinctive and still problematic identity. The emergence in recent decades of a startlingly sharp construction called "Islam" is one such deformation; others include "Communism," "Japan," and the "West," each of them possessing styles of polemic, batteries of discourse, and an unsettling profusion of opportunities for dissemination. In mapping the vast domains commanded by these gigantic caricatural essentializations, we can more fully appreciate and interpret the modest gains made by smaller literate groups that are bound together not by insensate polemic but by affinities, sympathies, and compassion.

Few people during the exhilarating heyday of decolonization and early Third World nationalism were watching or paying close attention to how a carefully nurtured nativism in the anti-colonial ranks grew and grew to inordinately large proportions. All those nationalist appeals to pure or authentic Islam, or to Afrocentrism, *négritude,* or Arabism had a strong response, without sufficient consciousness that those ethnicities and spiritual essences would come back to exact a very high price from their successful adherents. Fanon was one of the few to remark on the dangers posed to a great socio-political movement like decolonization by an untutored national consciousness. Much the same could be said about the dangers of an untutored religious consciousness. Thus the appearance of various mullahs, colonels, and one-party regimes who pleaded national security risks and the need to protect the foundling revolutionary state as their platform, foisted a new set of problems onto the already considerably onerous heritage of imperialism.

It is not possible to name many states or regimes that are exempt from active intellectual and historical participation in the new post-colonial international configuration. National security and a separatist identity are the watchwords. Along with authorized figures—the ruler, the national heroes and martyrs, the established religious authorities—the newly triumphant politicians seemed to require borders and passports first of all. What had once been the imaginative liberation of a people—Aimé Césaire's "inventions of new souls"—and the audacious metaphoric charting of spiritual territory usurped by colonial masters were quickly translated into and accommodated by a world system of barriers, maps, frontiers, police forces, customs and exchange controls. The finest, most elegiac commentary on this dismal state of affairs was provided by Basil Davidson in the course of a memorial reflection on the legacy of Amílcar Cabral. Rehearsing the questions that were never asked about what would happen after liberation, Davidson concludes that a deepening crisis brought on neo-imperialism and put petit bourgeois rulers firmly in command. But, he continues, this brand of

> reformist nationalism continues to dig its own grave. As the grave deepens fewer and fewer persons in command are able to get their own heads above the edge of it. To the tune of requiems sung in solemn

chorus by hosts of foreign experts or would be *fundi* of one profession or another, often on very comfortable (and comforting) salaries, the funeral proceeds. The frontiers are there, the frontiers are sacred. What else, after all, could guarantee privilege and power to ruling elites?[29]

Chinua Achebe's most recent novel, *Anthills of the Savannah*, is a compelling survey of this enervating and dispiriting landscape.

Davidson goes on to modify the gloom of his own description by pointing to what he calls the people's "own solution to this carapace accepted from the colonial period."

What the peoples think upon this subject is shown by their incessant emigration across these lines on the map, as well as by their smuggling enterprises. So that even while a "bourgeois Africa" hardens its frontiers, multiplies its border controls, and thunders against the smuggling of persons and goods, a "peoples' " Africa works in quite another way.[30]

The cultural correlative of that audacious but often costly combination of smuggling and emigration is, of course, familiar to us; it is exemplified by that new group of writers referred to as cosmopolitan recently in a perceptive analysis by Tim Brennan.[31] And crossing borders as well as the representative deprivations and exhilarations of migration has become a major theme in the art of the post-colonial era.

Although one may say that these writers and themes constitute a new cultural configuration and one may point admiringly to regional aesthetic achievements all over the world, I believe we should study the configuration from a somewhat less attractive but, in my opinion, more realistic and political point of view. While we should rightly admire both the material and the achievements of Rushdie's work, say, as part of a significant formation within Anglophone literature, we should at the same time note that it is encumbered, that aesthetically valuable work may be part of a threatening, coercive, or deeply anti-literary, anti-intellectual formation. Before *The Satanic Verses* appeared in 1988, Rushdie was already a problematic figure for the English thanks to his essays and earlier novels; to many Indians and Pakistanis in England and in the subcontinent, however, he was not only a celebrated author they were proud of but also a champion of immigrants' rights and a severe critic of nostalgic imperialists. After the *fatwa* his status changed drastically, and he became anathema to his former admirers. To have provoked Islamic fundamentalism when once he had been a virtual representative of Indian Islam—this testifies to the urgent conjunction of art and politics, which can be explosive.

"There is no document of civilization which is not at the same time a document of barbarism," said Walter Benjamin. Those darker connections are where today's interesting political and cultural conjunctures are to be found. They affect our individual and collective critical work no less than the hermeneutic and utopian work we feel easier about when we read, discuss, and reflect on valuable literary texts.

Let me be more concrete. It is not only tired, harassed, and dispossessed refugees who cross borders and try to become acculturated in new environments; it is also the whole gigantic system of the mass media that is ubiquitous, slipping by most barriers and settling in nearly everywhere. I have said that Herbert Schiller and Armand Mattelart have made us aware of the domination by a handful of multinationals of the production and distribution of journalistic representations; Schiller's most recent study, *Culture, Inc.*, describes how it is that all departments of culture, not just news broadcasting, have been invaded by or enclosed within an ever-expanding but small circle of privately held corporations.[32]

This has a number of consequences. For one, the international media system has in actuality done what idealistic or ideologically inspired notions of collectivity—imagined communities—aspire to do. When, for instance, we speak about and research something we call Commonwealth literature or world literature in English, our efforts are at a putative level, really; discussions of magic realism in the Caribbean and African novel, say, may allude to or at best outline the contours of a "post-modern" or national field that unites these works, but we know that the works and their authors and readers are specific to, and articulated in, local circumstances, and these circumstances are usefully kept separate when we analyze the contrasting conditions of reception in London or New York on the one hand, the peripheries on the other. Compared with the way the four major Western news agencies operate, the mode by which international English-language television journalists select, gather, and rebroadcast pictorial images from all over the world, or the way Hollywood programs like *Bonanza* and *I Love Lucy* work their way through even the Lebanese civil war, our critical efforts are small and primitive, for the media are not only a fully integrated practical network, but a very efficient *mode of articulation* knitting the world together.

This world system, articulating and producing culture, economics, and political power along with their military and demographic coefficients, has an institutionalized tendency to produce out-of-scale trans-national images that are now reorienting international social discourse and process. Take as a case in point the emergence of "terrorism" and "fundamentalism" as two key terms of the 1980s. For one, you could hardly begin (in the public space provided by international discourse) to analyze political conflicts involving

Sunnis and Shi'is, Kurds and Iraqis, or Tamils and Sinhalese, or Sikhs and Hindus—the list is long—without eventually having to resort to the categories and images of "terrorism" and "fundamentalism," which derived entirely from the concerns and intellectual factories in metropolitan centers like Washington and London. They are fearful images that lack discriminate contents or definition, but they signify moral power and approval for whoever uses them, moral defensiveness and criminalization for whomever they designate. These two gigantic reductions mobilized armies as well as dispersed communities. Not Iran's official reaction to Rushdie's novel, or the unofficial enthusiasm for him among Islamic communities in the West, or the public and private expression of outrage in the West against the *fatwa* is intelligible, in my opinion, without reference to the overall logic and the minute articulations and reactions set in motion by the overbearing system I have been trying to describe.

So it is that in the fairly open environment of communities of readers interested, for example, in emergent post-colonial Anglophone or Francophone literature, the underlying configurations are directed and controlled not by processes of hermeneutic investigation, or by sympathetic and literate intuition, or by informed reading, but by much coarser and more instrumental processes whose goal is to mobilize consent, to eradicate dissent, to promote an almost literally blind patriotism. By such means the governability of large numbers of people is assured, numbers whose potentially disruptive ambitions for democracy and expression are held down (or narcotized) in mass societies, including, of course, Western ones.

The fear and terror induced by the overscale images of "terrorism" and "fundamentalism"—call them the figures of an international or transnational imaginary made up of foreign devils—hastens the individual's subordination to the dominant norms of the moment. This is as true in the new post-colonial societies as it is in the West generally and the United States particularly. Thus to oppose the abnormality and extremism embedded in terrorism and fundamentalism—my example has only a small degree of parody—is also to uphold the moderation, rationality, executive centrality of a vaguely designated "Western" (or otherwise local and patriotically assumed) ethos. The irony is that far from endowing the Western ethos with the confidence and secure "normality" we associate with privilege and rectitude, this dynamic imbues "us" with a righteous anger and defensiveness in which "others" are finally seen as enemies, bent on destroying our civilization and way of life.

This is a mere sketch of how these patterns of coercive orthodoxy and self-aggrandizement further strengthen the power of unthinking assent and unchallengeable doctrine. As these are slowly perfected over time and much repetition, they are answered, alas, with corresponding finality by the designated enemies. Thus Muslims or Africans or Indians or Japanese, in their idioms and from within their own threatened localities, attack the West, or Americanization, or imperialism, with little more attention to detail, critical differentiation, discrimination, and distinction than has been lavished on them by the West. The same is true for Americans, to whom patriotism is next to godliness. This is an ultimately senseless dynamic. Whatever the "border wars" have as aims, they are impoverishing. One must join the primordial or constituted group; or, as a subaltern Other, one must accept inferior status; or one must fight to the death.

These border wars are an expression of essentializations—Africanizing the African, Orientalizing the Oriental, Westernizing the Western, Americanizing the American, for an indefinite time and with no alternative (since African, Oriental, Western essences can only remain essences)—a pattern that has been held over from the era of classic imperialism and its systems. What resists it? One obvious instance is identified by Immanuel Wallerstein as what he calls anti-systemic movements, which emerged as a consequence of historical capitalism.[33] There have been enough cases of these latecoming movements in recent times to hearten even the most intransigent pessimist: the democracy movements on all sides of the socialist divide, the Palestinian *intifada*, various social, ecological, and cultural movements throughout North and South America, the women's movement. Yet it is difficult for these movements to be interested in the world beyond their own borders, or to have the capacity and freedom to generalize about it. If you are part of a Philippine, or Palestinian, or Brazilian oppositional movement, you must deal with the tactical and logistical requirements of the daily struggle. Yet I do think that efforts of this kind are developing, if not a general theory, then a common discursive readiness or, to put it territorially, an underlying world map. Perhaps we may start to speak of this somewhat elusive oppositional mood, and its emerging strategies, as an internationalist counter-articulation.

What new or newer kind of intellectual and cultural politics does this internationalism call for?[34] What important transformations and transfigurations should there be in our traditionally and Eurocentrically defined ideas of the writer, the intellectual, the critic? English and French are world languages, and the logics of borders and warring essences are totalizing, so we should begin by acknowledging that the map of the world has no divinely or dogmatically sanctioned spaces, essences, or privileges. However, we may speak of secular space, and of humanly constructed and interdependent histories that are fundamentally knowable, although not through grand theory or systematic totalization. Throughout this book, I have been saying that human experience is finely textured, dense, and accessible enough *not* to need extra-historical or extra-worldly agencies to illuminate or explain it. I am talking about a way of regarding our world as amenable to investigation and interrogation without magic keys, special jargons and instruments, curtained-off practices.

We need a different and innovative paradigm for humanistic research. Scholars can be frankly engaged in the politics and interests of the present— with open eyes, rigorous analytical energy, and the decently social values of those who are concerned with the survival neither of a disciplinary fiefdom or guild nor of a manipulative identity like "India" or "America," but with the improvement and non-coercive enhancement of life in a community struggling to exist among other communities. One must not minimize the inventive excavations required in this work. One is not looking for uniquely original essences, either to restore them or to set them in a place of unimpeachable honor. The study of Indian history is viewed by *Subaltern Studies,* for example, as an ongoing contest between classes and their disputed epistemologies; similarly, "Englishness" for the contributors to the three-volume *Patriotism* edited by Raphael Samuel is not given priority before history, any more than "Attic civilization" in Bernal's *Black Athena* is made simply to serve as an ahistorical model of a superior civilization.

The idea behind these works is that orthodox, authoritatively national and institutional versions of history tend principally to freeze provisional and highly contestable versions of history into official identities. Thus the official version of British history embedded, say, in the durbars arranged for Queen Victoria's Indian Viceroy in 1876 pretends that British rule had an almost mythical longevity over India; traditions of Indian service, obeisance, and subordination are implicated in these ceremonies so as to create the image of an entire continent's trans-historical identity pressed into compliance before the image of a Britain whose own constructed identity is that it has ruled and must always rule both the waves and India.[35] Whereas these official versions of history try to do this for identitarian authority (to use Adornian terms)—the caliphate, the state, the orthodox clerisy, the Establishment—the disenchantments, the disputatious and systematically skeptical investigations in the innovative work I have cited submit these composite, hybrid identities to a negative dialectic which dissolves them into variously constructed components. What matters a great deal more than the stable identity kept current in official discourse is the contestatory force of an interpretative method whose material is the disparate, but intertwined and interdependent, and above all overlapping streams of historical experience.

A superbly audacious instance of this force can be found in interpretations of the Arabic literary and cultural tradition ventured by today's leading Arab poet, Adonis, the pen name of Ali Ahmed Said. Since the three volumes of *Al-Thabit wa al-Mutahawwil* were published between 1974 and 1978, he has almost single-handedly been challenging the persistence of what he regards as the ossified, tradition-bound Arab-Islamic heritage, stuck not only in the past but in rigid and authoritarian rereadings of that past. The purpose of these rereadings, he has said, is to keep the Arabs from truly encountering modernity *(al-hadatha)*. In his book on Arab poetics Adonis associates literal, hard-bound readings of great Arab poetry with the ruler, whereas an imaginative reading reveals that at the heart of the classical tradition—even including the Koran—a subversive and dissenting strain counters the apparent orthodoxy proclaimed by the temporal authorities. He shows how the rule of law in Arab society separates power from critique and tradition from innovation, thereby confining history to an exhausting code of endlessly reiterated precedents. To this system he opposes the dissolving powers of critical modernity:

> Those in power designated everyone who did not think according to the culture of the caliphate as "the people of innovation" *(ahl al-ihdath)*, excluding them with this indictment of heresy from their Islamic affiliation. This explains how the terms *ihdath* (modernity) and *muhdath* (modern, new), used to characterize the poetry which violated the ancient poetic principles, came originally from the religious lexicon. Consequently we can see that the modern in poetry appeared to the ruling establishment as a political or intellectual attack on the culture of the regime and a rejection of the idealized standards of the ancient, and how, therefore, in Arab life the poetic has always been mixed up with the political and religious, and indeed continues to be so.[36]

Although the work of Adonis and his associates in the journal *Mawaqif* is scarcely known outside the Arab world, it can be seen as part of a much larger international configuration that includes the Field Day writers in Ireland, the *Subaltern Studies* group in India, most of the dissenting writers in Eastern Europe, and many Caribbean intellectuals and artists whose heritage is traced to C.L.R. James (Wilson Harris, George Lamming, Eric Williams, Derek Walcott, Edward Braithwaite, the early V. S. Naipaul). For all these movements and individuals, the clichés and patriotic idealizations of official history can be dissolved, along with their legacy of intellectual bondage and defensive recriminations. As Seamus Deane put it for the Irish case, "The myth of Irishness, the notion of Irish unreality, the notions surrounding Irish eloquence, are all political themes upon which the literature has battened to an extreme degree since the nineteenth century when the idea of national character was invented."[37] The job facing the cultural intellectual is therefore not to accept the politics of identity as given, but to show how all representations are constructed, for what purpose, by whom, and with what components.

This is far from easy. An alarming defensiveness has crept into America's official image of itself, especially in its representations of the national past. Every society and official tradition defends itself against interferences with its sanctioned narratives; over time these acquire an almost theological status, with founding heroes, cherished ideas and values, national allegories having an inestimable effect in cultural and political life. Two of these elements—America as a pioneering society and American political life as a direct reflection of democratic practices—have come under recent scrutiny, with a resulting furor that has been quite remarkable. In both cases there has been some but by no means enough serious and secular intellectual effort by intellectuals themselves to accept critical views; rather like the media anchorpersons who internalize the norms of power, they have internalized norms of official self-identity.

Consider "America as West," an exhibition mounted at the National Gallery of American Art in 1991; the gallery is part of the Smithsonian Institution, maintained in part by the federal government. According to the exhibit, the conquest of the West and its subsequent incorporation into the United States had been transformed into a heroic meliorist narrative that disguised, romanticized, or simply eliminated the many-sided truth about the actual process of conquest, as well as the destruction of both native Americans and the environment. Images of the Indian in nineteenth-century American paintings, for example—noble, proud, reflective—were set against a running text on the same wall that described the native American's degradations at the hands of the white man. Such "deconstructions" as this stirred the ire of members of Congress, whether they had seen the exhibition or not; they found its unpatriotic or un-American slant unacceptable, especially for a federal institution, to exhibit. Professors, pundits, and journalists attacked what they considered a malign slur on the United States' "uniqueness," which, in the words of a *Washington Post* writer, is the "hope and optimism of its founding, the promise of its bounty, and the persevering efforts of its government."[38] There were only a few exceptions to this view, for example Robert Hughes, who wrote in *Time* (May 31, 1991) about the art exhibited as "a foundation myth in paint and stone."

That a strange mixture of invention, history, and self-aggrandizement had gone into this national origin story as it does into all of them was ruled by a semi-official consensus to be not fit for America. Paradoxically, the United

States, as an immigrant society composed of many cultures, has a public discourse more policed, more anxious to depict the country as free from taint, more unified around one iron-clad major narrative of innocent triumph. This effort to keep things simple and good disaffiliates the country from its relationship with other societies and peoples, thereby reinforcing its remoteness and insularity.

Another extraordinary case was the controversy surrounding Oliver Stone's seriously flawed film *JFK*, released in late 1991, the premise of which was that Kennedy's assassination had been planned in a conspiracy of Americans who opposed his desire to end the war in Vietnam. Granted that the film was uneven and confused, and granted that Stone's main reason for making it may have been only commercial, why did so many unofficial agencies of cultural authority—newspapers of record, establishment historians, politicians—think it important to attack the film? It takes very little for a non-American to accept as a starting point that most, if not all, political assassinations *are* conspiracies, because that is the way the world is. But a chorus of American sages takes acres of print to deny that conspiracies occur in America, since "we" represent a new, and better, and more innocent world. At the same time there is plentiful evidence of official American conspiracies and assassination attempts against the sanctioned "foreign devils" (Castro, Qaddafi, Saddam Hussein, and so on). The connections are not made, and the reminders remain unpronounced.

A set of major corollaries derives from this. If the chief, most official, forceful, and coercive identity is of a state with its borders, customs, ruling parties and authorities, official narratives and images, and if intellectuals consider that that identity is in need of constant criticism and analysis, then it must follow that other similarly constructed identities need similar investigation and interrogation. The education of those of us who are interested in literature and the study of culture has for the most part been organized under various rubrics—the creative writer, the self-sufficient and autonomous work, the national literature, the separate genres—that have acquired almost fetishistic presence. Now it would be insane to argue that individual writers and works do not exist, that French, Japanese, and Arabic are not separate things, or that Milton, Tagore, and Alejo Carpentier are only trivially different variations on the same theme. Neither am I saying that an essay about *Great Expectations* and Dickens's actual novel *Great Expectations* are the same thing. But I am saying that "identity" does not necessarily imply ontologically given and eternally determined stability, or uniqueness, or irreducible character, or privileged status as something total and complete in and of itself. I would prefer to interpret a novel as the choice of one mode of writing from among many others, and the activity of writing as one social mode among several, and the category of literature as something created to serve various worldly aims, including and perhaps even mainly aesthetic ones. Thus the focus in the destabilizing and investigative attitudes of those whose work actively opposes states and borders is on how a work of art, for instance, begins *as* a work, begins *from* a political, social, cultural situation, begins *to do* certain things and not others.

The modern history of literary study has been bound up with the development of cultural nationalism, whose aim was first to distinguish the national canon, then to maintain its eminence, authority, and aesthetic autonomy. Even in discussions concerning culture in general that seemed to rise above national differences in deference to a universal sphere, hierarchies and ethnic preferences (as between European and non-European) were held to. This is as true of Matthew Arnold as it is of twentieth-century cultural and philological critics whom I revere—Auerbach, Adorno, Spitzer, Blackmur. For them all, their culture was in a sense the only culture. The threats against it were largely internal—for the modern ones they were fascism and communism—and what they upheld was European bourgeois humanism. Neither the ethos nor the rigorous training required to install that *bildung* nor the extraordinary discipline it demanded has survived, although occasionally one hears the accents of admiration and retrospective discipleship; but no critical work done now resembles work on the order of *Mimesis*. Instead of European bourgeois humanism, the basic premise now is provided by a residue of nationalism, with its various derivative authorities, in alliance with a professionalism that divides material into fields, subdivisions, specialties, accreditations, and the like. The surviving doctrine of aesthetic autonomy has dwindled into a formalism associated with one or another professional method—structuralism, deconstruction, etc.

A look at some of the new academic fields that have been created since World War Two, and especially as a result of non-European nationalist struggles, reveals a different topography and a different set of imperatives. On the one hand, most students and teachers of non-European literatures today must from the outset take account of the politics of what they study; one cannot postpone discussions of slavery, colonialism, racism in any serious investigations of modern Indian, African, Latin and North American, Arabic, Caribbean, and Commonwealth literature. Nor is it intellectually responsible to discuss them without referring to their embattled circumstances either in post-colonial societies or as marginalized and/or subjugated subjects confined to secondary spots in the curricula in metropolitan centers. Nor can one hide in positivism or empiricism and offhandedly "require" the weapons of theory. On the other hand, it is a mistake to argue that the "other" non-European literatures, those with more obviously worldly affiliations to power and politics, can be studied "respectably," as if they were in actuality as high, autonomous, aesthetically independent, and satisfying as Western literatures have been made to be. The notion of black skin in a white mask is no more serviceable and dignified in literary study than it is in politics. Emulation and mimicry do not get one very far.

Contamination is the wrong word to use here, but some notion of literature and indeed all culture as hybrid (in Homi Bhabha's complex sense of that word)[39] and encumbered, or entangled and overlapping with what used to be regarded as extraneous elements—this strikes me as *the* essential idea for the revolutionary realities today, in which the contests of the secular world so provocatively inform the texts we both read and write. We can no longer afford conceptions of history that stress linear development or Hegelian transcendence, any more than we can accept geographical or territorial assumptions that assign centrality to the Atlantic world and congenital and even delinquent peripherality to non-Western regions. If configurations like "Anglophone literature" or "world literature" are to have any meaning at all, it is therefore because by their existence and actuality today they testify to the contests and continuing struggles by virtue of which they emerged both as texts and as historical *experiences,* and because they challenge so vigorously the nationalist basis for the composition and study of literature, and the lofty independence and indifference with which it had been customary to regard the metropolitan Western literatures.

Once we accept the actual configuration of literary experiences overlapping with one another and interdependent, despite national boundaries and coercively legislated national autonomies, history and geography are transfigured in new maps, in new and far less stable entities, in new types of connections. Exile, far from being the fate of nearly forgotten unfortunates who are dispossessed and expatriated, becomes something closer to a norm, an experience of crossing boundaries and charting new territories in defiance of the classic canonic enclosures, however much its loss and sadness should be acknowledged and registered. Newly changed models and types jostle against the older ones. The reader and writer of literature—which itself loses its perdurable forms and accepts the testimonials, revisions, notations of the post-colonial experience, including underground life, slave narratives, women's literature, and prison—no longer need to be tied to an image of the poet or scholar in isolation, secure, stable, national in identity, class, gender, or profession, but can think and experience with Genet in Palestine or Algeria, with Tayeb Salih as a Black man in London, with Jamaica Kincaid in the white world, with Rushdie in India and Britain, and so on.

We must expand the horizons against which the questions of *how* and *what* to read and write are both posed and answered. To paraphrase a remark made by Erich Auerbach in one of his last essays, our philological home is the world, and not the nation or even the individual writer. This means that we professional students of literature must take account of a number of astringent issues here, at the risk of both unpopularity and accusations of megalomania. For in an age of the mass media and what I have called the manufacture of consent, it is Panglossian to imagine that the careful reading of a few works of art considered humanistically, professionally, or aesthetically significant is anything but a private activity with only slender public consequences. Texts are protean things; they are tied to circumstances and to politics large and small, and these require attention and criticism. No one can take stock of everything, of course, just as no one theory can explain or account for the connections among texts and societies. But reading and writing texts are never neutral activities: there are interests, powers, passions, pleasures entailed no matter how aesthetic or entertaining the work. Media, political economy, mass institutions—in fine, the tracings of secular power and the influence of the state—are part of what we call literature. And just as it is true that we cannot read literature by men without also reading literature by women—so transfigured has been the shape of literature—it is also true that we cannot deal with the literature of the peripheries without also attending to the literature of the metropolitan centers.

Instead of the partial analysis offered by the various national or systematically theoretical schools, I have been proposing the contrapuntal lines of a global analysis, in which texts and worldly institutions are seen working together, in which Dickens and Thackeray as London authors are read also as writers whose historical experience is informed by the colonial enterprises in India and Australia of which they were so aware, and in which the literature of one commonwealth is involved in the literatures of others. Separatist or nativist enterprises strike me as exhausted; the ecology of literature's new and expanded meaning cannot be attached to only one essence or to the discrete idea of one thing. But this global, contrapuntal analysis should be modelled not (as earlier notions of comparative literature were) on a symphony but rather on an atonal ensemble; we must take into account all sorts of spatial or geographical and rhetorical practices—inflections, limits, constraints, intrusions, inclusions, prohibitions—all of them tending to elucidate a complex and uneven topography. A gifted critic's intuitive synthesis, of the type volunteered by hermeneutic or philological interpretation (whose prototype is Dilthey), is still of value, but strikes me as the poignant reminder of a serener time than ours.

This brings us once again to the question of politics. No country is exempt from the debate about what is to be read, taught, or written. I have often envied American theorists for whom radical skepticism or deferential reverence of the status quo are real alternatives. I do not feel them as such, perhaps because my own history and situation do not allow such luxury, detachment, or satisfaction. Yet I do believe that some literature is actually good, and that some is bad, and I remain as conservative as anyone when it comes to, if not the redemptive value of reading a classic rather than staring at a television screen, then the potential enhancement of one's sensibility and consciousness by doing so, by the exercise of one's mind. I suppose the issue reduces itself to what our humdrum and pedestrian daily work, what we do as readers and writers, is all about, when on the one hand professionalism and patriotism will not serve and on the other waiting for apocalyptic change will not either. I keep coming back—simplistically and idealistically—to the notion of opposing and alleviating coercive domination, transforming the present by trying rationally and analytically to lift some of its burdens, situating the works of various literatures with reference to one another and to their historical modes of being. What I am saying is that in the configurations and by virtue of the transfigurations taking place around us, readers and writers are now in fact secular intellectuals with the archival, expressive, elaborative, and moral responsibilities of that role.

For American intellectuals considerably more is at stake. We are formed by our country, and it has an enormous global presence. There is a serious issue posed by the opposition of, say, Paul Kennedy's work—arguing that all great empires decline because they overextend themselves[40]—and Joseph Nye's, in whose new preface to *Bound to Lead* the American imperial claim to be number one, especially after the Gulf War, is reasserted. The evidence is in Kennedy's favor, but Nye is too intelligent not to understand that "the problem for United States power in the twenty-first century will not be new challenges for hegemony but the new challenges of transnational interdependence."[41] Yet he concludes that "the United States remains the largest and richest power with the greatest capacity to shape the future. And in a democracy, the choices are the people's."[42] The question is, though, do "the people" have direct access to power? Or are the presentations of that power so organized and culturally processed as to require a different analysis?

To speak of relentless commodification and specialization in *this* world, is, I think, to begin to formulate the analysis, especially since the American cult of expertise and professionalism, which has hegemony in cultural discourse, and the hypertrophy of vision and will are so advanced. Rarely before in human history has there been so massive an intervention of force and ideas from one culture to another as there is today from America to the rest of the world (Nye is right about this), and I shall return to the issue a little later. Yet it is also true that in the main we have rarely been so fragmented, so sharply reduced, and so completely diminished in our sense of what our true (as opposed to asserted) cultural identity is. The fantastic explosion of specialized and separatist knowledge is partly to blame: Afrocentrism, Eurocentrism, Occidentalism, feminism, Marxism, deconstructionism, etc. The schools disable and disempower what was empowering and interesting about the original insights. And this in turn has cleared the space for a sanctioned rhetoric of national cultural purpose, well-embodied in such documents as the Rockefeller Foundation–commissioned study *The Humanities in American Life*,[43] or, more recently and more politically, the various expostulations of the former secretary of education (and former head of the National Endowment for the Humanities) William Bennett, speaking (in his "To Reclaim a Heritage") not simply as a cabinet officer in the Reagan administration, but as self-designated spokesman for the West, a sort of Head of the Free World. He was joined by Allan Bloom and his followers, intellectuals who consider the appearance in the academic world of women, African-Americans, gays, and Native Americans, all of them speaking with genuine multiculturalism and new knowledge, as a barbaric threat to "Western Civilization."

What do these "state of the culture" screeds tell us? Simply that the humanities are important, central, traditional, inspiring. Bloom wants us to read only a handful of Greek and Enlightenment philosophers in keeping with his theory about higher education in the United States being for "the elite." Bennett goes as far as saying that we can "have" the humanities by "reclaiming" our traditions—the collective pronouns and the proprietary accents are important—through twenty or so major texts. If every American student were required to read Homer, Shakespeare, the Bible, and Jefferson, then we would achieve a full sense of national purpose. Underlying these epigonal replications of Matthew Arnold's exhortations to the significance of culture is the social authority of patriotism, the fortifications of identity brought to us by "our" culture, whereby we can confront the world defiantly and self-confidently; in Francis Fukuyama's triumphalist proclamation, "we" Americans can see ourselves as realizing the end of history.

This is an extremely drastic delimitation of what we have learned about culture—its productivity, its diversity of components, its critical and often contradictory energies, its radically antithetical characteristics, and above all its rich worldliness and complicity with imperial conquest *and* liberation. We are told that cultural or humanistic study is the recovery of the Judeo-Christian or Western heritage, free from native American culture (which the Judeo-Christian tradition in its early American embodiments set about to massacre) and from that tradition's adventures in the non-Western world.

Yet the multicultural disciplines have in fact found a hospitable haven in the contemporary American academy, and this is a historical fact of extraordinary magnitude. To a great degree, William Bennett has had this as his target, as do Dinesh D'Souza, Roger Kimball, and Alvin Kernan; whereas we would have thought that it has always been a legitimate conception of the modern university's secular mission (as described by Alvin Gouldner) to be a place where multiplicity and contradiction co-exist with established dogma and canonical doctrine. This is now refuted by a new conservative dogmatism claiming "political correctness" as its enemy. The neo-conservative supposition is that in admitting Marxism, structuralism, feminism, and Third World studies into the curriculum (and before that an entire generation of refugee scholars), the American university sabotaged the basis of its supposed authority and is now ruled by a Blanquist cabal of intolerant ideologues who "control" it.

The irony is that it has been the university's practice to admit the subversions of cultural theory in order to some degree to neutralize them by fixing them in the status of academic subspecialties. So now we have the curious spectacle of teachers teaching theories that have been completely displaced—wrenched is the better word—from their contexts; I have elsewhere called this phenomenon "travelling theory."[44] In various academic departments—among them literature, philosophy, and history—theory is taught so as to make the student believe that he or she can become a Marxist, a feminist, an Afrocentrist, or a deconstructionist with about the same effort and commitment required in choosing items from a menu. Over and above that trivialization is a steadily more powerful cult of professional expertise, whose main ideological burden stipulates that social, political, and class-based commitments should be subsumed under the professional disciplines, so that if you are a professional scholar of literature or critic of culture, all your affiliations with the real world are subordinate to your professing in those fields. Similarly, you are responsible not so much to an audience in your community or society, as to and for your corporate guild of fellow experts, your department of specialization, your discipline. In the same spirit and by the same law of the division of labor, those whose job is "foreign affairs" or "Slavic or Middle Eastern area studies" attend to those matters and keep out of yours. Thus your ability to sell, market, promote, and package your expertise—from university to university, from publisher to publisher, from market to market—is protected, its value maintained, your competence enhanced. Robert McCaughey has written an interesting study of how this process works in international affairs; the title tells the whole story: *International Studies and Academic Enterprise: A Chapter in the Enclosure of American Learning.*[45]

I am not discussing here *all* cultural practices in contemporary American society—very far from it. But I am describing a particularly influential

formation that has a decisive bearing on the relationship, inherited historically by the United States from Europe in the twentieth century, between
culture and imperialism. Expertise in foreign policy has never been more
profitable than it is today—hence never as sequestered from public tamper-
ing. So on the one hand we have the co-optations of foreign-area expertise
by the academy (only experts on India can talk about India, only Africanists
about Africa), and on the other reaffirmations of these co-optations by both
the media and the government. These rather slow and silent processes are
put in startling evidence, revealed impressively and suddenly, during periods of foreign crisis for the United States and its interests—for example, the
Iranian hostage crisis, the shooting down of Korean Airlines flight 007, the
Achille Lauro affair, the Libyan, Panamanian, and Iraqi wars. Then, as if by
an open sesame as unarguably obeyed as it is planned to the last detail,
public awareness is saturated with media analysis and stupendous coverage.
Thus experience is emasculated. Adorno says:

> The total obliteration of the war by information, propaganda, commen-
> taries, with cameramen in the first tanks and war reporters dying heroic
> deaths, the mishmash of an enlightened manipulation of public opinion
> and oblivious activity: all this is another expression for the withering
> of experience, the vacuum between men and their fate, in which their
> real fate lies. It is as if the reified, hardened plaster-cast of events takes
> the place of events themselves. Men are reduced to walk-on parts in a
> monster documentary-film.[46]

It would be irresponsible to dismiss the effects that American electronic
media coverage of the non-Western world—and the consequent displacements in print culture—has on American attitudes to, and foreign policy
toward, that world. I argued the case in 1981[47] (and it is more true today) that
limited public effect on the media's performance coupled with an almost
perfect correspondence between prevailing government policy and the ideology ruling news presentation and selection (an agenda set by certified
experts hand in hand with media managers) keeps the United States' imperial perspective toward the non-Western world consistent. As a result
United States policy has been supported by a dominant culture that does not
oppose its main tenets: support for dictatorial and unpopular regimes, for a
scale of violence out of all proportion to the violence of native insurgency
against American allies, for a steady hostility to the legitimacy of native
nationalism.

The concurrence between such notions and the world-view promulgated
by the media is quite exact. The history of other cultures is non-existent

until it erupts in confrontation with the United States; most of what counts about foreign societies is compressed into thirty-second items, "sound-bites," and into the question of whether they are pro- or anti-America, freedom, capitalism, democracy. Most Americans today know and discuss sports with greater skill than they do their own government's behavior in Africa, Indochina, or Latin America; a recent poll showed that 89 percent of high school juniors believed that Toronto was in Italy. As framed by the media, the choice facing professional interpreters of, or experts on, "other" peoples is to tell the public whether what is happening is "good" for America or not—as if what is "good" could be articulated in fifteen-second sound bites—and then to recommend a policy for action. Every commentator or expert a potential secretary of state for a few minutes.

The internalization of norms used in cultural discourse, the rules to follow when statements are made, the "history" that is made official as opposed to the history that is not: all these of course are ways to regulate public discussion in all societies. The difference here is that the epic scale of United States global power and the corresponding power of the national domestic consensus created by the electronic media have no precedents. Never has there been a consensus so difficult to oppose nor so easy and logical to capitulate to unconsciously. Conrad saw Kurtz as a European in the African jungle and Gould as an enlightened Westerner in the South American mountains, capable of both civilizing and obliterating the natives; the same power, on a world scale, is true of the United States today, despite its declining economic power.

My analysis would be incomplete were I not to mention another important element. In speaking of control and consensus, I have used the word "hegemony" purposely, despite Nye's disclaimer that the United States does not now aim for it. It is not a question of a directly imposed regime of conformity in the correspondence between contemporary United States cultural discourse and United States policy in the subordinate, non-Western world. Rather, it is a system of pressures and constraints by which the whole cultural corpus retains its essentially imperial identity and its direction. This is why it is accurate to say that a mainstream culture has a certain regularity, integrity, or predictability over time. Another way of putting this is to say that one can recognize new patterns of dominance, to borrow from Fredric Jameson's description of post-modernism,[48] in contemporary culture. Jameson's argument is yoked to his description of consumer culture, whose central features are a new relationship with the past based on pastiche and nostalgia, a new and eclectic randomness in the cultural artefact, a reorganization of space, and characteristics of multinational capital. To this we must add the culture's phenomenally incorporative capacity, which makes it possible for anyone in fact to say anything at all, but everything is processed either toward the dominant mainstream or out to the margins.

Marginalization in American culture means a kind of unimportant provinciality. It means the inconsequence associated with what is not major, not central, not powerful—in short, it means association with what are considered euphemistically as "alternative" modes, alternative states, peoples, cultures, alternative theaters, presses, newspapers, artists, scholars, and styles, which may later become central or at least fashionable. The new images of centrality—directly connected with what C. Wright Mills called the power elite—supplant the slower, reflective, less immediate and rapid processes of print culture, with its encoding of the attendant and recalcitrant categories of historical class, inherited property, and traditional privilege. The executive presence is central in American culture today: the president, the television commentator, the corporate official, celebrity. Centrality is identity, what is powerful, important, and *ours*. Centrality maintains balance between extremes; it endows ideas with the balances of moderation, rationality, pragmatism; it holds the middle together.

And centrality gives rise to semi-official narratives that authorize and provoke certain sequences of cause and effect, while at the same time preventing counter-narratives from emerging. The commonest sequence is the old one that America, a force for good in the world, regularly comes up against obstacles posed by foreign conspiracies, ontologically mischievous and "against" America. Thus American aid to Vietnam and Iran was corrupted by communists on the one hand and terrorist fundamentalists on the other, leading to humiliation and bitter disappointment. Conversely, during the Cold War, the valiant Afghanistani *moujahidin* (freedom fighters), Poland's Solidarity movement, Nicaraguan "contras," Angolan rebels, Salvadoran regulars—all of whom "we" support—left to our proper devices would be victorious with "our" help, but the meddlesome efforts of liberals at home and disinformation experts abroad reduced our ability to help. Until the Gulf War, when "we" finally rid ourselves of the "Vietnam syndrome."

These subliminally available capsule histories are refracted superbly in the novels of E. L. Doctorow, Don DeLillo, and Robert Stone, and mercilessly analyzed by journalists like Alexander Cockburn, Christopher Hitchens, Seymour Hersh, and in the tireless work of Noam Chomsky. But these official narratives still have the power to interdict, marginalize, and criminalize alternative versions of the same history—in Vietnam, Iran, the Middle East, Africa, Central America, Eastern Europe. A simple empirical demonstration of what I mean is what happens when you are given the opportunity to express a more complex, less sequential history: in fact you are compelled to retell the "facts" in such a way as to be inventing a language from scratch, as was the case with the Gulf War examples I discussed earlier. The most difficult thing to say during the Gulf War was that foreign societies in history and at present may not have assented to the imposition of Western political and military power, not because there was anything inherently evil about that power but because they felt it to be alien. To venture so apparently uncontroversial a truth about how all cultures in fact behave was nothing less than an act of delinquency; the opportunity offered you to say something in the name of pluralism and fairness was sharply restricted to inconsequential bursts of facts, stamped as either extreme or irrelevant. With no acceptable narrative to rely on, with no sustained permission to narrate, you feel crowded out and silenced.

To complete this rather bleak picture, let me add a few final observations about the Third World. Obviously we cannot discuss the non-Western world as disjunct from developments in the West. The ravages of colonial wars, the protracted conflicts between insurgent nationalism and anomalous imperialist control, the disputatious new fundamentalist and nativist movements nourished by despair and anger, the extension of the world system over the developing world—these circumstances are directly connected to actualities in the West. On the one hand, as Eqbal Ahmad says in the best account of these circumstances we have, the peasant and pre-capitalist classes that predominated during the era of classical colonialism have dispersed in the new states into new, often abruptly urbanized and restless classes tied to the absorptive economic and political power of the metropolitan West. In Pakistan and Egypt, for example, the contentious fundamentalists are led not by peasant or working-class intellectuals but by Western-educated engineers, doctors, lawyers. Ruling minorities emerge with the new deformations in the new structures of power.[49] These pathologies, and the disenchantment with authority they have caused, run the gamut from the neo-fascist to the dynastic-oligarchic, with only a few states retaining a functioning parliamentary and democratic system. On the other hand, the crisis of the Third World does present challenges that suggest considerable scope for what Ahmad calls "a logic of daring."[50] In having to give up traditional beliefs, the newly independent states recognize the relativism of, and possibilities inherent in, all societies, systems of belief, cultural practices. The experience of achieving independence imparts "optimism—the emergence and diffusion of a feeling of hope and power, of the belief that what exists does not have to exist, that people can improve their lot if they try [and] . . . rationalism . . . the spread of the presumption that planning, organization and the use of scientific knowledge will resolve social problems."[51]

(III)

Movements and Migrations

F or all its apparent power, this new overall pattern of domination, developed during an era of mass societies commanded at the top by a powerfully centralizing culture and a complex incorporative economy, is unstable. As the remarkable French urban sociologist Paul Virilio has said, it is a polity based on speed, instant communication, distant reach, constant emergency, insecurity induced by mounting crises, some of which lead to war. In such circumstances the rapid occupation of real as well as public space—colonization—becomes the central militaristic prerogative of the modern state, as the United States showed when it dispatched a huge army to the Arabian Gulf, and commandeered the media to help carry out the operation. As against that, Virilio suggests that the modernist project of liberating language/speech *(la libération de la parole)* has a parallel in the liberation of critical spaces—hospitals, universities, theaters, factories, churches, empty buildings; in both, the fundamental transgressive act is to inhabit the normally uninhabited.[52] As examples, Virilio cites the cases of people whose current status is the consequence either of decolonization (migrant workers, refugees, *Gastarbeiter*) or of major demographic and political shifts (Blacks, immigrants, urban squatters, students, popular insurrections, etc.). These constitute a real alternative to the authority of the state.

If the 1960s are now remembered as a decade of European and American mass demonstrations (the university and anti-war uprisings chief among them), the 1980s must surely be the decade of mass uprisings outside the Western metropolis. Iran, the Philippines, Argentina, Korea, Pakistan, Algeria, China, South Africa, virtually all of Eastern Europe, the Israeli-occupied territories of Palestine: these are some of the most impressive crowd-activated sites, each of them crammed with largely unarmed civilian populations, well past the point of enduring the imposed deprivations, tyranny, and inflexibility of governments that had ruled them for too long. Most memorable are, on the one hand, the resourcefulness and the startling symbolism of the protests themselves (the stone-throwing Palestinian youths, for example, or the swaying dancing South African groups, or the wall-traversing East Germans) and, on the other, the offensive brutality or collapse and ignominious departure of the governments.

Allowing for great differences in ideology, these mass protests have all challenged something very basic to every art and theory of government, the principle of confinement. To be governed people must be counted, taxed, educated, and of course ruled in regulated places (house, school, hospital, work site), whose ultimate extension is represented at its most simple and severe by the prison or mental hospital, as Michel Foucault argued. True, there was a carnivalesque aspect to the milling crowds in Gaza or in Wenceslas and Tiananmen squares, but the consequences of sustained mass unconfinement and unsettled existence were only a little less dramatic (and dispiriting) in the 1980s than before. The unresolved plight of the Palestinians speaks directly of an undomesticated cause and a rebellious people paying a very heavy price for their resistance. And there are other examples: refugees and "boat people," those unresting and vulnerable itinerants; the starving populations of the Southern Hemisphere; the destitute but insistent homeless who, like so many Bartlebys, shadow the Christmas shoppers in Western cities; the undocumented immigrants and exploited "guest workers" who provide cheap and usually seasonal labor. Between the extremes of discontented, challenging urban mobs and the floods of semi-forgotten, uncared-for people, the world's secular and religious authorities have sought new, or renewed, modes of governance.

None has seemed so easily available, so conveniently attractive as appeals to tradition, national or religious identity, patriotism. And because these appeals are amplified and disseminated by a perfected media system addressing mass cultures, they have been strikingly, not to say frighteningly effective. When in the spring of 1986 the Reagan administration decided to deal "terrorism" a blow, the raid on Libya was timed to occur exactly as prime-time national evening news began. "America strikes back" was answered resoundingly throughout the Muslim world with bloodcurdling appeals to "Islam," which in turn provoked an avalanche of images, writings, and postures in the "West" underscoring the value of "our" Judeo-Christian (Western, liberal, democratic) heritage and the nefariousness, evil, cruelty, and immaturity of theirs (Islamic, Third World, etc.).

The raid on Libya is instructive not only because of the spectacular mirror reflection between the two sides, but also because they both combined righteous authority and retributive violence in a way that was unquestioned and then often replicated. Truly this has been the age of Ayatollahs, in which a phalanx of guardians (Khomeini, the Pope, Margaret Thatcher) simplify and protect one or another creed, essence, primordial faith. One fundamentalism invidiously attacks the others in the name of sanity, freedom, and goodness. A curious paradox is that religious fervor seems almost always to obscure notions of the sacred or divine, as if those could not survive in the overheated, largely secular atmosphere of fundamentalist combat. You would not think of invoking God's merciful nature when you were mobilized by Khomeini (or for that matter, by the Arab champion against "the Persians" in the nastiest of the 1980s wars, Saddam): you served, you fought, you fulminated. Similarly, oversize champions of the Cold War like Reagan and Thatcher demanded, with a righteousness and power that few clerics could match, obedient service against the Empire of Evil.

The space between the bashing of other religions or cultures and deeply conservative self-praise has not been filled with edifying analysis or discussion. In the reams of print about Salman Rushdie's *Satanic Verses,* only a tiny proportion discussed the book *itself;* those who opposed it and recommended its burning and its author's death refused to read it, while those who supported his freedom to write left it self-righteously at that. Much of the passionate controversy about "cultural literacy" in the United States and Europe was about what *should* be read—the twenty or thirty essential books—not about *how* they should be read. In many American universities, the frequent right-thinking response to the demands of newly empowered marginal groups was to say "show me the African (or Asian, or feminine) Proust" or "if you tamper with the canon of Western literature you are likely to be promoting the return of polygamy and slavery." Whether or not such *hauteur* and so caricatural a view of historical process were supposed to exemplify the humanism and generosity of "our" culture, these sages did not volunteer.

Their assertions joined a mass of other cultural affirmations whose feature was that they had been pronounced by experts and professionals. At the same time, as often noted on the Left and the Right, the general secular intellectual disappeared. The deaths in the 1980s of Jean-Paul Sartre, Roland Barthes, I. F. Stone, Michel Foucault, Raymond Williams, and C.L.R. James, mark the passing of an old order; they had been figures of learning and authority, whose general scope over many fields gave them more than professional competence, that is, a critical intellectual style. The technocrats, in contrast, as Lyotard says in *Postmodern Condition,*[53] are principally competent to solve local problems, not to ask the big questions set by the grand narratives of emancipation and enlightenment, and there are also the carefully accredited policy experts who serve the security managers who have guided international affairs.

With the virtual exhaustion of grand systems and total theories (the Cold War, the Bretton Woods entente, Soviet and Chinese collectivized economies, Third World anti-imperialist nationalism), we enter a new period of vast uncertainty. This is what Mikhail Gorbachev so powerfully represented until he was succeeded by the far less uncertain Boris Yeltsin. *Perestroika* and *glasnost,* the key words associated with Gorbachev's reforms, expressed dissatisfaction with the past and, at most, vague hopes about the future, but they were neither theories nor visions. His restless travels gradually revealed a new map of the world, most of it almost frighteningly interdependent, most of it intellectually, philosophically, ethnically, and even imaginatively uncharted. Large masses of people, greater in number and hopes than ever before, want to eat better and more frequently; large numbers also want to move, talk, sing, dress. If the old systems cannot respond to those demands, the gigantic media-hastened images that provoke administered violence and rabid xenophobia will not serve either. They can be counted on to work for a moment, but then they lose their mobilizing power. There are too many contradictions between reductive schemes and overwhelming impulses and drives.

The old invented histories and traditions and efforts to rule are giving way to newer, more elastic and relaxed theories of what is so discrepant and intense in the contemporary moment. In the West, *post-modernism* has seized upon the ahistorical weightlessness, consumerism, and spectacle of the new order. To it are affiliated other ideas like post-Marxism and post-structuralism, varieties of what the Italian philosopher Gianni Vatimo describes as "the weak thought" of "the end of modernity." Yet in the Arab and Islamic world many artists and intellectuals like Adonis, Elias Khoury, Kamal Abu Deeb, Muhammad Arkoun, and Jamal Ben Sheikh are still concerned with *modernity* itself, still far from exhausted, still a major challenge in a culture dominated by *turath* (heritage) and orthodoxy. This is similarly the case in the Caribbean, East Europe, Latin America, Africa, and the Indian subcontinent; these movements intersect culturally in a fascinating cosmopolitan space animated by internationally prominent writers like Salman Rushdie, Carlos Fuentes, Gabriel García Márquez, Milan Kundera, who intervene forcefully not only as novelists but also as commentators and essayists. And their debate over what is modern or post-modern is joined by the anxious, urgent question of how we are to modernize, given the cataclysmic upheavals the world is experiencing as it moves into the *fin de siècle*, that is, how we are going to keep up life itself when the quotidian demands of the present threaten to outstrip the human presence?

The case of Japan is extraordinarily symptomatic, as it is described by the Japanese-American intellectual Masao Miyoshi. Remark, he says, that, as everyone knows, according to studies of "the enigma of Japanese power," Japanese banks, corporations, and real-estate conglomerates now far overshadow (indeed dwarf) their American counterparts. Real-estate values in Japan are many times higher than in the United States, once considered the very citadel of capital. The world's ten largest banks are mostly Japanese, and much of the United States' huge foreign debt is held by Japan (and

Taiwan). Although there was some prefiguring of this in the brief ascendancy of Arab oil-producing states in the 1970s, Japanese international economic power is unparalleled, especially, as Miyoshi says, in being tied to an almost total absence of international cultural power. Japan's contemporary verbal culture is austere, even impoverished—dominated by talk shows, comic books, relentless conferences and panel discussions. Miyoshi diagnoses a new problematic for culture as a corollary to the country's staggering financial resources, an absolute disparity between the total novelty and global dominance in the economic sphere, and the impoverishing retreat and dependence on the West in cultural discourse.[54]

From the details of daily life to the immense range of global forces (including what has been called "the death of nature")—all these importune the troubled soul, and there is little to mitigate their power or the crises they create. The two general areas of agreement nearly everywhere are that personal freedoms should be safeguarded, and that the earth's environment should be defended against further decline. Democracy and ecology, each providing a local context and plenty of concrete combat zones, are set against a cosmic backdrop. Whether in the struggle of nationalities or in the problems of deforestation and global warming, the interactions between individual identity (embodied in minor activities like smoking or using of aerosol cans) and the general framework are tremendously direct, and the time-honored conventions of art, history, and philosophy do not seem well-suited to them. Much of what was so exciting for four decades about Western modernism and its aftermath—in, say, the elaborate interpretative strategies of critical theory or the self-consciousness of literary and musical forms—seems almost quaintly abstract, desperately Eurocentric today. More reliable now are the reports from the front line where struggles are being fought between domestic tyrants and idealist oppositions, hybrid combinations of realism and fantasy, cartographic and archeological descriptions, explorations in mixed forms (essay, video or film, photograph, memoir, story, aphorism) of unhoused exilic experiences.

The major task, then, is to match the new economic and socio-political dislocations and configurations of our time with the startling realities of human interdependence on a world scale. If the Japanese, East European, Islamic, and Western instances express anything in common, it is that a new critical consciousness is needed, and this can be achieved only by revised attitudes to education. Merely to urge students to insist on one's own identity, history, tradition, uniqueness may initially get them to name their basic requirements for democracy and for the right to an assured, decently humane existence. But we need to go on and to situate these in a geography of other identities, peoples, cultures, and then to study how, despite their differences, they have always overlapped one another, through unhierarchical influence, crossing, incorporation, recollection, deliberate forgetfulness, and, of course, conflict. We are nowhere near "the end of history," but we are still far from free from monopolizing attitudes toward it. These have not been much good in the past—notwithstanding the rallying cries of the politics of separatist identity, multiculturalism, minority discourse—and the quicker we teach ourselves to find alternatives, the better and safer. The fact is, we are mixed in with one another in ways that most national systems of education have not dreamed of. To match knowledge in the arts and sciences with these integrative realities is, I believe, the intellectual and cultural challenge of moment.

The steady critique of nationalism, which derives from the various theorists of liberation I have discussed, should not be forgotten, for we must not condemn ourselves to repeat the imperial experience. In the redefined and yet very close contemporary relationship between culture and imperialism, a relationship that enables disquieting forms of domination, how can we sustain the liberating energies released by the great decolonizing resistance movements and the mass uprisings of the 1980s? Can these energies elude the homogenizing processes of modern life, hold in abeyance the interventions of the new imperial centrality?

"All things counter, original, spare, strange": Gerard Manley Hopkins in "Pied Beauty." The question is, *Where?* And where too, we might ask, is there a place for that astonishingly harmonious vision of time intersecting with the timeless that occurs at the end of "Little Gidding," a moment that Eliot saw as words in

> *An easy commerce of the old and the new,*
> *The common word exact without vulgarity,*
> *The formal word precise but not pedantic,*
> *The complete consort dancing together.*[55]

Virilio's notion is counter-habitation: to live as migrants do in habitually uninhabited but nevertheless public spaces. A similar notion occurs in *Mille Plateaux* (volume 2 of the *Anti-Oedipe*) by Gilles Deleuze and Félix Guattari. A great deal of this immensely rich book is not easily accessible, but I have found it mysteriously suggestive. The chapter entitled "Traité de nomadologie: La Machine de guerre," builds on Virilio's work by extending his ideas on movement and space to a highly eccentric study of an itinerant war machine. This quite original treatise contains a metaphor about a disciplined kind of intellectual mobility in an age of institutionalization, regimentation, co-optation. The war machine, Deleuze and Guattari say, can be assimilated to the military powers of the state—but, since it is fundamentally a separate entity, need not be, any more than the spirit's nomadic wanderings need always be put at the service of institutions. The war machine's source of strength is not only its nomadic freedom but also its metallurgical art—which Deleuze and Guattari compare to the art of musical composition—by which materials are forged, fashioned "beyond separate forms; [this metallurgy, like music] stresses the continuing development of form itself, and beyond individually differing materials it stresses the continuing variation within matter itself."[56] Precision, concreteness, continuity, form—all these have the attributes of a nomadic practice whose power, Virilio says, is not aggressive but transgressive.[57]

We can perceive this truth on the political map of the contemporary world. For surely it is one of the unhappiest characteristics of the age to have produced more refugees, migrants, displaced persons, and exiles than ever before in history, most of them as an accompaniment to and, ironically enough, as afterthoughts of great post-colonial and imperial conflicts. As the struggle for independence produced new states and new boundaries, it also produced homeless wanderers, nomads, and vagrants, unassimilated to the emerging structures of institutional power, rejected by the established order for their intransigence and obdurate rebelliousness. And insofar as these people exist between the old and the new, between the old empire and the new state, their condition articulates the tensions, irresolutions, and contradictions in the overlapping territories shown on the cultural map of imperialism.

There is a great difference, however, between the optimistic mobility, the intellectual liveliness, and "the logic of daring" described by the various theoreticians on whose work I have drawn, and the massive dislocations, waste, misery, and horrors endured in our century's migrations and mutilated lives. Yet it is no exaggeration to say that liberation as an intellectual mission, born in the resistance and opposition to the confinements and ravages of imperialism, has now shifted from the settled, established, and domesticated dynamics of culture to its unhoused, decentered, and exilic energies, energies whose incarnation today is the migrant, and whose consciousness is that of the intellectual and artist in exile, the political figure between domains, between forms, between homes, and between languages. From this perspective then all things are indeed counter, original, spare, strange. From this perspective also, one can see "the complete consort dancing together" contrapuntally. And while it would be the rankest Panglossian dishonesty to say that the bravura performances of the intellectual exile and the miseries of the displaced person or refugee are the same, it is possible, I think, to regard the intellectual as first distilling then articulating

the predicaments that disfigure modernity—mass deportation, imprisonment, population transfer, collective dispossession, and forced immigrations.

"The past life of emigrés is, as we know, annulled," says Adorno in
Minima Moralia, subtitled *Reflections from a Damaged Life (Reflexionen aus dem
beschädigten Leben)*. Why? "Because anything that is not reified, cannot be
counted and measured, ceases to exist"[58] or, as he says later, is consigned to
mere "background." Although the disabling aspects of this fate are manifest,
its virtues or possibilities are worth exploring. Thus the emigré consciousness—a mind of winter, in Wallace Stevens's phrase—discovers in its marginality that "a gaze averted from the beaten track, a hatred of brutality, a
search for fresh concepts not yet encompassed by the general pattern, is the
last hope for thought."[59] Adorno's general pattern is what in another place
he calls the "administered world" or, insofar as the irresistible dominants in
culture are concerned, "the consciousness industry." There is then not just
the negative advantage of refuge in the emigré's eccentricity; there is also
the positive benefit of challenging the system, describing it in language
unavailable to those it has already subdued:

> In an intellectual hierarchy which constantly makes everyone answera-
> ble, unanswerability alone can call the hierarchy directly by its name.
> The circulation sphere, whose stigmata are borne by intellectual out-
> siders, opens a last refuge to the mind that it barters away, at the very
> moment when refuge no longer exists. He who offers for sale something
> unique that no one wants to buy, represents, even against his will,
> freedom from exchange.[60]

These are certainly minimal opportunities, although a few pages later
Adorno expands the possibility of freedom by prescribing a form of expression whose opacity, obscurity, and deviousness—the absence of "the full
transparency of its logical genesis"—move away from the dominant system,
enacting in its "inadequacy" a measure of liberation:

> This inadequacy resembles that of life, which describes a wavering,
> deviating line, disappointing by comparison with its premises, and yet
> which only in this actual course, always less than it should be, is able,
> under given conditions of existence, to represent an unregimented
> one.[61]

Too privatized, we are likely to say about this respite from regimentation.
Yet we can rediscover it not only in the obdurately subjective, even negative
Adorno, but in the public accents of an Islamic intellectual like Ali Shariati,

a prime force in the early days of the Iranian Revolution, when his attack on "the true, straight path, this smooth and sacred highway"—organized orthodoxy—contrasted with the deviations of constant migration:

> man, this dialectical phenomenon, is compelled to be always in motion. . . . Man, then, can never attain a final resting place and take up residence in God. . . . How disgraceful, then, are all fixed standards. Who can ever fix a standard? Man is a "choice," a struggle, a constant becoming. He is an infinite migration, a migration within himself, from clay to God; he is a migrant within his own soul.[62]

Here we have a genuine potential for an emergent non-coercive culture (although Shariati speaks only of "man" and not of "woman"), which in its awareness of concrete obstacles and concrete steps, exactness without vulgarity, precision but not pedantry, shares the sense of a beginning which occurs in all genuinely radical efforts to start again[63]—for example, the tentative authorization of feminine experience in Virginia Woolf's *A Room of One's Own,* or the fabulous reordination of time and character giving rise to the divided generations of *Midnight's Children,* or the remarkable universalizing of the African-American experience as it emerges in such brilliant detail in Toni Morrison's *Tar Baby* and *Beloved.* The push or tension comes from the surrounding environment—the imperialist power that would otherwise compel you to disappear or to accept some miniature version of yourself as a doctrine to be passed out on a course syllabus. These are not new master discourses, strong new narratives, but, as in John Berger's program, another way of telling. When photographs or texts are used merely to establish identity and presence—to give us merely representative images of *the* Woman, or *the* Indian—they enter what Berger calls a control system. With their innately ambiguous, hence negative and anti-narrativist waywardness *not* denied, however, they permit unregimented subjectivity to have a social function: "fragile images [family photographs] often carried next to the heart, or placed by the side of the bed, are used to refer to that which historical time has no right to destroy."[64]

From another perspective, the exilic, the marginal, subjective, migratory energies of modern life, which the liberationist struggles have deployed when these energies are too toughly resilient to disappear, have also emerged in what Immanuel Wallerstein calls "anti-systemic movements." Remember that the main feature of imperialist expansion historically was accumulation, a process that accelerated during the twentieth century. Wallerstein's argument is that at bottom capital accumulation is irrational; its additive, acquisitive gains continue unchecked even though its costs—in maintaining the process, in paying for wars to protect it, in "buying off" and co-opting "intermediate cadres," in living in an atmosphere of permanent crisis—are exorbitant, not worth the gains. Thus, Wallerstein says, "the very superstructure [of state power and the national cultures that support the idea of state power] that was put in place to maximize the free flow of the factors of production in the world-economy is the nursery of national movements that mobilize against the inequalities inherent in the world system."[65] Those people compelled by the system to play subordinate or imprisoning roles within it emerge as conscious antagonists, disrupting it, proposing claims, advancing arguments that dispute the totalitarian compulsions of the world market. Not everything can be bought off.

All these hybrid counter-energies, at work in many fields, individuals, and moments provide a community or culture made up of numerous anti-systemic hints and practices for collective human existence (and neither doctrines nor complete theories) that is not based on coercion or domination. They fuelled the uprisings of the 1980s, about which I spoke earlier. The authoritative, compelling image of the empire, which crept into and overtook so many procedures of intellectual mastery that are central in modern culture, finds its opposite in the renewable, almost sporty discontinuities of intellectual and secular impurities—mixed genres, unexpected combinations of tradition and novelty, political experiences based on communities of effort and interpretation (in the broadest sense of the word) rather than classes or corporations of possession, appropriation, and power.

I find myself returning again and again to a hauntingly beautiful passage by Hugo of St. Victor, a twelfth-century monk from Saxony:

> It is therefore, a source of great virtue for the practiced mind to learn, bit by bit, first to change about in visible and transitory things, so that afterwards it may be able to leave them behind altogether. The person who finds his homeland sweet is still a tender beginner; he to whom every soil is as his native one is already strong; but he is perfect to whom the entire world is as a foreign place. The tender soul has fixed his love on one spot in the world; the strong person has extended his love to all places; the perfect man has extinguished his.[66]

Erich Auerbach, the great German scholar who spent the years of World War Two as an exile in Turkey, cites this passage as a model for anyone—man *and* woman—wishing to transcend the restraints of imperial or national or provincial limits. Only through this attitude can a historian, for example, begin to grasp human experience and its written records in all their diversity and particularity; otherwise one would remain committed more to the exclusions and reactions of prejudice than to the negative freedom of real knowledge. But note that Hugo twice makes it clear that the "strong" or "perfect" person achieves independence and detachment by *working through* attachments, not by rejecting them. Exile is predicated on the existence of, love for, and a real bond with one's native place; the universal truth of exile is not that one has lost that love or home, but that inherent in each is an unexpected, unwelcome loss. Regard experiences then *as if* they were about to disappear: what is it about them that anchors or roots them in reality? What would you save of them, what would you give up, what would you recover? To answer such questions you must have the independence and detachment of someone whose homeland is "sweet," but whose actual condition makes it impossible to recapture that sweetness, and even less possible to derive satisfaction from substitutes furnished by illusion or dogma, whether deriving from pride in one's heritage or from certainty about who "we" are.

No one today is purely *one* thing. Labels like Indian, or woman, or Muslim, or American are not more than starting-points, which if followed into actual experience for only a moment are quickly left behind. Imperialism consolidated the mixture of cultures and identities on a global scale. But its worst and most paradoxical gift was to allow people to believe that they were only, mainly, exclusively, white, or Black, or Western, or Oriental. Yet just as human beings make their own history, they also make their cultures and ethnic identities. No one can deny the persisting continuities of long traditions, sustained habitations, national languages, and cultural geographies, but there seems no reason except fear and prejudice to keep insisting on their separation and distinctiveness, as if that was all human life was about. Survival in fact is about the connections between things; in Eliot's phrase, reality cannot be deprived of the "other echoes [that] inhabit the garden." It is more rewarding—and more difficult—to think concretely and sympathetically, contrapuntally, about others than only about "us." But this also means not trying to rule others, not trying to classify them or put them in hierarchies, above all, not constantly reiterating how "our" culture or country is number one (or *not* number one, for that matter). For the intellectual there is quite enough of value to do without *that*.

Notes

INTRODUCTION

1. Robert Hughes, *The Fatal Shore: The Epic of Australia's Founding* (New York: Knopf, 1987), p. 586.

2. Paul Carter, *The Road to Botany Bay: An Exploration of Landscape and History* (New York: Knopf, 1988), pp. 202–60. As a supplement to Hughes and Carter, see Sneja Gunew, "Denaturalizing Cultural Nationalisms: Multicultural Readings of 'Australia,' " in *Nation and Narration*, ed. Homi K. Bhabha (London: Routledge, 1990), pp. 99–120.

3. Joseph Conrad, *Nostromo: A Tale of the Seaboard* (1904; rprt. Garden City: Doubleday, Page, 1925), p. 77. Strangely, Ian Watt, one of Conrad's best critics, has next to nothing to say about United States imperialism in *Nostromo*: see his *Conrad: "Nostromo"* (Cambridge: Cambridge University Press, 1988). Some suggestive insights into the relationship between geography, trade, and fetishism are found in David Simpson, *Fetishism and Imagination: Dickens, Melville, Conrad* (Baltimore: Johns Hopkins University Press, 1982), pp. 93–116.

4. Lila Abu-Lughod, *Veiled Sentiments: Honor and Poetry in a Bedouin Society* (Berkeley: University of California Press, 1987); Leila Ahmed, *Women and Gender in Islam: Historical Roots of a Modern Debate* (New Haven: Yale University Press, 1992); Fedwa Malti-Douglas, *Woman's Body, Woman's World: Gender and Discourse in Arabo-Islamic Writing* (Princeton: Princeton University Press, 1991).

5. Sara Suleri, *The Rhetoric of English India* (Chicago: University of Chicago Press, 1992); Lisa Lowe, *Critical Terrains: French and British Orientalisms* (Ithaca: Cornell University Press, 1991).

6. Arthur M. Schlesinger, Jr., *The Disuniting of America: Reflections on a Multicultural Society* (New York: Whittle Communications, 1991).

CHAPTER ONE
OVERLAPPING TERRITORIES, INTERTWINED HISTORIES

1. T. S. Eliot, *Critical Essays* (London: Faber & Faber, 1932), pp. 14–15.

2. See Lyndall Gordon, *Eliot's Early Years* (Oxford and New York: Oxford University Press, 1977), pp. 49–54.

3. C. C. Eldridge, *England's Mission: The Imperial Idea in the Age of Gladstone and Disraeli, 1868–1880* (Chapel Hill: University of North Carolina Press, 1974).

4. Patrick O'Brien, "The Costs and Benefits of British Imperialism," *Past and Present*, No. 120, 1988.

5.   Lance E. Davis and Robert A. Huttenback, *Mammon and the Pursuit of Empire: The Political Economy of British Imperialism, 1860–1920* (Cambridge: Cambridge University Press, 1986).

6.   See William Roger Louis, ed., *Imperialism: The Robinson and Gallagher Controversy* (New York: New Viewpoints, 1976).

7.   For example, André Gunder Frank, *Dependent Accumulation and Underdevelopment* (New York: Monthly Review, 1979), and Samir Amin, *L'Accumulation à l'echelle mondiale* (Paris: Anthropos, 1970).

8.   O'Brien, "Costs and Benefits," pp. 180–81.

9.   Harry Magdoff, *Imperialism: From the Colonial Age to the Present* (New York: Monthly Review, 1978), pp. 29 and 35.

10.   William H. McNeill, *The Pursuit of Power: Technology, Armed Forces and Society Since 1000 A.D.* (Chicago: University of Chicago Press, 1983), pp. 260–61.

11.   V. G. Kiernan, *Marxism and Imperialism* (New York: St. Martin's Press, 1974), p. III.

12.   Richard W. Van Alstyne, *The Rising American Empire* (New York: Norton, 1974), p. I. See also Walter LaFeber, *The New Empire: An Interpretation of American Expansion* (Ithaca: Cornell University Press, 1963).

13.   See Michael H. Hunt, *Ideology and U.S. Foreign Policy* (New Haven: Yale University Press, 1987).

14.   Michael W. Doyle, *Empires* (Ithaca: Cornell University Press, 1986), p. 45.

15.   David Landes, *The Unbound Prometheus: Technological Change and Industrial Development in Western Europe from 1750 to the Present* (Cambridge: Cambridge University Press, 1969), p. 37.

16.   Tony Smith, *The Pattern of Imperialism: The United States, Great Britain, and the Late Industrializing World Since 1815* (Cambridge: Cambridge University Press, 1981), p. 52. Smith quotes Gandhi on this point.

17.   Kiernan, *Marxism and Imperialism*, p. III.

18.   D. K. Fieldhouse, *The Colonial Empires: A Comparative Survey from the Eighteenth Century* (1965; rprt. Houndmills: Macmillan, 1991), p. 103.

19.   Frantz Fanon, *The Wretched of the Earth*, trans. Constance Farrington (1961; rprt. New York: Grove, 1968), p. 101.

20.   J. A. Hobson, *Imperialism: A Study* (1902; rprt. Ann Arbor: University of Michigan Press, 1972), p. 197.

21.   *Selected Poetry and Prose of Blake*, ed. Northrop Frye (New York: Random House, 1953), p. 447. One of the few works to deal with Blake's anti-imperialism is David V. Erdman, *Blake: Prophet Against Empire* (New York: Dover, 1991).

22.   Charles Dickens, *Dombey and Son* (1848; rprt. Harmondsworth: Penguin, 1970), p. 50.

23.   Raymond Williams, "Introduction," in Dickens, *Dombey and Son*, pp. II–12.

24.   Martin Bernal, *Black Athena: The Afroasiatic Roots of Classical Civilization*, Vol. I (New Brunswick: Rutgers University Press, 1987), pp. 280–336.

25.   Bernard S. Cohn, "Representing Authority in Victorian India," in Eric Hobsbawm and Terence Ranger, eds., *The Invention of Tradition* (Cambridge: Cambridge University Press, 1983), pp. 185–207.

26.   Quoted in Philip D. Curtin, ed., *Imperialism* (New York: Walker, 1971), pp. 294–95.

27.   Salman Rushdie, "Outside the Whale," in *Imaginary Homelands: Essays and Criticism, 1981–1991* (London: Viking/Granta, 1991), pp. 92, 101.

28.   This is the message of Conor Cruise O'Brien's "Why the Wailing Ought to Stop," *The Observer*, June 3, 1984.

29.   Joseph Conrad, "Heart of Darkness," in *Youth and Two Other Stories* (Garden City: Doubleday, Page, 1925), p. 82.

30.   For Mackinder, see Neil Smith, *Uneven Development: Nature, Capital and the Production of Space* (Oxford: Blackwell, 1984), pp. 102–3. Conrad and triumphalist geography are at the

heart of Felix Driver, "Geography's Empire: Histories of Geographical Knowledge," *Society and Space*, 1991.

31. Hannah Arendt, *The Origins of Totalitarianism* (1951; new ed. New York: Harcourt Brace Jovanovich, 1973), p. 215. See also Fredric Jameson, *The Political Unconscious: Narrative as a Socially Symbolic Act* (Ithaca: Cornell University Press, 1981), pp. 206–81.

32. Jean-François Lyotard, *The Postmodern Condition: A Report on Knowledge*, trans. Geoff Bennington and Brian Massumi (Minneapolis: University of Minnesota Press, 1984), p. 37.

33. See especially Foucault's late work, *The Care of the Self*, trans. Robert Hurley (New York: Pantheon, 1986). A bold new interpretation arguing that Foucault's entire *oeuvre* is about the self, and his in particular, is advanced in *The Passion of Michel Foucault* by James Miller (New York: Simon & Schuster, 1993).

34. See, for example, Gérard Chaliand, *Revolution in the Third World* (Harmondsworth: Penguin, 1978).

35. Rushdie, "Outside the Whale," pp. 100–101.

36. Ian Watt, *Conrad in the Nineteenth Century* (Berkeley: University of California Press, 1979), pp. 175–79.

37. Eric Hobsbawm, "Introduction," in Hobsbawm and Ranger, *Invention of Tradition*, p. 1.

38. Jean-Baptiste-Joseph Fourier, *Préface historique*, Vol. 1 of *Description de l'Egypte* (Paris: Imprimerie royale, 1809–1828), p. 1.

39. 'Abd al-Rahman al-Jabarti, *'Aja'ib al-Athar fi al-Tarajum wa al-Akhbar*, Vol. 4 (Cairo: Lajnat al-Bayan al-'Arabi, 1958–1967), p. 284.

40. See Christopher Miller, *Blank Darkness: Africanist Discourse in French* (Chicago: University of Chicago Press, 1985), and Arnold Temu and Bonaventure Swai, *Historians and Africanist History: A Critique* (Westport: Lawrence Hill, 1981).

41. Johannes Fabian, *Time and the Other: How Anthropology Makes Its Object* (New York: Columbia University Press, 1983); Talal Asad, ed., *Anthropology and the Colonial Encounter* (London: Ithaca Press, 1975); Brian S. Turner, *Marx and the End of Orientalism* (London: Allen & Unwin, 1978). For a discussion of some of these works, see Edward W. Said, "Orientalism Reconsidered," *Race and Class* 27, No. 2 (Autumn 1985), 1–15.

42. Peter Gran, *The Islamic Roots of Capitalism: Egypt, 1760–1840* (Austin: University of Texas Press, 1979); Judith Tucker, *Women in Nineteenth Century Egypt* (Cairo: American University in Cairo Press, 1986); Hanna Batatu, *The Old Social Classes and the Revolutionary Movements of Iraq* (Princeton: Princeton University Press, 1978); Syed Hussein Alatas, *The Myth of the Lazy Native: A Study of the Image of the Malays, Filipinos, and Javanese from the Sixteenth to the Twentieth Century and Its Function in the Ideology of Colonial Capitalism* (London: Frank Cass, 1977).

43. Gauri Viswanathan, *The Masks of Conquest: Literary Study and British Rule in India* (New York: Columbia University Press, 1989).

44. Francis Fergusson, *The Human Image in Dramatic Literature* (New York: Doubleday, Anchor, 1957) pp. 205–6.

45. Erich Auerbach, "Philology and *Weltliteratur*," trans. M. and E. W. Said, *Centennial Review* 13 (Winter 1969); see my discussion of this work in *The World, the Text, and the Critic* (Cambridge, Mass.: Harvard University Press, 1983), pp. 1–9.

46. George E. Woodberry, "Editorial" (1903), in *Comparative Literature: The Early Years, An Anthology of Essays*, eds. Hans Joachim Schulz and Phillip K. Rein (Chapel Hill: University of North Carolina Press, 1973), p. 211. See also Harry Levin, *Grounds for Comparison* (Cambridge, Mass.: Harvard University Press, 1972), pp. 57–130; Claudio Guillérn, *Entre lo uno y lo diverso: Introducción a la literatura comparada* (Barcelona: Editorial Critica, 1985), pp. 54–121.

47. Erich Auerbach, *Mimesis: The Representation of Reality in Western Literature*, trans. Willard Trask (Princeton: Princeton University Press, 1953). See also Said, "Secular Criticism," in *The World, the Text, and the Critic*, pp. 31–53 and 148–49.

48.   The National Defense Education Act (NDEA). An act of the United States Congress passed in 1958, it authorized the expenditure of $295 million for science and languages, both deemed important for national security. Departments of Comparative Literature were among the beneficiaries of this act.

49.   Cited in Smith, *Uneven Development*, pp. 101–2.

50.   Antonio Gramsci, "Some Aspects of the Southern Question," in *Selections from Political Writings, 1921–1926*, trans. and ed. Quintin Hoare (London: Lawrence & Wishart, 1978), p. 461. For an unusual application of Gramsci's theories about "Southernism," see Timothy Brennan, "Literary Criticism and the Southern Question," *Cultural Critique*, No. 11 (Winter 1988–89), 89–114.

51.   John Stuart Mill, *Principles of Political Economy*, Vol. 3, ed. J. M. Robson (Toronto: University of Toronto Press, 1965), p. 693.

CHAPTER TWO
CONSOLIDATED VISION

1.   Richard Slotkin, *Regeneration Through Violence: The Mythology of the American Frontier, 1600–1860* (Middletown: Wesleyan University Press, 1973); Patricia Nelson Limerick, *The Legacy of Conquest: The Unbroken Past of the American West* (New York: Norton, 1988); Michael Paul Rogin, *Fathers and Children: Andrew Jackson and the Subjugation of the American Indian* (New York: Knopf, 1975).

2.   Bruce Robbins, *The Servant's Hand: English Fiction from Below* (New York: Columbia University Press, 1986).

3.   Gareth Stedman Jones, *Outcast London: A Study in the Relationship Between the Classes in Victorian Society* (1971; rprt. New York: Pantheon, 1984).

4.   Eric Wolf, *Europe and the People Without History* (Berkeley: University of California Press, 1982).

5.   Martin Green, *Dreams of Adventure, Deeds of Empire* (New York: Basic Books, 1979); Molly Mahood, *The Colonial Encounter: A Reading of Six Novels* (London: Rex Collings, 1977); John A. McClure, *Kipling and Conrad: The Colonial Fiction* (Cambridge, Mass.: Harvard University Press, 1981); Patrick Brantlinger, *The Rule of Darkness: British Literature and Imperialism, 1830–1914* (Ithaca: Cornell University Press, 1988). See also John Barrell, *The Infection of Thomas de Quincey: A Psychopathology of Imperialism* (New Haven: Yale University Press, 1991).

6.   William Appleman Williams, *Empire as a Way of Life* (New York and Oxford: Oxford University Press, 1980), pp. 112–13.

7.   Jonah Raskin, *The Mythology of Imperialism* (New York: Random House, 1971); Gordon K. Lewis, *Slavery, Imperialism, and Freedom: Studies in English Radical Thought* (New York: Monthly Review, 1978); V. G. Kiernan, *The Lords of Human Kind: Black Man, Yellow Man, and White Man in an Age of Empire* (1969; rprt. New York: Columbia University Press, 1986), and *Marxism and Imperialism* (New York: St. Martin's Press, 1974). A more recent work is Eric Cheyfitz, *The Poetics of Imperialism: Translation and Colonization from* The Tempest *to* Tarzan (New York: Oxford University Press, 1991). Benita Parry, *Conrad and Imperialism* (London: Macmillan, 1983), cogently discusses these and other works in the context provided by Conrad's fiction.

8.   E. M. Forster, *Howards End* (New York: Knopf, 1921), p. 204.

9.   Raymond Williams, *Politics and Letters: Interviews with New Left Review* (London: New Left, 1979), p. 118.

10.   Williams's *Culture and Society, 1780–1950*, was published in 1958 (London: Chatto & Windus).

11.   Joseph Conrad, "Heart of Darkness," in *Youth and Two Other Stories* (Garden City: Doubleday, Page, 1925), pp. 50–51. For a demystifying account of the connection between modern culture and redemption, see Leo Bersani, *The Culture of Redemption* (Cambridge, Mass.: Harvard University Press, 1990).

12.   Theories and justifications of imperial style—ancient versus modern, English versus French, and so on—were in plentiful supply after 1880. See as a celebrated example Evelyn Baring (Cromer), *Ancient and Modern Imperialism* (London: Murray, 1910). See also C. A. Bodelsen, *Studies in Mid-Victorian Imperialism* (New York: Howard Fertig, 1968), and Richard Faber, *The Vision and the Need: Late Victorian Imperialist Aims* (London: Faber & Faber, 1966). An earlier but still useful work is Klaus Knorr, *British Colonial Theories* (Toronto: University of Toronto Press, 1944).

13.   Ian Watt, *The Rise of the Novel* (Berkeley: University of California Press, 1957); Lennard Davis, *Factual Fictions: The Origins of the English Novel* (New York: Columbia University Press, 1983); John Richetti, *Popular Fiction Before Richardson* (London: Oxford University Press, 1969); Michael McKeon, *The Origin of the English Novel, 1600–1740* (Baltimore: Johns Hopkins University Press, 1987).

14.   J. R. Seeley, *The Expansion of England* (1884; rprt. Chicago: University of Chicago Press, 1971), p. 12; J. A. Hobson, *Imperialism: A Study* (1902; rprt. Ann Arbor: University of Michigan Press, 1972), p. 15. Although Hobson implicates other European powers in the perversions of imperialism, England stands out.

15.   Raymond Williams, *The Country and the City* (New York: Oxford University Press, 1973), pp. 165–82 and *passim*.

16.   D.C.M. Platt, *Finance, Trade and Politics in British Foreign Policy, 1815–1914* (Oxford: Clarendon Press, 1968), p. 536.

17.   *Ibid.*, p. 357.

18.   Joseph Schumpeter, *Imperialism and Social Classes*, trans. Heinz Norden (New York: Augustus M. Kelley, 1951), p. 12.

19.   Platt, *Finance, Trade and Politics*, p. 359.

20.   Ronald Robinson and John Gallagher, with Alice Denny, *Africa and the Victorians: The Official Mind of Imperialism* (1961; new ed. London: Macmillan, 1981), p. 10. But for a vivid sense of what effects this thesis has had in scholarly discussion of empire, see William Roger Louis, ed., *Imperialism: The Robinson and Gallagher Controversy* (New York: Franklin Watts, 1976). An essential compilation for the whole field of study is Robin Winks, ed., *The Historiography of the British Empire-Commonwealth: Trends, Interpretations, and Resources* (Durham: Duke University Press, 1966). Two compilations mentioned by Winks (p. 6) are *Historians of India, Pakistan and Ceylon*, ed. Cyril H. Philips, and *Historians of South East Asia*, ed. D.G.E. Hall.

21.   Fredric Jameson, *The Political Unconscious: Narrative as a Socially Symbolic Act* (Ithaca: Cornell University Press, 1981); David A. Miller, *The Novel and the Police* (Berkeley: University of California Press, 1988). See also Hugh Ridley, *Images of Imperial Rule* (London: Croom Helm, 1983).

22.   In John MacKenzie, *Propaganda and Empire: The Manipulation of British Public Opinion, 1880–1960* (Manchester: Manchester University Press, 1984), there is an excellent account of how popular culture was effective in the official age of empire. See also MacKenzie, ed., *Imperialism and Popular Culture* (Manchester: Manchester University Press, 1986); for more subtle manipulations of the English national identity during the same period, see Robert Colls and Philip Dodd, eds., *Englishness: Politics and Culture, 1880–1920* (London: Croom Helm, 1987). See also Raphael Samuel, ed., *Patriotism: The Making and Unmaking of British National Identity*, 3 vols. (London: Routledge, 1989).

23.   E. M. Forster, *A Passage to India* (1924; rprt. New York: Harcourt, Brace & World, 1952), p. 231.

24. For the attack on Conrad, see Chinua Achebe, "An Image of Africa: Racism in Conrad's *Heart of Darkness,"* in *Hopes and Impediments: Selected Essays* (New York: Doubleday, Anchor, 1989), pp. 1–20. Some of the issues raised by Achebe are well discussed by Brantlinger, *Rule of Darkness,* pp. 269–74.

25. Deirdre David, *Fictions of Resolution in Three Victorian Novels* (New York: Columbia University Press, 1981).

26. Georg Lukacs, *The Historical Novel,* trans. Hannah and Stanley Mitchell (London: Merlin Press, 1962), pp. 19–88.

27. *Ibid.,* pp. 30–63.

28. A few lines from Ruskin are quoted and commented on in R. Koebner and H. Schmidt, *Imperialism: The Story and Significance of a Political World, 1840–1866* (Cambridge: Cambridge University Press, 1964), p. 99.

29. V. G. Kiernan, *Marxism and Imperialism* (New York: St. Martin's Press, 1974), p. 100.

30. John Stuart Mill, *Disquisitions and Discussions,* Vol. 3 (London: Longmans, Green, Reader & Dyer, 1875), pp. 167–68. For an earlier version of this see the discussion by Nicholas Canny, "The Ideology of English Colonization: From Ireland to America," *William and Mary Quarterly* 30 (1973), 575–98.

31. Williams, *Country and the City,* p. 281.

32. Peter Hulme, *Colonial Encounters: Europe and the Native Caribbean, 1492–1797* (London: Methuen, 1986). See also his anthology with Neil L. Whitehead, *Wild Majesty: Encounters with Caribs from Columbus to the Present Day* (Oxford: Clarendon Press, 1992).

33. Hobson, *Imperialism,* p. 6.

34. This is most memorably discussed in C.L.R. James's *The Black Jacobins: Toussaint L'Ouverture and the San Domingo Revolution* (1938; rprt. New York: Vintage, 1963), especially Chapter 2, "The Owners." See also Robin Blackburn, *The Overthrow of Colonial Slavery, 1776–1848* (London: Verso, 1988), pp. 149–53.

35. Williams, *Country and the City,* p. 117.

36. Jane Austen, *Mansfield Park,* ed. Tony Tanner (1814; rprt. Harmondsworth: Penguin, 1966), p. 42. The best account of the novel is in Tony Tanner's *Jane Austen* (Cambridge, Mass.: Harvard University Press, 1986).

37. *Ibid.,* p. 54.

38. *Ibid.,* p. 206.

39. Warren Roberts, *Jane Austen and the French Revolution* (London: Macmillan, 1979), pp. 97–98. See also Avrom Fleishman, *A Reading of* Mansfield Park: *An Essay in Critical Synthesis* (Minneapolis: University of Minnesota Press, 1967), pp. 36–39 and *passim.*

40. Austen, *Mansfield Park,* pp. 375–76.

41. John Stuart Mill, *Principles of Political Economy,* Vol. 3, ed. J. M. Robson (Toronto: University of Toronto Press, 1965), p. 693. The passage is quoted in Sidney W. Mintz, *Sweetness and Power: The Place of Sugar in Modern History* (New York: Viking, 1985), p. 42.

42. Austen, *Mansfield Park,* p. 446.

43. *Ibid.,* p. 448.

44. *Ibid.,* p. 450.

45. *Ibid.,* p. 456.

46. John Gallagher, *The Decline, Revival and Fall of the British Empire* (Cambridge: Cambridge University Press, 1982), p. 76.

47. Austen, *Mansfield Park,* p. 308.

48. Lowell Joseph Ragatz, *The Fall of the Planter Class in the British Caribbean, 1763–1833: A Study in Social and Economic History* (1928; rprt. New York: Octagon, 1963), p. 27.

49. Eric Williams, *Capitalism and Slavery* (New York: Russell & Russell, 1961), p. 211. See

also his *From Columbus to Castro: The History of the Caribbean, 1492–1969* (London: Deutsch, 1970), pp. 177–254.

50. Austen, *Mansfield Park,* p. 213.

51. Tzvetan Todorov, *Nous et les autres: La réflexion sur la diversité humaine* (Paris: Seuil, 1989).

52. Raoul Girardet, *L'Idée coloniale en France, 1871–1962* (Paris: La Table Ronde, 1972), pp. 7, 10–13.

53. Basil Davidson, *The African Past: Chronicles from Antiquity to Modern Times* (London: Longmans, 1964), pp. 36–37. See also Philip D. Curtin, *Image of Africa: British Ideas and Action, 1780–1850,* 2 vols. (Madison: University of Wisconsin Press, 1964); Bernard Smith, *European Vision and the South Pacific* (New Haven: Yale University Press, 1985).

54. Stephen Jay Gould, *The Mismeasure of Man* (New York: Norton, 1981); Nancy Stepan, *The Idea of Race in Science: Great Britain, 1800–1960* (London: Macmillan, 1982).

55. See the thorough account of these currents in early anthropology by George W. Stocking, *Victorian Anthropology* (New York: Free Press, 1987).

56. Excerpted in Philip D. Curtin, *Imperialism* (New York: Walker, 1971), pp. 158–59.

57. John Ruskin, "Inaugural Lecture" (1870), in *The Works of John Ruskin,* Vol. 20, ed. E. T. Cook and Alexander Weddenburn (London: George Allen, 1905), p. 41, n. 2.

58. *Ibid.,* pp. 41–43.

59. V. G. Kiernan, "Tennyson, King Arthur and Imperialism," in his *Poets, Politics and the People,* ed. Harvey J. Kaye (London: Verso, 1989), p. 134.

60. For a discussion of one major episode in the history of the hierarchical relationship between West and non-West, see E. W. Said, *Orientalism* (New York: Pantheon, 1978), pp. 48–92, and *passim.*

61. Hobson, *Imperialism,* pp. 199–200.

62. Cited in Hubert Deschamps, *Les Méthodes et les doctrines coloniales de la France du XVIe siècle à nos jours* (Paris: Armand Colin, 1953), pp. 126–27.

63. See Anna Davin, "Imperialism and Motherhood," in Samuel, ed., *Patriotism,* Vol. I, pp. 203–35.

64. Michael Rosenthal, *The Character Factory: Baden-Powell's Boy Scouts and the Imperatives of Empire* (New York: Pantheon, 1986), especially pp. 131–60. See also H. John Field, *Toward a Programme of Imperial Life: The British Empire at the Turn of the Century* (Westport: Greenwood Press, 1982).

65. Johannes Fabian, *Time and the Other: How Anthropology Makes Its Object* (New York: Columbia University Press, 1983), pp. 25–69.

66. See Marianna Torgovnick, *Gone Primitive: Savage Intellects, Modern Lives* (Chicago: University of Chicago Press, 1990), and for the study of classification, codification, collecting, and exhibiting, James Clifford, *The Predicament of Culture: Twentieth Century Ethnography, Literature, and Art* (Cambridge, Mass.: Harvard University Press, 1988). Also Street, *Savage in Literature,* and Roy Harvey Pearce, *Savagism and Civilization: A Study of the Indian and the American Mind* (1953; rev. ed. Berkeley: University of California Press, 1988).

67. K. M. Panikkar, *Asia and Western Dominance* (1959; rprt. New York: Macmillan, 1969), and Michael Adas, *Machines as the Measure of Men: Science, Technology, and Ideologies of Western Dominance* (Ithaca: Cornell University Press, 1989). Also of interest is Daniel R. Headrick, *The Tools of Empire: Technology and European Imperialism in the Nineteenth Century* (New York: Oxford University Press, 1981).

68. Henri Brunschwig, *French Colonialism, 1871–1914: Myths and Realities,* trans. W. G. Brown (New York: Praeger, 1964), pp. 9–10.

69. See Brantlinger, *Rule of Darkness;* Suvendrini Perera, *Reaches of Empire: The English*

Novel from Edgeworth to Dickens (New York: Columbia University Press, 1991); Christopher Miller, *Blank Darkness: Africanist Discourse in French* (Chicago: University of Chicago Press, 1985).

70. Quoted in Gauri Viswanathan, *The Masks of Conquest: Literary Study and British Rule in India* (New York: Columbia University Press, 1989), p. 132.

71. Alfred Crosby, *Ecological Imperialism: The Biological Expansion of Europe, 900–1900* (Cambridge: Cambridge University Press, 1986).

72. Guy de Maupassant, *Bel-Ami* (1885); Georges Duroy is a cavalryman who has served in Algeria and makes a career as a Parisian journalist who (with some assistance) writes about life in Algeria. Later he is involved in financial scandals that attend the conquest of Tangiers.

73. Johannes Fabian, *Language and Colonial Power: The Appropriation of Swahili in the Former Belgian Congo, 1880–1938* (Cambridge: Cambridge University Press, 1986); Ranajit Guha, *A Rule of Property for Bengal: An Essay on the Idea of Permanent Settlement* (Paris and The Hague: Mouton, 1963); Bernard S. Cohn, "Representing Authority in Victorian India," in Eric Hobsbawm and Terence Ranger, eds., *The Invention of Tradition* (Cambridge: Cambridge University Press, 1983), pp. 185–207, and his *An Anthropologist Among the Historians and Other Essays* (Delhi: Oxford University Press, 1990). Two related works are Richard G. Fox, *Lions of the Punjab: Culture in the Making* (Berkeley: University of California Press, 1985), and Douglas E. Haynes, *Rhetoric and Ritual in Colonial India: The Shaping of Public Culture in Surat City, 1852–1928* (Berkeley: University of California Press, 1991).

74. Fabian, *Language and Colonial Power,* p. 79.

75. Ronald Inden, *Imagining India* (London: Blackwell, 1990).

76. Timothy Mitchell, *Colonising Egypt* (Cambridge: Cambridge University Press, 1988).

77. Leila Kinney and Zeynep Çelik, "Ethnography and Exhibitionism at the Expositions Universelles," *Assemblages* 13 (December 1990), 35–59.

78. T. J. Clark, *The Painting of Modern Life: Paris in the Art of Manet and His Followers* (New York: Knopf, 1984), pp. 133–46; Malek Alloula, *The Colonial Harem,* trans. Myrna and Wlad Godzich (Minneapolis: University of Minnesota Press, 1986); and see also Sarah Graham-Brown, *Images of Women: The Portrayal of Women in Photography of the Middle East, 1860–1950* (New York: Columbia University Press, 1988).

79. See, for example, Zeynep Çelik, *Displaying the Orient: Architecture of Islam at Nineteenth Century World's Fairs* (Berkeley: University of California Press, 1992), and Robert W. Rydell, *All the World's a Fair: Visions of Empire at American International Expositions, 1876–1916* (Chicago: University of Chicago Press, 1984).

80. Herbert Lindenberger, *Opera: The Extravagant Art* (Ithaca: Cornell University Press, 1984), pp. 270–80.

81. Antoine Goléa, *Gespräche mit Wieland Wagner* (Salzburg: SN Verlag, 1967), p. 58.

82. *Opera* 13, No. 1 (January 1962), 33. See also Geoffrey Skelton, *Wieland Wagner: The Positive Sceptic* (New York: St. Martin's Press, 1971), pp. 159 ff.

83. Joseph Kerman, *Opera as Drama* (New York: Knopf, 1956), p. 160.

84. Paul Robinson, *Opera and Ideas: From Mozart to Strauss* (New York: Harper & Row, 1985), p. 163.

85. *Ibid.,* p. 164.

86. *Verdi's "Aida": The History of an Opera in Letters and Documents,* trans. and collected by Hans Busch (Minneapolis: University of Minnesota Press, 1978), p. 3.

87. *Ibid.,* pp. 4, 5.

88. *Ibid.,* p. 126.

89. *Ibid.,* p. 150.

90. *Ibid.,* p. 17.

91. *Ibid.*, p. 50. See also Philip Gossett, "Verdi, Ghislanzoni, and *Aida:* The Uses of Convention," *Critical Inquiry* 1, No. 1 (1974), 291–334.

92. *Verdi's "Aida,"* p. 153.

93. *Ibid.*, p. 212.

94. *Ibid.*, p. 183.

95. Stephen Bann, *The Clothing of Clio* (Cambridge: Cambridge University Press, 1984), pp. 93–111.

96. Raymond Schwab, *The Oriental Renaissance,* trans. Gene Patterson-Black and Victor Reinking (New York: Columbia University Press, 1984), p. 86. See also Said, *Orientalism,* pp. 80–88.

97. Martin Bernal, *Black Athena: The Afroasiatic Roots of Classical Civilization,* Vol. 1 (New Brunswick: Rutgers University Press, 1987), pp. 161–88.

98. Schwab, *Oriental Renaissance,* p. 25.

99. Jean Humbert, "A propos de l'egyptomanie dans l'oeuvre de Verdi: Attribution à Auguste Mariette d'un scénario anonyme de l'opéra *Aida,"* *Revue de Musicologie* 62, No. 2 (1976), 229–55.

100. Kinney and Çelik, "Ethnography and Exhibitionism," p. 36.

101. Brian Fagan, *The Rape of the Nile* (New York: Scribner's, 1975), p. 278.

102. *Ibid.*, p. 276.

103. Kinney and Çelik, "Ethnography and Exhibitionism," p. 38.

104. *Verdi's "Aida,"* p. 444.

105. *Ibid.*, p. 186.

106. *Ibid.*, pp. 261–62.

107. *Opera,* 1986.

108. Skelton, *Wieland Wagner,* p. 160. See also Goléa, *Gespräche mit Wieland Wagner,* pp. 62–63.

109. *Verdi's "Aida,"* p. 138.

110. Muhammd Sabry, *Episode de la question d'Afrique: L'Empire egyptian sous Ismail et l'ingérence anglo-française (1863–1879)* (Paris: Geuthner, 1933), pp. 391 ff.

111. As in Roger Owen, *The Middle East and the World Economy, 1800–1914* (London: Methuen, 1981).

112. *Ibid.*, p. 122.

113. David Landes, *Bankers and Pashas* (Cambridge, Mass.: Harvard University Press, 1958).

114. Sabry, p. 313.

115. *Ibid.*, p. 322.

116. Georges Douin, *Histoire du règne du Khedive Ismail,* Vol. 2 (Rome: Royal Egyptian Geographic Society, 1934).

117. Landes, *Bankers and Pashas,* p. 209.

118. Owen, *Middle East,* pp. 149–50.

119. *Ibid.*, p. 128.

120. Janet L. Abu-Lughod, *Cairo: 1001 Years of the City Victorious* (Princeton: Princeton University Press, 1971), p. 98.

121. *Ibid.*, p. 107.

122. Jacques Berque, *Egypt: Imperialism and Revolution,* trans. Jean Stewart (New York: Praeger, 1972), pp. 96–98.

123. Bernard Semmel, *Jamaican Blood and Victorian Conscience: The Governor Eyre Controversy* (Boston: Riverside Press, 1963), p. 179. A comparable occlusion is studied in Irfan Habib, "Studying a Colonial Economy—Without Perceiving Colonialism," *Modern Asian Studies* 19, No. 3 (1985), 355–81.

124. Thomas Hodgkin, *Nationalism in Colonial Africa* (London: Muller, 1956), pp. 29–59.

125. See Adas, *Machines as the Measure of Men*, pp. 199–270.

126. As a sample of this sort of thinking, see J. B. Kelly, *Arabia, the Gulf and the West* (London: Weidenfeld & Nicolson, 1980).

127. Rosenthal, *Character Factory*, p. 52 and *passim*.

128. J. A. Mangan, *The Games Ethic and Imperialism: Aspects of the Diffusion of an Ideal* (Harmondsworth: Viking, 1986).

129. J.M.S. Tompkins, "Kipling's Later Tales: The Theme of Healing," *Modern Language Review* 45 (1950), 18–32.

130. Victor Turner, *Dramas, Fields, and Metaphors: Symbolic Action in Human Society* (Ithaca: Cornell University Press, 1974), pp. 258–59. For a subtle meditation on the problems of color and caste, see S. P. Mohanty, "Kipling's Children and the Colour Line," *Race and Class*, 31, No. 1 (1989), 21–40, also his "Us and Them: On the Philosophical Bases of Political Criticism," *Yale Journal of Criticism* 2, No. 2 (1989), 1–31.

131. Rudyard Kipling, *Kim* (1901; rprt. Garden City: Doubleday, Doran, 1941), p. 516.

132. *Ibid.*, pp. 516–17.

133. *Ibid.*, p. 517.

134. *Ibid.*, p. 523.

135. George Eliot, *Middlemarch*, ed. Bert G. Hornback (New York: Norton, 1977), p. 544.

136. Mark Kinkead-Weekes, "Vision in Kipling's Novels," in *Kipling's Mind and Art*, ed. Andrew Rutherford (London: Oliver & Boyd, 1964).

137. Edmund Wilson, "The Kipling that Nobody Read," *The Wound and the Bow* (New York: Oxford University Press, 1947), pp. 100–1, 103.

138. Kipling, *Kim*, p. 242.

139. *Ibid.*, p. 268.

140. *Ibid.*, p. 271.

141. Francis Hutchins, *The Illusion of Permanence: British Imperialism in India* (Princeton: Princeton University Press, 1967), p. 157. See also George Bearce, *British Attitudes Towards India, 1784–1858* (Oxford: Oxford University Press, 1961), and for the unravelling of the system, see B. R. Tomlinson, *The Political Economy of the Raj, 1914–1947: The Economics of Decolonization in India* (London: Macmillan, 1979).

142. Angus Wilson, *The Strange Ride of Rudyard Kipling* (London: Penguin, 1977), p. 43.

143. George Orwell, "Rudyard Kipling," in *A Collection of Essays* (New York: Doubleday, Anchor, 1954), pp. 133–35.

144. Michael Edwardes, *The Sahibs and the Lotus: The British in India* (London: Constable, 1988), p. 59.

145. See Edward W. Said, "Representing the Colonized: Anthropology's Interlocutors," *Critical Inquiry* 15, No. 2 (Winter 1989), 205–25. See also Lewis D. Wurgaft, *The Imperial Imagination: Magic and Myth in Kipling's India* (Middletown: Wesleyan University Press, 1983), pp. 54–78, and of course the work of Bernard S. Cohn, *Anthropologist Among the Historians*.

146. See Eric Stokes, *The English Utilitarians and India* (Oxford: Clarendon Press, 1959), and Bearce, *British Attitudes Towards India*, pp. 153–74. On Bentinck's educational reform, see Viswanathan, *Masks of Conquest*, pp. 44–47.

147. Noel Annan, "Kipling's Place in the History of Ideas," *Victorian Studies* 3, No. 4 (June 1960), 323.

148. See notes 11 and 12.

149. Geoffrey Moorhouse, *India Britannica* (London: Paladin, 1984), p. 103.

150. *Ibid.*, p. 102.

151. Georg Lukacs, *The Theory of the Novel*, trans. Anna Bostock (Cambridge, Mass.: MIT Press, 1971), pp. 35 ff.

152.   Kipling, *Kim*, p. 246.

153.   *Ibid.*, p. 248.

154.   Lukacs, *Theory of the Novel*, pp. 125–26.

155.   Kipling, *Kim*, p. 466.

156.   Frantz Fanon, *The Wretched of the Earth*, trans. Constance Farrington (1961; rprt. New York: Grove, 1968), p. 77. For substantiation of this claim, and the role of legitimizing and "objective" discourse in imperialism, see Fabiola Jara and Edmundo Magana, "Rules of Imperialist Method," *Dialectical Anthropology* 7, No. 2 (September 1982), 115–36.

157.   Robert Stafford, *Scientist of Empire: Sir Roderick Murchison, Scientific Exploration and Victorian Imperialism* (Cambridge: Cambridge University Press, 1989). For an earlier example, in India, see Marika Vicziany, "Imperialism, Botany and Statistics in Early Nineteenth-Century India: The Surveys of Francis Buchanan (1762–1829)," *Modern Asian Studies* 20, No. 4 (1986), 625–60.

158.   Stafford, *Scientist of Empire*, p. 208.

159.   J. Stengers, "King Leopold's Imperialism," in Roger Owen and Bob Sutcliffe, eds., *Studies in the Theory of Imperialism* (London: Longmans, 1972), p. 260. See also Neil Ascherson, *The King Incorporated: Leopold II in the Age of Trusts* (London: Allen & Unwin, 1963).

160.   Achebe, *Hopes and Impediments*; see note 24.

161.   Linda Nochlin, "The Imaginary Orient," *Art in America* (May 1983), 118–31, 187–91. In addition, as an extension of Nochlin's essay, see the remarkably interesting Boston University doctoral dissertation by Todd B. Porterfield, *Art in the Service of French Imperialism in the Near East, 1798–1848: Four Case Studies* (Ann Arbor: University Microfilms, 1991).

162.   A. P. Thornton, *The Imperial Idea and Its Enemies: A Study in British Power* (1959; rev. ed. London: Macmillan, 1985); Bernard Porter, *Critics of Empire: British Radical Attitudes to Colonialism in Africa, 1895–1914* (London: Macmillan, 1968); Hobson, *Imperialism*. For France see Charles Robert Ageron, *L'Anticolonialisme en France de 1871 à 1914* (Paris: Presses Universitaires de France, 1973).

163.   See Bodelsen, *Studies in Mid-Victorian Imperialism*, pp. 147–214.

164.   Stephen Charles Neill, *Colonialism and Christian Missions* (London: Lutterworth, 1966). Neill's is a very general work whose statements have to be supplemented and qualified by the large number of detailed works about missionary activity, for example, the work of Murray A. Rubinstein on China: "The Missionary as Observer and Imagemaker: Samuel Wells Williams and the Chinese," *American Studies* (Taipei) 10, No. 3 (September 1980), 31–44; and "The Northeastern Connection: American Board Missionaries and the Formation of American Opinion Toward China: 1830–1860," *Bulletin of the Modern History* (Academica Sinica), Taiwan, July 1980.

165.   See Bearce, *British Attitudes Towards India*, pp. 65–77, and Stokes, *English Utilitarians and India*.

166.   Quoted in Syed Hussein Alatas, *The Myth of the Lazy Native: A Study of the Image of the Malays, Filipinos, and Javanese from the Sixteenth to the Twentieth Century and Its Function in the Ideology of Colonial Capitalism* (London: Frank Cass, 1977), p. 59.

167.   *Ibid.*, p. 62.

168.   *Ibid.*, p. 223.

169.   Romila Thapar, "Ideology and the Interpretation of Early Indian History," *Review* 5, No. 3 (Winter 1982), 390.

170.   Karl Marx and Friedrich Engels, *On Colonialism: Articles from the* New York Tribune *and Other Writings* (New York: International, 1972), p. 156.

171.   Katherine George, "The Civilized West Looks at Africa: 1400–1800. A Study in Ethnocentrism," *Isis* 49, No. 155 (March 1958), 66, 69–70.

172.   For the definition of "primitives" through this technique, see Torgovnick, *Gone*

Primitive, pp. 3–41. See also Ronald L. Mees, *Social Science and the Ignoble Savage* (Cambridge: Cambridge University Press, 1976), for an elaborated version of the four-stage theory of the savage based on European philosophy and cultural thought.

173. Brunschwig, *French Colonialism,* p. 14.

174. Robert Delavigne and Charles André Julien, *Les Constructeurs de la France d'outre-mer* (Paris: Corea, 1946), p. 16. An interestingly different volume, although it deals with similar figures, is *African Proconsuls: European Governors in Africa,* eds. L. H. Gann and Peter Duignan (New York: Free Press, 1978). See also Mort Rosenblum, *Mission to Civilize: The French Way* (New York: Harcourt Brace Jovanovich, 1986).

175. Agnes Murphy, *The Ideology of French Imperialism, 1817–1881* (Washington: Catholic University of America Press, 1968), p. 46 and *passim.*

176. Raoul Girardet, *L'Idée coloniale en France, 1871–1962* (Paris: La Table Ronde, 1972), pp. 44–45. See also Stuart Michael Persell, *The French Colonial Lobby* (Stanford: Hoover Institution Press, 1983).

177. Quoted in Murphy, *Ideology of French Imperialism,* p. 25.

178. Raymond F. Betts, *Assimilation and Association in French Colonial Theory, 1840–1914* (New York: Columbia University Press, 1961), p. 88.

179. I discuss this material with regard to theories of national identity mobilized for use in late-nineteenth-century imperialism in "Nationalism, Human Rights, and Interpretation," in *Freedom and Interpretation,* ed. Barbara Johnson (New York: Basic Books, 1992).

180. Betts, *Association and Assimilation,* p. 108.

181. *Ibid.,* p. 174.

182. Girardet, *L'Idée coloniale en France,* p. 48.

183. For one small episode in the imperial competition with England, see the fascinating glimpse afforded by Albert Hourani, "T. E. Lawrence and Louis Massignon," in his *Islam in European Thought* (Cambridge: Cambridge University Press, 1991), pp. 116–28. See also Christopher M. Andrew and A. S. Kanya-Forstner, *The Climax of French Imperial Expansion, 1914–1924* (Stanford: Stanford University Press, 1981).

184. David Prochaska, *Making Algeria French: Colonialism in Bône, 1870–1920* (Cambridge: Cambridge University Press, 1990), p. 85. For a fascinating study of the way French social scientists and urban planners used Algeria as a place to experiment on, and to redesign, see Gwendolyn Wright, *The Politics of Design in French Colonial Urbanism* (Chicago: University of Chicago Press, 1991), pp. 66–84. Later sections of the book discuss the effect of these plans on Morocco, Indochina, and Madagascar. The definitive study, however, is Janet Abu-Lughod, *Rabat: Urban Apartheid in Morocco* (Princeton: Princeton University Press, 1980).

185. *Ibid.,* p. 124.

186. *Ibid.,* pp. 141–42.

187. *Ibid.,* p. 255.

188. *Ibid.,* p. 254.

189. *Ibid.,* p. 255.

190. *Ibid.,* p. 70.

191. Roland Barthes, *Le Degré zéro de l'écriture* (1953; rprt. Paris: Gonthier, 1964), p. 10.

192. Raymond Williams, *George Orwell* (New York: Viking, 1971), especially pp. 77–78.

193. Christopher Hitchens, *Prepared for the Worst* (New York: Hill & Wang, 1989), pp. 78–90.

194. Michael Walzer makes of Camus an exemplary intellectual, precisely because he was anguished and wavered and opposed terrorism and loved his mother: see Walzer, "Albert Camus's Algerian War," in *The Company of Critics: Social Criticism and Political Commitment in the Twentieth Century* (New York: Basic Books, 1988), pp. 136–52.

195. Conor Cruise O'Brien, *Albert Camus* (New York: Viking, 1970), p. 103.

196. Joseph Conrad, *Last Essays*, ed. Richard Curle (London: Dent, 1926), pp. 10–17.

197. The later O'Brien, with views noticeably like these and different from the gist of his book on Camus, has made no secret of his antipathy for the lesser peoples of the "Third World." See his extended disagreement with Said in *Salmagundi* 70–71 (Spring–Summer 1986), 65–81.

198. Herbert R. Lottman, *Albert Camus: A Biography* (New York: Doubleday, 1979). Camus's actual behavior in Algeria during the colonial war itself is best chronicled in Yves Carrière's *La Guerre d'Algérie II: Le Temps des léopards* (Paris: Fayard, 1969).

199. "Misère de la Kabylie" (1939), in Camus, *Essais* (Paris: Gallimard, 1965) pp. 905–38.

200. O'Brien, *Camus,* pp. 22–28.

201. Camus, *Exile and the Kingdom*, trans. Justin O'Brien (New York: Knopf, 1958), pp. 32–33. For a perspicacious reading of Camus in the North African context, see Barbara Harlow, "The Maghrib and *The Stranger*," *Alif* 3 (Spring 1983), 39–55.

202. Camus, *Essais*, p. 2039.

203. Quoted in Manuela Semidei, "De L'Empire à la decolonisation à travers les manuels scolaires," *Revue française de science politique* 16, No. 1 (February 1961), 85.

204. Camus, *Essais*, pp. 1012–13.

205. Semidei, "De L'Empire à la decolonisation," 75.

206. Jean-Paul Sartre, *Literary Essays*, trans. Annette Michelson (New York: Philosophical Library, 1957), p. 32.

207. Emir Abdel Qader, *Ecrits spirituels*, trans. Michel Chodkiewicz (Paris: Seuil, 1982).

208. Mostafa Lacheraf, *L'Algérie: Nation et societé* (Paris: Maspéro, 1965). A wonderful fictional and personal reconstruction of the period is in Assia Djebar's novel *L'Amour, la fantasia* (Paris: Jean-Claude Lattès, 1985).

209. Quoted in Abdullah Laroui, *The History of the Magreb: An Interpretive Essay*, trans. Ralph Manheim (Princeton: Princeton University Press, 1977), p. 301.

210. Lacheraf, *L'Algérie*, p. 92.

211. *Ibid.*, p. 93.

212. Theodore Bugeaud, *Par l'Epée et par la charrue* (Paris: PUF, 1948). Bugeaud's later career was equally distinguished: he commanded the troops who fired on the insurgent crowds on February 23, 1848, and was repaid by Flaubert in *L'Education sentimentale*, where the unpopular marshal's portrait is pierced in the stomach during the storming of the Palais Royal, February 24, 1848.

213. Martine Astier Loutfi, *Littérature et colonialisme: L'Expansion coloniale vue dans la littérature romanesque française, 1871–1914* (Paris: Mouton, 1971).

214. Melvin Richter, "Tocqueville on Algeria," *Review of Politics* 25 (1963), 377.

215. *Ibid.*, 380. For a fuller and more recent account of this material, see Marwan R. Buheiry, *The Formation and Perception of the Modern Arab World*, ed. Lawrence I. Conrad (Princeton: Darwin Press, 1989), especially Part 1, "European Perceptions of the Orient," which has four essays on nineteenth-century France and Algeria, one of which concerns Tocqueville and Islam.

216. Laroui, *History of the Magreb*, p. 305.

217. See Alloula, *Colonial Harem.*

218. Fanny Colonna and Claude Haim Brahimi, "Du bon usage de la science coloniale," in *Le Mal de voir* (Paris: Union Générale d'éditions, 1976).

219. Albert Sarraut, *Grandeur et servitude coloniales* (Paris: Editions du Sagittaire, 1931), p. 113.

220. Georges Hardy, *La Politique coloniale et le partage du terre aux XIXe et XXe siècles* (Paris: Albin Michel, 1937), p. 441.

221. Camus, *Théâtre, Récits, Nouvelles* (Paris: Gallimard, 1962), p. 1210.

222. *Ibid.*, p. 1211.

223. Seeley, *Expansion of England*, p. 16.

224. Albert O. Hirschman, *The Passions and the Interests: Political Arguments for Capitalism Before Its Triumph* (Princeton: Princeton University Press, 1977), pp. 132–33.

225. Seeley, *Expansion of England*, p. 193.

226. See Alec G. Hargreaves, *The Colonial Experience in French Fiction* (London: Macmillan, 1983), p. 31, where this strange elision is noted and explained interestingly as the result of Loti's peculiar psychology and Anglophobia. The formal consequences for Loti's fiction are not noted however. For a fuller account, see the unpublished Princeton University dissertation, Panivong Norindr, *Colonialism and Figures of the Exotic in the Work of Pierre Loti* (Ann Arbor: University Microfilms, 1990).

227. Benita Parry, *Delusions and Discoveries: Studies on India in the British Imagination, 1880–1930* (London: Allen Lane, 1972).

CHAPTER THREE
RESISTANCE AND OPPOSITION

1. André Gide, *L'Immoraliste* (Paris: Mercure de France, 1902), pp. 113–14.

2. Gide, *The Immoralist*, trans. Richard Howard (New York: Knopf, 1970), pp. 158–59. For the connection between Gide and Camus, see Mary Louise Pratt, "Mapping Ideology: Gide, Camus, and Algeria," *College Literature* 8 (1981), 158–74.

3. As used by Christopher Miller, *Blank Darkness: Africanist Discourse in French* (Chicago: University of Chicago Press, 1985); a profound philosophical critique of "Africanist" philosophy is found in Paulin J. Hountondji, *Sur la "philosophie africaine"* (Paris: Maspéro, 1976). Hountondji gives special priority in his critique to the work of Placide Tempels.

4. V. Y. Mudimbe, *The Invention of Africa: Gnosis, Philosophy, and the Order of Knowledge* (Bloomington: Indiana University Press, 1988).

5. Raymond Schwab, *The Oriental Renaissance*, trans. Gene Patterson-Black and Victor Reinking (New York: Columbia University Press, 1984).

6. Frantz Fanon, *The Wretched of the Earth*, trans. Constance Farrington (1961; rprt. New York: Grove, 1968), p. 314.

7. Basil Davidson, *Africa in Modern History: The Search for a New Society* (London: Allen Lane, 1978), pp. 178–80.

8. Jean-Paul Sartre, "Le Colonialisme est un système," in *Situations V: Colonialisme et néo-colonialisme* (Paris: Gallimard, 1964).

9. Sartre, "Preface" to Fanon, *Wretched of the Earth*, p. 7.

10. Davidson, *Africa in Modern History*, p. 200.

11. Fanon, *Wretched of the Earth*, p. 96.

12. *Ibid.*, p. 102.

13. Sartre, "Preface," p. 26.

14. Henri Grimal, *Decolonization: The British, French, Dutch and Belgian Empires, 1919–1963*, trans. Stephan de Vos (1965; rprt. London: Routledge & Kegan Paul, 1978), p. 9. There is a massive literature on decolonization of which some noteworthy titles are R. F. Holland, *European Decolonization, 1918–1981: An Introductory Survey* (London: Macmillan, 1985); Miles Kahler, *Decolonization in Britain and France: The Domestic Consequences of International Relations* (Princeton: Princeton University Press, 1984); Franz Ansprenger, *The Dissolution of the Colonial Empires* (1981; rprt. London: Routledge, 1989); A. N. Porter and A. J. Stockwell, Vol. 1, *British Imperial Policy and Decolonization, 1938–51*, and Vol. 2, *1951–64* (London: Macmillan, 1987, 1989); John Strachey, *The End of Empire* (London: Gollancz, 1959).

15.   Terence Ranger, "Connexions Between Primary Resistance Movements and Modern Mass Nationalisms in East and Central Africa," pts. 1 and 2, *Journal of African History* 9, No. 3 (1968), 439. See also Michael Crowder, ed., *West African Resistance: The Military Response to Colonial Occupation* (London: Hutchinson, 1971), and the later chapters (pp. 268 ff.) of S. C. Malik, ed., *Dissent, Protest and Reform in Indian Civilization* (Simla: Indian Institute of Advanced Study, 1977).

16.   Michael Adas, *Prophets of Rebellion: Millenarian Protest Movements Against the European Colonial Order* (Chapel Hill: University of North Carolina, 1979). For another example, see Stephen Ellis, *The Rising of the Red Shawls: A Revolt in Madagascar, 1895–1899* (Cambridge: Cambridge University Press, 1985).

17.   Ranger, "Connexions," p. 631.

18.   Quoted in Afaf Lutfi al-Sayyid, *Egypt and Cromer* (New York: Praeger, 1969), p. 68.

19.   E. M. Forster, *A Passage to India* (1924; rprt. New York: Harcourt, Brace & World, 1952), p. 322.

20.   See the final pages, 314–20, of Benita Parry, *Delusions and Discoveries: Studies on India in the British Imagination, 1880–1930* (London: Allen Lane, 1972). By contrast, in *The Rhetoric of English India* (Chicago: University of Chicago Press, 1992), Sara Suleri reads the relationship between Aziz and Fielding in psycho-sexual terms.

21.   Forster, *Passage to India*, p. 86.

22.   *Ibid.*, p. 136.

23.   *Ibid.*, p. 164.

24.   Quoted in Francis Hutchins, *The Illusion of Permanence: British Imperialism in India* (Princeton: Princeton University Press, 1967), p. 41.

25.   Forster, *Passage to India*, p. 76.

26.   Hutchins, *Illusion of Permanence*, p. 187.

27.   In Syed Hussein Alatas, *The Myth of the Lazy Native: A Study of the Image of the Malays, Filipinos, and Javanese from the Sixteenth to the Twentieth Century and Its Function in the Ideology of Colonial Capitalism* (London: Frank Cass, 1977). See also James Scott, *Weapons of the Weak: Everyday Forms of Peasant Resistance* (New Haven: Yale University Press, 1985).

28.   Sidney and Beatrice Webb, *Indian Diary* (Delhi: Oxford University Press, 1988), p. 98. On the oddly insulating atmosphere of colonial life, see Margaret MacMillan, *Women of the Raj* (London: Thames & Hudson, 1988).

29.   Parry, *Delusions and Discoveries*, p. 274.

30.   Forster, *Passage to India*, pp. 106–7.

31.   Quoted in Anil Seal, *The Emergence of Indian Nationalism: Competition and Collaboration in the Later Nineteenth Century* (Cambridge: Cambridge University Press, 1971), p. 140.

32.   *Ibid.*, p. 141.

33.   *Ibid.*, p. 147. Ellipses in the original.

34.   *Ibid.*, p. 191.

35.   Edward Thompson, *The Other Side of the Medal* (1926; rprt. Westport: Greenwood Press, 1974), p. 26.

36.   *Ibid.*, p. 126. See also Parry's sensitive account of Thompson in *Delusions and Discoveries*, pp. 164–202.

37.   Fanon, *Wretched of the Earth*, p. 106.

38.   Frantz Fanon, *Black Skin, White Masks,* trans. Charles Lam Markmann (1952; rprt. New York: Grove Press, 1967), p. 222. As a complement to Fanon's early, psychologizing style, see Ashis Nandy, *The Intimate Enemy: Loss and Recovery of Self Under Colonialism* (Delhi: Oxford University Press, 1983).

39.   Raoul Girardet, *L'Idée coloniale en France, 1871–1962* (Paris: La Table Ronde, 1972), p. 136.

40.   *Ibid.*, p. 148.

41.   *Ibid.,* pp. 159–72. On Griaule see the excellent pages on his career and contribution in James Clifford, *The Predicament of Culture: Twentieth Century Ethnography, Literature, and Art* (Cambridge, Mass.: Harvard University Press, 1988), pp. 55–91; see also Clifford's account of Leiris, pp. 165–74. In both cases, however, Clifford does not connect his authors with decolonization, a global political context eminently present in Girardet.

42.   André Malraux, *La Voie royale* (Paris: Grasset, 1930), p. 268.

43.   Paul Mus, *Viet-Nam: Sociologie d'une guerre* (Paris: Seuil, 1952), pp. 134–35. Frances FitzGerald's prizewinning 1972 book on the American war against Vietnam, *Fire in the Lake,* is dedicated to Mus.

44.   Davidson, *Africa in Modern History,* p. 155.

45.   *Ibid.,* p. 156.

46.   Fanon, *Black Skin, White Masks,* p. 220.

47.   Philip D. Curtin, *The Image of Africa: British Ideas and Action, 1780–1850,* 2 vols. (Madison: University of Wisconsin Press, 1964).

48.   Daniel Defert, "The Collection of the World: Accounts of Voyages from the Sixteenth to the Eighteenth Centuries," *Dialectical Anthropology* 7 (1982), 11–20.

49.   Pratt, "Mapping Ideology." See also her remarkable *Imperial Eyes: Travel Writing and Transculturation* (New York and London: Routledge, 1992).

50.   James Joyce, *Ulysses* (1922; rprt. New York: Vintage, 1966), p. 212.

51.   James Ngugi, *The River Between* (London: Heinemann, 1965), p. 1.

52.   Tayeb Salih, *Season of Migration to the North,* trans. Denys Johnson-Davies (London: Heinemann, 1970), pp. 49–50.

53.   Peter Hulme, *Colonial Encounters: Europe and the Native Caribbean, 1492–1797* (London: Methuen, 1986).

54.   George Lamming, *The Pleasures of Exile* (London: Allison & Busby, 1984), p. 107.

55.   *Ibid.,* p. 119.

56.   Roberto Fernández Retamar, *Caliban and Other Essays,* trans. Edward Baker (Minneapolis: University of Minnesota Press, 1989), p. 14. See as a corollary, Thomas Cartelli, "Prospero in Africa: *The Tempest* as Colonialist Text and Pretext," in *Shakespeare Reproduced: The Text in History and Ideology,* eds. Jean E. Howard and Marion F. O'Connor (London: Methuen, 1987), pp. 99–115.

57.   Ngugi wa Thiongo, *Decolonising the Mind: The Politics of Language in African Literature* (London: James Curry, 1986).

58.   Barbara Harlow, *Resistance Literature* (New York: Methuen, 1987), p. xvi. In this regard a pioneering work is Chinweizu, *The West and the Rest of Us: White Predators, Black Slaves and the African Elite* (New York: Random House, 1975).

59.   Aimé Césaire, *The Collected Poetry,* eds. and trans. Clayton Eshleman and Annette Smith (Berkeley: University of California Press, 1983), p. 46.

60.   Rabindranath Tagore, *Nationalism* (New York: Macmillan, 1917), p. 19 and *passim.*

61.   W.E.B. Du Bois, *The Souls of Black Folk* (1903; rprt. New York: New American Library, 1969), pp. 44–45.

62.   Tagore, *Nationalism,* p. 62.

63.   Benedict Anderson, *Imagined Communities: Reflections on the Origin and Spread of Nationalism* (London: New Left, 1983), p. 47.

64.   *Ibid.,* p. 52.

65.   *Ibid.,* p. 74.

66.   Bill Ashcroft, Gareth Griffiths, and Helen Tiflin, *The Empire Writes Back: Theory and Practice in Post-Colonial Literatures* (London and New York: Routledge, 1989).

67.   Eric Hobsbawm, *Nations and Nationalism Since 1780: Programme, Myth, Reality* (Cam-

bridge: Cambridge University Press, 1990); Ernest Gellner, *Nations and Nationalism* (Ithaca: Cornell University Press, 1983).

68. Partha Chatterjee, *Nationalist Thought and the Colonial World: A Derivative Discourse?* (London: Zed, 1986), p. 79. See also Rajat K. Ray, "Three Interpretations of Indian Nationalism," in *Essays in Modern India,* ed. B. Q. Nanda (Delhi: Oxford University Press, 1980), pp. 1–41.

69. Chatterjee, *Nationalist Thought,* p. 100.

70. *Ibid.,* p. 161.

71. Davidson, *Africa in Modern History,* especially p. 204. See also *General History of Africa,* ed. A. Adu Boaher, Vol. 7, *Africa Under Colonial Domination, 1880–1935* (Berkeley, Paris, and London: University of California Press, UNESCO, James Currey, 1990), and *The Colonial Moment in Africa: Essays on the Movement of Minds and Materials, 1900–1940,* ed. Andrew Roberts (Cambridge: Cambridge University Press, 1990).

72. Kumari Jayawardena, *Feminism and Nationalism in the Third World* (London: Zed, 1986), especially pp. 43–56, 73–108, 137–54 and *passim.* For emancipatory perspectives on feminism and imperialism, see also Laura Nader, "Orientalism, Occidentalism and the Control of Women," *Cultural Dynamics* 2, No. 3 (1989), 323–55; Maria Mies, *Patriarchy and Accumulation on a World Scale: Women in the International Division of Labour* (London: Zed, 1986). See also Helen Callaway, *Gender, Culture and Empire: European Women in Colonial Nigeria* (Urbana: University of Illinois Press, 1987) and eds. Nupur Chandur and Margaret Strobel, *Western Women and Imperialism: Complicity and Resistance* (Bloomington: Indiana University Press, 1992).

73. Angus Calder, *Revolutionary Empire: The Rise of the English-Speaking Empires from the Eighteenth Century to the 1780's* (London: Cape, 1981), p. 14. A philosophical and ideological accompaniment is provided (alas, in a terrible jargon) by Samir Amin, *Eurocentrism,* trans. Russell Moore (New York: Monthly Review, 1989). By contrast, a liberationist account—also on a world scale—is in Jan Nederveen Pietersee, *Empire and Emancipation* (London: Pluto Press, 1991).

74. Calder, *Revolutionary Empire,* p. 36.

75. *Ibid.,* p. 650.

76. Eqbal Ahmad, "The Neo-Fascist State: Notes on the Pathology of Power in the Third World," *Arab Studies Quarterly* 3, No. 2 (Spring 1981), 170–80.

77. James Joyce, *A Portrait of the Artist as a Young Man* (1916; rprt. New York: Viking, 1964), p. 189.

78. Thomas Hodgkin, *Nationalism in Colonial Africa* (London: Muller, 1956), pp. 93–114.

79. Alfred Crosby, *Ecological Imperialism: The Biological Expansion of Europe, 900–1900* (Cambridge: Cambridge University Press, 1986), pp. 196–216.

80. Neil Smith, *Uneven Development: Nature, Capital, and the Production of Space* (Oxford: Blackwell, 1984), p. 102.

81. *Ibid.,* p. 146. Further differentiations of space, with consequences for art and leisure, occur in landscape and the project for national parks. See W.J.T. Mitchell, "Imperial Landscape," in *Landscape and Power,* ed. W.J.T. Mitchell (Chicago: University of Chicago Press, 1993), and Jane Carruthers, "Creating a National Park, 1910 to 1926," *Journal of South African Studies* 15, No. 2 (January 1989), 188–216. In a different sphere compare with Mark Bassin, "Inventing Siberia: Visions of the Russian East in the Early Nineteenth Century," *American Historical Review* 96, No. 3 (June 1991), 763–94.

82. Mahmoud Darwish, "A Lover from Palestine," in *Splinters of Bone,* trans. B. M. Bannani (Greenfield Center, N.Y.: Greenfield Review Press, 1974), p. 23.

83. Mary Hamer, "Putting Ireland on the Map," *Textual Practice* 3, No. 2 (Summer 1989), 184–201.

84.   *Ibid.*, p. 195.

85.   Seamus Deane, *Celtic Revivals: Essays in Modern Irish Literature* (London: Faber & Faber, 1985), p. 38.

86.   *Ibid.*, p. 49.

87.   *Ibid.*

88.   Wole Soyinka, *Myth, Literature and the African World* (Cambridge: Cambridge University Press, 1976), p. 127. See also Mudimbe, *Invention of Africa*, pp. 83–97.

89.   *Ibid.*, pp. 129, 136.

90.   Fanon, *Wretched of the Earth*, p. 203.

91.   Césaire, *Collected Poetry*, p. 72.

92.   *Ibid.*, pp. 76 and 77.

93.   R. P. Blackmur, *Eleven Essays in the European Novel* (New York: Harcourt, Brace & World, 1964), p. 3.

94.   Mahmoud Darwish, *The Music of Human Flesh*, trans. Denys Johnson-Davies (London: Heinemann, 1980), p. 18.

95.   Pablo Neruda, *Memoirs*, trans. Hardie St. Martin (London: Penguin, 1977), p. 130. This passage may come as a surprise to anyone who had once been influenced by Conor Cruise O'Brien's essay "Passion and Cunning: An Essay on the Politics of W. B. Yeats," collected in his *Passion and Cunning* (London: Weidenfeld & Nicolson, 1988). Its claims and information are inadequate, especially when compared with Elizabeth Cullingford's *Yeats, Ireland and Fascism* (London: Macmillan, 1981); Cullingford also refers to the Neruda passage.

96.   W. B. Yeats, *Collected Poems* (New York: Macmillan, 1959), p. 146.

97.   Pablo Neruda, *Fully Empowered*, trans. Alastair Reid (New York: Farrar, Straus & Giroux, 1986), p. 131.

98.   Yeats, *Collected Poetry*, p. 193.

99.   Fanon, *Wretched of the Earth*, p. 59.

100.   Gary Sick, *All Fall Down: America's Tragic Encounter with Iran* (New York: Random House, 1985).

101.   Chinua Achebe, *Things Fall Apart* (1959; rprt. New York: Fawcett, 1969).

102.   Lawrence J. McCaffrey, "Components of Irish Nationalism," in *Perspectives on Irish Nationalism*, eds. Thomas E. Hachey and Lawrence J. McCaffrey (Lexington: University of Kentucky Press, 1989), p. 16.

103.   Yeats, *Collected Poetry*, p. 212.

104.   *Ibid.*, p. 342.

105.   Quoted in Hachey and McCaffrey, *Perspectives on Irish Nationalism*, p. 117.

106.   *Ibid.*, p. 106.

107.   See David Lloyd, *Nationalism and Minor Literature: James Clarence Mangan and the Emergence of Irish Cultural Nationalism* (Berkeley: University of California Press, 1987).

108.   For a collection of some of their writings see *Ireland's Field Day* (London: Hutchinson, 1985). This collection includes Paulin, Heaney, Deane, Kearney, and Kiberd. See also W. J. McCormack, *The Battle of the Books* (Gigginstown, Ireland: Lilliput Press, 1986).

109.   R. P. Blackmur, *A Primer of Ignorance*, ed. Joseph Frank (New York: Harcourt, Brace & World, 1967), pp. 21–37.

110.   Joseph Leerssen, *Mere Irish and Fior-Ghael: Studies in the Idea of Irish Nationality, Its Development, and Literary Expression Prior to the Nineteenth Century* (Amsterdam and Philadelphia: Benjamins, 1986).

111.   Fanon, *Wretched of the Earth*, p. 210.

112.   *Ibid.*, p. 214.

113.   Yeats, *Collected Poetry*, p. 343.

114. R. P. Blackmur, *Language as Gesture: Essays in Poetry* (London: Allen & Unwin, 1954), p. 118.

115. *Ibid.*, p. 119.

116. Gordon K. Lewis, *Slavery, Imperialism, and Freedom* (New York: Monthly Review, 1978); and Robin Blackburn, *The Overthrow of Colonial Slavery, 1776–1848* (London: Verso, 1988).

117. Thomas Hodgkin, "Some African and Third World Theories of Imperialism," in *Studies in the Theory of Imperialism*, eds. Roger Owen and Bob Sutcliffe (London: Longman, 1977), p. 95.

118. Marcel Merle, ed., *L'Anticolonialisme Européen de Las Casas à Karl Marx* (Paris: Colin, 1969). Also Charles Robert Ageron, *L'Anticolonialisme en France de 1871 à 1914* (Paris: Presses Universitaires de France, 1973).

119. Harry Bracken, "Essence, Accident and Race," *Hermathena* 116 (Winter 1973), 81–96.

120. Gerard Leclerc, *Anthropologie et colonialisme: Essai sur l'histoire de l'africanisme* (Paris: Seuil, 1972).

121. J. A. Hobson, *Imperialism: A Study* (1902; rprt. Ann Arbor: University of Michigan Press, 1972), pp. 223–84.

122. Another example, caustically analyzed by C.L.R. James, is the case of Wilberforce, manipulated by Pitt, in the cause of abolition: *The Black Jacobins: Toussaint L'Ouverture and the San Domingo Revolution* (1938; rprt. New York: Vintage, 1963), pp. 53–54.

123. See Noam Chomsky, *American Power and the New Mandarins* (New York: Pantheon, 1969), pp. 221–366.

124. Girardet, *L'Idée coloniale en France*, p. 213.

125. See Hue-Tam Ho Tai, *Radicalism and the Origins of the Vietnamese Revolution* (Cambridge, Mass.: Harvard University Press, 1992), for an excellent account of young Vietnamese intellectuals in Paris between the wars.

126. This is well described in Janet G. Vaillant, *Black, French, and African: A Life of Léopold Sédar Senghor* (Cambridge, Mass.: Harvard University Press, 1990), pp. 87–146.

127. Raymond Williams, *Culture* (London: Fontana, 1981), pp. 83–5.

128. Ali Haroun, *La 7e Wilaya: La Guerre de FLN en France, 1954–1962* (Paris: Seuil, 1986).

129. Alatas, *Myth of the Lazy Native*, p. 56.

130. *Ibid.*, p. 96.

131. James, *Black Jacobins*, p. 198.

132. George Antonius, *The Arab Awakening: The Story of the Arab National Movement* (1938; rprt. Beirut: Librairie du Liban, 1969), pp. 305–6.

133. Albert Hourani, *The Emergence of the Modern Middle East* (Berkeley: University of California Press, 1981), pp. 193–234. See also the Georgetown University doctoral dissertation of Susan Silsby, *Antonius: Palestine, Zionism and British Imperialism, 1929–1939* (Ann Arbor: University Microfilms, 1986), which has an impressive amount of information on Antonius's life.

134. Paul Buhle, *C.L.R. James: The Artist as Revolutionary* (London: Verso, 1988), pp. 56–57.

135. "An Audience with C.L.R. James," *Third World Book Review* 1, No. 2 (1984), 7.

136. Antonius, *Arab Awakening*, p. 43.

137. Alatas, *Myth of the Lazy Native*, p. 152.

138. Ranajit Guha, *A Rule of Property for Bengal: An Essay on the Idea of Permanent Settlement* (Paris and The Hague: Mouton, 1963), p. 8.

139. Guha, "On Some Aspects of the Historiography of Colonial India," in *Subaltern Studies I* (Delhi: Oxford University Press, 1982), pp. 5, 7. For the later development of Guha's thought, see his "Dominance Without Hegemony and Its Historiography," *Subaltern Studies VI* (Delhi: Oxford University Press, 1986), pp. 210–309.

140. A. L. Tibawi, *A Modern History of History, Including Lebanon and Palestine* (London:

Macmillan, 1969); Albert Hourani, *Arabic Thought in the Liberal Age, 1798–1939* (Cambridge: Cambridge University Press, 1983); Hisham Sharabi, *Arab Intellectuals and the West: The Formative Years, 1875–1914* (Baltimore: Johns Hopkins University Press, 1972); Bassam Tibi, *Arab Nationalism: A Critical Analysis,* trans. M. F. and Peter Sluglett (New York: St. Martin's Press, 1990); Mohammad Abed al-Jabry, *Naqd al-Aql al-'Arabi,* 2 vols. (Beirut: Dar al-Tali'ah, 1984, 1986).

141.   A. A. Duri, *The Historical Formation of the Arab Nation: A Study in Identity and Consciousness,* trans. Lawrence I. Conrad (1984; London: Croom Helm, 1987).

142.   Walter Rodney, "The African Revolution," in *C.L.R. James: His Life and Work,* ed. Paul Buhle (London: Allison & Busby, 1986), p. 35.

143.   Guha, *Rule of Property for Bengal,* p. 38.

144.   *Ibid.,* p. 62.

145.   *Ibid.,* p. 145.

146.   *Ibid.,* p. 92.

147.   Eric Williams, *Capitalism and Slavery* (New York: Russell & Russell, 1961), p. 211.

148.   Alatas, *Myth of the Lazy Native,* p. 200.

149.   James, *Black Jacobins,* p. x.

150.   *Ibid.,* p. 391.

151.   Quoted in Silsby, *Antonius,* p. 184.

152.   Tariq Ali, *The Nehrus and the Gandhis: An Indian Dynasty* (London: Pan, 1985).

153.   Theodor Adorno, *Minima Moralia: Reflections from a Damaged Life,* trans. E.F.N. Jephcott (1951; trans. London: New Left, 1974), p. 102.

154.   Conor Cruise O'Brien, "Why the Wailing Ought to Stop," *The Observer,* June 3, 1984.

155.   Fanon, *Wretched of the Earth,* p. 77.

156.   See S. P. Mohanty, "Us and Them: On the Philosophical Bases of Political Criticism," *Yale Journal of Criticism* 2, No. 2 (1989), 1–31. Three examples of such a method in action are Timothy Brennan, *Salman Rushdie and the Third World: Myths of the Nation* (New York: St. Martin's Press, 1989); Mary Layoun, *Travels of a Genre: The Modern Novel and Ideology* (Princeton: Princeton University Press, 1990); Rob Nixon, *London Calling: V. S. Naipaul, Postcolonial Mandarin* (New York: Oxford University Press, 1992).

157.   Embodied in the following remark made by British Foreign Secretary Lord Balfour in 1919, which has remained generally true so far as Western liberal opinion has been concerned:

> For in Palestine we do not propose even to go through the form of consulting the wishes of the present inhabitants of the country, though the American Commission has been going through the form of asking what they are. The four great powers are committed to Zionism and Zionism, be it right or wrong, good or bad, is rooted in age-long tradition, in present needs, in future hopes, of far profounder import than the desires and prejudices of the 700,000 Arabs who now inhabit that ancient land. In my opinion that is right.

Quoted in Christopher Sykes, *Crossroads to Israel, 1917–1948* (1965; rprt. Bloomington: Indiana University Press, 1973), p. 5.

158.   Raphael Patai, *The Arab Mind* (New York: Scribner's, 1983); David Pryce-Jones, *The Closed Circle: An Interpretation of the Arabs* (New York: Harper & Row, 1989); Bernard K. Lewis, *The Political Language of Islam* (Chicago: University of Chicago Press, 1988); Patricia Crone and Michael Cook, *Hagarism: The Making of the Islamic World* (Cambridge: Cambridge University Press, 1977).

159.   Ronald Robinson, "Non-European Foundations of European Imperialism: Sketch for a Theory of Collaboration," in Owen and Sutcliffe, *Studies in the Theory of Imperialism,* pp. 118, 120.

160. Masao Miyoshi, *As We Saw Them: The First Japanese Embassy to the United States (1860)* (Berkeley: University of California Press, 1979); Ibrahim Abu-Lughod, *The Arab Rediscovery of Europe: A Study in Cultural Encounters* (Princeton: Princeton University Press, 1963).

161. Homi K. Bhabha, "Signs Taken for Wonders: Questions of Ambivalence and Authority Under a Tree Outside Delhi May 1817," *Critical Inquiry* 12, No. 1 (1985), 144–65.

162. Afghani's response to Renan is collected in Nikki R. Keddie, *An Islamic Response to Imperialism: Political and Religious Writings of Sayyid Jamal ad-Din "al-Afghani"* (1968; rprt. Berkeley: University of California Press, 1983), pp. 181–87.

163. Albert Hourani, "T. E. Lawrence and Louis Massignon," in *Islam in European Thought* (Cambridge: Cambridge University Press, 1991), pp. 116–28.

164. Yeats, *Collected Poetry*, p. 49.

165. Chatterjee, *Nationalist Thought*, p. 147.

166. *Ibid.*, p. 169.

167. V. S. Naipaul, *Among the Believers: An Islamic Journey* (New York: Alfred A. Knopf, 1981); and *Guerrillas* (New York: Alfred A. Knopf, 1975). Also his *India: A Wounded Civilization* (New York: Vintage, 1977) and *An Area of Darkness* (New York: Vintage, 1981).

168. Claude Liauzu, *Aux origines des tiers-mondismes: Colonisés et anti-colonialistes en France (1919–1939)* (Paris: L'Harmattan, 1982), p. 7.

169. V. S. Naipaul, *A Bend in the River* (New York: Knopf, 1979), p. 244.

170. Davidson, *Africa in Modern History*, p. 374.

171. Fanon, *Wretched of the Earth*, p. 88.

172. *Ibid.*, p. 51.

173. *Ibid.*, p. 47.

174. *Ibid.*, p. 204.

175. *Ibid.*, p. 106. On the subject of "re-introducing mankind into the world" as treated by Fanon, see the perceptive discussion by Patrick Taylor, *The Narrative of Liberation: Perspectives on Afro-Caribbean Literature, Popular Culture and Politics* (Ithaca: Cornell University Press, 1989), pp. 7–94. On Fanon's misgiving about national culture, see Irene Gendzier, *Frantz Fanon, a Biography* (1973; rprt. New York: Grove Press, 1985), pp. 224–30.

176. Georg Lukacs, *History and Class Consciousness: Studies in Marxist Dialectics*, trans. Rodney Livingstone (London: Merlin Press, 1971), p. 199.

177. Fanon, *Wretched of the Earth*, p. 52.

178. *Ibid.*, p. 51.

179. *Ibid.*, pp. 88, 93.

180. *Ibid.*, p. 93.

181. *Ibid.*, p. 94.

182. Albert Memmi, *The Colonizer and the Colonized* (1957; trans. New York: Orion Press, 1965).

183. Fanon, *Wretched of the Earth*, p. 107.

184. *Ibid.*, p. 124.

185. *Ibid.*, p. 125.

186. *Ibid.*, p. 131.

187. *Ibid.*, p. 148.

188. *Ibid.*, p. 159.

189. *Ibid.*, p. 203.

190. *Ibid.*, p. 247.

191. Amílcar Cabral, *Unity and Struggle: Speeches and Writings*, trans. Michael Wolfers (New York: Monthly Review, 1979), p. 143.

192. Michel Chodkiewicz, "Introduction," to Emir Abdel Kader, *Ecrits spirituels*, trans. Chodkiewicz (Paris: Seuil, 1982), pp. 20–22.

193. Jalal Ali Ahmad, *Occidentosis: A Plague from the West,* trans. R. Campbell (1978; Berkeley: Mizan Press, 1984).

194. Wole Soyinka, "Triple Tropes of Trickery," *Transition,* No. 54 (1991), 178–83.

195. Anwar Abdel-Malek, "Le Project de civilisation: Positions," in *Les Conditions de l'independence nationale dans le monde moderne* (Paris: Editions Cujas, 1977) pp. 499–509.

196. Abdullah Laroui, *The Crisis of the Arab Intellectuals* (Berkeley: University of California Press, 1976), p. 100.

197. Chinua Achebe, *Hopes and Impediments: Selected Essays* (New York: Doubleday, Anchor, 1989), p. 76.

198. The phrase first turns up in Michel Foucault, *Discipline and Punish: The Birth of the Prison,* trans. Alan Sheridan (New York: Pantheon, 1977), p. 26. Later ideas related to this notion are throughout his *The History of Sexuality, Vol. 1,* trans. Robert Hurley (New York: Pantheon, 1978), and in various interviews. It influences Chantal Mouffe and Ernest Laclau, *Hegemony and Socialist Strategy: Towards a Radical Democratic Politics* (London: Verso, 1985). See my critique in "Foucault and the Imagination of Power," in *Foucault: A Critical Reader,* ed. David Hoy (London: Blackwell, 1986), pp. 149–55.

199. I discuss this possibility in "Michel Foucault, 1926–1984," in *After Foucault: Humanistic Knowledge, Postmodern Challenges,* ed. Jonathan Arac (New Brunswick: Rutgers University Press, 1988), pp. 8–9.

200. Jürgen Habermas, *Autonomy and Solidarity: Interviews,* ed. Peter Dews (London: Verso, 1986), p. 187.

201. James, *Black Jacobins,* p. 401.

202. *Ibid.*

203. *Ibid.,* p. 402.

CHAPTER FOUR

FREEDOM FROM DOMINATION IN THE FUTURE

1. Michael Barratt-Brown, *After Imperialism* (rev. ed. New York: Humanities, 1970), p. viii.

2. Arno J. Mayer, *The Resistance of the Old Regime: Europe to the Great War* (New York: Pantheon, 1981). Mayer's book, which deals with the reproduction of the old order from the nineteenth to the early twentieth century, should be supplemented by a work that details the passing on of the old colonial system, and trusteeship, from the British empire to the United States, during World War Two: William Roger Louis, *Imperialism at Bay: The United States and the Decolonization of the British Empire, 1941–1945* (London: Oxford University Press, 1977).

3. *North-South: A Program for Survival* (Cambridge, Mass.: MIT Press, 1980). For a bleaker, and perhaps truer, version of the same reality, see A. Sivananden, "New Circuits of Imperialism," *Race and Class* 30, No. 4 (April–June 1989), 1–19.

4. Cheryl Payer, *The Debt Trap: The IMF and the Third World* (New York: Monthly Review, 1974).

5. *North-South,* p. 275.

6. For a useful history of the three worlds classification, see Carl E. Pletsch, "The Three Worlds, or the Division of Social Scientific Labor, circa 1950–1975," *Comparative Studies in Society and History* 23 (October 1981), 565–90. See also Peter Worlsley's now classic *The Third World* (Chicago: University of Chicago Press, 1964).

7. Noam Chomsky, *Towards a New Cold War: Essays on the Current Crisis and How We Got There* (New York: Pantheon, 1982), pp. 84–85.

8. Ronald Steel, *Walter Lippmann and the American Century* (Boston: Little, Brown, 1980), p. 496.

9. See Anders Stephanson, *Kennan and the Art of Foreign Policy* (Cambridge, Mass.: Harvard University Press, 1989), pp. 167, 173.

10. Richard J. Barnet, *The Roots of War* (New York: Atheneum, 1972), p. 21. See also Eqbal Ahmad, "Political Culture and Foreign Policy: Notes on American Interventions in the Third World," in *For Better or Worse: The American Influence in the World*, ed. Allen F. Davis (Westport: Greenwood Press, 1981), pp. 119–31.

11. V. G. Kiernan, *America: The New Imperialism: From White Settlement to World Hegemony* (London: Zed, 1978), p. 127.

12. Albert K. Weinberg, *Manifest Destiny: A Study of Nationalist Expansionism in American History* (Gloucester, Mass.: Smith, 1958). See also Reginald Horsman, *Race and Manifest Destiny: The Origin of American Racial Anglo-Saxonism* (Cambridge, Mass.: Harvard University Press, 1981).

13. Richard Slotkin, *Regeneration Through Violence: The Mythology of the American Frontier, 1600–1860* (Middletown: Wesleyan University Press, 1973), p. 557. See also its sequel, *The Fatal Environment: The Myth of the Frontier in the Age of Industrialization, 1800–1890* (Middletown: Wesleyan University Press, 1985).

14. C.L.R. James, *Mariners, Renegades and Castaways: The Story of Herman Melville and the World We Live In* (1953; new ed. London: Allison & Busby, 1985), p. 51 and *passim*. Also Kiernan, *America*, pp. 49–50.

15. See J. Michael Dash, *Haiti and the United States: National Stereotypes and the Literary Imagination* (London: Macmillan, 1988), pp. 9, 22–25 and *passim*.

16. Kiernan, *America*, p. 206.

17. *Ibid.*, p. 114.

18. Irene Gendzier, *Managing Political Change: Social Scientists and the Third World* (Boulder and London: Westview Press, 1985), especially pp. 40–41, 127–47.

19. *Many Voices, One World* (Paris: UNESCO, 1980).

20. Anthony Smith, *The Geopolitics of Information: How Western Culture Dominates the World* (New York: Oxford University Press, 1980), p. 176.

21. Herbert I. Schiller, *The Mind Managers* (Boston: Beacon Press, 1973) and *Mass Communications and American Empire* (Boston: Beacon Press, 1969); Armand Mattelart, *Transnationals and the Third World: The Struggle for Culture* (South Hadley, Mass.: Bergin & Garvey, 1983). These are only three works among several produced on the subject by these writers.

22. Munif's five novels in the series appeared in Arabic between 1984 and 88; two volumes have appeared in excellent English translations by Peter Theroux, *Cities of Salt* (New York: Vintage, 1989) and *The Trench* (New York: Pantheon, 1991).

23. James A. Field, Jr., *America and the Mediterranean World, 1776–1882* (Princeton: Princeton University Press, 1969), especially Chapters 3, 6, 8, and 11.

24. Richard W. Van Alstyne, *The Rising American Empire* (New York: Norton, 1974), p. 6.

25. Fouad Ajami, "The Summer of Arab Discontent," *Foreign Affairs* 69, No. 5 (Winter 1990–91), 1.

26. One of the leading historians of Islamic art, Oleg Grabar, discusses the city of Baghdad as one of three foundational monuments of the artistic heritage: *The Formation of Islamic Art* (1973; rev. ed. New Haven: Yale University Press, 1987), pp. 64–71.

27. Kiernan, *America*, pp. 262–63.

28. Arnold Krupat, *For Those Who Came After: A Study of Native American Autobiography* (Berkeley: University of California Press, 1985).

29. Basil Davidson, "On Revolutionary Nationalism: The Legacy of Cabral," *Race and Class* 27, No. 3 (Winter 1986), 43.

30. *Ibid.*, 44. Davidson amplifies and develops this theme in his deeply reflective *The Black Man's Burden: Africa and the Curse of the Nation-State* (New York: Times, 1992).

31. Timothy Brennan, "Cosmopolitans and Celebrities," *Race and Class* 31, No. 1 (July–September 1989), 1–19.

32. In Herbert I. Schiller, *Culture, Inc.: The Corporate Takeover of Public Expression* (New York: Oxford University Press, 1989).

33. Immanuel Wallerstein, *Historical Capitalism* (London: Verso, 1983), p. 65 and *passim*. See also Giovanni Arrighi, Terence K. Hopkins, and Immanuel Wallerstein, *Antisystemic Movements* (London and New York: Verso, 1989).

34. A very compelling account of this is given by Jonathan Rée in "Internationality," *Radical Philosophy*, 60 (Spring 1992), 3–11.

35. Bernard S. Cohn, "Representing Authority in Victorian India," in *The Invention of Tradition*, eds. Eric Hobsbawm and Terence Ranger (Cambridge: Cambridge University Press, 1983), pp. 192–207.

36. Adonis, *An Introduction to Arab Poetics*, trans. Catherine Cobban (London: Saqi, 1990), p. 76.

37. Seamus Deane, "Heroic Styles: The Tradition of an Idea," in *Ireland's Field Day* (London: Hutchinson, 1985), p. 58.

38. Ken Ringle, *The Washington Post*, March 31, 1991. The caricatural attacks on the exhibition have an excellent antidote in the massive and intellectually compelling catalogue *The West as America: Reinterpreting Images of the Frontier, 1820–1970*, ed. William H. Truettner (Washington and London: Smithsonian Institution Press, 1991). A sampling of visitors' responses to the exhibition is reproduced in *American Art* 5, No. 2 (Summer 1991), 3–11.

39. This notion is explored with extraordinary subtlety in Homi K. Bhabha, "The Postcolonial Critic," *Arena* 96 (1991), 61–63, and "DissemiNation: Time, Narrative, and the Margins of the Modern Nation," *Nation and Narration*, ed. Homi K. Bhabha (London and New York: Routledge, 1990), pp. 291–322.

40. Paul Kennedy, *The Rise and Fall of the Great Powers: Economic Change and Military Conflict from 1500–2000* (New York: Random House, 1987).

41. Joseph S. Nye, Jr., *Bound to Lead: The Changing Nature of American Power* (1990; rev. ed. New York: Basic, 1991), p. 260.

42. *Ibid.*, p. 261.

43. *The Humanities in American Life: Report of the Commission on the Humanities* (Berkeley: University of California Press, 1980).

44. In Edward W. Said, *The World, the Text, and the Critic* (Cambridge, Mass.: Harvard University Press, 1983), pp. 226–47.

45. Robert A. McCaughey, *International Studies and Academic Enterprise: A Chapter in the Enclosure of American Learning* (New York: Columbia University Press, 1984).

46. Theodor Adorno, *Minima Moralia: Reflections from a Damaged Life*, trans. E.F.N. Jephcott (1951; trans. London: New Left, 1974), p. 55.

47. In Edward W. Said, *Covering Islam* (New York: Pantheon, 1981).

48. Fredric Jameson, "Postmodernism and Consumer Society," in *The Anti-Aesthetic: Essays on Postmodern Culture*, ed. Hal Foster (Port Townsend, Wash.: Bay Press, 1983), pp. 123–25.

49. Eqbal Ahmad, "The Neo-Fascist State: Notes on the Pathology of Power in the Third World," *Arab Studies Quarterly* 3, No. 2 (Spring 1981), 170–80.

50. Eqbal Ahmad, "From Potato Sack to Potato Mash: The Contemporary Crisis of the Third World," *Arab Studies Quarterly* 2, No. 3 (Summer 1980), 230–32.

51. *Ibid.*, p. 231.

52. Paul Virilio, *L'Insécurité du territoire* (Paris: Stock, 1976), p. 88 ff.

53. Jean-François Lyotard, *The Postmodern Condition: A Report on Knowledge*, trans. Geoff Bennington and Brian Massumi (Minneapolis: University of Minnesota Press, 1984), pp. 37, 46.

54. Masao Miyoshi, *Off Center: Power and Culture Relations Between Japan and the United States* (Cambridge, Mass.: Harvard University Press, 1991), pp. 623–24.

55. T. S. Eliot, "Little Gidding," in *Collected Poems, 1909–1962* (New York: Harcourt, Brace & World, 1963), pp. 207–8.

56. Gilles Deleuze and Félix Guattari, *Mille Plateaux* (Paris: Minuit, 1980), p. 511 (translation mine).

57. Virilio, *L'Insecurité du territoire*, p. 84.

58. Adorno, *Minima Moralia*, pp. 46–47.

59. *Ibid.*, pp. 67–68.

60. *Ibid.*, p. 68.

61. *Ibid.*, p. 81.

62. Ali Shariati, *On the Sociology of Islam: Lectures by Ali Shariati*, trans. Hamid Algar (Berkeley: Mizan Press, 1979), pp. 92–93.

63. This is described at length in my *Beginnings: Intention and Method* (1975; rprt. New York: Columbia University Press, 1985).

64. John Berger and Jean Mohr, *Another Way of Telling* (New York: Pantheon, 1982), p. 108.

65. Immanuel Wallerstein, "Crisis as Transition," in Samir Amin, Giovanni Arrighi, André Gunder Frank, and Immanuel Wallerstein, *Dynamics of Global Crisis* (New York: Monthly Review, 1982), p. 30.

66. Hugo of St. Victor, *Didascalicon*, trans. Jerome Taylor (New York: Columbia University Press, 1961), p. 101.

Index

A NOTE ABOUT THE AUTHOR

An internationally renowned literary and cultural critic, Edward W. Said is
University Professor at Columbia University. He is the author of ten previous
books, including *Orientalism,* which was nominated for the National Book
Critics Circle Award.

A NOTE ON THE TYPE

This book was set in a digitized version of Janson. The hot-metal version of Janson was a recutting made direct from type cast from matrices long thought to have been made by the Dutchman Anton Janson, who was a practicing type founder in Leipzig during the years 1668–1687. However, it has been conclusively demonstrated that these types are actually the work of Nicholas Kis (1650–1702), a Hungarian, who most probably learned his trade from the master Dutch type founder Dirk Voskens. The type is an excellent example of the influential and sturdy Dutch types that prevailed in England up to the time William Caslon (1692–1766) developed his own incomparable designs from them.

Composed by ComCom,
a division of The Haddon Craftsmen, Allentown, Pennsylvania
Printed and bound by Haddon Craftsmen, Scranton, Pennsylvania
Typography and binding design by
Dorothy Schmiderer Baker